THE CONTROL OF OIL

THE CONTROL
OF OIL

JOHN M. BLAIR

PANTHEON BOOKS
New York

Library of Congress Cataloging in Publication Data

Blair, John Malcolm, 1914–
    The Control of Oil.

    Includes bibliographical references and index.
    1. Petroleum industry and trade. 2. Petroleum industry and trade—United States. 3. Energy policy—United States. I. Title.
HD9560.6.B55   338.2′7′282   75–38116
ISBN 0–394–49470–9

Manufactured in the United States of America

987654

Since this copyright page cannot accommodate all acknowledgments, they are to be found on the following page.

Grateful acknowledgment is made to the following for permission to reprint previously published material:

Ballinger Publishing Company: Excerpts from "Firm Size and Technological Change in the Petroleum and Bituminous Coal Industries," by Edwin Mansfield, from *Competition in the U.S. Energy Industry*. Copyright © 1974 by The Ford Foundation.

CBS News: Excerpt from discussion between Clifton C. Garvin, Jr., and Morton Mintz on "Face the Nation," November 16, 1975.

Daedalus, Journal of the American Academy of Arts and Sciences, Boston, Mass.: Excerpts from "The OPEC Process," by Zuhayr Mikdashi, from *Daedalus*, Fall 1975, *The Oil Crisis: In Perspective*.

E. P. Dutton & Co., Inc., and International Creative Management: Brief excerpts from pages 22–23 and 25 of the *Elusive Bonanza: The Story of Oil Shale*, by Chris Welles. Copyright © 1970 by Christopher J. Welles.

Macmillan Publishing Co., Inc.: Excerpt from pages 76–77 of *The Modern Corporation and Private Property*, by Adolf A. Berle and Gardiner C. Means, rev. ed., 1967.

The New York Times: Oriana Fallaci's interview with Sheik Yamani of September 14, 1975 (*Magazine*). Copyright © 1975 by The New York Times Company.

Peter R. Odell and Professor Edith Penrose: Excerpts from pages 296–297 of *The Large International Firms in Developing Countries*, by Edith Penrose. George Allen & Unwin Ltd.

Oil and Gas Journal: Table entitled "Exploratory Successes in U.S. Oil and Gas Fields, 1972," July 2, 1973, issue. Also excerpts from *Annual Refining Report*, March 1976.

The Petroleum Economist: Excerpts from issues of *The Petroleum Economist*, January 1974 through November 1975.

Shrade F. Radtke: Quote from paper entitled "Charging Up for a Changing World," delivered at Battery Council International Convention, May 7, 1970.

The Wall Street Journal: Excerpts from the March 15, 1976, *Wall Street Journal*. Copyright © 1976 by Dow Jones & Company, Inc. All rights reserved.

The Washington Post: Excerpts from an article by Bernard Nossiter from the July 16, 1970, issue. Copyright © 1970 by The Washington Post.

Preface

This book had its genesis in a proposal in June 1973 by the Ford Foundation's Energy Policy Project that I prepare "an independent appraisal of the entire competition problem in petroleum." Correctly anticipating what is today referred to as the "energy crisis," the Ford Foundation had several years earlier established the Project to support research and finance the publication of studies on various aspects of the energy problem. Although over two-score studies have subsequently been published, they are for the most part technical monographs, directed toward some particular, narrowly defined issue. My task was to supplement these technical contributions with an overall or general analysis. By the latter part of the year, however, it had become clear that I would be unable to meet the Project's deadline. Because of this and other reasons, the proposed undertaking was terminated by mutual consent.

At about this same time the world was being rocked by a veritable upheaval in oil prices. In October 1973–January 1974 a fourfold rise in the price of oil was unilaterally imposed by the Organization of Petroleum Exporting Countries. Not only was this increase utterly unprecedented; it flew in the face of expectations by economists expert in the oil industry, whose general point of view was accurately expressed in 1969 by Professor M. A. Adelman: "Thus, the prospect is: continued decline of prices but at a very slow and gradual rate."[1] At first the precipitous price rise was attributed to shortages occasioned by what was loosely termed "the Arab embargo." Within a few months, however, all signs of shortage had disappeared, but the price remained at its new, stratospheric level. Equally puzzling was the dramatic increase in the oil companies' profits. If, as was widely assumed, the majors were buyers of foreign crude oil, the sharp rise in their raw material's cost should, under competitive conditions, have narrowed their profit margin. Then, as the 1974–75 recession worsened, price was stabilized by substantial curtailments in output—

again contrary to the expectations of many economists who had based their expectations on the comforting dogma that "cartels always break down."

It is true that in the petroleum industry there have been recurrent periods of price weaknesses, both at home and abroad. In the constant pull-and-haul between the natural forces of supply and demand on the one hand and attempts to control the market on the other, prices have periodically moved downward, as cartels have in fact come apart, newcomers have been able to circumvent established channels, and ways and means have been devised of getting around governmental restraints on supply. But as a guide to public policy, belief in the impermanence of market restraints overlooks the rapidity with which such breakdowns have usually been repaired, often through the imposition of some new and more effective form of governmental control.

That price was not only quadrupled in 1973–74 but maintained in the face of the subsequent recession implies either a capability on the part of OPEC to implement a "prorationing" system or responsibility by the other party capable of taking the action—the oil companies. This was a type of activity which OPEC had attempted in the past but without any measure of success. In 1969 Professor Edith Penrose noted: "OPEC has twice attempted a 'prorationing' system under which an overall target was set for production and quotas were assigned to the participating countries. Both attempts failed."[2] Obviously something new had been added both in the form of market control and in the manner in which it was being exercised. What was past may have continued as the foundation, but it was no longer the explanation for current developments. If the effort to make an "appraisal of the entire competition problem in petroleum" was to continue, a wide range of new topics would have to be explored.

Yet, such an undertaking would require a wide variety of types of information, most of which are nonexistent, inaccessible, or, at best, difficult to obtain. No other industry begins to offer the data problems that are presented by petroleum. Statistical time series are few and far between, and even those that appear to relate to the same subject often differ in their definitions, with the result that they can neither be combined nor compared. The financial statements of the integrated companies reveal next to nothing about profits in the industry's successive stages or in their operations outside petroleum. The use of the techniques of "creative accounting," particularly the revaluation of inventories, gives to the companies considerable leeway in understating earnings compared to those of previous years. In terms of both quantitative importance and essentiality, energy is outranked only by agriculture. Yet, although there are dozens of colleges of agricultural economics, scores of courses on various aspects of the subject, and hundreds of textbooks, there are no colleges of energy economics, virtually no courses, and thus no textbooks.

On the supply side the informational problem was compounded by the U.S. Geological Survey, *the* authoritative source of figures on domestic reserves, which, beginning in the mid-fifties, persisted for over a decade and a half in issuing wildly inflated estimates of the supply of petroleum ultimately recoverable in the United States. Inasmuch as the major oil companies were at the same time greatly underestimating the proved reserves of the Middle East, the result was to overstate the ability of the United States to meet its own needs and to understate the magnitude of alternative sources. On the demand side the essential difficulty is that the industry has grown to such a size that slight differences in predicted growth rates yield strikingly different forecasts of demand, conveying, in relation to anticipated supply, quite different implications for public policy. For example, raising the projected U.S. population for the year 2000 from 252 million to 285 million persons increases the expected gross energy consumption by 13 percent. Raising the per capita consumption from the actual use in 1970 (429 million BTUs) to the level assumed in the "Dixie Lee Ray" report (680 million BTUs)[3] increases gross consumption by 101 percent. And the combination of both has the effect of increasing estimated consumption by 134 percent.[4] Inasmuch as long-term growth rates were interrupted in 1974–75, plausible rationales are available for each of the extremes, as well as for any value in between.

Although difficult to secure for any industry, information on market control in petroleum is particularly hard to come by. In domestic oil monopoly power does not stem from a simple, highly concentrated, oligopolistic structure but rather from an amalgam of a moderately high level of concentration, an extraordinary maze of interlocking corporate relationships, an extreme degree of vertical integration, and governmental interventions to limit supply. And in foreign oil, company concentration has been supplemented by the Organization of Petroleum Exporting Countries. Concerning this highly complex pattern the principal source of information consists of the hearings (and materials in appendices) of Congressional committees. Though it is used much too sparingly, the very existence of the subpoena power enables such bodies to secure information not obtainable from any other source. Particularly valuable are the hearings conducted by the Subcommittee on Multinational Corporations, headed by Senator Frank Church, of the Senate Foreign Relations Committee. Important information is also to be found in hearings conducted by the Senate

Interior Committee, the Senate Committee on Government Operations, and the Senate Subcommittee on Antitrust and Monopoly. Other
types of useful information can occasionally be obtained from the
industry's trade journals, notably *Oil Week* and the *Oil and Gas
Journal*. Particularly valuable have been the analyses of contemporary
developments appearing in *The Petroleum Economist*. Although frequently quite different from the interpretations offered in this volume,
its analyses are invariably knowledgeable and thoughtful.

To aid in understanding, a few words on nomenclature are necessary. Traditionally, companies in the oil industry have been classified
as "majors" and "independents." Another basis of differentiation is
between "integrated" and "nonintegrated," i.e., between those companies engaged in each of the industry's successive stages of operations
(crude production, refining, and marketing) and those limited to
just one of the stages. In the United States there are somewhat less
than twenty integrated companies, all of whom are "majors." But
within this group a clear differentiation exists between the eight largest companies and some eight or nine others. In this volume the former
are referred to as the "top eight" and the latter as "lesser" or "other"
majors. In the world industry it has long been customary to make a
distinction between the seven largest firms (often referred to as "the
seven sisters") and "independents," which include a number of the
integrated, "lesser" majors. Six of the "seven sisters" are among the
"top eight" in the United States; the other two are Standard of Indiana
and Atlantic-Richfield (ARCO), which do not hold important positions in the world industry.

A related problem concerns the nomenclature to be used in desig-
nating the leading companies. Four of the "top eight" and three of
the "seven sisters" were originally part of the old Standard Oil
"Trust," dissolved by the Supreme Court in 1911; two of these enterprises have subsequently undergone a series of name changes. Thus,
the company currently known as Mobil was first known as Standard
Oil of New York (Socony), then after a merger as Socony-Vacuum,
and then as Socony-Mobil. Similarly the firm now designated as Exxon
was originally Standard Oil of New Jersey, later as Humble Oil Co.,
selling its products in most markets under the trade name "Esso."
Because their current trade names ("Amoco" and "Chevron") are
not as readily identifiable with their companies, the other two members of the old trust are referred to here by their respective corporate
names: Standard of Indiana and Standard of California (or SoCal).
British Petroleum, now called BP, was originally known as Anglo-
Persian Oil Co. and then as Anglo-Iranian. In this work the companies
will, wherever possible, be designated by their current names. The

following listings indicate which companies are grouped in which categories. Under the "top eight" and the "seven sisters" the companies are *not* ranked in accordance with size; rather, there are shown first the "Standard" companies, next other American majors (Texaco and Gulf), and finally foreign-owned concerns (Shell and BP). The domestic "lesser majors" are ranked by their shares of proved domestic reserves in 1970. There is no particular order to the listing of leading international independents.

U.S.		International	
"Top Eight"	**"Lesser Majors"**	**"Seven Sisters"**	**Leading "Independents"**
Exxon	Getty	Exxon	Compagnie Française
Mobil	Phillips	Mobil	Pétrole
SoCal	Signal	SoCal	Continental
Stand. (Ind.)	Union	Texaco	Marathon
Texaco	Continental	Gulf	Amerada Hess
Gulf	Sun	Royal Dutch Shell	Occidental
Shell	Amerada Hess	BP	
ARCO	Cities Service		
	Marathon		

Finally, I wish to express my deepest gratitude and appreciation to Dr. Walter Measday of the Senate Subcommittee on Antitrust and Monopoly and to Mr. Jack Blum of the Senate Subcommittee on Multinational Corporations for their helpful suggestions and insights; to Professor George Steinike for his technical assistance in preparing the growth-rate analysis; to Mrs. Emily Zayanni, Mrs. Sunne Brandmeyer, and Miss Karen Kroger for their editorial and clerical assistance; to Mr. Don Meares for drafting the charts; and to Mrs. Kathy Schoonmaker for her skill and patience in typing and retyping an interminable series of drafts and redrafts.

John M. Blair
University of South Florida

July 1976

Contents

List of Charts

List of Tables

Table

THE CONTROL OF OIL

THE ENERGY CRISIS

1

WHEN OIL SHIPMENTS were restricted and even embargoed by the Arab producing countries following the Egyptian invasion of Israel on October 6, 1973, the world suddenly found itself confronted with what has come to be referred to as the "energy crisis." This was not the first occasion on which oil deliveries from the Middle East had been cut off. It was, however, the first occasion on which the curtailment was accompanied by an explosion in prices.

During the first Suez crisis Egypt, on July 26, 1957, nationalized the Suez Canal, and on October 31 closed it to traffic, thereby cutting off about two-thirds of Europe's supply of oil. According to a report of May 21, 1957, to the Administrator of the Middle East Emergency Committee, 2,165,000 barrels per day of the Eastern Hemisphere supply (west of Suez) had been "moved via the canal and the Middle East pipelines."[1] Nonetheless, no shortage developed, as the affected areas received "slightly more than 90 percent of the supplies prior to the stoppage."[2] These additional supplies were made possible by increased production, by heavy stock withdrawals during November and December, and by "numerous unusual operations . . . particularly in the United States."[3] The cause of price stability was considerably strengthened by the opening of Congressional hearings and the filing of an antitrust suit directed against the use of the crisis as a pretext for price increases. During the second Suez conflict, according to the informed trade journal *The Petroleum Economist*, "the U.S.A. was able to help the Free World with a dramatic increase in domestic production; this made over 1 million barrels a day available to Western Europe, by exports and the diversion of supplies previously intended for the U.S.A."[4] Again, the ability of the United States to offset most of the shortfall from the Middle East prevented any abrupt increase in price.

But by the time of the third Suez crisis, the excess capacity that had

3

given the United States the power to offset interruptions in supply elsewhere in the world had ceased to exist. Indeed, by 1973 the United States had itself become quite dependent upon foreign sources, and insofar as its own reserves were concerned, was rapidly running out of oil. The "energy crisis" is thus the logical consequence of the limited and declining size of U.S. reserves and the resultant vulnerability of oil consumers everywhere to those controlling foreign oil, consisting of above a dozen members of the Organization of Petroleum Exporting Countries (OPEC) and a small group of giant international oil companies (known as the "seven sisters").

U.S. RESERVES

Although to most of the world the energy crisis came as a complete and shattering surprise, a few petroleum geologists and economists had for years been calling attention to the approaching exhaustion of U.S. reserves; but their analyses, published in academic journals or congressional hearings, were ignored or soon forgotten. Warnings of an impending shortage were highly inconvenient to a government embarked on a program designed to enlarge the oil producers' profits by excluding what were then low-cost foreign imports. This was the purpose and effect of the mandatory import quota, introduced in 1957 and continued for fourteen years. To make acceptable a policy of restricting imports and maximizing domestic production, it was necessary to portray a roseate vision of ample domestic reserves. As one persistent critic of the industry's estimates has put it: "Contemporaneously, one of the most widely publicized dicta of the public relations arm of the U.S. petroleum industry was the statement 'the United States has all the oil it will need for the foreseeable future.' "[5]

On May 20, 1969, E. Wayles Browne, formerly economist of the Senate Subcommittee on Antitrust and Monopoly, introduced into the record a series of charts showing the trends from 1945 to 1968 on proved reserves, production, and new discoveries. The extrapolation of those trends clearly pointed to the development of a domestic shortage within the near future. Chart 1-1 reproduces his trend lines for proved reserves (defined by the American Petroleum Institute as the quantities of crude oil which "geologic and engineering data demonstrate with reasonable certainty to be recoverable from known reservoirs under existing economic and operating conditions"). It also shows the "reserve production ratio" (the number of years' supply derived by dividing proved reserves by annual production). The chart extends his actual observations to 1974 (indicated by dotted lines), and, in addition, shows the trends both with and without the reserves in the North Slope of Alaska.

CHART 1-1
United States Crude Oil Reserves

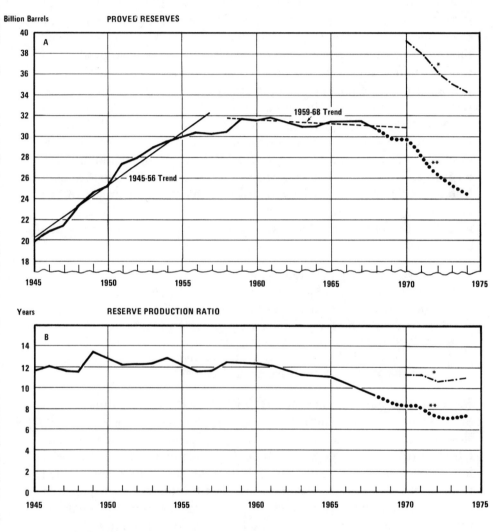

Billion Barrels   PROVED RESERVES

A

1959-68 Trend

1945-56 Trend

Years   RESERVE PRODUCTION RATIO

B

* Including North Slope of Alaska (9.6 billion barrels).
** Excluding North Slope.
Source: API and Bureau of Mines.

After rising during the first dozen years following World War II by over 1 billion barrels a year, proved reserves in 1961 began to decline, falling slowly but perceptibly during the next decade. In the coterminous forty-eight states this moderate downward trend understated the severity of the post-1968 decline, as proved reserves fell between 1968 and 1974 at about the same rate that they had risen during 1945–56—approximately 1 billion barrels a year. During the earlier period, the increase in domestic production closely paralleled the rise in proved reserves, with the result that the reserve production ratio remained relatively stable at around twelve years' supply, long considered a "comfortable" supply. In the late 1950's, however, the ratio turned downward, the number of years' supply falling from 12.4 years in 1958 to 7.7 years in 1974. This downward trend flattened out during 1972–74, not so much, however, from any rise in new discoveries as from a decline in domestic production, stemming from an increase in imports and the recession-induced decline in demand. The bleak prospect has been relieved only by the appearance of the Alaskan reserves, introduced into proved reserves in 1970 and estimated by the Bureau of Mines at 9.6 billion barrels. Referring to the discoveries in Alaska, M. A. Adelman has testified:

> Some rather wildly extravagant statements have been made about it, such as the center of gravity of the world oil trade shifting to the Arctic zones. I do think we need to keep a sense of proportion in these matters. The 5 to 10 billion barrels reserves expected to be developed over the next few years, large as they are, are only a small fraction of the new gross additions to reserves made every year in the Middle East and North Africa.[6]

Moreover, getting the Alaskan oil to where it is needed in the United States in the quantities anticipated is by no means a foregone conclusion. The task of constructing the 798-mile pipeline in this inhospitable clime is proving to be incredibly difficult. In September 1975, a 5-mile-long convoy of barges, carrying $5 billion worth of equipment, failed to reach the oil fields at Prudhon Bay.[7] In addition to the problems of terrain, climate, and permafrost, ice from glaciers may endanger the pipeline and disrupt shipping in the terminal port of Valdez. On October 14, 1975, a glacierologist of the U.S. Geological Survey reported that "unusually large" ice discharges were coming from the Columbia Glacier and expressed apprehension that the glacier might discharge icebergs into shipping lanes to be used by tankers carrying Alaskan oil.[8] But the principal problem will be in getting the Alaskan oil to those areas of the "lower forty-eight" where it is needed. By 1976 FEA officials were publicly acknowledging what proponents of the proposed alternative trans-Canadian route had stressed four years earlier: that the Alaskan line would saturate the West Coast while providing little relief to the Midwest and East. Without some way of getting the oil over, through, or under the Rocky Mountains, the West Coast will be deluged with a daily surplus of as much as 400,000 barrels—a third of the pipeline's daily capacity.[9]

If the amount of oil produced exceeds the amount discovered, an increase in demand can be supported only by a rise in imports or a drawing down of reserves. Inasmuch as imports were restricted during 1959–73 to 12.2 percent of domestic production, the decline in domestic reserves implies a failure of new discoveries ("new oil found") to keep pace with production. As can be seen in Chart 1-2, not only did new discoveries fail to keep up with production; the two series moved in opposite directions.[10] During the twenty-year period 1946–65, an upward trend in production, averaging 54.4 million barrels a year, was accompanied by a downward trend in new oil found, averaging 22.89 million barrels a year. At the time, Browne observed that the gap between production and new oil found was "widening at the rate of over 77 million barrels a year. This gap represents the drawing down of proved reserves. By 1980 the projected gap amounts to 1,234 million barrels in one year."[11]

In retrospect, it can be seen that the projections understated the severity of the problem, as actual production exceeded the forecast from the mid-sixties to the early seventies. The surge in output was the product of a variety of stimuli to demand, many of which could not have been accurately anticipated; e.g., automobiles of increasingly irrational weight and size, automotive engines with increasingly irrational horsepower, the rapidity of the "white flight" to suburbs and the attendant increases in commuter traffic, two- and three-car families, and the near-collapse of mass transportation. By the early 1970's, however, the combination of the upward trend of the projection and the decline after 1970 in actual output had brought the two into close juxtaposition. In 1974, for example, the level of output indicated by the estimate was 3.4 billion barrels; actual production turned out to be 3.2 billion barrels. Although the series on new oil found fluctuates more widely around the trend line than production, a long-term downward tendency is clearly evident. What is most alarming is the fact that since 1971 actual new discoveries have fallen well below the historical trend. Thus, as compared to a predicted level of 2.6 billion barrels, the actual amount of new oil found in the coterminous states was 2.3 billion barrels in 1973 and 2.1 billion in 1974. The United States appears to be running out of oil at an even more rapid rate than had been predicted in 1968.

CHART 1-2
Crude Oil: New Oil Found* and Production in the United States

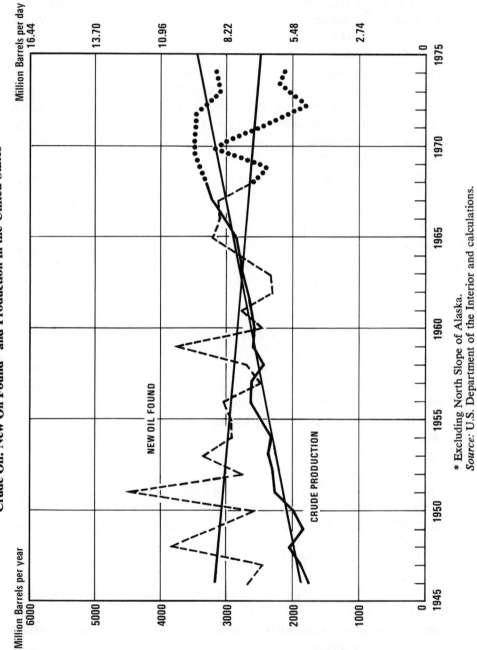

* Excluding North Slope of Alaska.
Source: U.S. Department of the Interior and calculations.

Although their import was made abundantly clear, these historical trends and projections, when introduced into the record, were greeted by the Congress, the administration, the press, and indeed the academic world with profound indifference. The oil companies for their part did not quarrel with the predictions,[12] arguing instead that even though they were correct, the import quotas should be retained, since the needed new supplies would be forthcoming from Alaska and offshore drilling. Indeed, by the end of the 1960's some industry officials had come to acknowledge that the oil regarded as recoverable from *known* reservoirs would meet only a small proportion of this country's future needs. In testimony before the Senate Antitrust Subcommittee, M. A. Wright, vice-president of Exxon, projected demand and supply to 1985, dividing domestic production into two categories: "booked" reserves and reserves "to be discovered." "Crude oil reserves now [1969] on the books are 31 billion barrels. Under the future reserve part we show the oil that in the future must come from crude oil reserves which will be found post–January 1 of this year, and booked post–January 1 of this year. This shows that to do this [i.e., meet the expanding demand without increasing imports] we have to book 72 billion barrels of oil in the future." Senator Hart then intervened:

SENATOR HART: Mr. Wright, let me interrupt you. You say that this future reserve—which by 1985 must be relied on for *85 percent* of our needs—represents oil which *will* be found. That is the way you put it.

MR. WRIGHT: That is true.

SENATOR HART: How do the bookmakers quote the odds? That is an awful lot of oil that somebody says will be found . . . are you not playing sort of Russian roulette with national security?

MR. WRIGHT: I do not think so, Senator.[13]

The proration authorities of the nation's largest producing state, Texas, were well aware that domestic production could not possibly meet the rising demand. The Subcommittee's chief economist asked Judge Jim C. Langdon, chairman of the Texas Railroad Commission, whether the state could meet its proportionate share of the then anticipated demand of 18 million barrels a day:

DR. BLAIR: In order to meet an estimated demand of 18.0 million while holding imports constant at 20 percent, which consists of 12.2 percent for crude and the remainder for residual, domestic production would have to run to 11.4 million barrels a day for crude oil and 2.9 for natural gas liquids. But to reach 11.4 million barrels a day, production would have to increase by 2.3 million barrels above the 1968 level of 9.1 million barrels. . . . At a total U.S. production of 14.4 million barrels a day . . . it would be necessary for the State of Texas, if it were to maintain its 35 percent share of total U.S. output, to produce 5 million barrels a day. . . .

MR. LANGDON: We would not even pretend to try to produce that much oil simply because under existing conditions *we could not produce this much oil.* . . . We are not going to contest one iota the statement that we are going to be more dependent in 1975 and 1980 on foreign crude than we are today.[14]

In addition to proved reserves, there are two other classes of petroleum resources: "prospective reserves" and "undiscovered potential." The former are reserves which have been discovered but are not considered to be proved; consisting of the difference between ultimate production actually obtainable from a given reservoir and the proved resources assigned to it, they are usually estimated to average about 50 percent of proved reserves. The task of estimating the "undiscovered potential" is particularly difficult, since the needed information is at best fragmentary, usually closely held, and often exaggerated. Petroleum geologists are constantly expanding our knowledge of the locations of those deposits most likely to be repositories of oil, while engineering advances, particularly in offshore drilling, are making it feasible to tap reserves considered inaccessible only a few years ago. Nonetheless, the quantity of oil placed by nature under the earth's surface is not impossible to estimate, since it is to be found only in a certain type of geological formation whose size and general location is fairly well known—the sedimentary sandstones, shales, and limestones in which ancient plants and animals (the repositories of stored energy from the sun) were buried eons ago. These unmetamorphosed deposits are found as a veneer in basin-like depressions above the upper surface of granite and other dense "basement" rock covering the earth. Oil is to be found in those particular sedimentary deposits where the decomposed flora and fauna displaced water from the porous strata and in effect were captured by the surrounding nonporous formations. While the presence of such deposits by no means guarantees discovery, the fact that they are the only sources of oil greatly simplifies the problem of estimation. As the eminent petroleum geologist M. King Hubbert has put it: "This knowledge provides us with a powerful geological basis against unbridled speculations as to the occurrence of oil and gas. The initial supply is finite; the rate of renewal is negligible; and the occurrences are limited to those areas of the earth where the basement rocks are covered by thick sedimentary deposits."[15]

Unfortunately, beginning in the latter 1950's total domestic petroleum resources did become a subject of "unbridled speculation." Up to

1957, a consensus had developed among petroleum geologists that the amount of oil ultimately recoverable in the coterminous United States and adjacent continental shelves would be roughly 150–200 billion barrels.[16] Referred to as "Estimated Ultimate Recovery" (EUR), this represented the sum total of the amount already produced, plus "proved reserves," plus "probable" reserves, plus "future discoveries." Then, inexplicably, rapidly escalating estimates began to appear. To use Hubbert's language, "Shortly after 1956 . . . all consistency in the estimates of petroleum reserves vanished." The earlier lower estimates, with their implications of impending shortage, came to have only a "negligible influence on national policy with respect to oil and gas during the next decade, largely because estimates three to four times higher of the resources of oil and gas were issued repeatedly by members of the U.S. Geological Survey and by representatives of the petroleum industry."[17] In 1957, the Chase Manhattan Bank published an estimate of 250 billion barrels; in 1958, a private research firm, Resources for the Future, came out with an estimate of 372 billion; and in 1959, an Exxon geologist revised a previous estimate of 240 billion to 391 billion. In the first of a series of extremely high estimates, A. D. Zapp of the U.S. Geological Survey arrived at a figure of 590 billion barrels.* In addition to some 90–100 billion barrels that had already been produced, estimates for undiscovered reserves of crude oil and natural gas liquids of 346 billion barrels were made by Hendricks (1965),[18] 458 billion by Theobold, et al. (1972),[19] and 200–400 billion by McKelvey (1974).[20]

Not surprisingly, the industry made good use of these new higher estimates in fending off attacks on the import quota. Drains on our natural resources could be accepted with equanimity if domestic reserves were adequate for our future needs. This line of argument was exemplified by the testimony of Robert G. Dunlop, president of the Sun Oil Co.: ". . . reports of the U.S. Geological Survey show that we are a long way from exhausting our petroleum resources . . . enormous supplies are still available for development."[21]

The Geological Survey arrived at its estimates by identifying as

---

* Because of its use in subsequent estimates by the Geological Survey, Zapp's methodology is of particular interest. Completely adequate exploration, he assumed, would require that one well be drilled to 20,000 feet (or the basement rock) for every 2 miles of sedimentary basin. This would require some 5 billion feet of exploratory drilling. By the end of 1961, the 1.1 billion feet of exploratory drilling had resulted in the discovery of 130 billion barrels of crude oil—a ratio of 118 bbl/ft. At this same rate of discovery, 5 billion feet of drilling should result in the discovery of 590 billion barrels. Underlying this methodology is the extraordinary assumption that the rate of discovery in the least promising areas, yet to be explored, will be as high as in the most promising areas where oil has been found. As Hubbert demonstrated, the success ratio has been anything but constant, falling from 240 bbl/ft. during 1860–1920 to 30 bbl/ft. in recent years. (Hubbert, "Energy Resources," p. 56.)

"promising" those parts of a basin which had not yet been developed and estimating their oil content through the use of a "discovery ratio." Initially, the Survey assumed a ratio of 1 to 1, i.e., that a basin's undeveloped areas would yield as much oil as its developed areas. This of course implied that the geological surveys conducted by both oil companies and wildcatters in order to identify the more promising areas of a basin were simply a waste of time and money; or, in the words of the National Academy of Sciences, that "the richest parts of the basins that were selected for drilling by oil companies were typical of the entire basin."[22] Yet, such an assumption runs counter not only to common sense but to the available evidence: ". . . the amount of oil to be produced, according to the U.S. Geological Survey, would be proportional only to the number of wells drilled, with no importance attached to differences in the geology within different parts of the basins. Actual drilling experience, however, shows that the oil produced per well in a given field or region decreases with the number of wells drilled. . . ."[23]

In 1975, the Survey published the results of a new study, based on a review of "a large amount of geological and geophysical information gathered on more than 100 different provinces by over 70 specialists . . . applying a variety of resource appraisal techniques to each potential petroleum province."[24] Of its latest forecast the Survey states: ". . . the current appraisals indicate that the estimated statistical mean of undiscovered recoverable resources of crude oil in the United States, on shore and off shore, amounts to 82 billion barrels."[25] Together with the 103 billion already produced, this yields an ultimate recoverable supply of 185 billion barrels—or about the same magnitude as the estimates nearly twenty years earlier.

One possible explanation for the rise and fall of the official estimates might be that their inflation had served its purpose. Since the import quota had been terminated in 1973, the need for excessive estimates had ceased to exist. Or, perhaps confronted with the hard reality of declining domestic production, the Geological Survey was forced to recognize the utter untenability of its assumption that the discovery rate in unexplored areas would be the same as, or even approach, the rate in producing areas. Whatever the motivation, the very publication of the inflated "official" estimates had seriously aggravated the current energy crisis. Had it not been for their reassuring implications, public policy might well have been the reverse of that actually followed from 1959 to 1973. Instead of accelerating the depletion of our limited reserves by a forced reliance on domestic production, public policy could have been directed toward the rational objective of conserving in peacetime our limited supply by using foreign imports. Throughout this period the foreign producing countries, particularly in the Middle East, were more than anxious to gain entry into the U.S. market. As compared to the present posted price of over $12 a barrel, they would undoubtedly have been willing to sell for the then posted price of $1.80 and probably for the actual "armslength" price of only $1.30. Had they been able to do so, strong ties with American consuming interests would have been cemented, weakening the motivation to form a separate producer cartel of their own. The United States could have gradually phased out its almost complete reliance on domestic reserves and thus avoided the potential for skyrocketing prices inherent in the sudden realization that it could no longer supply its own needs, much less those of other consuming nations.

How many years of use is implied by an ultimate recoverable supply of 150–200 billion barrels? This is a question to which Hubbert first addressed himself in 1956. Based on the assumption that the exponential rise in crude production would be followed by a roughly correlative decline, resulting from the "slowing rates of extraction from depleting reservoirs," he constructed a bell-shaped curve that rose steadily until 1970 and then began a sustained and irreversible decline.[26] His forecast has proved to be astonishingly accurate, as domestic production did reach its high point in 1970 and since then has been steadily declining. The reception accorded his original prediction ranged from skepticism to disbelief. As Hubbert has recalled, "The universal intuitive judgment of the U.S. petroleum industry at that time was that there was plenty of oil left. The propaganda dictum of the American Petroleum Institute was that the United States has all the oil it needs."[27] Chart 1-3 shows a recent version of Hubbert's bell-shaped curve which assumes an ultimate recoverable domestic supply of 170–172 billion barrels, consisting of 96 billion barrels of cumulative production through 1971, 47 billion for "reserves of recoverable oil from fields already discovered" (i.e., "proved" and "probable" reserves), and 27–29 billion for future discoveries. Hubbert's technique has been to design a curve which on a chart will envelop squares, each representing a given amount of oil (20 billion bbls. as indicated in the upper right-hand quadrant) and totaling ultimate recoverable supply (170 billion bbls.). The 96 billion barrels of past consumption (through 1971) are represented by the squares with downward-sloping, left-to-right diagonal lines; the 74 billion remaining by squares with upward-sloping lines. After reaching a peak of 3.5 billion barrels in 1970, the curve indicates a steady decline to 2.5 billion by 1980, to slightly over 1.5 billion by 1990, and to only 1 billion by the year 2000. Calling particular attention to the sixty-seven-year time period required to produce the middle 80 percent (i.e., from 1932 to 2000), Hubbert

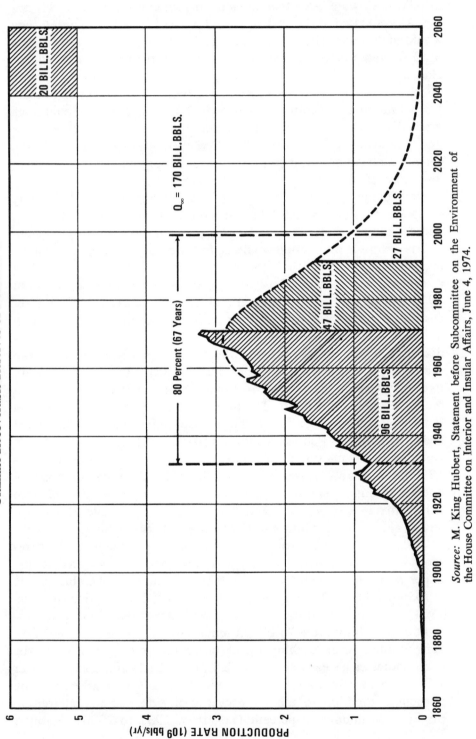

CHART 1-3

Ultimate Recoverable Reserves of Domestic Oil

Source: M. King Hubbert, Statement before Subcommittee on the Environment of the House Committee on Interior and Insular Affairs, June 4, 1974.

noted: "A child born in the 1930's, if he lives a normal life expectancy, will see the United States consume most of its oil during his lifetime."[28]

WORLD RESERVES

In contrast to the grim picture presented for the United States of falling production, declining proved reserves, and a limited ultimate recoverable supply, the prospects for the world as a whole are decidedly more favorable. Production has yet to be curtailed by physical constraints, proved reserves have been rising, and total resources appear adequate to meet probable demand for at least a generation. If a worldwide shortage of petroleum develops before then, the probabilities are that it will be the result not of the "niggardliness of nature" but of "manmade" commercial or political restrictions. It is true that, like any finite resource, the world's petroleum reserves will ultimately be exhausted. But by then the world's dependence on petroleum should have given way to other sources of energy (e.g., hydrogen) and more efficient ways of utilizing them.

Although the earth's total reserves are of course depleted by each year's production, proved reserves have steadily risen since World War II, the amount taken out of the ground having been more than offset by what has been added through new discoveries. In the Middle East, for example, nearly 100 billion barrels were added to the area's proved reserves in the short span 1967–71. In other words, its reserves in known reservoirs considered to be recoverable under existing economic and operating conditions *increased* by more than twice the total existing proved reserves of North America. The trends in proved reserves over the past quarter of a century are shown in Chart 1-4.

As can be seen, the long-term upward trend in the world total is largely the result of the continuing increase in the Middle East reserves. In the two decades before the development of the "energy crisis" proved reserves had increased sevenfold, while their share of the world total mounted from 51.5 to 60.9 percent. At the same time, North American reserves fell from 30.0 to only 8.6 percent, and beginning in the 1970's began to decline in absolute terms. These diverging trends clearly portended an increasing dependence by the United States on Middle East supplies.[29]

Until 1968, however, North America led the Middle East (and the other continents as well) in actual production. Even in 1971, when the Middle East was producing 34.2 percent of world output, North America, with less than a tenth of the world's reserves, was the second largest producing area, accounting for 23.3 percent. As Chart 1-5

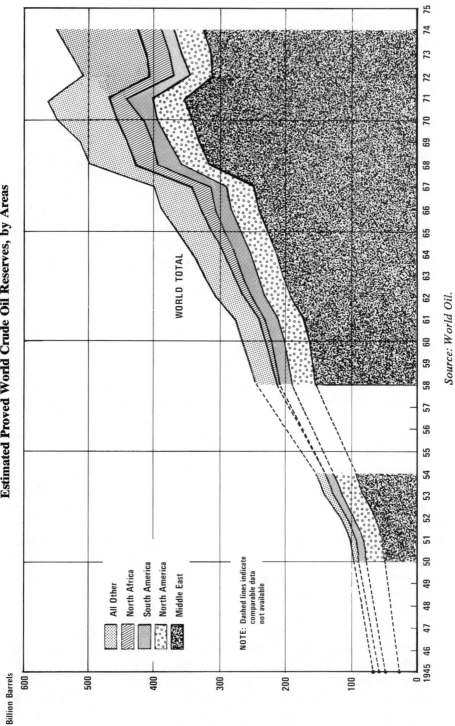

CHART 1-4

Estimated Proved World Crude Oil Reserves, by Areas

Billion Barrels

WORLD TOTAL

All Other
North Africa
South America
North America
Middle East

NOTE: Dashed lines indicate
comparable data
not available

Source: World Oil.

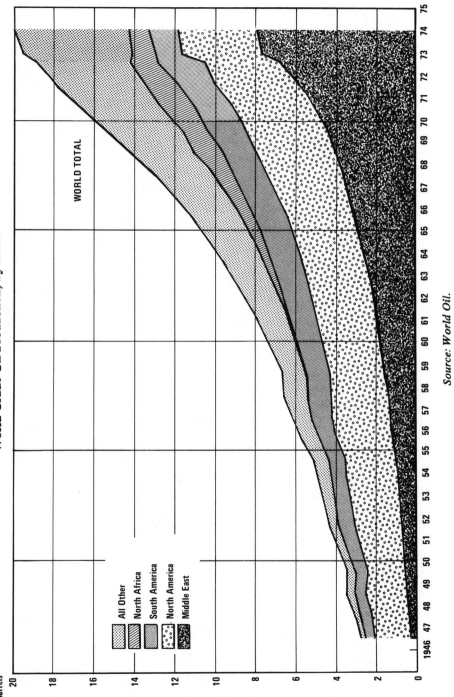

CHART 1-5
World Crude Oil Production, by Areas

Billion Barrels

WORLD TOTAL

All Other
North Africa
South America
North America
Middle East

Source: World Oil.

shows, production in the Middle East rose at a moderate but steady pace until the mid-sixties. Thereafter, its rate of increase noticeably accelerated, output rising from 3.051 billion in 1965 to 6.036 billion barrels in 1971 and 7.948 in 1974.

But the importance of the Middle East is even greater than would be inferred from the published figures on proved reserves. Referring to the "enormous reserves and high producibility of certain oil fields, especially in the Middle East," Paul H. Frankel, probably the world's leading petroleum economist, observed: ". . . the reserve figures, proved reserve figures . . . I have no doubt, nor does anybody else, are vastly understated."[30] Reporting a conversation on August 3, 1973, with a Saudi official, H. J. Johnston of Aramco noted: "I told him while it is unlikely we would find any more Ghawars, I thought that Aramco for the foreseeable future would continue to find number of accumulations on order of size of that discovered by Marjan 25, which . . . preliminary estimates indicated contains in excess of 5 billion barrels of oil in place."[31] Along the same lines, Annon M. Burd of Aramco notified J. M. Voss of Caltex of the displeasure of Saudi officials that only slightly more than a third of the "discovered reservoirs" were "developed and producing":

> It has been brought to our attention that for some time now, representatives of the Saudi Arabian government have been critical of Aramco for producing Arabian light crude at such a high rate and Arabian Medium and Heavy at much lower rates. They complain that the Aramco shareholders preferentially lift the most valuable crude and leave the others behind.
>
> We understand that the Saudi Oil ministry has pointed out that Aramco has at present over 85 discovered reservoirs out of which only 40 are developed and producing. They have indicated much concern about activity concentrated in Abqaig, Ghawar, and Berri (all Arabian Light fields) which according to Aramco plans would produce more than 50% of total Aramco oil production. . . .[32]

In describing a conversation with Saudi Arabia's oil minister, Sheik Yamani, Aramco's Johnston revealed the astonishing information that Saudi Arabia's "true reserves" were more than two and a half times the "ultra conservative numbers" at which "proven reserves" were being carried:

> I told him . . . that really the gist of the matter was, up until now, not very important to determine what our reserves actually were and you could view this in any way you like, true enough *in the past we have given ultra conservative numbers as proven reserves of 90 billion barrels,* and there were a number of reasons why we didn't have to worry about what they truly were, they were big

enough even at that rate . . . he had asked for a depletion study and when we attempted to make this study we found ourselves arguing here in Aramco on what our true reserves were. And we finally came to the position that *our true reserves were 245 billion based on the method that is commonly accepted for determining these figures.*[33]

This 155 billion difference between the reported and the "true" figures is nearly three times the total proved reserves of North America. But Saudi Arabia is not the only Mideast country whose proved reserves are known to be vastly understated. An even more conspicuous example is Iraq, whose untapped reservoirs have been stated by a U.S. "intelligence report" to be "fantastic."[34] Moreover, figures on proved reserves do not include all of the recently discovered new fields outside the OPEC countries that have yet to come "onstream" but which are confidently expected to be in production within a few years. By 1980, according to *The Petroleum Economist*, new fields in the North Sea, the North Slope of Alaska, Brazil, and Malaysia may be producing more than 2.5 billion barrels a year, increasing the non-Communist world's crude oil output as of 1973 by 10.5 percent.[35] And of course there may be others to come: "The discovery of so many new oil fields of at least medium significance within a relatively short time should encourage the hope or further significant finds in widely spread parts of the world."[36]

At the Ninth World Petroleum Congress, held in Tokyo during May 1975, J. D. Moody of Mobil Oil presented estimates of ultimate recoverable crude oil resources. Although trying to estimate what has not as yet been discovered is a most uncertain art (particularly where unexplored areas are involved), *The Petroleum Economist* observed that these estimates "deserve respect."[37] Moody placed the world total at 2,000 billion barrels, of which only 297 billion (15%) had been used through 1973, 740 billion (37%) are in the form of "proved and prospective" reserves, and 963 billion (48%) of "undiscovered potential" remain to be found.

Moody's figures are compared in Table 1-1 with earlier estimates by L. G. Weeks and W. P. Ryman of Exxon. The totals of all three are about the same—2,000 billion barrels for Weeks and Moody, and 2,090 billion barrels for Ryman. In each of the estimates the Middle East is shown to be the largest source of supply, followed by the Communist countries and the United States. As is also indicated by Moody's figures, however, nearly half of the estimated supply in the United States (45%) has already been recovered, whereas the corresponding percentages for the Middle East and the Communist countries are only 11 and 9 percent, respectively. As compared to Ryman's estimates,

TABLE 1-1

Estimates of Ultimate Recovery of Crude Oil
(billions of barrels)

Area	L. G. Weeks (1962)	W. P. Ryman (1967)	J. D. Moody (1974)			
			Total	Cum. Prod. to 1973	Proved & Pros.	Undiscovered Potential
North America	355	295	315	110	58	147
U.S.	270	200	230	103	51	76
Canada	85	95	85	7	7	71
Latin America	221	225	174	44	39	91
W. Europe (incl. N. Sea)	19	20	69	3	21	45
Middle East	780	606	630	69	430	131
Africa	100	250	163	16	61	86
Far East	85	200	129	9	27	93
Communist Countries	440	500	500	46	104	350
Other			20			20
Total	2,000	2,090	2,000	297	740	963

Sources: Weeks and Ryman as presented by M. King Hubbert, "Energy Resources," in *Resources and Man*, National Academy of Sciences—National Research Council, 1969, p. 194; J. D. Moody, *The Petroleum Economist*, June 1975, p. 204.

the principal differences are downward revisions for Latin America, Africa, and the Far East, and increases for the United States (reflecting Alaska) and Western Europe (resulting from the North Sea). In Moody's distribution by geographic area, the Middle East is the largest future source of oil, with 430 billion barrels in the form of proved and prospective reserves and 131 billion in undiscovered potential, or a third of the world's ultimate recoverable reserves (excluding past production). Next in importance are the Communist countries, with a little more than a quarter of the total. By way of contrast, the share estimated for the United States is only 8 percent.

According to *The Petroleum Economist,* Moody believes that his estimates, particularly for offshore reserves, may substantially understate the available supply:

> . . . Mr. Moody refers to certain recent developments which could make it possible eventually to upgrade the potential of the as yet unexplored deeper oceans, and thereby conceivably to *double his own current estimate of ultimate world reserves.* There have been highly promising new preliminary studies of the geology of certain deep ocean areas, among them a Russian study of an area extending from the Voring Plateau offshore Norway to the waters north of Iceland. The Deep Sea Drilling Project has revealed that there are traces of various hydrocarbons at numerous sites in very deep waters, and it has also been found that organic rich sediments in deep oceans are more widespread than previously anticipated. Finally, it has been proved that turbidites (one of the most typical of the deep-ocean sediments) often have a high content of substances which either resemble crude oil or which appear to be convertible to crude under favorable geological conditions.[38]

That current estimates of ultimate recoverable reserves, such as Moody's, are indeed understatements—at least for the Middle East— is also indicated by a new and comprehensive study of the area's reserves, *The Petroleum Geology and Resources of the Middle East,* by Professor C. R. Bedoun of the American University of Beirut and Dr. H. V. Dunnington.[39] According to their analysis, the area's ultimate recoverable reserves should be raised from current estimates of 600–650 billion barrels to at least 900 billion barrels, and probably well beyond. In their view, the current estimates suffer from three downward biases. They understate the amount of oil in known reservoirs that can be brought to the surface by conventional secondary recovery methods (water flooding and gas reprocessing), as well as by sophisticated tertiary techniques involving the injection of chemicals. They disregard known reservoirs of heavy and sulphurous oils that can be made usable by current technologies. And, finally, they do not adequately allow for discoveries of new fields and of new pools in old fields. In the authors' view, the first of these biases is the most important.

It should also be recognized that in other parts of the world there are promising geological structures which have so far remained singularly free of intensive exploration. Noting their prevalence along many continental shelves, the National Academy of Sciences comments on the "absence or rarity of producing fields off Eastern Asia (except Indonesia), southern Asia, eastern Africa, northwestern Africa, eastern United States, eastern South America, western South America, northern North America and Asia, and off Antarctica, even though many of these shelves appear to have high potential."[40] In some of these areas the lack of production is attributed to climatic inhospitality; in others to "politically inhospitable host nations." But spectacular progress has been made during recent years in extracting oil under even the most arduous climatic and geographical conditions. And, as the Academy notes, "politics change." What makes the continental shelves such rich repositories is the entrapment of decaying organic matter between continental runoff and underwater dams or reefs: "Belts of thick marine sediments of Mesozoic or Tertiary Age contain fields that produce about 60 percent of the world's oil and gas. Most of these belts underlie coastal regions, where they have been localized by marginal troughs bounded on their oceanward sides by dams of tectonic, diapiric, or reefal origin. Because the sediments in these troughs are thick and contain much organic matter produced from nutrients in continental runoff, the quantity of oil and gas in them may well exceed the average for continental areas that are underlain by sediments."[41]

The Academy regards as "particularly promising" the ancient deltas of the world's large rivers. Noting that "Many of these deltas are major producing areas of the world," it calls attention to other deltas that have been "inadequately explored"—notably off South America, India, and the Far East—expressing its opinion that "when explored," the undeveloped deltas "should materially increase oil production and reserves."

*   *   *

Behind every energy policy, program, or legislative proposal put forth by the practical men of affairs lie assumptions (usually implicit) concerning the adequacy of petroleum reserves. These assumptions range from the alarmist position which envisions an imminent exhaustion to the euphoric view that reserves are adequate to last indefinitely. For the United States, the pessimistic position under any reasonable forecast of demand is very definitely in order. For the world, it will take a somewhat longer period before reserves are seriously depleted. In addition to the problems of estimation on the supply side, predictions of world demand are exercises in uncertainty. Straight-line projections of past use, characterized by the National Academy of Sciences as "primitive," "unsophisticated," "untested," "inadequate," and neglectful of "considerations which are difficult to incorporate into numerical models," have had the effect of creating "a tendency toward upward bias that exaggerates demand."[42] An important complication is the refusal of per capita consumption to remain constant. As Wilfred Malenbaum has pointed out, "For energy (and for most minerals) the U.S. and other rich lands show declining intensities: such nations tend to use less energy per unit of GNP as GNP per capita increases."[43] Nonetheless, the world's long-range supply-demand situation can hardly be regarded as comfortable.

The implications for public policy in the United States are in the nature of immediate requirements. For the world as a whole, the objectives are the same but the urgency of action less demanding. The objectives should be: (1) to increase supply by stimulating exploration, improving recovery, and developing alternative fuels (particularly for motor vehicle transportation); (2) to reduce demand; (3) to lessen the ability of the major companies to aggravate the shortage to their own advantage; and (4) to infuse competition if possible among the producing countries. Even under the best of circumstances, however, the consuming countries will become more and more dependent on a few large-scale suppliers. And this, as the distributions of reserves have shown, will mean increasing involvement with the Middle East.

Part
ONE

THE CONTROL OF FOREIGN OIL

Most of the world's known reserves outside the Communist countries and North America happen to be found in a few locales—the Middle East, parts of Africa (Libya, Algeria, and Nigeria), Venezuela, and Indonesia. And within these countries the reserves are centralized in a few large pools. In addition to this geological condition, certain institutional arrangements have contributed to centralized control. The early concession agreements granted monopoly rights for the exploration of oil in huge areas, extending over long periods of time. Ownership of subsoil mineral rights has resided in the state or ruler, thereby making it unnecessary (as in the United States) for a company seeking exploration rights to deal with numerous private owners of the surface land. Moreover, the inaccessibility of the oil-bearing lands and their remoteness from the principal consumption centers required substantial capital outlays for production, gathering, refining, and transportation facilities. To retain control all the way to the ultimate consumer, the companies holding the concessions elected to bear the further costs of establishing their own retail outlets.

But, although a large measure of centralized control was more or less inevitable, the degree of concentration inherent in the nature of things has been insufficient to provide effective control of the markets. The nature of the industry is such that stability of price requires almost complete control over markets, since, as has been repeatedly demonstrated, it takes only a relatively small amount of "uncontrolled" supply to disrupt the market. And the generous spread between price and production costs has constantly held out the lure of generous profits at prices well below the prevailing levels. When independents secured concessions in Venezuela and later in Libya, it did not take long for their supplies to depress world prices. Control over supply through jointly owned operating companies and restrictive long-term contracts has had to be supplemented in a variety of ways. In these efforts, the major international oil companies have received the enthusiastic cooperation of governments in both the producing *and* the consuming countries. By means of a web of cartel arrangements set up in most of the world's consuming countries, they secured control over most of the world markets. Through boycotts, intimidation, and the active support of governmental bodies, particularly the U.S. State Department, they have been remarkably successful in keeping outsiders out. And by perfecting highly effective control "systems" they have been able to limit world output almost exactly to a predetermined growth rate, and, in addition, to eliminate differences in delivered prices at any given destination throughout the world. These "systems" provide the instruments by which effective control over the supply and distribution of oil can be continued into the future by the companies, the producing countries, or, some combination of both.

THE EVOLUTION OF CONTROL: Supply

2

FOR THE FORESEEABLE FUTURE, control over the movement of oil in world trade will hinge largely on control in the Middle East—principally Saudi Arabia, Iran, Kuwait, and Iraq. The overwhelming importance of this area in supplying crude petroleum to the world's principal consuming areas is shown in Chart 2-1. Of the 13,700 thousand barrels a day (m b/d) imported in 1974 by Western Europe, 9,480 m b/d, or 69 percent, was shipped from the Middle East, most of it (8,500 m b/d) coming by supertanker around the Cape of Good Hope. The remainder was made up almost entirely by shipments from African countries (Libya, Nigeria, and Algeria), totaling 3,454 m b/d, or 26 percent of Western Europe's imports. The Middle East was of even greater importance to Japan, supplying 3,711, or 77 percent, of the 4,810 m b/d imported by that country. Though exceeded by shipments from other Western Hemisphere countries (principally Canada and Venezuela), crude oil from the Middle East made up 29 percent of U.S. imports; moreover, they are rapidly rising, while this country's imports from other Western Hemisphere countries are declining.[1] In view of the area's dominant position in current world oil movements, as well as in reserves for the future, it should be clear that any understanding of the control over world oil must begin with the evolution of control over Mideast supply.

The discovery of oil in the Middle East traces back to the efforts, not of corporations or governments but of individuals. C. S. Gulbenkian, an Armenian, made a "comprehensive report" on the oil possibilities of Mesopotamia, prompting the Turkish Sultan, Abdul Hamid, in 1904 to transfer the ownership of immense tracts of land from the Minister of Mines to the Liste Civile: "This in fact was a transfer from the government to his personal account."[2] In Persia an Australian, William D'Arcy, obtained in 1901 a sixty-year concession covering 500,000 square miles or five-sixths of what is now Iran. There

29

CHART 2-1

World Crude Oil Movements to Major Consuming Areas, 1974 (Preliminary)

(THOUSAND BARRELS PER DAY)

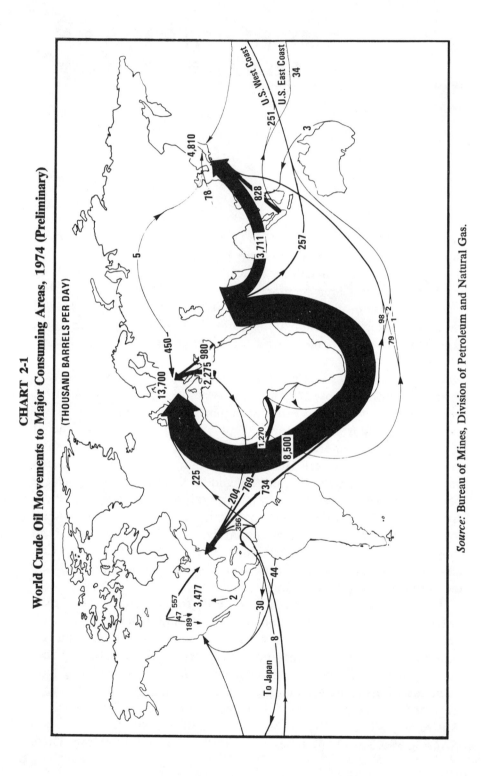

Source: Bureau of Mines, Division of Petroleum and Natural Gas.

he established the Anglo-Persian Oil Co., later to become Anglo-Iranian, and, still later, British Petroleum (BP). An interested party was the Deutsche Bank, which secured mining rights extending 20 kilometers on both sides of the projected Baghdad railway. But according to a commission of experts sent by the bank to examine the area, ". . . it seemed doubtful whether the discovered oil was worth exploiting, since considerable transportation problems had to be solved, and the Deutsche Bank, which would have had to bear the main burden of all exploitation costs, owned promising oil resources in Rumania. . . ."[3] The Deutsche Bank lost its foothold to the French as a spoil of World War I, while the direct corporate beneficiaries of the Gulbenkian and D'Arcy discoveries were the British-European firms, BP and Royal Dutch Shell.

Not until the latter half of the twenties were the first American companies admitted into the area. On July 31, 1928, Exxon and Mobil became part owners of the Iraq Petroleum Co. Later entrants into the Middle East were Gulf (through Kuwait) and Standard of California and Texaco (through Bahrein and Saudi Arabia). Until 1973, when the host governments began to exercise varying degrees of influence over the disposition of their mineral wealth, control over Mideast oil remained firmly in the hands of these companies—the "seven sisters." Their control was rooted in a series of jointly owned operating companies established in each of the area's principal producing countries: Iraq, Iran, Saudi Arabia, and Kuwait. Supplementing and reinforcing these joint ventures were supply contracts covering very large volumes of oil, extending over periods of many years, and containing highly restrictive provisions relating to terms and conditions of sale. The pattern of control through joint ventures was first established by the formation of the Iraq Petroleum Company.

THE IRAQ PETROLEUM COMPANY

Formed in 1914, the Iraq Petroleum Company (originally Turkish Petroleum Co.) brought together interests who for over a decade had been contesting each other for a firm foothold in the Middle East. From the outset, the purposes of IPC were to consolidate existing rights under common ownership and to preclude competitive rivalry for future rights. Under an agreement adopted at the British Foreign Office on March 19, 1914, the British-Dutch groups accepted a "self-denying clause, stipulating that they "would not be interested, directly or indirectly, in the production or manufacture of crude oil in the Ottoman Empire . . . otherwise than through the Turkish Petroleum Co."[4]

Conspicuous by their absence were the American companies, who had remained profoundly disinterested in the Middle East. But scattered shortages during World War I gave rise to a deep-seated fear that the United States might be running out of oil. According to an industry source, "Fear of an oil shortage in the United States was uppermost as a factor in international relations after World War I. It was a hold-over fear from a narrow escape from scarcity in 1917–1918 when in the midst of war." Moreover, even before the use of the foreign tax credit, the cost of leasing from private landowners (usually at a one-eighth royalty rate) was generally higher than securing rights from governments. There was also widespread concern over a foreign monopoly of all foreign oil resources. The Senate launched an investigation, which found that American interests were indeed being systematically excluded from foreign oil fields.[5] In 1920, Senator Phelan of California introduced a bill to establish a government corporation to develop oil resources in foreign countries.[6] Negotiations looking toward American entrance into the Middle East as a participant in the Iraq Petroleum Company began in 1922 and continued for six years, with the American firms represented by Exxon (Standard of New Jersey).[7] The U.S. companies, however, were frustrated in their efforts to secure access to the new sources of supply, which were being discovered with increasing frequency in Rumania, India, the Dutch East Indies, Iran, and elsewhere:

> Because of these factors, by the end of World War I nearly all of the important American oil companies were actively seeking foreign reserves. In this search, however, they were confronted in the Eastern Hemisphere with formidable obstacles, the most important ones being the national and colonial policies of Great Britain and the activities of British-Dutch oil companies which were, themselves, engaged in the search for foreign reserves. The British-Dutch companies were endeavoring to prevent the surrender of Empire reserves to the American "oil trust," while at the same time they were busily protecting a similar trust of their own. The national and colonial policies of other European countries were directed to similar objectives.[8]

These restrictionist policies were dramatized by the British refusal in 1919 to permit American oil companies to send exploration parties into Mesopotamia (now Iraq). Formerly part of the old Ottoman Empire under Turkish control, Mesopotamia after the war had become a "mandated" area under British control. Arguing that the war had been won by all of the allies fighting together, the U.S. companies and their government insisted upon an "open door" policy, specifically that favored treatment not be accorded nationals of any one country, that concessions not be so large as to be exclusive, and that no monopolistic concession be granted. Although it was the British-Dutch interests which had the concessions, the American firms supplied nearly three-fifths of total foreign demand, with Exxon alone controlling over 50 percent of the U.K. market, and hence were in a strong bargaining position. In July 1922, negotiations began looking toward American entrance into the Iraq Petroleum Co.; with the U.S. companies represented by W. C. Teagle, president of Exxon. After six years of seemingly interminable haggling, the U.S. firms, on July 31, 1928, were granted a combined 23.75 percent share (divided equally between Exxon and Mobil), with 23.75 percent shares, each, going to British Petroleum, Shell, Compagnie Française Pétrole, and the remaining 5 percent to Gulbenkian. IPC was not operated as an independent profit-making company, but was essentially a partnership for producing and sharing crude oil among its owners. Profits were kept at a nominal level by charging the member groups an arbitrarily low price for crude—a practice which reduced IPC's tax liability to the British government and permitted the refining and marketing subsidiaries of the groups to capture most of the profits resulting from IPC's operations. This arrangement proved to be the source of considerable friction between the large integrated companies on the one hand and the French and Gulbenkian on the other. The French had only limited refining and marketing facilities, while Gulbenkian owned none.

Between 1922, when the "open door" policy was first advanced, and 1927, when it was in the process of being discarded, radical changes took place in the world oil situation. The fears of a shortage, so widespread in 1922, were drowned in a surplus of oil. Instead of competing for the development of oil resources, the international companies turned their attention to limiting output and allocating world oil markets. Reflecting this change in economic conditions, the American companies lost their enthusiasm for the "open door" policy, particularly after their entrance into IPC had been assured. One of the key provisions of the policy was the right of *any* responsible concern to obtain by competitive bidding concessions on plots to be selected each year by the Iraqi government. Originally backed by the American companies, this feature was subsequently nullified by a clause permitting IPC itself to be a bidder, thereby enabling the company to outbid any prospective lessee at no cost to itself, since the proceeds from the sale were to be returned to IPC. Three years after the American companies had been admitted, the concession was revised to eliminate all provisions for sharing the concession with third parties.

The "open door," in the words of one industry observer, had been "bolted, barred, and hermetically sealed."

> In the early twenties when the American oil companies first became interested in oil concessions in the Middle East, they placed great emphasis on what was termed the "open door" policy, and, in fact, made the acceptance of this policy a sine qua non of their participation in IPC. In this they were actively supported by the Ameriman Government. In its initial stages the "open door" policy was broadly interpreted to mean freedom for any company to obtain, without discrimination, oil concessions, in mandated areas, particularly in Mesopotamia. . . . The "open door" policy which had been so strongly advanced was discarded in subsequent years without a single test of its adequacy as a practical operating principle.[9]

Competition among the owners themselves was precluded by retaining the "self-denying" clause of the 1914 Foreign Office agreement. Within an area circumscribed on a map by a "Red Line" encompassing most of the old Ottoman Empire (including Turkey, Iraq, Saudi Arabia, and adjoining sheikdoms, but excluding Iran, Kuwait, Israel, and Trans-Jordan), the owners agreed to be interested in oil only through the IPC (see Chart 2-2). When Gulf Oil, a member of the American group, sought permission to exercise an option to purchase a concession in Bahrein, IPC denied the request.

As one writer commented, the Red Line Agreement ". . . is an outstanding example of a restrictive combination for the control of a large portion of the world's supply by a group of companies which together dominate the world market for this commodity." In a confidential memorandum, the French described the objectives of the agreement: "The execution of the Red Line Agreement marked the beginning of a long-term plan for the world control and distribution of oil in the Near East." IPC was so operated as "to avoid any publicity which might jeopardize the long-term plan of the private interests of the group. . . ."

THE ENTRANCE INTO ARAMCO

While providing adequate protection against independent action by the groups within IPC, the Red Line Agreement could not prevent *nonmembers* from seeking concessions within the red-line area. When an independent organization, the British Oil Development Co. (BOD), obtained a concession in the Mosul area of Iraq, IPC began to secure as many concessions as possible within the red-line area, principally for the purpose of keeping them out of the hands of competitors. IPC

CHART 2-2
Oil Concessions and Facilities in the Middle East, January 1951

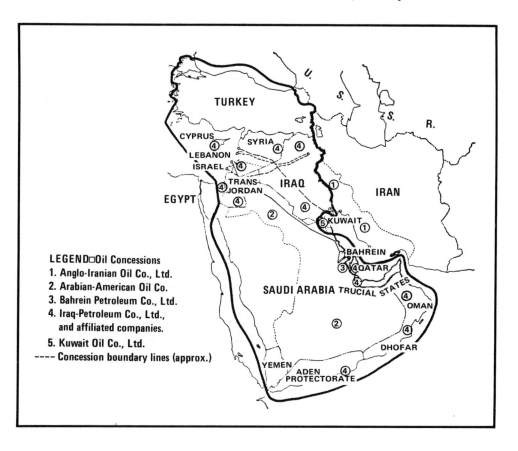

subsequently obtained control of the BOD concession by secretly purchasing its shares.

The same type of problem on a far larger scale developed when
another outsider, SoCal (Standard Oil of California), discovered oil
initially on the island of Bahrein and later in Saudi Arabia. Standard
of California was a newcomer to the world oil scene, and as *The
Petroleum Times* put it, ". . . what each large oil group fears more
than anything else is the entry of a powerful newcomer in the established order of world oil markets."[10] A confidential memorandum
found by the Department of Justice in Exxon's files discussed the

problem, stating: "It would seem a mistake to allow even a small quantity of this [Bahrein] crude to find a direct market, and the question of taking 100,000 or 150,000 barrels . . . ought to be considered."[11] In their efforts to arrive at some accommodation with this new entrant BP, Shell and Exxon were seriously handicapped by the refusal of the French and Gulbenkian to waive their rights entitling them to their pro rata share of output produced within the Red Line area. The Big Three tried for almost seven years to alter the Red Line Agreement in such a way that they would be able to neutralize the competitive effects of Standard of California's operations, but with only partial success. The problem was frankly discussed in another Exxon internal memorandum: ". . . unfortunate repercussions [of the Red Line Agreement] resulting for some of the groups, including ourselves, is that as long as [SoCal] would not sell and was not in a position to trade with any of the Iraq partners now interested in selling products in the Far East, they would be obliged to become competitive; and in forcing an entry into these markets, would adversely affect the price structure in these markets."[12] Or as the FTC staff report on the International Petroleum Cartel put it: "As long as the red-line agreement hung around their necks like a millstone, the Big Three were placed in the role of unwilling outsiders, watching Standard of California develop this great new area [Saudi Arabia] with possible disastrous consequences on world price and markets."[13]

Having relied for some years on Mobil (Socony-Vacuum) to market its products in the Far East, SoCal had not itself developed any foreign marketing facilities—or what the industry refers to as a marketing "position": "The Big Three international oil companies were fearful that SoCal would force Bahrein products into world markets by reducing prices, a course of action which, however, could be detrimental to SoCal's own interests in the United States."[14] Confronted with such possible repercussions as an international price war, the company opted for an arrangement "which would make it possible to market Bahrein products without having to grant price concessions."[15] On July 1, 1936, an agreement was entered into establishing a new jointly owned company, Caltex, under which SoCal received a one-half interest in Texaco's marketing positions east of Suez, and Texaco a one-half interest in the Bahrein concession and facilities. Under this joint venture, later superseded for Saudi Arabia by the Arabian American Oil Co. (Aramco), SoCal was provided with outlets for Bahrein production by a company with a recognized market position. On its part, the Texas Company gained a more advantageous source of supply for its foreign markets. Meanwhile, SoCal had also gained the concession for Saudi Arabia, to which the provisions of the Bahrein agreement were extended. The world oil trade breathed an almost audible sigh of relief, *The Petroleum Times* observing that the agreement: ". . . assures that Bahrein production, as well as any output that may eventually come from countries now being developed by Standard of California, will have assured and regulated outlets and will so lessen any possible danger of upsetting the equilibrium of international markets."[16]

But the feeling of relief was short-lived. It soon became apparent that Saudi Arabia's reserves were far greater than had been anticipated and certainly far larger than could be accommodated by SoCal's newly acquired marketing position. By 1941, up to 200,000 barrels a day could reportedly have been produced in Saudi Arabia, whereas the available market position "east of Suez" absorbed only 12,000 to 15,000 barrels. To compound the problem King Ibn Saud, ruler of Saudi Arabia, was insisting that production be expanded to increase his royalty payments: "In short, Aramco's production could not be readily shut in or retarded."[17] The available alternatives have been described as follows:

> The owners of Aramco (Standard of California and the Texas Co.) were apparently faced with the choice of either forcing their way by competitive means into markets which, before the war, had been closed to them because of international cartel arrangements; i.e., the "as is" position; or permitting companies which did have marketing outlets and positions in areas *west of Suez* to acquire a proprietary interest in Aramco.
>
> If the former choice were made and the international companies refused to make way for Aramco's output, the stability of all oil concessions in the Middle East might be upset, particularly since King Ibn-Saud was unlikely to accept a program of limited output. Moreover, in view of the various pressures to produce, Aramco might attempt to force its way into international markets by competing price-wise.
>
> But if the latter choice were made, Aramco's output would not unstabilize existing world prices and markets, as the production could be fitted into markets over a wide area without the need of price competition. Also, if necessary, adjustments could be made in the production rates of other areas operated by the purchasing companies in order to make room for Aramco's output.[18]

Some resolution of the problem had to be found. During 1946, Aramco was selling crude for about 90 cents per barrel at a time when the lowest price prevailing on the U.S. Gulf for oil of comparable quality was $1.28. That there existed ample room for further price cutting was indicated by the fact that both SoCal and Texas estimated the cost of producing Aramco oil to be only 33 cents a barrel.[19] From Exxon's point of view, Aramco would be a better source of profits than IPC; and, in addition, its participation in Aramco would arrest the price cutting. An Exxon document stated, "A deal through which Jersey would obtain a substantial interest in Saudi Arabia would not only have the advantage of providing additional supplies to Jersey which could probably be converted into cash and profits more rapidly than IPC oil, but would have the further advantage of easing the pressure that would otherwise come from Caltex in their efforts to expand their outlets."[20]

Within SoCal a strong faction argued against allowing Exxon in as a partner in Aramco and indeed for competing against Exxon wherever possible. In a memorandum of June 10, 1946, SoCal Director Ronald C. Stoner observed that affiliation with Exxon would link Caltex to a company which in turn was tied to Shell in joint ventures in all of its overseas production: "Jersey, therefore, could never get ahead of Shell because the more Venezuelan, Iraqi and Indonesian crude oil available to Jersey, the more became available to Shell."[21]

> The more they [Jersey] develop and produce in these areas, the greater they allow the Shell position to build up. Once they equalize their position with us, then they can go ahead with the Shell as they have been doing, competing very effectively against us. They are dominated by foreign groups in the area. We, the California-Texas, the only solely American group in the area, therefore are in a position to expand rapidly; not because we already have the markets, but because we have a cheap oil available right now; i.e., with relatively little investment we can put more oil into the Blue Line Area (East of Suez) and other areas, and by obtaining tankers we can put oil any place in the world until it seems advisable to lay the Trans Arabian pipeline. Our earnings in Arabia are tremendous and are going to be greater, deal or no deal with Standard-Vacuum for the simple reason that it will take such a small investment to put our crude from the oil fields of Arabia to the port of Ras Tanura and then to the world.[22]

Instead of becoming enmeshed in a web of restrictive agreements, Caltex should become the supplier to the independent sector of the U.S. market, which could readily supply the capital necessary to develop the Saudi Arabia concession:

> It is common knowledge that all large companies in the United States are seeking foreign oil, such as Phillips, Barnsdall, Atlantic Refining, Standard of Indiana, and Sinclair, and hundreds of millions of dollars are being spent to augment the decline in domestic production. It is barely possible that any and all of these

companies could afford to buy Arabian oil at a profit to us rather than seek foreign oil by drilling. Should we desire capital, it would seem this avenue should be investigated with the view to making sales or exchange contracts with those companies, which might help us in our expansion on the Atlantic seaboard. They could advance us on the contracts and it would give a number of American companies an interest in Arabian oil, which would be political protection for us in the future. This, I believe, is no small thing to consider since there has been criticism in the United States that this concession is too big for one company and also there has been strong thought in the world of petroleum that all countries and more companies should have access to foreign petroleum.[23]

The Senate Subcommittee on Multinational Corporations commented that the acceptance of Stoner's recommendation "would have radically changed the international oil industry by giving the U.S. domestic oil industry a large—if not deciding—say in how the majors set production levels in the Middle East."[24] There can be little question but that had SoCal followed Stoner's recommendation, Caltex would have become the largest supplier of oil in the world, able to beat any rival or combination of rivals in free and open competition for markets. But the cause of merger prevailed, for, as the Subcommittee observed, "Exxon remained in command throughout the merger negotiations."[25]

By becoming part of the company cartel and bound by its restriction, SoCal has never been able to market the oil that otherwise would have been available to it. The amount allotted to SoCal as a 30 percent owner of Aramco has had to be fitted into a world total made up in large part of supplies with considerably higher costs. One possible explanation for the subordination of Stoner's persuasive arguments to the "command" position of Exxon may lie in the fact that the same financial interest group was by far the leading stockholder in both SoCal and Exxon (as well as Mobil). The sole study ever made that traces ownership of large corporations back through "owners of record" to the ultimate "beneficial owners" was the report of the Securities and Exchange Commission to the Temporary National Economic Committee; the data relate to 1939, only seven years before the negotiations over the entrance of Exxon into Aramco.[26] With respect to the three corporations involved here, the report found that the combined holdings of the Rockefeller family and family foundations should in the case of Exxon "carry with it an amount of influence equal to working control"; that in the case of Mobil, "the Rockefeller interests seemed to have safe working control"; and that in the case of SoCal, the block of stock owned by the Rockefeller family and family foundations "appeared to carry working control."[27]

The ultimate objective of the elaborate maneuvers[28] to free Exxon and Mobil from the Red Line Agreement was an arrangement which, in the words of a Mobil official, would "lead to the stabilization of the world market price of oil by preventing distress oil from being offered on the market."[29] After the Red-Line problem had been resolved, meetings were initiated between Exxon and SoCal as a result of which the form of the joint venture was changed:

> Discussions with Standard of California and the Texas Co. were initiated by Jersey [Standard of N.J.] and Socony [Mobil] sometime before mid-1946. By December of that year an agreement in principle had been reached whereby Jersey Standard and Socony-Vacuum would obtain a 30-percent and a 10-percent interest, respectively, in Aramco and Trans-Arabian Pipe Line Co. By March 12, 1947, all details were worked out, and the formal documents were signed on that date. . . .
>
> Aramco's output could now be marketed not only in Europe through the marketing outlets formerly owned by the Texas Co. . . . but also through the extensive marketing outlets of Jersey and Socony, which were world-wide. Even before the agreements between Jersey-Socony and Aramco were consummated, Jersey and Socony began to purchase crude and refined products from Aramco.[30]

As in Bahrein, the joint venture provided a handy alternative to competition. The beneficiaries were the established international oil companies, who thus avoided the rigors of price rivalry; the losers included SoCal and Texaco, their potential oil company customers, and consumers generally. "Thus, while new markets were opened up to Aramco, the recognized marketing positions of the international oil companies were preserved. The principal change was a shift in their sources of supply on the part of three of the four American companies which now own Aramco in order to make room for Aramco's production, which they are now in a position to control."[31]

But the acceptance of Exxon and Mobil into ownership gave rise to a whole new set of controversies between the old and the new owners. For one thing, there was the price to be charged for Aramco crude. The position of the new owners revealed, in the words of Barbara Svedberg, attorney of the Antitrust Division who had worked on the cartel case, "the unusual and unlikely spectacle of a customer complaining about paying too low a price for what they are buying." According to her testimony, an Exxon spokesman stated: "If an arbitrarily low price is set for Arabian crude for sale to the partners, say 90 cents a barrel, it would in all probability result in price cutting to obtain business." An increase in price to $1.02 was objected to on the grounds that it still left Aramco's quotation well below the "competitive world market price" of $1.40 f.o.b. the Persian Gulf. SoCal and Texaco took the position that the price of Aramco crude should be related to its cost, contending that "tying the price to . . . world market prices would restrict the area in which Aramco crude could be profitably resold and as a result limit production." It was stressed that Aramco's costs were considerably lower than costs in the Texas Gulf, on which "world" prices were based, and also below costs in other Mideast countries. A document in the SoCal files stated: "Attempting to tie the price of crude to Offtakers to world market prices involves directly or indirectly U.S. gulf prices and assumptions as to transportation costs. This is not logical as U.S. crude prices may increase because of the demand in this country whereas Middle East crude prices should decrease as more of that area's tremendous reserves are developed. Aramco's competition is other Middle East sources, not the Western Hemisphere." Another reason for basing Aramco's price on its own costs was expressed in a letter found in the Texaco files marked "Personal and Confidential": "If the crude price is determined by agreement among Aramco Directors and not on a cost-plus basis, there may be danger of violation of U.S. Anti-Trust laws . . . it may be contended that any agreement as to price arrived at by the Aramco Directors, who are also directors of four large oil companies doing business in the United States, is in effect an agreement in restraint of trade with the United States."[32]

On this, as on other issues, the Exxon-Mobil position prevailed. A sense of discouragement among the expansion-minded officials of Aramco set in, and their leaders resigned. A lengthy internal State Department memorandum from Parker T. Hart, resident consul general in Dhahran, Saudi Arabia, dated July 2, 1949, discusses the imminent retirement of James MacPherson, vice-president of Aramco, who had been in charge of its field operations since 1945. According to this document, "The accession of two new ownership companies, Standard Oil of New Jersey and Socony-Vacuum, brought about changes of policy which undoubtedly were the direct cause of Mr. 'Mac's' decision to leave Aramco." The principal factor cited was a "cutback" ordered by the parent companies, which was a severe blow to MacPherson's sense of initiative. "It placed a wall before him. . . . He refuses to accept in his own mind the justifications given (scarcity of dollar markets) and argues that arrangements should have been made to sell for sterling. He is convinced that all ownership companies are now holding back to avoid Aramco competition with other subsidiaries. . . . Mr. 'Mac' is essentially a pioneer, and the retrenchment to a goal of 500,000 barrels a day did violence to his instincts and convinced him that his real work in Dhahran was now finished." The memorandum concluded by citing MacPherson to the effect that ". . . the attitude of the Board in general is characterized by primary attention to world-wide oil balance sheets and profit before all else, rather than the realities of the Near East and particularly the special factors present in Arabia."[33]

KUWAIT: CONTROL THROUGH CONTRACTS

With proved reserves that are second in size only to those of Saudi Arabia, the tiny sheikdom of Kuwait was left outside the Red-Line area and therefore open to exploitation by the owners of IPC. In 1931 two of the participants, Gulf and BP, began negotiating for a concession in Kuwait. After about three years, during which time oil had been discovered in nearby Bahrein, they made common cause, obtaining an exclusive concession dividing the whole of Kuwait on a fifty-fifty basis. The contract establishing the Kuwait Oil Co., Ltd., contained the unusual provision that neither party would use oil from Kuwait to upset or injure the other's "trade or marketing position directly or indirectly at any time or place," and that they would confer from time to time to settle any questions that might arise between them regarding the marketing of Kuwait oil. It also provided that the oil to be produced in Kuwait would consist of two parts: (1) such quantity as the two owners agreed to provide and share equally; and (2) such additional quantity as either party might order out for its own account. Oil ordered by Gulf, however, could actually be supplied by BP "from Persia and/or Iraq in lieu of requiring the company to produce additional oil in Kuwait." This in effect gave BP a continuing option, subject to Gulf's consent, to control the quantity of oil produced in Kuwait by substituting oil from its other sources.

Further restrictions were contained in a long-term contract, under which Gulf agreed to supply Shell more than 1.5 billion barrels of Kuwait crude over a period of at least twenty-two years, and in another contract under which BP agreed to provide Exxon with 1.3 billion barrels of oil from Iran or Kuwait over a twenty-year period. Under the Gulf-Shell contract, profits derived by both companies from the production, transportation, refining, and marketing of the Kuwait crude were to be shared. In addition to the stipulation under the 1933 joint-ownership agreement with BP that it would not disturb BP's marketing position at any time or place, Gulf in its 1947 contract with Shell agreed that if it should use Kuwait oil to increase its business in any Eastern Hemisphere market, it would be penalized by an equivalent reduction of its deliveries to Shell. Under the profit-sharing arrangement, Gulf would also share in any losses occasioned by price cutting in any Eastern Hemisphere market. And price cutting would be anticipated if Gulf, using Kuwait (or any other) crude, tried to invade new markets or increase its share in established markets.

In the agreements that BP entered into with Exxon and Mobil, it was likewise provided that no more than 5 percent of the Kuwait (or Iranian) oil could be distributed "east of Suez." Under supplementary agreements to go into effect on January 1, 1952, Exxon was limited in the distribution of the oil to Europe and North and West Africa (where it had established market positions) and Mobil to the United States, to the countries bordering on the eastern Mediterranean, and to any other areas in which it already had a marketing position.

In the words of the report on the International Petroleum Cartel:

> Thus the crude oil supply contracts, not only because of the large quantities of oil and the long periods of time that were specified, but also because of the unusual provisions as to price and marketing, constitute effective instruments for the control of Middle East oil. As such, they complement and increase the degree of joint control over Middle East oil resulting from the pattern of joint ownership. . . . The operation of these two instruments of control, in effect, brings the seven international oil companies, controlling practically all of the Middle East oil resources, together into a mutual community of interest.[34]

THE IRANIAN CONSORTIUM

In 1901 William K. D'Arcy, a speculator in mining ventures in Australia and elsewhere, obtained a sixty-year oil concession from the Shah of Persia which covered 500,000 square miles, or five-sixths, of the Persian Empire (now Iran). In 1933 the concession was revised to give the Anglo-Iranian Oil Co., Ltd. (BP), a sixty-year concession covering over 100,000 square miles. More than half (56%) of the stock of Anglo-Iranian was owned by the British government, 22 percent by Burmah Oil Co. (a British-Shell affiliate), and the remaining 22 percent by various individuals. Anglo-Iranian realized that it did not have the market outlets to accommodate this potentially large source of supply, which would be in addition to its sizable holdings in Iraq and Kuwait. The logical partners would be the crude-short U.S. firms, notably Exxon and Mobil. To supply its far-flung international markets, Exxon had only its 11.8 percent share of the Iraq concession, plus its recently acquired 30 percent share of Saudi Arabia, but at the time the full size of the latter could hardly have been anticipated. With the same share of the Iraq concession plus only a 10 percent

share of Aramco, Mobil was in an even worse position. In addition
to their natural desire to secure long-term substantial supplies, Exxon
and Mobil shared with BP the common objective of preventing the
inevitable increase in Iranian production from being funneled into
world markets by companies less concerned in maintaining the stability
of world prices.

Like the purchase and sales agreements for Kuwait oil, the resulting
agreements differed from the usual run-of-the-mill contact in that they
involved very large quantities (800 million barrels for Exxon and 500
million barrels for Mobil), covered a lengthy period of time (twenty
years), and contained highly restrictive provisions. To protect BP's
markets in the Far East, neither Exxon nor Mobil were to market
more than 5 percent of the Iranian oil "east of Suez." European markets were open to Exxon since in most of these countries it had an
established "market position," but foreclosed to Mobil which generally did not. Mobil, however, was permitted to market in the United
States and "in the countries bordering on the eastern Mediterranean
(including any islands within or adjacent to these areas)."[35] But these
arrangements had hardly been entered into before they became moot.
On May 1, 1951, the properties of the Anglo-Iranian Oil Company
were nationalized by the Iranian government under the leadership
of its Prime Minister, Dr. Mossadeq. After the overthrow of the Mossadeq régime and the restoration of the Shah, a new government came
into power.

Before Iranian oil could again start flowing into world markets, two
immediate problems had to be dealt with: first, how to bring about a
reduction in oil output in those other Mideast countries whose production had been expanded to fill up the void left by Iran; and, second,
how to determine which companies were to participate in future
Iranian production. To meet the first, the strategy adopted was to
appeal to the anti-Communist feelings of the countries' conservative
rulers. The line of argument made to King Ibn Saud of Saudi Arabia
was recounted by Howard W. Page, vice-president of Exxon:

> . . . this is verbal and I have to give it to you hearsay, but it is, I
> think, on good hearsay . . . this was discussed with the King in
> Saudi Arabia, the old King, Ibn Saud, and he was told that the
> Aramco partners were being asked to get into this and that we
> would have to tell him that as a result we would not be able to
> increase our liftings appreciably for a while in Aramco, and we
> were going in solely on the basis that there might be chaos out in
> the area if we didn't, and would he agree with this and recognize
> that we weren't doing this because we wanted more oil anywhere,
> because we have adequate oil in the Aramco concession but we

were doing it as a political matter at the request of our government. . . . "Yes, but," he said, "In no case should you lift more than you are obligated to lift to satisfy the requirements of doing that job."[36]

On the question of participation, a determined effort was made within the American government to secure for independent companies a significant share of Iranian supply. Although his viewpoint was definitely not shared by his superiors, the State Department's petroleum attaché strongly urged a greater role for independents:

> The U.S. government should promote the entry of new competition into the Middle East, particularly the competition of U.S. companies and particularly U.S. independent companies. U.S. oil policy objectives in the area can best be fulfilled by and with American companies and American personnel and American methods. . . .
>
> The control of Middle East resources by the major international companies is subject to serious criticism by both friendly and unfriendly states. The successful participation of independent U.S. companies is a requisite to elimination of that criticism.[37]

At the Department of Justice the Antitrust Division's specialist on petroleum, Watson Snyder, recommended that a sizable specified proportion of Iranian output be set aside for American independents. The State Department arranged for Price Waterhouse to "pass upon the eligibility" of U.S. independents "desirous of joining in the venture." On March 4, 1955, Price Waterhouse "certified" eleven companies as reliable applicants. The firms with their requested percentage participations were: Cities Service, Richfield, Tidewater, Pacific Western (5%), Sinclair, Standard of Ohio, Signal, Hancock (3%), Atlantic (2%), Anderson Pritchard, and San Jacinto Petroleum (1%).

Snyder objected to the use of Price Waterhouse as the certifying agent: "Price Waterhouse and Co. [were] accountants for . . . most of the participants in the consortium. All through the documentary material delivered by the five defendants in the cartel case, you will find that Price Waterhouse and Company is the medium through which all the accounting is done for the participants in the various illegal arrangements. . . . Whenever either the domestic or foreign branches of the petroleum industry carry out any joint operations Price Waterhouse is chosen to do the accounting."[38] Under these circumstances he implied that Price Waterhouse was not likely to certify any firm strongly objected to by the majors. Incidentally, one reason for the boycott's success was alluded to by Snyder. The president of one independent claimed to have received a promise from the Secretary of State for a 5 percent participation on the condition that "prior to the setting up of the consortium he would have no dealings with the Iranian government directly and that he would not be a party to purchasing any Iranian oil whatsoever."[39]

But the arguments of such government officials as Funkhouser and Snyder (and there were others) went for naught. The total allotted to the American independents turned out to be not 36 percent but 5 percent. What had begun as a serious effort to inject competition into the international oil industry ended up as a gesture worth little more than amused contempt from the majors. Their attitude was graphically expressed by Page of Exxon. In replying to Senator Case's question as to why the independents were given any share whatever, the following colloquy took place:

MR. PAGE: I don't know their reasons for it but they had a feeling, well, "Because people were always yacking about it we had better put some independents in there."

SENATOR CHURCH: Put a few independents in?

MR. PAGE: Yes.

SENATOR CHURCH: Window-dressing?

MR. PAGE: That's right.[40]

The ultimate distribution was 40 percent for BP, 14 percent for Shell, 7 percent each for Exxon, Mobil, SoCal, Texaco, and Gulf, 6 percent for Compagnie Française Pétrole, and 5 percent for the American independents organized as "Iricon." In 1974, Iricon's membership was made up of: American Independents (2/12), Getty Oil (2/12), Arco (4/12), Sohio (1/12), Charter (2/12), and Conoco (1/12).[41] As to the way in which the ownership of the consortium was arrived at, Page testified:

> Well, I have some notion in the sense that, as I understand it, the 40 percent for BP was the maximum that would be politically allowable within Iran. In other words, that the politics of it were such that they felt it would be impossible to renegotiate the thing if BP had a majority interest or even 50 percent interest, and, therefore, that more or less established the 40.
>
> Now, exactly how the others shaped out, I don't know, except that Shell had very large markets and not much crude in the Middle East and . . . they could certainly handle their 14% with no problem at all. How the others were decided on I am not quite sure.[42]

When Senator Muskie asked why "Exxon, Mobil, Texaco, Gulf, SoCal . . . were given 40 percent of the whole, which is more than you wanted, you say," whereas the independents, "Richfield, Signal, Hancock, Sohio, Getty, and so on . . . wanted more and got less,"[43] the answer was that only the majors could market the oil "in the quantities necessary to restore the Iranian economy." As Page put it, ". . . they were selected by the State Department on the basis they were the five companies and the only five American that could provide outlets in the foreign area."[44] In the full context of his testimony, Page appeared to be implying that these were the only five companies whose established market positions were sufficient to accommodate such a large increase in world supply without disturbing the market; and that if such a disturbance were to be avoided, even these companies would have to persuade other Mideast countries to reduce their output. Certainly, the subsequent success of the independents in Libya demonstrated what must have been realized at the time: that an independent wholly lacking in established market positions can penetrate world markets very rapidly if it is willing to cut prices. An apprehension that with a greater share of Iranian output the independents might do just that seems implicit in Page's remark, ". . . they were getting something and didn't have to *back up anywhere to do it*."[45] Senator Muskie thought it curious that the four concession-holders in Saudi Arabia (Exxon, Mobil, SoCal, and Texaco) plus the U.S. co-holder in Kuwait (Gulf) happened to be selected as the participants in Iran. Again, the answer was the same: ". . . that was for the sole reason that it was those companies *who naturally had the outlets for crude oil and products abroad*."[46]

COSTS AND PROFITS OF MIDDLE EAST OIL

It was of course the fabulous profits arising from extraordinarily low costs that induced the major oil companies to go to such lengths to control oil in the Middle East.

Among the earliest estimates on costs in the Middle East were data presented to a congressional committee in 1947 headed by Senator Owen Brewster, investigating purchases of Middle East oil during World War II by the U.S. Navy. During the hearings it was revealed that the cost of production of Saudi Arabian crude oil was about 19 cents a barrel (excluding a royalty of 21 cents). The cost of production for nearby Bahrein crude was estimated to be 10 cents a barrel (excluding a royalty of 15 cents). At this time the Navy was paying $1.05 per barrel and upward for crude from Saudi Arabia and Bahrein.[47] In 1955, the Economic Commission for Europe reported costs of 10 cents a barrel for Bahrein crude.[48] According to Leeman, costs for Iraq under the 1952 oil agreement were 24 cents a barrel, and for Kuwait 10 cents.[49] Issawi and Yeganeh cited early estimates of

10 cents for Bahrein (1945), 14 cents for Kuwait (1946), 19 cents for Saudi Arabia (1945), 20 cents for Iran (after 1955), and 24 cents for Iraq (1952).[50] In a time series presented by Mikdashi for the period 1950–63, costs averaged 14 cents but by 1963 were down to 7 cents.[51] One of the most revealing insights into costs was provided by John Warder, chairman of the Iranian Consortium, in an address before the Central Bank of Tehran. Citing crude oil production costs in Iran as 14 cents a barrel—as against 8–9 cents in Saudi Arabia and 6 cents in Kuwait—Warder was quoted as saying that "this relatively high production cost was Iran's major problem in competitive oil industry. He attributed it mainly to high proportion of surplus personnel and expressed the view that work force could safely be reduced by 50%—which, he indicated, would help cut production costs sharply."[52]

A breakdown between "development" and "operating" or "lifting" costs for the period 1953–62 was made by Paul G. Bradley: "To produce known reserves it is necessary to invest substantial sums to develop the fields; that is, to drill wells and install gathering, processing and shipping facilities. Once a field is developed further expenditures are required to produce the crude; these cover such items as operating labor and maintenance."[53] In the Middle East, his estimate for operating costs ranged from 3 to 5 cents a barrel. For Saudi Arabia, his estimates for development costs—i.e., the costs of drilling wells and installing the necessary gathering, processing, and shipping facilities— plus operating costs, was 16–17 cents a barrel (assuming the need for a 15% rate of return to attract the necessary capital) or 19–21 cents (assuming a 20% rate of return). His estimates were 1 cent higher for Kuwait and 3 cents higher for Iraq. The relationship of Bradley's cost estimates to price was brought out in hearings:

DR. BLAIR: If Middle East oil were sold to domestic buyers at the same f.o.b. price at which it is now [1969] sold to independent foreign buyers, it could be laid down on the eastern seaboard at around $2, of which transportation would be about 60 cents and the duty 10 cents.

The development costs, as you have delineated here, are around 15 cents; in fact, 15 is the upper limit of the range for the principal producing countries of the Middle East. The upper limit of the range for operating costs is 5 cents. Thus, the gross margin would be $1.30 minus $0.20, or $1.10, out of which would come the costs of exploration, royalties, and the other expenses of doing business, as well as profits. Is my arithmetic correct?

DR. BRADLEY: I believe I followed you, Dr. Blair, and I didn't find any fault with it.[54]

That costs have fallen to even lower levels is implied in an estimate by M. A. Adelman. Testifying in 1969, he stated: "The current production cost—meaning current operating expense plus a 20 percent return on the necessary development investment—is about 12 cents per barrel in the most expensive of the big five producing countries of the Eastern Hemisphere."[55] In the words of Helmut J. Frank, ". . . there is sufficient evidence to support the conclusion that production costs in the Middle East typically have been very low, relative to both costs in other producing areas and to the level of posted prices."[56] At the current price level of $11.00–$12.00 per barrel, they are obviously so low as to be irrelevant to the determination of price.

With costs so low, the ability of the "seven sisters" to control the market inevitably resulted in profits beyond the dreams of avarice. As early as 1917, the annual report of Anglo-Persian Oil Co. (predecessor to British Petroleum) noted that the production obtainable from just one Persian field was larger than the entire prewar production from the whole of the Rumanian and Galician oil fields with ten times the number of wells and invested capital.[57] Four years later, Anglo-Persian observed that the cost of producing oil in Persia was not a "tithe of the average cost obtaining in other fields yielding light gravity oil of equal quality." In 1924, the company asserted that no matter how low petroleum prices might fall, they could not fall in the long run below the production costs of Persian oil. In 1923 Sir Winston Churchill—who nine years earlier had been instrumental in the British government's purchase for £2 million of a controlling interest in Anglo-Persian—placed the financial benefits to the government at £25.6 million, consisting of £16 million appreciation in the shares of the original investment, £6.5 million in dividends, and other payments of £3 million in savings in the purchase of oil.[58]

Even officials from the international majors have occasionally acknowledged the extraordinary profitability of Mideast production and commented on its contribution to their companies' earnings. In 1952, for example, the president of Exxon declared at a meeting of stockholders, "I assure you that the history as a whole of the foreign investments has been very good." And in 1960, the company's president revealed that about 28 percent of the company's earnings came from the Eastern Hemisphere, and that a fairly substantial part of that 28 percent came from the Arab world, where the investment represented a much smaller proportion of the company's total investment: "We're very fortunate in having an extremely sizable and potentially important stake in the Arab world with a relatively very small investment."[59] The chairman of Gulf revealed in 1957 that over half of the company's profits were derived from Kuwait's crude oil.[60]

Estimates of the rate of return on investment for the four leading Middle East oil companies have been prepared by Zuhayr Mikdashi.[61] Covering varying intervals between the early fifties and mid-sixties, these profit rates are shown on Chart 2-3. For the Iraq Petroleum Company and the Iranian Consortium, the figures were compiled by Mikdashi from the companies' balance sheets on file at the Companies Registration Office in London. For the Kuwait Oil Company, he used the annual reports published by Gulf for its operations in the Eastern Hemisphere (principally Kuwait), on the grounds that the great bulk of Gulf's supply of crude in that area came from Kuwait. And for Saudi Arabia, he used profit rates compiled by A. H. Tariki.[62]

Over the period 1952–63, net profits for the Iraq Petroleum Co. averaged 56.6 percent of net assets. After the ill-fated nationalization effort in 1951, operations in Iran did not again became profitable for several years; but for the period 1955–64, the net profits of the Iranian Consortium averaged 69.3 percent of its net assets. For 1952–64, net income on Gulf's Eastern Hemisphere operations averaged 40.7 percent of its ownership interest. And for 1952–61, Aramco's profits averaged 57.6 percent of its invested capital.[63] In view of these extraordinary rates it is not surprising that "the payout period of one of Consortium's shareholders on its original investment was less than two years";[64] or that "Executives consider Kuwait to be the source of 'very remarkable profits'"; or that "Executives of Aramco and its parent companies have declared on several occasions, that their investment in Saudi Arabia is very profitable."[65]

These remarkable showings predated the shutting off of the U.S. market to imported oil, the emergence of Libya as a large-scale supplier, and the deterioration in world oil prices resulting from price cutting by Libyan newcomers—all of which had an adverse effect on the majors' profit showings. Nonetheless, costs have been so low that even after the price erosion of the 1960's production of Mideast oil remained a highly profitable investment.

In the Middle East, and indeed in most other oil-producing areas as well, the instrument traditionally used to control production and distribute income therefrom was the jointly owned operating company. In the form that came to be adopted elsewhere, the joint venture made its first appearance in 1928 with the formation, principally by BP and Shell, of the Iraq Petroleum Co., into which Exxon and Mobil were later admitted. To these four, Aramco added SoCal and Texaco, while the Kuwait Oil Co. added Gulf, bringing to seven the number of international majors accounting for the great bulk of the area's production. Most of this output was controlled through joint operating companies,

CHART 2-3
Middle East Oil Companies: Net Profit as Percent of
Net Assets, 1952–64*

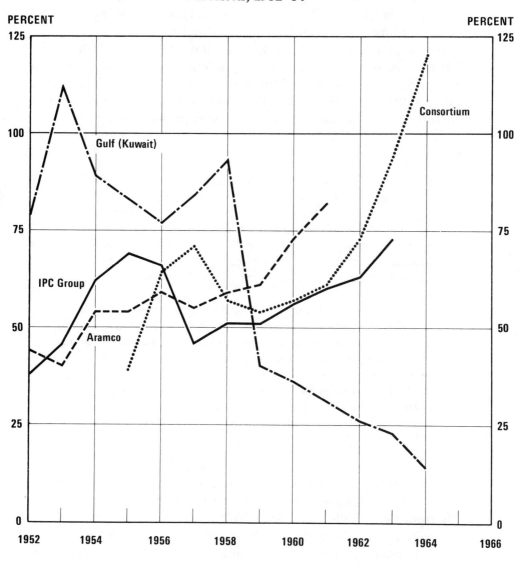

* As available.
Source: Zuhayr Mikdashi, *A Financial Analysis of Middle Eastern Oil Concessions;*
1901-65, Praeger, 1966, pp. 182, 195, 212, 221.

which performed the functions of exploration, development, and production; distributed income to the parent companies in accordance with their ownership shares; and effected sales or transfers (also based on ownership shares) only to their companies' owners, except under specific contracts with other members of the seven, covering very long periods of time and containing highly restrictive provisions.

Although some erosion in their position took place during the 1960's,[66] as late as 1972 the seven international majors were still producing 91 percent of the Middle East's crude oil and 77 percent of the Free World's supply outside the United States.[67] That this pattern of control persisted without significant change for so long is a tribute to what Paul H. Frankel has described as the "workmanlike manner" in which it was put together:

> By a number of far-reaching agreements, concluded in 1947, one of them involving equity participations, the other being long-term sales contracts, the "new" producers, Texaco, Standard of Calif., Gulf Oil Co., and Anglo-Iranian secured large-scale outlets by making use of the facilities and old-established market positions of those of the traditional international major oil companies who, at that time at least, found themselves short of oil: Esso, Socony-Mobil and Shell.
>
> By virtue of all this, the need for the (comparative) newcomers to fight their way into the markets was obviated or at least limited, and the position of those who took their oil was consolidated; also some of the prices at which the crude oils were sold depended on the price level of products disposed of by the buyer of the crude oil. Thus companies like Gulf Oil had for many years no strong incentive to behave aggressively at any place where their buyer— Shell—sold products made from Gulf's crude. One cannot sell the same oil twice.[68]

*   *   *

Although by the 1930's the seven sisters, through jointly owned companies and long-term contracts, had pretty well sewed up the supply from the Middle East, uncontrolled oil from other areas would intermittently appear and delay the attainment of "orderly" marketing. Thus, not only to achieve an "equitable" distribution among themselves but to accommodate the uncontrolled supplies, the international majors were forced to supplement their control over Mideast output with a parallel complex of controls in the world's consuming markets. Otherwise, the uncontrolled output of independent producers in the United States (then the world's largest exporter), Rumania, and Venezuela would have utterly wrecked all efforts toward price stability. Oil is no exception to the general principle that any attempt to eliminate "destructive" competition can have a reasonable chance of success only if both the dominant firms and the independent producers are tolerably content with their market shares. Today, if an important OPEC country were to bypass the majors and sell directly at discount prices to independent refiners (as both Saudi Arabia and Iran have on occasion threatened to do), a compelling need would again arise to fit the resulting increment to supply into established distribution patterns.

THE EVOLUTION OF
CONTROL: Marketing

3

AT THE SAME TIME that the international oil majors were gaining control over the vast reserves of the Middle East, they were also busily engaged in devising complicated cartel agreements to assure "orderly" marketing. Beginning in the late 1920's, four international agreements were entered into, designed to establish the principles, guidelines, and general *modus operandi* to be applied through national or "local" cartels in most of the world's consuming countries.

THE ACHNACARRY AGREEMENT

The first of the four international agreements had its genesis in a price war that arose from a dispute between Standard Oil of New York (Mobil) and Royal Dutch Shell over the Indian market, and quickly spread to the important markets of America and Great Britain. Over Shell's protests, Mobil had persisted in buying crude from the Russian government, which earlier had seized Shell's properties.

> On Sept. 19, 1927, Royal Dutch Shell announced that the price of kerosene in India would be reduced immediately, should any more Russian oil arrive at Indian ports. But Standard was not deterred; and on Sept. 23, 1927, price reductions were made. Further reductions followed, developing into a price war in India between Standard of New York and Shell. Steps were taken by each to broaden the conflict. Shell intensified competition in the United States, while Standard of New York intensified its advertising of ethyl fuel in England. As the competition between the two companies spread, other world markets were involved and other international marketing companies found it necessary to reduce prices to hold their respective positions. . . .
> Shell's action in carrying the price competition to the American market affected the operation of all American oil companies. On

the other hand, the action of Standard of New York in staying in India notwithstanding low prices, and in intensifying the promotion of its ethyl gasoline in England, brought sharply to the attention of Anglo-Persian [BP] and Royal Dutch-Shell the possibility that Standard might increase its sales in Great Britain and continental Europe, and that other American interests might take similar action. The relative positions of all international companies in the principal consuming markets of the world were jeopardized.[1]

Alarmed by the rapidity with which the price war had spread from India to America and then back to Europe, the heads of the three dominant international majors met at Achnacarry Castle in Scotland to prevent the recurrence of such disturbances. Walter C. Teagle, then president of Exxon, was quoted by a trade journal as saying, "Sir John Cadman, head of the Anglo-Persian Oil Co. [BP] and myself were guests of Sir Henri Deterding and Lady Deterding at Achnacarry for the grouse shooting, and while the game was a primary object of the visit, the problem of the world's petroleum industry naturally came in for a great deal of discussion."[2] Referred to generally as the "As Is Agreement of 1928," or the "Achnacarry Agreement," the product of this discussion was a document, dated September 17, 1928, setting forth a set of seven "principles" and outlining in general terms the policies and procedures to be followed in applying them. The principles provided for: (1) accepting and maintaining as their share of markets the status quo of each member; (2) making existing facilities available to competitors on a favorable basis, but not at less than actual cost to the owner; (3) adding new facilities only as actually needed to supply increased requirements of consumers; (4) maintaining for each producing area the financial advantage of its geographical location; (5) drawing supplies from the nearest producing area; and (6) preventing any surplus production in a given geographical area from upsetting the price structure in any other area. The last point asserted that observance of these principles would benefit not only the industry but consumers as well by eliminating practices that "materially increase costs with consequent reduction in consumption."* Although exports to the United States were specifically ex-

* As set forth in the agreement, the principles were as follows: 1. "The acceptance by the units of their present volume of business and their proportion of any future increases in consumption.

2. As existing facilities are amply sufficient to meet the present consumption these should be made available to producers on terms which shall be based on the principle of paying for the use of these facilities an amount which shall be less than that which it would have cost such producer had he created these facilities for his exclusive use, but not less than demonstrated cost to the owner of the facilities.

3. Only such facilities to be added as are necessary to supply the public with

empted in deference to its antitrust laws, the application of the "as is" principles to their foreign production by American companies would obviously limit imports by such companies into this country and thus bring them within the jurisdiction of the U.S. statutes.

From the outset it was emphasized that the purpose of the overall agreement was to achieve a consensus among the three on general principles which would serve as "enduring" guides for the operation of "local" cartels to be set up in the various consuming countries. In his original statement describing the meeting in Scotland, the head of Exxon emphasized that: "any attempt at regulation of overproduction of crude would obviously require cooperation of a vastly greater number and diversity of interests than were represented at Achnacarry Castle." The Big Three then turned their attention toward getting this "larger cooperation," which, it was clearly recognized, could be accomplished best on a country-by-country basis. In the words of E. J. Sadler, vice-president of Exxon, "The making of a world-wide agreement is more difficult to obtain than accomplishing the result piecemeal. Economically, there are local situations which can be consolidated with a much sounder economic basis than to immediately attempt to jump to a position of world-wide distribution."[3]

THE INSTRUCTIONAL AGREEMENTS

Having agreed on general principles, the companies then entered into a series of three further agreements, delineating in progressively greater detail the functions of local cartels to be set up in the various individual consuming countries: the Memorandum for European Markets (Jan. 20, 1930), the Heads of Agreement for Distribution (Dec. 15, 1932), and the Draft Memorandum of Principles (Jan. 1, 1934).

---

its increased requirements of petroleum products in the most efficient manner. The procedure now prevailing of producers duplicating facilities to enable them to offer their own products regardless of the fact that such duplication is neither necessary to supply consumption nor creates an increase in consumption should be abandoned.

4. Production shall retain the advantage of its geographical situation, it being recognized that the value of the basic products of uniform specifications are the same at all points of origin or shipment and that this gives to each producing area an advantage in supplying consumption in the territory geographically tributary thereto, which should be retained by the production in that area.

5. With the object of securing maximum efficiency and economy in transportation, supplies shall be drawn from the nearest producing area.

6. To the extent that production is in excess of the consumption in its geographical area then such excess becomes surplus production which can only be dealt with in one of two ways; either the producer to shut in such surplus production or offer it at a price which will make it competitive with production from another geographical area.

7. The best interests of the public as well as the petroleum industry will be served through the discouragement of the adoption of any measures the effect of which would be to materially increase costs with consequent reduction in consumption." Quoted from the *International Petroleum Cartel*, p. 200.

As the companies became increasingly familiar with the troublesome problems of trying to make a cartel operate successfully, the instructions had to cover a growing number of issues and at the same time become increasingly specific and precise. The principal topics with which they dealt were: (a) fixing quotas; (b) making adjustments for under- and overtrading; (c) fixing prices and other conditions of sale; and (d) dealing with outsiders.

The Memorandum for European Markets followed the Achnacarry Agreement in specifying 1928 as the base period for the determination of quotas, which were to be allotted for each petroleum product sold in the country. Quotas could be increased, but only at the expense of "outsiders," i.e., firms not parties to the agreement. The document explicitly stated:

> It is an essential part of these arrangements that each and every party thereto, having been allotted a quota, shall do his utmost to obtain the share of total trade represented by that quota, and to extend it where possible *but not at the expense of the parties to these arrangements.*[4]

To assure compliance with the quotas, the parties were to meet and report their own deliveries as well as giving estimates of total "outside" deliveries as a basis for determining the total consumption of each local market area. Monthly meetings were to be held by the local representatives to exchange statistics and to cooperate fully not only in relation to each other but also in their combined position to the market as a whole. In the Heads of Agreement for Distribution, these provisions were carried forward. Not all of the parties, it was revealed, had complete faith in the integrity of their rivals, since the trade figures submitted by each of the companies were to be certified by an independent auditor.

The Draft Memorandum of Principles set forth in great detail the precise rules to be established governing revision in quotas resulting from a variety of circumstances. Failure to meet a quota meant that the loss was transferred to a firm that had exceeded its quota. A quota could be increased through the acquisition of an outsider. Complex procedures were established to share the business of a firm retiring from the market. The procedure established to govern the displacement of an older by a newer petroleum product—e.g., gasoline by diesel fuel—was particularly interesting. Whether so intended, the procedure clearly had the effect of discouraging innovation, since the party who previously had control over the outlet for a displaced product "should be entitled to an equivalent outlet for the replaced product."[5]

It was fully recognized that because of a variety of circumstances—

interruptions in production, delivery problems, political disturbances, as well as lack of aggressiveness and plain inefficiency—some firms in a particular country would fail to achieve their quota. By the same token, owing to such considerations as a need to satisfy a Mideast ruler, an unusually large discovery, an exceptionally successful marketing program, as well as over-aggressiveness and outstanding efficiency, some firms would exceed their quotas. It was therefore necessary to develop systematic procedures to redistribute both the consequent losses and excessive gains.

In the first of the "how to" documents, rules for handling this problem were spelled out in detail. The preferred method was to make such adjustments by transferring customers among the parties. If adjustments could not be made in this way, the "undertrader" was to receive from the "overtrader" the "net proceeds" realized by the overtrader. To guard against any party becoming a habitual undertrader it was provided that, as a penalty, the undertrader's allotted quota for the ensuing year was to be reduced for the ensuing accounting period by distributing to the other participants "one-quarter of the amount by which his undertrading exceeds his 5-percent margin."[5a]

It was equally important that no party should obtain and hold a position as a heavy overtrader at the expense of the other parties. Therefore, provision was made for a sliding-scale system of penalties for overtrading, to be collected and distributed to the undertraders. These general provisions were carried over in the Heads of Agreement for Distribution, but the rules were made more explicit. Thus, the only basis for determining over- and undertrading was the percentage of the trade done by the parties during each trading period. Definite rules were also provided for determining when overtrading had occurred; in accordance with the "as is" principle, this was to be corrected by exchanging customers, giving cash compensation, and paying fines. A definite rule was also added for determining how much of an undertrader's volume was lost to parties to the agreement, as distinguished from that lost to outsiders. Undertraders were to have the option of supplying products to overtraders or of accepting cash compensation. Rules for determining the compensation to be paid by overtraders also were spelled out in somewhat greater detail than in the Memorandum for European Markets.

In the final document, the Draft Memorandum of Principles, these provisions were simply carried forward. The point was repeatedly emphasized that with real cooperation, "over and undertrading among the participants should not arise." If they did occur, they were to be adjusted by transfer of customers or by compensation to undertraders and fines against overtraders. In arriving at such compensation, the parties were to meet and agree upon a price to cover allowable expenses that the overtraders would retain in making compensation to the undertraders. In specifying how to determine that compensation, the document revealed a sophisticated awareness of the effect of volume on overhead costs: The intention was declared to be that the price paid as compensation would be such as to place the overtrader

> as closely as possible in the position in which he would have been had he not traded in excess of his quota and *that he should not get the benefit of the contribution to his overhead arising out of his increased volume.*[6]

The companies not only proscribed unilateral price determination but established a formal procedure to ensure that all price changes were the result of collective determination. Above all, no pricing activities should be allowed to disturb the "as is" positions of the participating companies. The Memorandum for European Markets stated:

> It is agreed between the parties that they shall maintain at least the share of the total trade which they held during the basic period, and to this end prices and selling conditions *shall be fully and frankly discussed and agreed* between the local representatives. In the event of disagreement between the parties the matter shall be settled by a simple majority vote, each party having one vote for each complete 1 percent of quota.[7]

The voting power of each participant, it should be noted, was to be proportional to its quota; this of course gave the participants with large quotas the dominant voting power to determine the prices which all participants agreed to observe. While such a procedure might give rise to dissatisfaction, particularly with the admission of other parties, disagreements were not to be permitted to upset the local cartel as long as the group maintained at least 90 percent of its joint share of the market during the base period. Independent price action was to be permitted only under two circumstances: either failure by the parties to maintain that 90 percent, or the occurrence of an all-out price war with independents. Because their loss to outsiders would obviously disturb the "as is" positions, large contracts were made the subject of special provisions. The document set forth the principle that the company

> . . . holding the business in the basic period shall retain it, but in any case prices and conditions for all such business *shall be discussed between the parties, and in the event of the party who, it has been agreed,* shall take the business, losing it to an outsider after quoting prices and conditions on which all are agreed, all the parties shall, without alteration of their quota rights, take their

share of the quantity lost pro rata to their respective quotas. But if, on the other hand, the party whose business it was to make the contract fails to quote the price and conditions which have been agreed with the other parties, and thereby loses the contract, he will have no claim to share the loss with the other parties.[8]

The Draft Memorandum of Principles provided for the first time a standard for price determination: "Prices should be maintained in all markets on a basis which should yield a fair return on a reasonable investment. . . ." Although no specific figure was suggested, the managers of local cartels were cautioned that the profit rate should have "due regard to encouraging the use of petroleum products." Moreover, the public interest should not be completely ignored: "It is important that prices should not be permitted to rise to a point where the buying public is exploited."[9] As on other issues, the final document spelled out in more detail the limited circumstances in which individual action on "prices, discounts or allowances" could be taken, but in general reemphasized the prohibition on individual freedom of price action except to restore "as is" quota positions. The effect of the pricing system was thus to combine open price reporting and open discussion of proposed prices with binding price agreements.

Of all the issues confronting the drafters of these manuals, none was more vexing than the problem raised by the existence of "outsiders"—independent crude suppliers and independent refiners. In addition to the original signatories of the Achnacarry Agreement, Shell, BP, and Exxon, all but one of what later became referred to as the "seven sisters" had by 1932 become participants; the Heads of Agreement for Distribution was adopted by representatives of Exxon, Mobil, BP, Shell, Gulf, and Texaco, as well as Atlantic.[10] One way of minimizing the problems raised by outsiders was simply to acquire them:

> *Purchase of outsiders.* It is recognized that it is desirable to convert uncontrolled outlets into the controlled class; in view of this *the purchase by the "as is" members of going distributing concerns outside "as is" is to be recommended* as tending to improve the stability of the markets.
>
> The purchase of such outsiders is in principle the equivalent of admitting new members to "as is" and should be treated accordingly. It is therefore recommended that where possible, such purchases shall be frankly discussed between parties interested before the purchase is completed.[11]

The most troublesome issues were whether independent refiners should be allowed to become members of the national cartels and, if so, who should supply them. On both issues the majors were confronted with a classic dilemma. If independents were not admitted, they could be expected to undercut the majors' prices, and the higher those prices, the greater the room for price cutting. On the other hand, if independents were admitted, they would have to be given quotas, which would have to come out of the majors' shares. Similarly, if the independent refiners were not to be supplied by the majors, they would obtain their crude oil from independent producers, thereby providing a market outlet for the latter. On the other hand, if they were to be supplied by the majors, some way of fitting them into the cartel would have to be found, since otherwise the anomalous situation would inevitably arise of majors supplying price-cutters.

Reflecting the complexities of the problem, the first of the manuals simply laid down the general principle that outsiders were to be admitted on conditions "not more favorable than those enjoyed by the original parties at the time when they were admitted."[12] But to those in the trade, even this vaguely worded doctrine could hardly have been taken seriously since the fractious Rumanians had just been conceded a 65 percent increase in crude oil production over what they would have been entitled to under quotas based on their 1928 performance. By 1934, however, a number of more specific rules had been formulated. Sales to outside refiners could be made to prevent them from being supplied by independent crude producers:

> It is recognized that there are certain refineries in various countries that have a position in the market and while it was not the intention to improve that position neither is it the intention to deny to the participants the right to sell crude to such refiners and thereby *forcing the crude supply outlet to outside suppliers.*[13]

The participants were to establish annually a list of outside refineries to whom they would sell crude oil to prevent "forcing the crude supply outlet to outside suppliers." They were also to determine, but not "improve," the market share of the outside refiners so supplied. And their share was to come out of the participants' share, in proportion to each participant's "overall percentage in the total consumption of all products in the market in question." A similar procedure was laid down to cover the sale of refined products to outside marketers. It was emphasized that "except as hereinbefore provided for, *no participant shall be free to sell to outsiders either crude oil or finished products.*"[14]

Summing up the import of the provisions relating to outsiders, the FTC Staff report stated: "The 'as is' position of independent refiners and marketers was to be recognized only to the extent necessary to prevent them from becoming market outlets for outside suppliers. If outside suppliers could be excluded, the control of the cartel over outside refiners and marketers would be complete, and no independent refiner or marketer could exist except by unanimous consent of the cartel members."[15]

The Draft Memorandum of Principles also contained an unusual provision designed to restrict claims of product superiority. While competition in price was to be eliminated, it was still possible for firms to improve their positions through other types of competition. Hence, the document stressed the need to eliminate "unnecessary" sales costs, particularly advertising expenses: ". . . advertising budgets should be, insofar as possible, agreed upon for each market by the participants in that market before being submitted for consideration to London with a view to eliminating duplication or expense. . . ." Among the types of advertising to be "eliminated," "reduced," or "kept within reasonable limits" were road signs or billboards, newspaper advertising, premiums to racing drivers, novelties such as cigarette lighters, and signs placed at dealers' garages.[16] Hence a cartel agreement which began as a general agreement to divide markets and stabilize prices became progressively more specific even to the point of including detailed restrictions on gifts of cigarette lighters.

Anticipating the need for some central authority to iron out differences that could not be resolved at the national level and to meet still further unanticipated contingencies, the majors in the Heads of Agreement for Distribution agreed that "to further the smooth working of 'as is' a central, full-time secretariat should be formed, with its functions to be divided between New York and London committees: 'New York should handle supply "as is" and . . . London, being in closer contact with the markets, should deal with distribution "as is." ' " Displaying a refreshing candor, the documents described what was being set up by its proper term: "The 'Heads of Agreement' which follow have been drawn up with a view that they should be used as a guide to representatives on the field for drawing up rules for local *cartels* or for local Agreements. It is the intention that all such local *cartels* or Agreements should be based on these 'Heads.' . . ." Commenting on the ultimate fate of the overall marketing agreements, Exxon in transmitting the documents to the FTC stated, "In or before the early part of 1938, *verbal* notice was given, in accordance with Clause I of the Draft Memorandum of Principles, of termination of that agreement."[17] The company went on to state, "Any activities that may have survived came to an end in September, 1939, as a result of the outbreak of the war. They were never resumed."[18] The *Cartel* report also observed, "Legal counsel for Standard Oil Co. (New Jersey) in submitting a copy of the agreement to the Federal Trade Commission, stated that there *were no papers* in the company's files indicating when the Achnacarry Agreement was *terminated. . . .*"[19] Once national cartels had been set up, however, the only reason to continue the issuance of overall agreements would be to keep *au courant* the instructions to the local groups. But the need to have some means of performing this function had already been anticipated with the establishment of a central secretariat. There is evidence that as recently as 1971 new and difficult issues were taken for resolution to two high-level committees—one in London and the other in New York. A point at issue was whether the companies should stand by their previous commitment to negotiate jointly with the Mideast countries and Libya as a group or whether the joint approach should be abandoned in favor of separate negotiations. Arguing for joint negotiations was George Henry Schuler, the representative of Bunker Hunt International Oil Co. which, with BP, held the largest concession in Libya. Testifying before the Senate Subcommittee on Multinational Corporations, Schuler recounted that at a critical point in the deliberations he was summoned on January 30, 1971, to a meeting of what he termed the "London Policy Group."[20] After speaking to the group, he was asked to present his argument via overseas conference call to a group that was meeting in the offices of Mobil Oil Corp. in New York City. Referred to as the "meeting of the chiefs," and headed by Mr. Jamieson, chief executive officer of Exxon, its function was described by Schuler as that of handling issues "too big for the London Policy Group." As later events were to demonstrate, both the London and the New York Committee rejected Schuler's arguments:

MR. HENRY: . . . Mr. Schuler is called downstairs to the telephone and it is at this point that he gets on the speaker system with Mr. Jamieson and the other chief executive officers back in New York.

After that was done, after you made your arguments to Mr. Jamieson, Mr. Schuler, can you tell us what happened from that point on?

MR. SCHULER: I made the arguments why this would destroy our entire credibility were we to acquiesce in the refusal to fix the Eastern Mediterranean postings, and Mr. Jamieson said, "Thank you," and words to the effect that it was a strong presentation.

SENATOR CHURCH: At that point you knew you were lost.

MR. SCHULER: I guess.[21]

THE NATIONAL CARTELS

With the benefit of hindsight it is possible to discern, and in a way admire, the enduring architectural design of the successive cartel agreements. Beginning with the statement of general principles in the Achnacarry Agreement, the next stage was the preparation of a series of instructional guidelines, which in turn were to be followed by local cartels to be established in the world's consuming countries. And it was these national cartels that were to serve as the operative bodies. In addition to decentralizing authority and handing it over to those most familiar with the local problems, this approach had the further advantage that, except for the United States, the activities contemplated for the national cartels would not contravene either the law or the public policy of the consuming countries; indeed in certain nations, France, for example, they would be actively encouraged.

In some cases the rudiments of a national cartel were already in existence, needing only perfection and refinement. Thus, in 1929, *The Economist* cited Great Britain as a commendable illustration of the attainment of price stability through "cooperation":

> An example of the effectiveness of international cooperation in oil marketing is Great Britain, where the three groups—Shell, Anglo-Persian, and Standard Oil of New Jersey . . . have not only agreed upon selling prices and the number of pump installations, but have secured an agreement with the Russian Oil Trust fixing its proportion of the British trade. The stability of petrol and other refined oil prices in the British, European, and Eastern markets is the measure of the cooperation between Royal Dutch-Shell, Burmah Oil, and Anglo-Persian on the one hand and the Standard Oil companies on the other.[22]

In other countries the cartel had to be established *de novo*. It is ironic that in Germany, the birthplace of cartels, no national cartels in petroleum existed prior to the introduction of the "as is" arrangements. In 1928, Standard (N.J.), Shell, and Anglo-Iranian, which had captured control of more than 60 percent of the domestic market, came to an agreement for the application of "as is" to the German market. In addition, important German firms cooperated with the three major companies in this 1928 agreement, including the Benzoleverband (an association of distributors) and the marketing subsidiaries of Leuna and I. G. Farben, which produced motor alcohol and gasoline blends. Despite the participation of German firms, the usually well-disciplined German consumer did not take kindly to the new arrangements. So strongly was the agreement criticized that the majors, through a subsidiary of BP, thought it necessary to issue a public statement denying that the German consumer was being exploited by a "close combine" of the major oil companies through inordinately high prices and onerous trade terms. It stated that, while there had been no understandings whatever among the companies prior to 1928, they had entered upon "limited arrangements" in that year in order to "safeguard" the interests of those in the oil trade and "to counteract the senseless competition" then prevalent.

But whether already in existence or recently formed, the national cartels were to follow the same principles in their operations. In the words of an addendum to the Memorandum for European Markets, "As there are many European countries which are now endeavoring to work out certain agreements, it is desirable to give a sketch of the charter which will fix the *main principles* for all European countries."[23] The principles to be followed related of course to the main topics covered in the international agreements: quotas, over- and undertrading, price fixing, and outsiders. Despite the varying circumstances presented by different countries, it would appear that a remarkable degree of uniformity was achieved, as can be illustrated by the activities of the national cartels in Great Britain and Sweden. The latter is of particular interest owing to information revealed in 1947 by a special investigating committee reporting to the Swedish Riksdag.

Contrary to the widespread and long-standing impression that cartels are somehow inherent in the nature of things, the fashioning and implementing of these arrangements was the product of a great deal of very hard work. According to the cartel's minutes, which came into the hands of the Swedish investigating committee, the group held 55 meetings in 1937 at which 897 subjects were discussed; in 1938, 49 meetings were held at which 656 subjects were discussed; and in 1939, 51 meetings were held at which 776 subjects were discussed.[24] Following the instructions of both the Memorandum for European Markets and the Draft Memorandum of Principles, the Swedish officials of the international companies submitted at these meetings duly audited and certified lists of deliveries made by the marketing subsidiaries, together with estimates of outsiders' sales. In France the setting up of the cartel was immeasurably facilitated by government policy.[25] Nearly all the French distributing companies of any size had been joined together in the Board of Liquid Fuel Distributors as a "voluntary" group, set up under the auspices of the government. Every company doing business in France in 1928 and subject to the quota system had been invited to join this "syndicate," and thereafter membership was closed by French law.

The fixing of quotas of course gave rise to the inevitable problem of over- and undertrading. Following the instructional agreements, adjustments were to be made by a system of fines and compensation paid to each other. Where a cartel member overtraded by making inroads on an outsider, he was to receive the full benefit of the gain. And by the same token, where a participant lost business to an outsider, the loss was not to be shared. Evidence secured by the Swedish committee revealed that such adjustments had in fact been made and fines paid as a result.

The Swedish committee reported that there were comparatively few negotiations over prices during 1936–37 since this was a period of relative price stability. It did, however, find a letter from a subsidiary to its parent, written in 1939, stating that gasoline prices were unduly high, but that they would not be reduced because during that year two of the companies wanted to recover their investments in new plant facilities. The minutes of the cartel group made it clear that such changes in price as did take place were the result of decisions made concertedly. For example, at a meeting on July 7, 1937, it was decided to increase the prices of illuminating kerosene, power kerosene, and automotive gas oil. The minutes record not only the decision to raise prices by fixed amounts in different localities, but also a decision that each company should send its sales organizations a prescribed telegram at 4 P.M. on the day of the meeting announcing the new prices which were to go into effect the following day. Similarly, it was decided in meetings on October 15 and 19, 1937, to increase benzene prices. Assurances were received from an association of cooperatives that it would try to induce its member associations to adhere to the new prices, and from an independent marketer that it would apply a corresponding increase in price.

Despite low and falling demand during much of the 1930's, the British cartel was able to demonstrate a remarkable record of price stability. Wholesale prices of gasoline in the United Kingdom changed only seventeen times during 1930–39. Aside from five changes in 1931 and six in 1937–38, reflecting changes in U.S. Gulf quotations, British gasoline prices changed on the average only about once a year, while there were two periods of twenty months with no price changes.[26]

Summarizing the price behavior of Great Britain during this period, the report on the International Petroleum Cartel states:

> The stability of gasoline prices in the United Kingdom reflects the solidity of the structure of control that had been erected there between 1928 and 1939. The long-term cooperation of the national companies—Standard (New Jersey), Shell, and Anglo-Iranian—and their predominance in the market provided the core of this control. Built around this core, and supported by it was a scheme of control that may be likened to private licensing of distributors and retailers, although the scheme was less successful in the control of retail trade. The national companies applied the "as is" principles among themselves, and these principles were, in effect, transmitted to the independent distributors through modi-

fied cartel-like arrangements. Except for sporadic rivalry among retailers, resulting largely from the activity of the "pirates," price competition had been almost completely eliminated from the petroleum industry by the latter thirties.[27]

The national cartels spent much of their time in classifying customers and establishing conditions of sale. The common practice of charging government agencies the highest possible price was systematically employed in Sweden. In a supplement to the Swedish "price system" agreement of January 31, 1936, it was agreed that no other rebates than those usually applied to the general public would be granted for purchases by state institutions which bought privately, such as regiments, hospitals, and the pilotage service. The Swedish "as is" agreement of October 15, 1937, specified that new offers for all transactions with state and municipal institutions should contain uniform prices and selling conditions. And on January 12, 1937, it was decided that offers to such institutions should not be submitted by retailers but by the "companies' own organizations," to ensure that the terms of the agreements were fully applied. The report cited the opinion of a former official of Texas Co. in Sweden that "the agreements were most dangerous to the state, since when making purchases, the state accepted the lowest price offered, even when they happened to be higher than that paid by certain other consumers."[28]

A number of typical cases were cited of negotiations over terms for special customers. According to the minutes of a meeting on January 31, 1936, it was decided that prices charged the Stockholm tramways for gasoline were far too low and should be raised by the tramway supplier, Gulf. In order to ensure that Gulf would not lose this large customer, it was agreed that the other oil companies, if invited to make offers, would quote the tramways an even higher price. Similarly, it was agreed on January 7, 1937, that Shell, which supplied the tramways with diesel fuel, should quote a price 20 percent higher than before. "Standard, Texaco, and BP declared their willingness to protect this price quoted by Shell in such a way that, in the event of the tramways applying to them with an inquiry, *they would quote a higher price, varying for the parties concerned.*" Gulf "promised not to disturb the customer in question," and agreed to quote a higher price, but pointed out that it had previously promised the tramways that it would meet the prices for diesel fuel offered by "any of the other oil enterprises in this country." If pressed by the tramways, Gulf promised to "get into contact with Mr. Gustafson of Shell, and settle the question of price in consultation with him."[29]

It was in dealing with outsiders that the national cartels had been given the greatest leeway. Recognizing the need for wide latitude in dealing with maverick suppliers, refiners, and distributors, the international majors had given their local officials a fairly free hand. And in meeting the challenge the latter appear to have been imaginative, resourceful, and largely successful. In Sweden the only competition encountered by the six majors came from a few small importer-marketers and consumer cooperatives. The investigating committee found that the oil companies had brought concerted pressure to bear on the importer-marketers to ensure their adherence to the established price policies. Minutes dated June 11, 1937, for example, record a case where a retail outlet of one of these independent competitors cut prices. The managing director of BP acted for the group in undertaking "to impress effectively on the supplier that the benzene prices fixed for the place in question shall be observed."

The Swedish agreements were liberally peppered with statements on the desirability of clearing up the existing "price chaos" or "unsound rebate conditions," or of achieving "a better order in respect of selling price." The purpose of the Swedish "as is" agreement of October 15, 1937, was stated as follows: "to arrive at and maintain a *stable and normal price level* in the Swedish market, and, *through better cooperation* make it possible for the companies to run their business as economically as possible."[30]

The committee also found that the countervailing power of consumer cooperatives—an important institution in Sweden's economy—had largely been neutralized by the oil companies. In a draft memorandum of May 5, 1937, Exxon, Shell, Texaco, and BP reached an agreement with IC (a large association of automobile owners' purchasing organizations) under which the four companies agreed to supply IC with its total requirements, while IC agreed to observe the companies' prices and selling conditions. Subsequent events revealed that the cooperative had indeed cooperated. For example, it agreed to prevent a member organization from expanding into a territory where Shell had eliminated rebates to a consumer's cooperative. And it agreed to require its member organizations to apply general increases in prices voted by the oil companies. Pressures were also brought to bear on other consumer organizations, such as associations of property holders, the National Association of Swedish Farmers, and the several fishery associations. The tactics used included lessening or eliminating discounts, rebates, bonuses, and commissions; refusal to make additional deliveries to associations which increased their membership; refusal to enter into contracts with new associations; and so on. It was agreed that every measure should be taken to avoid "the risk of such organizations growing too strong, whereby difficulties may be caused to the companies."

In Great Britain the independent distributors had for some time been supplied by independent importers, referred to unaffectionately by the trade as "pirates." Buying their supplies from private brokers who had picked up spot cargoes of American, Rumanian, Mexican, or Russian products, their purchase prices were sufficiently low to more than offset the irregularity of shipments, the lack of established trade names, and the uncertainty of quality. To combat this recurring source of competition, the strategy of the majors was to limit access to distributors. Insofar as their own retailers were concerned, the remedy was simple; upon a complaint of price cutting, they would immediately cut off supplies to the offending retailer. The problem of course lay in the retailers served by independent distributors who in turn secured their supplies from the "pirates." In 1936, the cartel members made a determined effort to secure the coöperation of the independent distributors. Joining the Motor Trade Association, it was agreed that the association would maintain a "segregated stop list" of all price cutters, and that the distributor members of the association would not supply any firm on this list. It was anticipated that the association would be able to induce the independent distributors, many of whom were among its members, to support the "stop list." In this way the price-maintenance program of the major oil companies was to be extended to the independents. The association readily undertook to maintain the "stop list" and announced early in 1937 that it would "conduct an intensive campaign to trace and put a stop to the cutting of petrol prices." In this campaign the association was fortified by a decision of the highest court in the United Kingdom, which affirmed the power of the association to discipline its members. It was expected, therefore, that the association would be able to fine or suspend distributor members who failed to observe the "stop list."

Despite the fact that "hundreds" of cases of price cutting were dealt with, the campaign was not a success. The major oil companies charged that while they had loyally supported the "stop list," losing business and incurring public disfavor as a result, the association had been unable or unwilling to penalize those distributors who had not done so. Affirming their loyalty to the "principles of price maintenance," the majors withdrew from the association two years later, continuing to protect the retail prices of their own brands. The episode illustrates the difficulty of eliminating competition through marketing cartels alone when low-cost supplies can be brought into the market. It should be recognized, however, that the amount of these uncontrolled supplies reaching the buying public represented only a small proportion of the British market. In 1935, companies other than the seven majors accounted for only 15.4 percent of the deliveries into consumption of all "controlled" products in the United Kingdom, of which 2.9 percent was supplied by Russian Oil Products, Ltd. This state-owned enterprise had previously entered into a restrictive agreement with the "as is" companies, designed in the words of Shell's Sir Henri Deterding to "put an end to the dumping policy of Russia . . ."[31]

DISTRIBUTION QUOTAS AND TRADING RESULTS

It is one thing for businessmen to sit around a table and divide up a market; it is something else for them to transform their intentions into reality. The best-laid plans will come to naught if one of the participants seeks to improve his position through secret price concessions, if outsiders are able to secure a significant share of the market, if the volume of supplies is greater than the market can absorb, if the vagaries of government policy tend to favor one group against another, etc. Because of such causes, concerted efforts to control prices come apart so frequently as to give rise to the widely held impression that "cartels always break down." Concerning the national cartels established in the oil industry, some light is shed on this issue by documents obtained from Exxon by the Federal Trade Commission. These documents (known as "Deliveries into Consumption") present comparisons of the "distribution quotas" with the "trading results" for gasoline and the country's second leading product. Comparisons between "quotas" and "results" of the "as is" companies[32]—Exxon, Mobil, Shell, and BP—were made for ten countries: France, Sweden, Italy, Switzerland, Algeria, Tunisia, Argentina, Curaçao, Colombia, and Peru.[33]

In view of all the factors that can prevent a cartel from achieving its objectives, the correspondence between the intended and the actual divisions of the market must be regarded as remarkably close. In only three of the twenty comparisons did the actual share of the "as is" group fall by more than 10 percentage points below their quota: gasoline and "black oils" in Italy and gasoline in France. Although the explanation for Italy is not known, in France the ability of the "as is" companies to capture only 42 percent of the gasoline market as against a quota of 55 percent was directly the consequence of government policy. Not only did the French government seek to promote the interests of its state-owned enterprise, Compagnie Française Pétrole; it also exempted from its mandatory import limitations all "small" importers, whose number and volume of imports thereupon increased greatly, undermining the cartel.[34] For Exxon alone the correspondence was even closer, the only conspicuous deviations being the two Italian products. Apparently Exxon was somewhat more successful than Shell and BP in meeting the intended objectives.

The Swedish investigating committee found evidence of "continued cooperation among the three major companies" after World War II.[35] And according to testimony by David Haberman of the Department of Justice, ". . . there was clear evidence in the Cartel Case (see Plaintiff's Statement of Claims, pp. 22–31) that cartels persisted in some form between 1945 and 1953 in some 13 countries of Europe, Latin America, Africa, the Near East, and the Far East."[36] But just as the need to update the overall agreements continuously would tend to disappear with the development of successful national cartels, so also would the cartels be expected to atrophy as these practices became ingrained in the local industry's customs and behavior patterns. What had previously required a formalized structure would become institutionalized as the normal way of doing business, accepted and in some cases required by the local government. And as the industry's normal way of doing business, the operation of a national or local cartel is not likely to arouse attention. It therefore came as something of a surprise when on January 18, 1974, an examining magistrate indicted the chief of British Petroleum's French subsidiary in a criminal action involving price-fixing and market-sharing arrangements with other companies in the Marseilles area. Also to appear before the magistrate were officials of the French subsidiaries of Exxon, Mobil, Shell, two French firms (CFP and ELF-ERAP), and the Belgian firm Petrofina. Two months earlier, these companies had been formally accused of organizing an illicit cartel. In fact their behavior, according to the prosecution's charges, conformed closely to the directions of the international agreements. The formal charge was "hindrance of freedom of bidding and public tenders on public markets and combining with a view to eliminating competition from the market by an illicit ring."[37] How many similar local cartels were in operation can only be a matter of conjecture. According to *The New York Times*, "For France, which does not have a history of tough antitrust enforcement like the United States, the case is unusual."[38]

THE CARTEL CASE

The summary of the restrictive supply and marketing agreements presented above is based primarily on material in the staff report to the Federal Trade Commission, *The International Petroleum Cartel*, supplemented by extracts from documents subsequently secured by the Department of Justice.[39] The principal purpose of the report—called for by a Commission resolution of December 2, 1949, and published on August 2, 1952, by the Senate Small Business Committee—was "to subject the activities of great concentrations of economic power to the spotlight of publicity." In making the report public, Senator John Sparkman, then chairman of the Small Business Committee, stated:

> It has long been the public policy of the United States to supplement the legal provisions of the antitrust laws with broad fact-finding powers. The fundamental purpose of fact finding is to prevent the abuse of power. Where power exists there also exists the possibility of its abuse. Some two decades ago the Federal Trade Commission, through an economic investigation, restrained the abuse of power by the private utility holding companies. Today the power of the international oil companies is so vast as to invite its abuse. By focusing the spotlight of publicity on the activities of these oil companies the present report of the Federal Trade Commission, like the earlier investigation of the utility companies, should prevent any possible abuse of power, either at home or abroad. . . .
>
> The Senate Small Business Committee, in publicizing the operations of the international oil companies, wishes to affirm the determination of the American people that American companies, whether at home or abroad, shall so conduct themselves as to promote the interests of all people everywhere.[40]

The report, like other FTC economic investigations, proved to be responsible for the launching of an antitrust case, although this was not its primary purpose. On June 23, 1952, President Truman wrote a memorandum to the Secretaries of State, Defense, Interior, Commerce, and the FTC, stating: "I have requested the Attorney General to institute appropriate legal proceedings with respect to the operations of the International Oil Cartel. I would like for you to cooperate with him in gathering the evidence required for these proceedings."[41] At the outset, the case gave every indication of becoming one of the most important actions ever brought by the Antitrust Division. Appointed to direct the investigation was one of the Department's most experienced and seasoned attorneys, Leonard J. Emmerglick. A special grand jury was convened, and subpoenas were served on twenty-one oil companies, including the seven international majors. Based in considerable part upon findings in the FTC report,[42] its specific objectives (as delineated in a later civil suit) were to bring to an end: (a) the monopolistic control of foreign production; (b) the curtailment of domestic production "to the extent necessary to maintain the level of domestic and world prices"; (c) the use of quotas to limit sales in foreign markets; (d) the limitation of U.S. imports and exports; and (e) the exclusion of American independents from foreign sources of supply.[43]

Attorneys for the oil companies promptly objected on the grounds that the documents were "sensitive," that they "involved the national security," and that the court lacked the jurisdictional power to require the production of documents from foreign subsidiaries of U.S. companies. But these arguments were not persuasive. In Emmerglick's words, "In largest part, the motions made by the companies were decided in favor of the United States. . . . The actions attacking the jurisdiction of the Court were denied as were the motions to change the venue. The bulk of the documentary production which we sought was ordered to be made."[44] Having lost in the judicial branch, the companies then turned their attention to the executive branch where they were far more successful.

Shortly before he was to leave office President Truman on January 12, 1953, directed the Attorney-General to replace the criminal suit with a civil case, thereby obviating the possibility of jail sentences for pillars of the corporate community and also making more difficult the process of securing the necessary documentary evidence.[45] Emmerglick received the bad news in a personal meeting with the President at the White House:

> On Sunday evening President Truman sent for me and we met in the living quarters of the White House. His purpose was to tell me and Charles Bohlen of the State Department who was present two things: first, that he reached his decision with great reluctance and he was constrained to take that decision, not on the advice of the Cabinet officers who attended the Security Council meeting, but solely on the assurance of General Omar Bradley that the national security called for that decision; and, second, that he wished the civil action to be vigorously prosecuted.[46]

From this point on it was downhill all the way; the case was finally closed out fifteen years later by virtually meaningless consent decrees. The means by which this was accomplished constitute a textbook example of how to bring about the evisceration of an antitrust case; they also provide a revealing insight into the influence of the major oil companies at the highest levels of government.

Shortly after President Eisenhower took office, Robert Cutler, Special Assistant to the President, sent a note to Secretary of State Dulles stating, "It will be assumed that the enforcement of the Antitrust laws of the United States against the Western oil companies operating in the Near East may be deemed secondary to the national security interest. . . ."[47] This was followed on August 6, 1953, by a policy directive of the National Security Council transferring primary responsibility over the case from the Department of Justice to the Department of State. Incidentally, it may be noted that the former law firm of Secretary of State Dulles, Sullivan and Cromwell, had been retained as defense counsel in the cartel case. In response to Senator Church's question whether the Secretary of State had "ever been put in charge of an antitrust case before," Emmerglick replied, "I have never heard of that before or since in my efforts to follow antitrust development."[48]

Ironically, at the very time when top policymakers at State, Defense, and the National Security Council were working to curb the cartel case, State's own petroleum attaché was urging a wholly different policy. In a memorandum dated September 11, 1950, Richard Funkhouser, the petroleum adviser to Under Secretary McGhee and later ambassador to Gabon, noted that such companies as the Iraq Petroleum Co., Aramco, and Anglo-Iranian Oil Co. held concessions of over 100,000 square miles each; he drew the analogy that "to have had Texas-Oklahoma-Louisiana oil fields controlled by one company would have had obvious disadvantages."[49] American independents, he argued, could gain a foothold in the Middle East if the majors would relinquish parts of their concession areas "in which no development is contemplated in the near future." Such a policy would have several advantages: "It would indicate to producing states that the company cannot be accused of hindering development of the concession, that the company is not monopolistic and that the company is not in a position to increase payments. These charges are familiar to oil companies operating in the Middle East." Allowing royalty rates to be determined by a free market would refute charges of exploitation: "If new competition is unwilling to pay increased royalties, it is indicative that present concessionaires are paying fair royalty rates. In turn, failure of concessionaires to reduce holdings is a strong indication to producing states that the value of the concession is greater than the royalties paid."[50] And Mr. Funkhouser cited the argument (also used later to no avail by critics of the import quota) that larger imports of Mideast oil would actually promote the national security of the United States: "Use of Middle East oil conserves Western Hemisphere resources which are vital to the Allied Nations in an emergency."[51]

Appearing in 1974 before the Senate Subcommittee on Multinational Corporations, Mr. Funkhouser was asked: "What happened when you presented this argument to the alternative policy of the companies in the Middle East relinquishing those parts of their concessions that were not currently in production? What was the reaction that you got?" His answer was, "Silence." Committee Counsel Blum pursued the point: "In effect, you are making an excellent national security argument for the cartel case going forward rather than cutting it back, as I read that. . . . Did you or anyone, to your recollection, at the Department of State go to Justice and say, 'Gee, it would be helpful, if you brought the cartel case'?" Funkhouser's explanation was to the effect that such action on his part would have involved going outside official channels: "On this point I have to say that we are—we are bureaucratized, if that is the word. There are other sections of the State Department . . . who see the big picture, the global picture, and are concerned much more with relations with other departments of the U.S. government. I do not think I ever stepped in another departmental office the whole time I was petroleum adviser."[52]

If Funkhouser's memoranda ever reached the policymakers, his arguments were obviously ignored, as the National Security Council dealt the case one crippling blow after another. First, it directed the Justice Department not to challenge the legality of joint production, joint refining, joint storage, and joint transportation ventures among the seven international majors. As described by Haberman, ". . . what was still left open for prosecution were the older 'As Is' market cartel arrangements which by then had become relatively incidental to the basic joint venture supply control system."[53]

After placing control over supply beyond the Department's reach, the National Security Council then prohibited it from using the single most effective remedy of antitrust enforcement—dissolution and divestiture. Emmerglick described the progressive deterioration of the case resulting from the change from a criminal to a civil action, the transference of primary responsibility to State, the immunization of joint ventures, the foreclosure of dissolution, and divestiture and other inhibitions: "The pressures were continuous from month to month, sometimes week to week, to downgrade the importance of prosecution of the cartel case. We did not give up at the staff level in our purpose to achieve the aims which we set out to achieve, but we realized that new impediments were being thrown in our way as each of these developments took place."[54] Or, in Barbara Svedberg's words, ". . . it did not take very long when anybody was assigned to that case to realize it was heading downhill, and that the real relief was not going to be allowed or perhaps was impossible, and that it was drudgery."[55]

Predictably, the end result took the form of consent decrees which, in the words of the Senate Subcommittee on Multinational Corporations, "did not impair the major companies' ability jointly to production, and through production, the world market."[56] As was to be expected from the National Security Council's directive, the decrees specifically permitted participation in joint production, joint refining and joint pipeline operations, and other engagements with competitors of a kind customarily regarded as inconsistent with competition. Moreover, participation in cartel arrangements was to be permitted where pursuant to either a "requirement of law of the foreign nation in which it takes place," or to a "policy of such foreign nations where failure to comply therewith would expose the defendant to the risk of loss of the particular business. . . ." This placed upon the Antitrust Division the virtually impossible burden of proving that the following by the defendants of something as vague and tenuous as a country's "policy" did not "expose them to the *risk* of loss." A similar, even weaker decree was entered in 1963 against Texaco. The cartel case remained pending, albeit inactive, against the remaining two defendants, SoCal and Mobil, until January 28, 1968, when the actions against them were dismissed. In a press release, the Justice Department explained that the main objectives of the suit had been realized through the consent judgments against the other defendants, and that since the complaint was nearly fifteen years old its continuation would not be in the public interest.

Weak as they were, the consent judgments apparently were still considered potentially troublesome by Exxon and Gulf and hence were further relaxed. According to a memorandum by Worth Rowley, formerly of the Antitrust Division, this took place "in mysterious and unexplained circumstances." Rowley pointed out:

> Pursuant to the Code of Federal Regulations . . . it is the policy of the Justice Department to afford persons who may be affected by consent judgments and who are not named as partners to the action to state comments, views or relevant allegations prior to its entry. Pursuant to this policy each proposed consent judgment is filed in court or otherwise made available upon request to interested persons as early as feasible but at least thirty days prior to entry by the court, so that the Department of Justice may receive and consider any written comments, views or relevant allegations relating to the judgment. . . . Here the policy was breached. Indeed the entry of these superseding judgments did not come to public notice until March 31, 1969, when they were published in Trade Regulation Reports.
>
> This lack of publicity is itself most unusual because important developments of this kind are normally announced by the Department in a carefully prepared press release. Here, public business was secretly conducted. No reason whatsoever appears in the public record or is otherwise available to justify the relaxation of the 1960 consent decrees.[57]

What had been launched with such high hopes more than a decade and a half earlier had finally been interred. In the interim the targets of the original complaint—the international agreements—had long since served their purpose, having spawned control of the market through national cartels, with the expectation that in most countries these would in turn become part of the normal way of doing business.

THE EXCLUSION OF OUTSIDERS

4

ALTHOUGH ATTEMPTS TO stabilize the price of any commodity can be upset by only a relatively small amount of uncontrolled production, certain characteristics of oil make it particularly vulnerable to market disruption. For one thing, large-scale storage is difficult and expensive. As a liquid it must be contained, usually in steel storage tanks; but steel is costly and the tanks must be constantly painted to prevent rust. Hence, it is an industry axiom that oil, once produced, must move. Moreover, oil is a fungible commodity ("any unit of which can replace another unit"). While differences in quality do exist, particularly in weight and sulphur content, quality differentials that are recognized by both buyers and sellers make it possible for oil from any source to compete directly with oil from any other source. Finally, oil's relatively low short-run elasticity of demand with respect to price means that any excess of total production will not, as a consequence of a lower price, be absorbed by a corresponding increase in consumption. On the supply side, independents who have been fortunate enough to obtain a concession have usually been under strong pressure by the host government to constantly increase production. The combination of this pressure with the other characteristics has made world oil prices peculiarly sensitive to any uncontrolled supply. And it has also led the international majors to be particularly vigorous in their efforts to keep outsiders out.

Opportunities for the entrance of newcomers have from time to time made their appearance. But, generally speaking, the efforts of newcomers to gain a viable foothold have either been frustrated or, if initially successful, short-lived. The problems encountered by newcomers are illustrated here by the inability of the Iranian government to market oil seized from a concessionaire; by the failure of the Iraqi government to induce independents to take concessions and produce in areas where oil had been discovered but not produced; and by

77

the ending of a competitive threat from Italy and the subsequent subordination of the Italian government to the majors.

IRAN

The abortive and short-lived attempt by the Iranian government to find outlets for oil seized in 1951 from the Anglo-Iranian Oil Co. (BP) presents a classic example of the virtually insurmountable obstacles encountered by an outsider—even one with the powers of a sovereign state. In 1951, the properties of Anglo-Iranian were nationalized by the Iranian government. The company had accepted a new supplemental oil agreement in 1949, providing for an increase in the royalty from 22 to 33 cents a barrel, but it flatly refused to accept the fifty-fifty profit-sharing arrangement conceded by American firms to the governments of Venezuela and Saudi Arabia. Thereupon, at the instigation of Dr. Muhammed Mossadeq the Iranian government in March 1951 passed a nationalization bill: "By May, Mossadeq was Prime Minister and the British were out of Iran."[1] Not unexpectedly, consternation reigned in the government of Great Britain. On July 4, 1952, Secretary of State Acheson, British Ambassador Oliver Franks, George McGhee, and Averell Harriman met at Harriman's Washington office to discuss the Iranian question. According to Acheson: "Sir Oliver left no doubt how seriously and angrily both the British government and public viewed what they regarded as the insolent defiance of decency, legality and reason by a group of wild men in Iran who proposed to despoil Britain."[2] On their part the Iranians were filled with anti-British resentment which had been mounting over many years. According to Zuhayr Mikdashi, unhappiness with oil revenues was not the only cause of the takeover, ". . . a crucial factor, yet not amenable to economic analysis, was Persian dissatisfaction with the predominance of a major British interest (viz. A.I.O.C.) in the country. Dr. Mossadeq himself acknowledged the importance of this social-political factor."[3] Similarly, in a "Background Paper" dated September 10, 1950 (before the takeover), the State Department's petroleum attaché, Richard Funkhouser, observed, "The Iranian Majlis [parliamentary body] refused the agreement in a 1949 session marked by emotional excesses and have since shown no disposition to sign. AIOC and the British are genuinely hated in Iran; approval of AIOC is treated as political suicide." Stressing the importance of Iran for strategic reasons, Funkhouser urged the acceptance of Mossadeq's request for the immediate initiation of payments under the higher royalty schedule: "Both U.S. and U.K. governments believe it important that

AIOC comply with this request because of the economic, political and strategic considerations involved. AIOC, however, refuses to pay until the agreement is ratified; progress is nil, the Prime Minister has threatened concession cancellation."[4]

The reaction to nationalization by the major oil companies took the form of a collective boycott on Iranian oil. Prospective buyers were warned of legal action on the grounds that without a compensation agreement the oil was still the property of Anglo-Iranian. Of course, the more effective the boycott, the less the ability of the Iranians to pay compensation and thus the brighter the prospect for ultimate capitulation. Mikdashi writes: "The embargo . . . was very effective due to the cooperation of the eight major oil companies. This embargo had, as intended, a punitive effect on Persia's economy."[5] Oil exports dropped from over $400 million in 1950 to less than $2 million in the two-year period from July 1951 to August 1953.

Little difficulty was experienced in making up the deficit with oil from Arab countries: "Oil was available—even to A.I.O.C.—in abundance in neighboring countries, and world surplus production capacity of crude oil was estimated then at about 1.5 million barrels per day pressing for outlets."[6] Unusually sharp increases between 1951 and 1955 were registered by Kuwait and Iraq, while the production of Saudi Arabia was also accelerated above its long-term trend.[7] If between 1951 and 1955 Iranian production had held at its 1950 level, the net loss (after deducting some 300 million barrels actually produced) would have totaled approximately 900 million barrels. About 800 million barrels was made up by the expansion above what would appear to be the long-term growth rates of Kuwait (300 million), Iraq (200 million), and Saudi Arabia (300 million). Miscellaneous increases from smaller Middle East countries completely closed the gap. In Mikdashi's words, Anglo-Iranian's total production "was substantially replaced by the end of 1954 with oil produced by subsidiaries from outside Persia."[8]

The U.S. State Department did what it could to bring the Iranian government to terms by persuading independent American oil companies to abstain from seeking concessions. On May 15, 1951, the Department of State issued a press release, stating that "U.S. oil companies . . . have indicated . . . that they would not, in the face of unilateral action by Iran against the British company, be willing to undertake operations in that country."[9]

Unable to market its oil and starved for revenues, the Mossadeq government faced a mounting financial crisis. The events of 1953 leading to its overthrow have been summarized by the Senate Subcommittee on Multinational Corporations as follows:

When the Parliament refused to grant Mossadeq's demand that it extend for one year his right to govern by decree, a wave of demonstrations swept the country. Mossadeq directly challenged the Shah, ordered a plebiscite to dissolve Parliament and won more than 99 percent of the votes cast and counted. In a swiftly moving series of events, the Shah attempted to oust Mossadeq by decree, failed, and fled the country as Mossadeq's supporters demonstrated in the streets smashing the statues of the Shah and his father. The military moved in, and in bloody street fighting deposed Mossadeq and restored the Shah to his throne, a move which was assisted clandestinely by the U.S. Central Intelligence Agency.[10]

The fact that the Iranian government took over, without compensation, concession rights previously awarded to BP does not necessarily mean that under international law legal proceedings alone would have prevented the independent firms from gaining concessions in Iran or purchasing oil directly from the Iranian government. In a memorandum of October 24, 1964, on the "Iraq Petroleum Situation," Andreas F. Lowenfeld of the State Department's legal staff summarized the U.S. position on the general issue of the nationalization of concessions:

> The United States Executive Branch, consistent with classical international law, has maintained the view that taking of alien property is improper under international law if it is not for a public purpose, is discriminatory, or is without provision for prompt, adequate and effective compensation. But as the Supreme Court recently said in the Sabbatino case, "There are few if any issues in international law today on which opinion seems to be so divided as the limitations of a State's power to expropriate the property of aliens. . . ." (376 U.S. 393 [1964])[11]

On the argument that a concession agreement is the fundamental law of the parties, granting rights which the government lacks legal authority to withdraw, Lowenfeld noted that ". . . in the Anglo-Iranian Oil Company case, the International Court of Justice held that a concession was not a treaty within the meaning of Article 36 of the Statute of the International Court. The inference arguably could be drawn that the breach of such a concession does not give rise to international responsibility at all, though the Courts did not deal with this question. . . ." On the question of whether the breach of a concession does "give rise to an international law violation," Lowenfeld concluded, "No conclusive answer can be given . . ."[12]

IRAQ

Although its original concession of March 14, 1925, covered all of Iraq, the Iraq Petroleum Co., under the ownership of BP (23.75%),

Shell (23.75%), CFP (23.75%), Exxon (11.85%), Mobil (11.85%), and Gulbenkian (5.0%), limited its production to fields constituting only one-half of 1 percent of the country's total area. During the Great Depression, the world was awash with oil and greater output from Iraq would simply have driven the price down to even lower levels. Delaying tactics were employed not only in actual drilling and development, but also in conducting negotiations on such matters as pipeline rights-of-way. While such tactics ensured the limitation of supply, they were not without their dangers. If the Iraqi government learned that IPC was neither actively seeking new fields nor exploiting proved and productive areas, it might withdraw or narrow IPC's concession, or worse, award it to some independent willing and anxious to maximize production.

*SUPPRESSION OF DISCOVERIES.** From almost the beginning of its operations IPC not only suppressed production in Iraq (as well as in nearby lands) but went to considerable lengths to conceal that fact from the Iraqi government.

Of the many concession areas exclusively preempted by IPC, none was rapidly developed. IPC had held the area east of the Tigris River in the Mosul and Baghdad vilayets since 1931, and by 1950 the only developed field was Kirkuk. Qatar is another illustration of "sitting on" a concession. Fearful that the area would fall to outside interests, Anglo-Iranian in 1932 obtained a two-year exclusive license for a geological examination of this peninsula. These exploration rights were expanded into a concession in 1935, and in 1936 were given to IPC under the terms of the Red Line Agreement. BP and Shell, however, were not anxious to develop more production in the Persian Gulf because of the effect this would have upon production in Iran. Although Mobil wanted more crude from the Persian Gulf, drilling did not start until three years and five months after the signing of the concession, and five years and two months after the completion of the geological survey. A productive well was completed in 1939, and a few others were drilled after the war began; but in 1941, an official (Mr. Sellers) wrote: ". . . as there is excess of petroleum products available from AIOC and Cal-Tex in Persian Gulf, it is obvious productive wells in Qatar will not be expedited at present time." Commercial production in substantial quantities did not begin until 1950— eighteen years after the first exploration of the area.

* This section is based on an Addendum to the Staff Report to the FTC, *The International Petroleum Cartel;* the Addendum was deleted before the publication of the report, but after being declassified by the State Department was introduced into the public record during hearings of the Senate Subcommittee on Multinational Corporations on July 25, 1974 (*Hearings*, Pt. 8, pp. 529–532). The italics are in the Addendum.

An interesting case of "technical compliance" is provided by IPC's actions concerning a concession in Syria. In 1933, IPC had obtained drilling permits in Syria, and two years later suggested that the Syrian government grant it a blanket concession over a large part of Syria, similar to the Iraq concession. Negotiations were opened for this purpose, but in view of the time which the negotiations would take, the IPC groups "agreed that *the Company should drill shallow holes which would constitute technical compliance with Company's obligations,* the Syrian government should be informed of the Company's intentions to do so." Negotiations dragged on and the British High Commissioner of Syria suspended the acceptance of any further drilling permits. But IPC was prepared to receive this blow with equanimity; the general manager wrote: ". . . we have been steadily complying with the letter of the Mining Law by drilling shallow holes on locations where there was no danger of striking oil. . . ." However, when IPC encountered difficulty in getting the Syrian Parliament to ratify the concession, *"serious drilling"* was recommended by the High Commissioner and by the general manager of IPC. The latter wrote the secretary of IPC: "You should explain to the Groups that *neither the High Commissioner, nor myself, are actuated by a hell for leather rush to find oil; we want to set up a convincing window dressing that we are actually working the concession* . . . the High Commissioner can exert far more justifiable pressure in getting our concession ratified by the succeeding ministry than he would be justified in exerting if we merely stood by, content to watch events, doing nothing. . . ."

In outlining to the groups the obstacles which stood in the way of obtaining better concession terms from Syria, the general manager of IPC also revealed the government's opinion of IPC: among the obstacles faced by IPC was the *"Government's conviction that we did not intend to find oil, and if we found it we would advance a thousand and one reasons for not producing it. In these circumstances my plan was to obtain terms that would be light to bear so long as we explored without result,* whilst conceding to Government that if we did find oil, we would produce or pay."

Not surprisingly, IPC's policies of "sitting on" concessions endowed the company with the stigma of restrictionism. In 1936, the question arose as to whether IPC should negotiate directly, or indirectly through an intermediary, for concessions in Turkey, Saudi Arabia, and Yemen; the general manager of IPC stated that in his opinion:

> . . . the indirect method . . . might in the long run produce rather better terms than would be given to a company whose proprietors already hold many oil concessions, *who have been identified with a policy of restrictive production, and whose object in obtaining*

fresh oil territory would not be associated with any irrepressible urge for intensive exploitation.

By 1938, IPC's reputation for obstructionism had become firmly established throughout the Middle East. The general manager of IPC, who had been engaged in discussions on the Bahrein and Basrah concessions, described the attitude of the "various authorities and rulers" toward the IPC in these words:

> From the earnestness of their address in my conversation with various authorities and rulers on the subject of production, they will brook no sitting on concessions, regardless of what loopholes the terms may give us, particularly *us*, whom, one and all, they suspect as capable of cheating on production, the future leaves them cold; they want money now.

The pressure of governments and of public opinion appears to have induced IPC to dispense with some of its restrictions. In 1938, one oil company official wrote:

> As regards the BOD and Basrah concessions it is the consensus of opinion of the Groups that it will be necessary to explore these concessions and if a satisfactory oil is found, that same should be exploited, even though the production and the reserves from the IPC concession would amply cover the crude oil requirements of the Groups. We are led to this conclusion since we do not believe that public opinion or the Government would permit that these large areas were either left unexplored or unexploited if production were found.

World War II interrupted the operations of IPC in most of its concessions, and political disturbances handicapped its activities since that time. Yet even after allowing for these difficulties, in 1948 production in Iran was seven times larger than in Iraq, while in 1936 production in Iran was a little more than double that in Iraq. In Saudi Arabia commercial production did not begin until 1938, but by 1948 it was almost six times the production of Iraq.

The restrictive policies of the Iraq Petroleum Company during its early years have been summarized as follows:

> Following the discovery of oil in Iraq in October, 1927, these three groups [BP, Shell, and Exxon-Mobil] employed a variety of methods to retard developments in Iraq and prolong the period before the entry of Iraq oil into world markets. Among the tactics used to retard the development of Iraq oil were the requests for an extension of time in which to make the selection plots for IPC's exclusive exploitation, the delays in constructing a pipeline, the practice of preempting concessions for the sole purpose of prevent-

ing them from falling into other hands, the deliberate reductions in drilling and development work, and the drilling of shallow holes without any intention of finding oil.

Restrictive policies were continued even after a pipeline was completed, for in 1935, IPC's production was shut back several hundred thousand tons. Moreover, for a time, a sales coordinating committee was established to work out a "common policy regarding the sale of Iraq oil." Again in 1938 and 1939, the Big Three opposed any "enlargement of the pipeline and the corresponding increase in production" on the ground that additional production would upset the world oil market. Although the Big Three eventually conceded to the demands of the French (CFP) for some expansion, no action was taken until after World War II.[13]

While the restriction of Iraqi production during the 1930's had its roots in the generally depressed economic conditions of the time, the continued curtailment of Iraq's output after World War II stemmed from different causes. With the development of Saudi Arabia and Kuwait, the U.S. firms—which owned 100 percent of the former and 50 percent of the latter—gained large-scale sources of supply that were far more attractive to them than Iraq, where their ownership interest was only 23.75 percent. A later complication was the emergence of Libya as an important and largely uncontrollable source of supply, portending reductions in the growth rates of all the major Middle East countries.[14] To the question of whether Libyan output could be accommodated within the limits of the overall growth rate (i.e., "Can you swallow this amount of oil?"), Exxon's vice-president Page answered, "Of course, with Iraq down."[15] Indeed, keeping Iraq "down" was the only means by which the high growth rates of Iran and Saudi Arabia could be sustained in the face of Libya's expansion without creating a price-reducing surplus.

That the IPC continued its restrictive practices into recent years is corroborated by an excerpt from what Senator Muskie referred to as "this intelligence report," which he read into the record of the Senate Subcommittee on Multinational Corporations on March 28, 1974. According to the Senator, the report was "dated February 1967 and it has to do with this question of the potential in Iraq."

In 1966 a study was made of the geological, geographical and other petroleum exploration data of the areas of Iraq relinquished by IPC, Iraq Petroleum Co. The purpose of the study was to help government let new concessions and obtain more advantageous terms from foreign oil firms. The study indicated that the untapped reservoirs of oil in Iraq appear to be fantastic.

There is every evidence that millions of barrels of oil will be found in the new concessions. Some of these new vast oil reservoirs had been discovered previously by IPC but they were not exploited because of the distance to available transportation, the heavy expense of building new pipelines *and the fact that IPC has had a surplus of oil in its fields that are already served by existing pipelines.*

The files yielded proof that IPC had drilled and found wildcat wells that would have produced 50,000 barrels of oil per day. The firm plugged these wells and did not classify them at all because the availability of such information would have made the companies' bargaining position with Iraq more troublesome. Many of these areas had been returned to the Government in settlement of the petroleum concession conflict between the Government and IPC.[16]

PUBLIC LAW 80. Word of IPC's restrictive practices could not be kept from the Iraqis indefinitely. The first concrete manifestation of their mounting unhappiness was the enactment in 1961 of Public Law 80, withdrawing IPC's rights to those areas in which it was not producing. The nature of the action was described in an internal State Department memorandum dated October 13, 1967, from Assistant Secretary Solomon to Under Secretary Katzenbach: "The Iraqis . . . in December, 1961, took away over 99.5 percent of the concession area (Law 80), including proven reserves of the North Rumaila field and suspected fields in other areas, but provided that 0.5 percent could be returned to the company. All subsequent discussions have shattered on the selection of this crucial 0.5 percent—the company insisting that it include North Rumaila and the government insisting that it not."[17]

In response to a request from the Under Secretary, Andreas Lowenfeld of the State Department's legal office submitted a memorandum on "the validity and effect of Law No. 80 of December 11, 1961."[18] Emphasizing the differences between the Iraqi action and "typical nationalizations, such as have recently occurred for example in Cuba or Indonesia," Lowenfeld pointed out: "Under Law No. 80, IPC's property as such has not been taken, and in fact IPC's operations have continued substantially unimpeded. What IPC has been deprived of is mineral rights granted in a number of concessions awarded by the government of Iraq. Thus, it may be argued that IPC's claim is at most a claim for breach of contract, and not a claim arising out of expropriation of property." None of the area expropriated, the memorandum stressed, was actually under production: "For the most part the area removed from the concession was unexplored territory, but the area included in several cases proven reserves. Our understanding is that

IPC's production capacity (at least in the short-run) was not affected by Law No. 80. . . . The question of whether and under what circumstances the breach of a concession gives rise to a violation of international law is very much in doubt." If the matter were brought before some international body for adjudication, Lowenfeld warned, IPC on at least one point would be "fairly vulnerable," i.e., that the company had not governed its exploitation of Iraq's oil "solely according to the requirements of Iraq and the intention of the concession, but in accordance with the overall interests of the participating companies":

> This issue could be raised with respect to the amount of exploration and production in Iraq; with respect to pricing and discounting policies followed by the company; and possibly also with respect to IPC's efforts to exclude competitors. Without in any way attempting to examine these charges or the arguments in defense of IPC, it is fair to conclude that any thorough airing of these charges in an international adjudication would not likely be beneficial either to the interests of the major western countries concerned—Great Britain, France, and the United States. . . .
>
> A fairly substantial case could be made (particularly in an arbitration) that IPC has followed a "dog in the manger" policy in Iraq, excluding or swallowing up all competitors, while at the same time governing its production in accordance with the overall worldwide interests of the participating companies and not solely in accordance with the interests of Iraq. This of course has been one of the principal charges of the government of Iraq against IPC.

The memorandum concluded by stating: "While the legal issues in the IPC-Iraq dispute are numerous and complicated, law does not appear to provide solutions . . . IPC's legal remedies are few, *and we have no firm legal basis for telling independent American companies—let alone foreign companies—to stay out of Iraq*."[19]

STATE DEPARTMENT PRESSURE ON INDEPENDENTS. Although lacking a "firm legal basis," top State Department officials were in fact exceedingly active in telling independent American companies to "stay out of Iraq," both before and after the submission of the legal memorandum. For example, on May 6, 1964, Governor Averell Harriman and other State Department officials met with E. L. Steiniger, chairman of the Board of Sinclair Oil Company, one of the largest companies without a Mideast concession.[20] According to the Department's Memorandum of Conversation, Governor Harriman said that: "In the IPC case proved and probable reserve areas were taken away. We wonder whether it is wise for U.S. oil companies to approve this type of action which the same companies condemn in other parts of the world. . . . We hope you will not take any action which will appear to condone unilateral acts." In reply, Mr. Steiniger cited other instances (Peru, Argentina) in which Sinclair "had refused to enter the petroleum picture since this would be to the detriment of an existing concessionaire," but he went on to refer to the danger that in Iraq "foreign companies—German, Japanese and Italian—would acquire concessions shutting Sinclair out." Governor Harriman replied: "We could not wish governments, such as Iraq, to get the impression that American oil companies can be pushed around." In return Mr. Steiniger alluded to the Achilles' heel of IPC's case: "Sinclair was not interested in taking proven areas which IPC wishes to exploit but Sinclair understands that many favorable areas in Iraq were drilled by IPC and then abandoned." Governor Harriman closed the meeting by suggesting that Sinclair "hint to the Iraqis that its offer is affected by what takes place between the GOI [Government of Iraq] and IPC." There is nothing in the record to indicate whether Steiniger conveyed this suggestion which, if accepted by the Iraqis, would have ruined his own chances of securing a concession.

Two weeks later, a similar meeting was held between Ambassador Jernegan of the State Department and James Richards of Standard Oil of Indiana, another large company lacking a Mideast concession. It would appear from the Memorandum of Conversation that this company (formerly a part of the old Standard Oil "Trust") evidenced a greater spirit of cooperativeness:[21] "Standard of Indiana, he [Richards] said, has been very careful not to appear to do anything until it is clear that the company's action would not be infringing on the rights of another company. Ambassador Jernegan replied, 'That's what I wanted to hear you say.' He noted the worldwide repercussions which would emanate from Iraq's getting away with expropriation of IPC's concession territory, particularly if other American companies reached agreement with the Iraq Government prior to an IPC-GOI settlement. The ambassador was assured that 'Standard of Indiana would do no such thing.' "

By early July, the Department was able to report that it had successfully "interceded with all American companies which to its knowledge or belief have expressed interest in Iraq land concessions in order to deter them from making offers to GOI while critical IPC-GOI negotiations in progress."* In an outgoing telegram of July 8, Under

* Awareness that the major oil companies "mark the sparrow's fall" is illustrated by a communication relating to a company engaged in drilling operations—the Santa Fe Drilling Co. According to a State Department telegram in September 1967, the assistant manager of Santa Fe for Mid- and Far-East "had been approached over a month ago by Iraq National Oil Co. for possible drilling contracts. Source quickly added Santa Fe would carefully check attitude of Iraq Petroleum Co. parents before signing a contract with INOC as it did not want to jeopardize other Santa Fe contracts with IPC parent majors." (Department of State, Incoming Telegram from Ambassador Middleton [Beirut], Subject: "Oil-Iraq.")

Secretary George Ball stated, "The firms to which Department has spoken are Sinclair, Union Oil, Standard of Indiana, Continental, Marathon, Pauly, and Phillips. These companies have been responsive to Department's urgings and it is therefore incumbent on us to make same effort with any new American or American-affiliated company which appears to be entering Iraq picture."[22]

Despite the fact that by the end of the year the Department had made its views known "forcefully and repeatedly to Sinclair, Continental and some 8 other companies," a cloud loomed on the horizon: "U.S. independents are becoming increasingly nervous lest other American or non-American companies get in ahead of them and cause them to lose out entirely."[23] During the next two years the problem subsided as a compromise agreement was reached in 1965 between IPC and the Government of Iraq. But the agreement was never ratified, and in 1967 the issue resurfaced. The principal aspiring "poachers" (to use Secretary Rusk's term)[24] were the Italians and the French. Here, the U.S. government had to exert its influence indirectly through the governments of the offending companies. Inasmuch as the U.S. majors were themselves important sellers in each of these countries, their governments could engage in "harassment of majors," which, as Rusk noted, "dictates cautious approach to problem."[25]

On May 13, the *Financial Times* of London reported a " 'clash' of U.K., U.S., France and Netherlands with Italy over reported ENI [the Italian state-owned oil company] negotiations to take 20 million tons of crude from INOC [the government-owned Iraq National Oil Company] in return for leading role in exploitation of concession areas which were to have been explored by BP, Shell, Mobil and CFP."[26] Protests were lodged with the Italian Foreign Office by ambassadors of the United States, the United Kingdom, France, and The Netherlands. According to Ambassador David Bruce, "Four companies and respective governments furious that Italians interfering with 1965 agreement." In this case, the gravamen of the Department's concern was made explicit: "Companies maintain ENI does not have outlets requiring 20 million tons. Thus their oil, taken as royalty in kind by INOC from IPC operations, *would be released on world markets.*"[27] At the same time, Ambassador Reinhardt in Rome called upon Foreign Minister Ortona to express the U.S. government's "particular concern." Ortona reported that ENI had "taken note" of the protests, but expressed the view that "in light of its own past experiences with major oil companies, it did not see why it should exercise self-restraint in this matter."[28] The mere fact that ENI was a state-owned company, Ortona pointed out, did not mean that it was under the control of the Italian government: "There were limits to pressure Foreign Ministry could bring on ENI," given the fact that "Italy's long quest for sources of oil was [a] matter of continuing and acute public and political interest." Nonetheless, Ortona said, a "warning" had been given to ENI by the Foreign Ministry.[29] Whether because of the warning or differences over terms, the deal fell through.

Keeping French interests out of Iraq proved more difficult, and ultimately impossible. In the summer of 1967, Iraq passed a new law (No. 97) specifically barring the return of any known reserves to the IPC and giving the country's own Iraq National Oil Company the right to exploit those reserves either by itself or in partnership with other companies. Shortly thereafter a smaller French firm, ERAP, was granted a concession on territory taken from IPC. This was followed by a proposal on the part of the major French Company, CFP, that it establish a joint venture with the Iraq National Oil Company to develop the highly productive North Rumaila field. To the other IPC owners it was bad enough for outsiders to produce on lands IPC claimed as its own, but for one of the owning companies to do so seemed little short of treasonous. On October 13, senior officials of Exxon and Mobil met with Under Secretary Katzenbach "to urge Department to protest formally to GOF [Government of France] recent activities of CFP and ERAP that are detrimental to the interests of the Iraq Petroleum Company. Company representatives expressed their conviction that CFP has been pressured by GOF . . . by threatening to have ERAP negotiate for the venture if CFP does not."[30]

A note was prepared, signed by the Secretary, for delivery to the French Foreign Office no later than October 18. While vigorously worded, its logic is somewhat difficult to follow. The fact that the Iraqi government would still entertain proposals from IPC relating to the disputed areas is somehow twisted into an argument that Iraq recognizes "a continuing right in IPC to the areas. . . ." The same conclusion is drawn from the fact that the Iraqi government "has not attempted to cede any of the territory to other foreign oil interests." Yet the note itself ascribes this forbearance simply to the exercise of pressure on aspiring independents: "That no other companies have been granted rights to the disputed territory is due to the vigor with which the IPC shareholders and their respective governments have asserted the continuing effect of the concession agreement between the IPC and the GOI. . . ." The note also emphasized the danger of establishing harmful precedents: "The GOF must appreciate that the acquisition by French companies of territories claimed by the IPC can create precedents elsewhere which can weaken the security of Western oil rights and thereby adversely affect the national interests of France as well as of the United States." Yet how could developments in Iraq serve as precedents for countries where the growth rate had *not* been held down to less than half that of other leading Mideast countries, where proven and productive fields had *not* been suppressed for years on end, where misleading information had *not* been deliberately supplied to the host government and where, in the words of the Department's own legal counsel, the company had *not* followed a "dog in the manger" policy?

The controversy escalated to a new height when on October 23, 1967, President Mostini of Mobil's French subsidiary met with Foreign Minister Giraud. Referring to protests lodged by Exxon and Mobil, Giraud commented that the "two letters had practically identical wording and seemed to have been written by same attorney." According to an account transmitted by the U.S. Embassy in Paris:

> He [Giraud] then strongly objected to part of letter raising possibility of legal action against CFP on oil eventually flowing from disputed areas. He asked how this should be interpreted. If this is simply a case of Mobil and Esso lawyers filing protests, French government would do nothing. However, if Mobil and Esso really contemplate legal action, the French government would consider this a declaration of hostilities and take appropriate action against the companies in France. Giraud stated frankly "This is a threat." . . .
>
> Mostini acknowledged to us that Dica [the French regulatory agency] has unlimited scope for harassing local affiliate, can do "anything and everything under 1928 law."[31]

It was not long, however, before the whole issue became moot, as Iraq moved inexorably toward complete nationalization, including the takeover of IPC's major producing property, the Kirkuk field. In 1964, the government established the Iraq National Oil Co. (INOC) for the express purpose of operating in those areas confiscated from IPC under Public Law 80; and three years later, the newly formed company was authorized to work in the expropriated areas. On June 1, 1972, *all* of IPC's properties were nationalized, and in March of the following year IPC formally accepted the nationalization. Perhaps because IPC realized that it had a weak case (as the State Department's legal counsel had predicted earlier), the company "desisted from taking legal action to prevent exports of Kirkuk crude."[32] Thus forty-five years after it had brought in its first well in Iraq, the Iraq Petroleum Co. lost its rights in a land that was not only the original source of Mideast oil but remains a repository of "fantastic" reserves.[33]

ITALY

The problems encountered by Iraq and Iran involved outsiders (governments of oil-producing countries) situated at the upstream stage of the industry's vertical flow. The problems faced by Enrico Mattei involved an outsider primarily engaged at the industry's opposite stage —marketing. As the restless and imaginative head of Italy's state-owned energy companies (ENI and AGIP), Mattei had no intention of simply presiding over a stagnant bureaucracy, subsisting on a stable share of the Italian market accorded to it by the majors. Because of its location, situated between the producing countries of the Middle East and the consuming markets of Western Europe, Italy was ideally suited to play a key role in the inevitable expansion of the petroleum industry. Moreover, Mattei shared with many of his countrymen a strong resentment against "imperialist" British-American interests, personified by the major oil companies. Italy, he felt, should have its own place in the energy sun. Supported by the Italian government and even more strongly by its populace, he set about in the 1950's and early 1960's to secure it.

His first step was to secure a supply of low-cost crude, which he was able to obtain from first Anglo-Iranian (BP) and later the Russians. In his perceptive biography of Mattei, Paul H. Frankel notes that, with far more crude than outlets, Anglo-Iranian was prepared to give large distributors, such as Mattei, "prices which were more advantageous for the buyer than were the official quotations on the strength of which smaller customers were paying for their crude oil at the time. Therefore . . . AGIP bought oil on terms which gave her a very substantial profit margin. . . ."* In view of Mattei's subsequent rapid expansion, this contract aroused no little resentment among the other majors: "Anglo-Iranian was afterwards criticized for having built up a competitor for the sake of gaining a momentary outlet, and it was said that Mattei was Anglo-Iranian's 'Frankenstein Monster.' "[34]

Next, Mattei embarked on an expensive and, for Italy, novel form of non-price competition. In Frankel's words, "Now Mattei (and this was really a personal contribution of his) hit on the idea of building bigger and better service stations than anybody had ever seen in those parts, to endow them with first-rate and well-kept toilet facilities— rare in Italy at the best of places—and to broaden this appeal by side-lines such as coffee bars and motels." Needless to say, this project became a further source of resentment: "The competitors said indignantly that all this was not necessary to sell gasoline. . . ."[35]

But Mattei did not confine himself to the more genteel forms of rivalry represented by non-price competition. According to Frankel, "Mattei pursued for several years the policy of taking the lead in

---

* Frankel, *op. cit.*, p. 89. On occasion Frankel had served as consultant to Mattei. Although a biography of Mattei, the book provides penetrating insights into the economics of the petroleum industry.

progressive reductions of gasoline prices at the pump, and he had the great satisfaction of succeeding in persuading the government to reduce apace the (inordinately high) excise taxes on gasoline. Thus, in the course of the years 1959 and 1961 gasoline prices, including tax, fell by about 25%, actually by a bigger amount than was the total value of the stuff (without tax) when it left the refinery." Coming at the crest of the Italian boom, the response to these lower prices was enthusiastic, except of course from his competitors "who, appearing to be dragged along by Mattei, did not cut too favorable a figure in the whole series of events." Frankel states that in 1962, shortly before his death, Mattei "toyed with the idea of yet another round of gasoline price cuts."[36]

Having established himself as a formidable rival in Italy, Mattei began to expand his operations into other parts of the world, starting with the miscellaneous underdeveloped oil-consuming countries of Africa and Asia. Apart from Japan, India, and South Africa, their demand for oil, individually, was too small to warrant much attention from the industry: "Consequently, there was no competition at all except for that between the few established major oil companies. . . . It was said, not without some justification, that the poorer a country was, the higher were the prices it paid for the oil."[37] Having formerly been directly or indirectly under the domain of Great Britain, "saturated with anti-imperialist sentiment and with the suspicion of being overcharged," these countries were ripe for the new approach offered by Mattei. Specifically, he proposed the construction of local oil refineries, thereby enabling the countries to earn the refinery margin themselves. From a purely cost standpoint, these refineries would obviously not be as efficient as the majors' large, centralized refineries; but in Mattei's view, the margin between costs and price was sufficient for the refining operation to be carried on at a somewhat higher cost and still yield a comfortable return.

The benefits to Mattei's enterprises included a guaranteed return on the capital invested, design and engineering contracts for the refinery, and establishment as an oil distributor. The benefits to the countries included a lessening of their foreign exchange payments (by virtue of preempting the refining margin), freedom to select the source of crude, and the foundation of a petrochemical complex.

Though holding much promise for the long run, the consummation of these projects would necessarily be a slow and laborious process. Impatient for bigger game, Mattei then sought to force his way into the huge, rapidly expanding markets of Central Europe and beyond. And it was here that he met his Waterloo. To the majors, his success in Italy and his projects for underdeveloped countries were bothersome

but little more than annoyances. The move to bring competition into
the markets of Western Europe was something else again. His plan of
assault was to build pipelines through the Alps which would carry
crude to refineries that he had constructed in Bavaria and Switzerland.
In Frankel's words, this concept was "sound and progressive and in
fact the oil companies had such plans on their mental drawing boards
to be carried out a few years hence." Confronted with the reality of
invasion, "the oil companies got frightened and the Mattei Initiative
acted once again as a catalyst; plans made for later years were rapidly
brought forward and a pipeline system plus a number of large refineries
were built somewhat in advance of their really being needed. Some of
these projects, having been rushed through unduly, proved to be ill-
conceived . . ."[38] In other words, Mattei was checkmated through a
form of cross-subsidization.

Deprived of his cost advantage, and having neglected to lay the
necessary groundwork by securing a captive market in the form of his
own filling station chains, Mattei found that his instrument for progress
had turned into an albatross around his neck: "The simple truth was
that, contrary to what Mattei had thought, a pipeline . . . is an extremely inflexible means of transport and, since almost all its costs
are fixed, depends on full and regular utilization of its capacity, is not
a suitable weapon of attack for the newcomer but can be simply a
boomerang."[39] In Frankel's judgment, this most ambitious of Mattei's
undertakings "failed . . . almost completely."[40]

On October 27, 1962, Enrico Mattei died in the crash of a small
plane under circumstances that have been the subject of continuing
speculation. Within a year and a half after his death the Italian government substantially increased the gasoline tax, prices were raised, and
"the whole policy of cheap gasoline was reversed."[41]

It may have been only a coincidence, but at about the same time as
Mattei's "policy of cheap gasoline" was being reversed, the international oil companies were beginning to make large-scale contributions
to parties and politicians covering almost the entire spectrum of Italian
politics. Not only did Mattei's old firm, the state-owned ENI, cease
its aggressive competitive invasions; it became the recipient of secret
kickbacks from Exxon. According to the prepared statement of Exxon's controller, Mr. Archie Monroe, presented to the Senate Subcommittee on Multinational Corporations on July 16, 1975, the head
of Exxon's Italian subsidiary, a Dr. Cazzaniga, "had made unauthorized secret commitments and $11 million in unauthorized payments
to SNAM, which was purchasing Exxon liquefied natural gas (LNG)
from Libya. SNAM is a subsidiary of ENI, an Italian State holding
company."[42] When this came to light in mid-March 1972, Exxon's

European regional office (Esso Europe) undertook a "full-scale" investigation of its Italian subsidiary (Esso Italiano), the results of which were set forth in an "Internal Audit Report."[43] Though Dr. Cazzaniga was held to be primarily responsible, it was conceded that members of Exxon's top management had been generally aware of the nature of his activities:

SENATOR CHURCH: But through that special budget between 1963 and 1972 $29 million was disbursed for purposes of political contributions.

MR. MONROE: Yes, sir.

SENATOR CHURCH: That was fully known to the top management of Exxon . . .

MR. MONROE: It was known to the member of management that was responsible for following the Italian operation. It was not fully known by the Board of Directors or all of the management of the Exxon Corporation.

SENATOR CHURCH: Well, did the head of the company, Mr. Jamieson, know?

MR. MONROE: At the time that Mr. Jamieson was contact for Esso on Europe he was aware we were making political contributions.[44]

In 1964, a procedure to record political payments, known as the "Special Budget," was set up, against which $29 million was disbursed from 1963 to 1972, the amounts ranging from $760,000 in 1963 to over $5 million by 1968. But, according to the Internal Audit Report, "The Special Budget was an illusion." Payments were used "for purposes other than those reported to Esso Europe management"; and, "In addition to the $29 million budgeted for such purposes, a further estimated $30 million was expended for payments of the same nature and charged to expenses or against capital projects."[45] Payments were effected against the Special Budget in two ways. Under the most widely used procedure, dummy invoices were processed through the books of Esso Standard Italiano and charged to either administrative or marketing expenses, thereby generating cash that could be used when required. In the words of the Internal Audit Report, the advantages of this procedure were "to gain tax relief on these business expenses, to negate the possibility of ESI having to report the names of recipients to the tax authorities and to disguise the fact that Esso was making such payments." At the time of their investigation, the auditors found "a file of such invoices totalling some $4.6 million, many of which were dated, stamped and receipted but not yet processed. No doubt they could have been used as the need arose." The payments against dummy invoices were "almost always against invoices of newspapers and other periodicals for journalistic services that had never been rendered." Between January 1963 and March 1972, payments of this nature totaled $20,616,639, of which over four-fifths went to recipients affiliated with Italy's two largest political parties—the Christian Democratic Party (58%) and the Social Democratic Party (25%). Recipients affiliated with Italy's other political parties received amounts ranging from 6 percent for the Italian Socialist Party, to 3 percent for the Liberal Party, down to 1 percent or less for the Italian Republican Party, the Italian Social Movement, and the Italian Socialist Party of the United Proletariat.[46] Even the Communist Party was not neglected. Commenting on the disclosure that it had received $85,000 in one year (1971), Exxon's comptroller was somewhat perplexed: "It was definitely against our policy to contribute to a Communist party."[47]

The second method of effecting payments was by processing cash payment requests with no supporting documentation. Such payments were made from a bank account not recorded on the company's books, to a company employee, usually Dr. Cazzaniga's assistant, who then passed them on to the intended recipient. These payments were "principally to individual politicians and ministries"—some were clearly related to specific governmental actions of benefit to Exxon; of others the auditors reported that they were "not in a position to establish whether the . . . payments made were for the purpose stated, were received by the person indicated, or achieved the objectives purported."

In the eyes of Exxon's Board Audit Committee, to which the auditors' report was submitted, "The principal factor which permitted the irregularities to occur and remain undiscovered for such a long period of time was the fact that higher levels of management in both the [European] Region and in Jersey condoned the falsification of records to obtain funds for confidential special payments."[48]

Exxon was by no means the only oil company which saw fit to aid the democratic process as practiced in Italy. The general manager of Mobil Oil Italiano decided in 1970 that his company's "best interests" would be served by "extending financial support to the major non-Communist Italian parties." As Mobil's executive vice-president, Everett S. Checkett, put it: "Accordingly, during 1970 and in each of the next three years, up through 1973, Mobil Oil Italiano did make financial contributions to the major political parties of the center-left coalition government—namely, the Christian Democrat, the Social Democrat, and the Socialist parties. The amount of these contributions averaged $534,000 per year over the four-year period."[49] In addition, according to the *London Times* of April 11, 1976, "Both Shell and BP, in one period of less than twelve months, paid about £500,000 each in secret Italian political contributions.

In exchange for their corporate munificence, the oil companies were the direct beneficiaries of a number of helpful measures adopted by the Italian government. One was the so-called Suez subsidy adopted by the Italian Parliament in 1967, under which the oil companies received government grants to offset added transportation costs arising from the closing of the Suez Canal. A second was the reduction in 1971 of the manufacturing tax on petroleum products. And a third granted the companies greater time in which to remit excise taxes; instead of requiring refineries to remit the tax when the product left the refinery, the Italian government in March 1968 modified the requirement to allow thirty days before remittance, and up to sixty days upon payment of interest.[50] Of even greater importance, however, was the creation of a more sympathetic and understanding attitude toward the oil companies than had existed under Mattei. Political parties of whatever persuasion that became dependent on them for a substantial part of their financial sustenance were not likely to become centers of agitation against the oil companies. The possibility that under a new "Mattei" a revived ENI might again launch attacks on the companies was rendered even more unlikely by the particular method employed in determining the political assessments. After being notified by the political parties "as to the level of support they deemed appropriate from the petroleum industry,"[51] the industry's trade association, the Unione Petrolifera, imposed assessments which in turn were based on the amount of oil sold to ENEL, the state-owned electric utility company. Any gains by a revived ENI in sales to ENEL would be at the companies' expense and would therefore, under the formula, have the effect of reducing their political contributions. Such losses to the parties' treasuries would probably not be offset by compensating increases from ENI, since, even in Italy, state-owned firms would not be expected to make political contributions. The relationship of the oil companies to the Italian government thus illustrates not only Lord Acton's celebrated dictum but its converse as well: Corruption is power and absolute corruption is absolute power.

*   *   *

Until the mid-sixties, when medium-size firms were able for a time to enjoy some measure of success in Libya, outsiders had failed almost completely in their efforts to secure a significant position in international oil. If suppliers, like Iraq and Iran, they had encountered boycotts, legal actions, and the dissuasion of potentially interested independents by governments of the consuming countries. If marketers, like Mattei, they had been plagued by difficulties in securing supplies, by cross-subsidization and other discriminatory tactics. But today there is an opportunity for the entrance of a new group of outsiders. By having taken over all or part of former concessions, the OPEC countries have it in their power to dispose of vast quantities of oil to companies other than the international majors. While aware of this power, the countries also recognize its dangers. As *The Petroleum Economist* has pointed out, "Attempts at nationalization over the years were generally not successful unless and until agreement was reached with the concessionary companies *to bring the state's activities within the framework of the existing world system.*"[52] As long as the OPEC countries continue this policy, the prospects for outsiders will probably continue to be no better in the future than they have been in the past.

THE INTERNATIONAL
CONTROL MECHANISM

5

IF THE INTERNATIONAL oil industry had followed the customary sequence of industry growth and development, its earlier era of market control through explicit price-fixing meetings and cartel agreements would by now have given way to the more sophisticated stage of oligopolistic interdependence. Such episodes as the Achnacarry or "As Is" Agreement, the Memorandum for European Markets, the Heads of Agreement for Distribution, the Draft Memorandum of Principles, and the Red Line Agreement would be regarded as relics of an earlier era, replaced by parallel, noncompetitive behavior stemming from an awareness of mutual self-interest. Between outright collusion and self-imposed restraint arising from an awareness of mutual self-interest, there is a third alternative—the techniques of "systems analysis." Through the observance of complex formulae and mechanisms, production can be curtailed, variations in price eliminated, and competition substantially lessened without either the need for collusive meetings and agreements or dependence upon a state of psychological awareness of rivals' probable reactions. It was against the suppression of competition through one such system that the Federal Trade Commission proceeded in its historic basing point cases.*

THE PREDETERMINED GROWTH RATE

In hearings before the Senate Subcommittee on Multinational Corporations, officials of the international oil companies expressed as an

---

* Among the very few economists who continued their interest in this important "middle ground" between explicit collusion and pure oligopolistic interdependence are Vernon Mund, *Government and Business,* Harper & Row, New York, 1965; and Samuel M. Loescher, "Geographic Pricing Policies and the Law," *Journal of Business,* vol. 27 (July 1954), pp. 211–224; "Inert Antitrust Administration: Formula Pricing and the Cement Industry," *Yale Law Journal,* vol. 65 (November 1955), pp. 1–22; *Imperfect Collusion in the Cement Industry,* Harvard University Press, Cambridge, Mass., 1959.

article of faith their conviction that oil in excess of what the market would absorb *at the existing price* simply could not be allowed to reach the market. Senator Percy addressed the following question to Howard W. Page, senior vice-president of Exxon: "If you had been using the production capacity up to the fullest extent obviously *it would have driven prices down considerably*," to which Page replied, ". . . I mean if we had used any one to capacity, then we would have to shut the other back. There was no place to go with it. You can't dump it in the sea. There is a law against it."[1] In other words, any expansion from one source that would cause overall supply to grow at an unduly rapid rate must be compensated for by a corresponding decrease somewhere else. George T. Piercy, also a senior vice-president of Exxon, stated, "Well, I think that if some capacity was brought on anywhere else in the world, as Mr. Page has said, it is like a balloon and you brought it on one place—you punch it in one place, something has to give somewhere else because the fact that oil was brought on here or there does not in any way mean there is any more consumption."[2]

The system of control over production developed by the companies has been designed to govern the individual rates of output of the various producing countries in such a way as to attain (*and not exceed*) a predetermined growth rate of overall supply. Chart 5-1 shows the yearly increase in aggregate output for 1950–72 of eleven members of the Organization of Petroleum Exporting Countries (OPEC)— Saudi Arabia, Iran, Kuwait, Iraq, Abu Dhabi, Qatar, Venezuela, Libya, Nigeria, Algeria, and Indonesia.* The compound growth rate and a measure of the "closeness of fit" have been computed by plotting the actual increase in aggregate output, fitting a regression line by least squares to logarithms of the data, determining the compound rate of increase in output (the "average growth rate"), and measuring the deviations between the regression line and the actual observations, thereby indicating by a coefficient of determination (r^2) the extent to which the actual increases are "explained" by the derived growth rate.

For the eleven countries as a group, the average annual percentage increase in output during 1950–72 (the "growth rate") works out at

---

* Of these eleven countries, six are in the Middle East (Saudi Arabia, Iran, Kuwait, Iraq, Abu Dhabi, and Qatar); three in Africa (Libya, Nigeria, and Algeria); one in South America (Venezuela); and one in the Far East (Indonesia). In 1972 production in these countries totaled 26,218,000 barrels a day, which represented 84.8% of the world production of 30,905,000 barrels a day, outside the U.S., Canada, the Soviet Union, China, and the East European Communist countries. The remaining 4,128,000 barrels a day were widely dispersed among some two dozen other countries in relatively small quantities, a substantial proportion of which was produced by subsidiaries or affiliates of the seven international majors.

CHART 5-1
OPEC Crude Production: Actual Versus Estimated Growth Rate, 1950–72

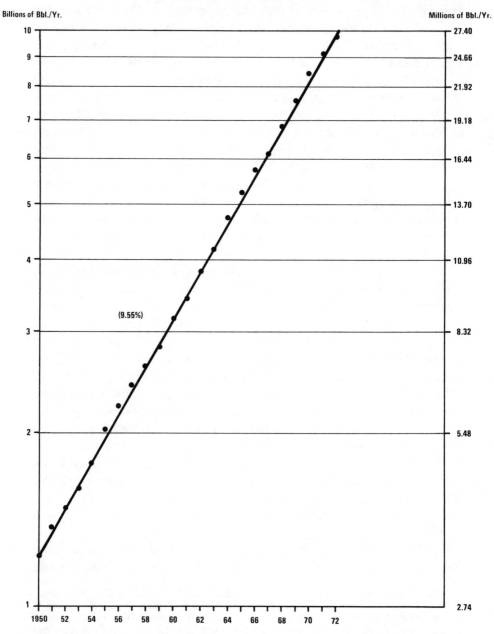

Billions of Bbl./Yr.   Millions of Bbl./Yr.

(9.55%)

Source: Derived from Organization of Petroleum Exporting Countries, Statistical Bulletins.

9.55 percent. The measure of the "closeness of fit" of the regression line to the actual observations (the "coefficient of determination") is an astonishing 99.9 percent. In other words, an assumption that oil production would increase at an average annual rate of 9.55 percent explains all but one-tenth of 1 percent of the actual change.

What makes the stable growth of supply so extraordinary is the widely diverse movements of its separate components. If each of the producing countries had been increasing its output at about the same rate, the steady rise in supply could be explained as merely the sum total of the behavior of the individual countries. But this explanation obviously falls if the different sources of supply have been expanding at widely varying rates, and even more strikingly, if some have been characterized by actual declines. That such has been the pattern of the international oil industry is apparent from Chart 5-2, which shows for 1950–73 the yearly change in total production for each of the nine leading producing countries. The international supply picture is revealed as a composite of long-sustained steady increases (Saudi Arabia and Iran); of much slower rates of increase (Venezuela, Kuwait, and Iraq); of precipitous rises (Libya until 1970, Nigeria, Abu Dhabi, Indonesia); and of occasional pronounced declines (Iran in 1951–54; Iraq in 1957, 1967, and 1972; Nigeria in 1968; and Venezuela and Libya since 1970). Somehow the major oil companies have been able to "orchestrate" these and other aberrations into a smooth and uninterrupted upward trend in overall supply. Indeed, a steady increase in supply was achieved despite such extreme changes as, on the one hand, the virtually complete loss of Iran's output, resulting from its nationalization of Anglo-Iranian's properties, and, on the other hand, the rapid rise of output in Libya, about half of which was in the hands of independents. Chart 5-1 shows that neither the former, which affected supply during 1951–54, nor the latter, which became important during 1965–70, had any discernible effect on the growth rate of overall supply.

THE PRODUCTION CONTROL MECHANISM

Both abroad and at home, the control of production has been initiated by forecasts of the supply needed to meet the expected level of demand. In international oil they have taken the form of predictions of annual growth rates, prepared by most, if not all, of the seven international majors. Forecasts have regularly been made for the Free World, for the Eastern Hemisphere, and, of greatest importance, for the Middle East. These "annual internal industry-wide supply-demand forecasts"[3] are set forth in what are referred to as Exxon's

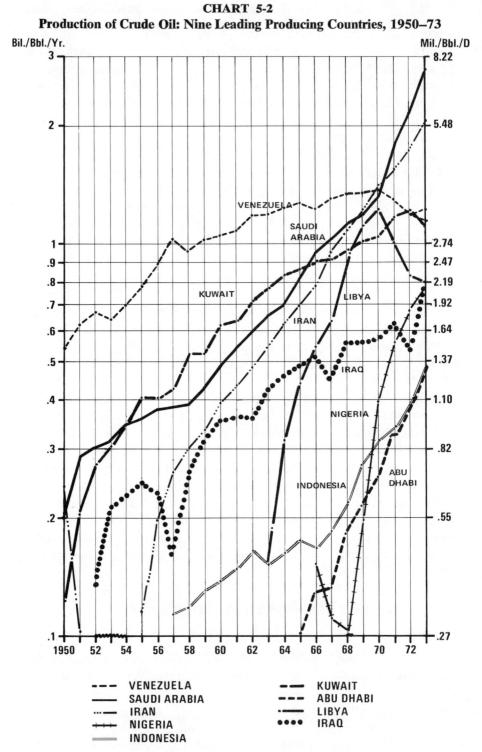

CHART 5-2
Production of Crude Oil: Nine Leading Producing Countries, 1950–73

Bil./Bbl./Yr.

Mil./Bbl./D

VENEZUELA

SAUDI ARABIA

KUWAIT

LIBYA

IRAN

IRAQ

NIGERIA

INDONESIA

ABU DHABI

- - - VENEZUELA
——— SAUDI ARABIA
···— IRAN
+++ NIGERIA
═══ INDONESIA

–— KUWAIT
- – ABU DHABI
·— LIBYA
●●●● IRAQ

Source: Derived from Organization of Petroleum Exporting Countries, Statistical Bulletins.

"Green Books," SoCal's "Blue Books," Gulf's "Orange Books," etc.[4] Describing what "has come to be known within Exxon as the Green Book," the company stated:

> There is obviously considerable effort involved in preparing the projections and analyses that are documented in the Green Book. The primary purpose of this activity is to anticipate changes in the industry supply/demand environment that should be considered in developing Exxon's forward plans. Emphasis is placed on identifying and studying problems that might be expected to arise if current demand and supply trends continue, without necessarily attempting to forecast how these problems will be resolved.
>
> . . . it is felt to be a benefit to use one consistent set of assumptions regarding long-term industry developments in planning future investments in the many parts of the world in which we operate. In addition, the Green Books serve as a data source for the analysis and development of policy positions on issues relating to the petroleum and energy industries.[5]

Exxon went on to say that it "has generally not made its Green Books publicly available."[6] Although its complete books, as well as the similar documents of the other majors, continue to be unavailable, the Senate Subcommittee on Multinational Corporations did get into the public record summaries of Exxon's forecasts from 1960 to 1972. On the basis of these forecasts it is readily possible to determine the total size of the pie, which can then be divided up among the various producing countries. In world oil this process has begun with establishing the production rate for Iran, which, it turns out, has also come to govern the production rate in Saudi Arabia.[7]

IRAN. Since the late 1950's, the pivotal role has been the production rate established for Iran. To bring Iranian production back into the flow of supply after the nationalization of 1951, an agreement in 1954 was negotiated under which Iranian output after three years was to keep pace with the "average growth rate" of the Middle East. Although no exact rate was specified, the desire of the U.S. government to build up Iran as a bastion against Communist influence was recognized by all.* It is therefore not surprising that of all the major producing countries, Iran during 1958–72 enjoyed the highest growth rate—12.46 percent a year. Interestingly enough, the growth rate calculated here turns out to be exactly the rate cited by Exxon in its internal forecasts: "Iranian production . . . would expand 12.5%

---

* Mr. G. L. Parkhurst, former vice-president, Standard Oil of Calif., testified: ". . . in Iran the agreement sponsored by the U.S. Government in 1954 obligated the participants in general terms to keep Iran's production rate up to the growth rate of the area." (*Hearings on Multinational Corporations,* Pt. 7, p. 354.)

per year during 1967 and 1968, *in accordance with agreements already made with the government.*"[8]

The precise means by which Iran's annual output has been determined was described by E. L. Shafer, vice-president of Continental Oil. The method employed by the Consortium is a complex system referred to as the "Average Program Quantity," or "APQ":[9]

> The first step in determining the APQ would occur in October when the operating companies would advise the holding company of crude availability and the holding company [the Consortium] would report to the participants the expected capacity of crude available for export in the coming year. Each of the participants would then nominate to the holding company the amount of oil that it expected to lift in the coming year.
>
> The holding company would divide each individual nomination by the equity percentage of the nominator to determine the total program which would be required in order to allow the nominator to lift his equity percentage and receive his nomination. The total program figures derived from each nomination were then listed in descending order of magnitude. The total program figure of the participants whose liftings fell at or above a cumulative total of 70 percent of equity percentages became the APQ.[10]

The operation of the system was illustrated by the experience of 1966, as shown in the following table:[11]

Example of APQ Procedure—1966 APQ

Participation	Share	Cumul.	Nomination	Total Program
Iricon	5%	5%	101 m b/d	2,030 m b/d
BP	40	45	811	2,027
Shell	14	59	284	2,027
Mobil	7	66	137	1,964
CFP	6	72	117	1,945
. . . . APQ				
Exxon	7	79	132	1,890
Texaco	7	86	120	1,712
Gulf	7	93	119	1,700
SoCal	7	100	117	1,644

Thus, for 1966 BP called for a total output for the Consortium of 2,027 m b/d, which, with a 40 percent equity share, meant that it wished to lift 811 m b/d. At the opposite extreme, SoCal called for a total program of only 1,644 m b/d, which with a 7 percent share meant that it wished to lift only 117 m b/d. The total program called for by these two companies ranged from 95 down to 77 percent of the Consortium's expected capacity. In 1966, the point of 70 percent was reached with the addition of the equity shares for Iricon, BP, Shell, Mobil, and CFP. The most peculiar feature of the system is that the marginal firm—the company whose submission brought the cumulative voting total up to (or over) 70 percent—*was given a weight of 100 percent*. In 1966, the marginal firm was CFP, whose submission of 1,945 m b/d thus became the Average Program Quantity.

Up to the amount represented by their equity shares of the APQ, the participating companies receive oil at "tax-paid-cost" or about two-thirds of the posted price. But for any excess they had to pay the full posted price, later modified to a "halfway" price (the tax-paid cost plus one-half the difference between tax-paid cost and the posted price), and still later to a "quarter-way" price. Neither, in Shafer's view, would have been considered economically attractive since, compared to a market price of about $1.30, a "halfway" price for Iranian light worked out to around $1.49, and a "quarter-way" price to $1.40.[12]

Reflecting its unique construction, the formula used in determining Iranian output has had a number of consequences that were undoubtedly anticipated when it was adopted. By keeping their nominations relatively low, the Aramco partners have been in a position to exert a downward influence on Iranian output, since with larger nominations the APQ, *ceteris paribus*, would have been higher. And, as can be seen from Table 5-1, in which the companies whose nominations were less than the APQ are shown within horizontal lines, this was indeed the course of action followed by the three "30 percent" owners of Aramco. Between 1957 and 1973, Exxon's nominations put it below the APQ in fourteen of the seventeen years; SoCal's put it below the APQ in fifteen; and Texaco was below in all seventeen. Commenting on the dual position of these companies, Senator Muskie remarked: "So the effect of the decision, for whatever reason the decision was given, would give to the same American companies that were dominant in Aramco the control of the American interest, at least, of the consortium in Iran."[13] On the other hand, companies whose nominations were greater than the APQ (shown within vertical lines) included chronically crude-short Shell (sixteen years) and Iricon (sixteen years).

The formula also gave both the American and the British-European groups the power to checkmate each other. Regardless of how high the submissions of BP, Shell, and CFP might be, their combined vote

TABLE 5-1
Historical APQ Tablings in Iranian Consortium
(in thousands of barrels per day)

1957 CO.	MBD	1958 CO.	MBD	1959 CO.	MBD	1960 CO.	MBD	1961 CO.	MBD	1962 CO.	MBD	1963 CO.	MBD	1964 CO.	MBD	1965 CO.	MBD
BP	750	CFP	827	Iricon	912	Mobil	1111	Mobil	1213	Iricon	1370	BP	1575	Iricon	1740	CFP	1863
CFP	750	Iricon	826	Mobil	890	Iricon	1023	Iricon	1201	BP	1370	CFP	1575	Mobil	1721	Iricon	1860
Shell	714	Shell	822	BP	850	BP	984	BP	1192	Shell	1370	Iricon	1535	Shell	1708	BP	1836
Iricon	700	Mobil	814	Shell	850	Shell	960	Shell	1192	CFP	1370	Shell	1534	BP	1680	Shell	1836
Exxon	690	BP	787	SoCal	850	CFP	911	CFP	1192	Mobil	1342	Mobil	1521	CFP	1680	Mobil	1836
SoCal	603	Exxon	759	Exxon	841	Exxon	900	Exxon	980	Texaco	1195	SoCal	1360	Texaco	1470	Gulf	1685
Gulf	574	SoCal	724	CFP	822	Gulf	880	Texaco	980	SoCal	1170	Texaco	1299	Exxon	1400	Texaco	1589
Texaco	528	Texaco	700	Texaco	805	Texaco	875	SoCal	973	Exxon	1115	Exxon	1200	Gulf	1314	Exxon	1575
Mobil	528	Gulf	655	Gulf	680	SoCal	874	Gulf	940	Gulf	1000	Gulf	1068	SoCal	1214	SoCal	1370

1966 CO.	MBD	1967 CO.	MBD	1968 CO.	MBD	1969 CO.	MBD	1970 CO.	MBD	1971 CO.	MBD	1972 CO.	MBD	1973 CO.	MBD
Iricon	2030	CFP	2274	Iricon	2698	Iricon	3062	Iricon	3547	Iricon	4054	Iricon	4678	Gulf	5428
BP	2027	Shell	2233	Shell	2678	BP	3014	Shell	3346	Mobil	3986	CFP	4645	Iricon	5342
Shell	2027	BP	2219	Gulf	2571	Shell	3014	Mobil	3342	BP	3973	Exxon	4638	CFP	5297
Mobil	1964	Mobil	2178	BP	2568	Mobil	3014	BP	3329	Shell	3973	Shell	4590	Exxon	5250
CFP	1945	Iricon	2178	CFP	2568	CFP	3014	CFP	3329	CFP	3973	Mobil	4516	BP	5137
Exxon	1890	Exxon	2100	Mobil	2568	Gulf	2900	Exxon	3205	Exxon	3973	SoCal	4500	Mobil	5068
Texaco	1712	Texaco	2005	SoCal	2391	Exxon	2849	Gulf	3200	SoCal	3767	BP	4372	Shell	5055
Gulf	1700	SoCal	1973	Exxon	2363	SoCal	2795	SoCal	3164	Texaco	3562	Gulf	4257	Texaco	5043
SoCal	1644	Gulf	1871	Texaco	2363	Texaco	2679	Texaco	3134	Gulf	3286	Texaco	4200	SoCal	4857

Companies tabling above APQ.
Company whose tabling sets APQ.
Companies tabling below APQ.

would still fall 10 percent short of the required 70 percent (and even with the addition of Iricon, 5% short). It would take the vote of one or the other of the five U.S. majors to reach the 70 percent figure, and its submission would then be *the APQ*. Conversely, any expansion sought by the U.S. firms but considered unwise by the British could simply be vetoed by BP, since only with the addition of BP's vote (40%) could the combined voting power of the American majors reach the required level.

In actual operation the system displayed several additional restrictive features. None of the participants would of course submit a total program exceeding the Consortium's capacity. Capacity, however, was not an independent variable, but was established at a level considered sufficient to meet forecast demands. Thus, the smaller the proposed liftings (which for capital budgeting were submitted two years in advance), the lower the capacity. As Senator Case put it, "So what you are doing is you are really controlling prospective production by controlling capacity."[14] Moreover, the amount actually lifted consistently fell below the Average Program Quantity. For the period 1962–66, actual liftings by Exxon and SoCal were 20 percent less than what they were entitled to; liftings by all participants averaged 8 percent below the APQ.[15] Noting that 1962–66 coincided "with the coming onstream of Libya as a major productive source," Subcommittee counsel raised the question whether the failure to lift their entitlements reflected the fact that "the companies which had interests elsewhere had to make room for Libyan production." Mr. Shafer indicated his agreement: "I think that is one of the factors that affected this situation."[16]

SAUDI ARABIA. The production increase for Iran, as determined by the APQ formula, also governed the rate of increase in the Middle East's largest producing country.* For the owners of Aramco, maintaining a roughly comparable rate in Saudi Arabia was a political necessity since to Exxon, SoCal, Texaco, and Mobil, the Aramco concession was far more important than their participation in the Iranian Consortium. Emphasizing the need to maintain good relationships with the ruler of Saudi Arabia, Howard Page of Exxon testified: ". . . if we hadn't played ball with him, we could have lost the

---

* As with the Iranian Consortium, Aramco employed a built-in restrictive device to dissuade owners from overlifting. As actual liftings rise above those warranted by equity ownership, dividends per barrel received from Aramco decline. During 1967–69 the decrease in dividends was from around $.80 with no overliftings to about $.60 a barrel with overliftings at least double the equity ownership. In each year the companies at the extremes were the same: SoCal, whose rights to crude exceeded its ability to market, and Mobil, whose need for crude was chronic.

Aramco concession, which is not something for us to lose. It is the biggest concession in the world, and we had 30 percent of it as against a concession one-quarter as big in which we had 7 percent. So you know what you had better do in these cases."[17]

Documents obtained by the Senate Subcommittee from the files of one of Aramco's owning firms[18] clearly reveal a linkage to the APQ of the Iranian Consortium. On February 14, 1973, J. J. Johnston, senior vice-president of Aramco, notified its four owners that for 1972: "The provisional Middle East industry growth ratio determined in accordance with the growth ratio guidelines letter dated May 18, 1971 is 136.4 percent. The data on which the provisional industry growth ratio was computed is the net exports of crude and crude equivalent of those countries/companies which *were participants in the 1964 Consortium.*"[19] The next day Johnston sent the owning companies a "schedule," headed "Growth Ratio Guidelines: Estimate of Minimum Lifting Obligation or Provision." This schedule sets forth for each company its "1970 Base Volume," the "Company or Industry Growth Ratio," and the "Minimum Lifting Obligations or Provision" derived by multiplying the "Base Volume" by the "Growth Ratio."[20] Here, the important point is that the "growth ratio" is *the figure of 136.4 percent* set forth in the letter of the previous day as "the provisional Middle East growth ratio, computed on the basis of the net exports of participants in the 1964 Consortium."[21]

IRAQ. With output growing at an extraordinary pace in both Iran and Saudi Arabia, the area's existing "glut of productive capacity" (to use Page's term) would soon have reached formidable proportions had production in the other Mideast countries been allowed to rise at anything like the same rates. But during 1958–72, the growth rates in output for Iraq and Kuwait averaged only 5.12 and 5.93 percent respectively, less than half the rates of Saudi Arabia and Iran and well below their own previous rates.

According to Page, the relatively slow growth rate in Iraq stemmed from a dispute between the oil companies and the Iraqi government. Feeling that efforts to develop the country's oil resources had left much to be desired, Iraq, as has been noted, enacted in 1961 the so-called Public Law 80 of the Kassim régime, restricting the concession held by the Iraq Petroleum Company to fields in which it was then producing and foreclosing it from a number of extremely promising areas. But this controversy was certainly not the only reason for the low rate of production. In response to the question, "what would have happened if Iraq production had also surged during the 1960's," Page responded:

I admit we would have been in one tough problem, and we would have had to lower our liftings from the [Iranian] Consortium down to the minimum we could possibly take there and meet the agreement. Remember we were taking more than the agreement called for out of Iran, you see, and we were taking an equal amount, though, from Saudi Arabia, we would have had to cut back on both of those and we would have had to slow down on our development of Libya, which nobody wanted to do, but this was discussed at a time when people came to me and said, "Can you swallow this amount of oil?" and "of course with Iraq down," the answer was, "Yes, I am going to have a lot of problems and some tough problems, but I will undertake to do it."

And I was successful, that is all I can say. But if Iraq had come on, it would have been that much harder.[22]

KUWAIT. According to Exxon's internal yearly forecasts, Kuwait has been used as what might be regarded as an "evener," by means of which actual Mideast output is brought into balance with the supply called for by the overall growth rate. Thus, "Kuwait production is estimated by difference after reviewing possible company supply positions" (1963); "Kuwait output is determined to be the difference between Eastern Hemisphere demand and supplies from all other sources" (1964); and "Kuwait outlet is assumed to be the marginal supply source for Eastern Hemisphere demand. . . ."[23] Quite apart from such major disturbances as the Libyan expansion, the international oil companies have constantly been confronted with unexpected occurrences, such as unusually mild (or severe) winters, interruptions in pipeline and tanker transportation, delays and breakdowns in refinery operations, and a multitude of problems involved in trying to achieve a nice articulation of supply with markets thousands of miles away. To prevent such interruptions from upsetting the smooth increase in overall supply, production in Kuwait has not infrequently been reduced when supplies from other sources appeared excessive and expanded when they seemed insufficient.[24] The performance of this function can be seen most clearly in Chart 5-2; unlike the steady, undeviating upward trends of Iran and Saudi Arabia, the increases in Kuwait's output have been recurrently interrupted by years of slow growth, e.g., 1958–59, 1960–61, and 1966–67.

For these four principal Mideastern producing countries (plus Abu Dhabi) the growth rate during 1958–72 averaged 9.9 percent a year, which incidentally turns out to be the identical rate cited by Exxon in its own internal 1970 forecast: "The region's oil production is forecast to average 9.9%/year growth through 1980, about the same as the 9.9%/year since 1960."[25]

OTHER OPEC COUNTRIES. What of the remaining countries which in 1972 accounted for 43 percent of OPEC's output? Countries with slow growth rates are unlikely to be the source of disturbances to the market. During 1958–72, Venezuelan production grew at an average rate of only 2.02 percent, and indeed since 1970 has moved noticeably downward; the addition of Venezuela to the four principal Mideast producers brings to 68 percent the share of OPEC production which can be said to have been readily controllable and predictable.

Two of the remaining OPEC countries—Nigeria and Abu Dhabi— have registered spectacular growth rates (33.36% and 35.39%, respectively), while production in a third, Indonesia, has also been moving up sharply since the mid-sixties. But two factors militate against the emergence of these countries as sources of uncontrollable excess supply. Independent producers are virtually nonexistent, accounting in 1972 for only 6 percent of the production of Nigeria, 3 percent of Abu Dhabi, and none in Indonesia. And it would appear that companies bringing on new sources of supply are expected to make more or less compensating reductions in their liftings from other sources. Thus, Exxon's 1964 *Forecast* observes, "Major participants in the IPC group, the Iranian Consortium, and Nigerian production, are also the major offtakers of Kuwait crude. Therefore, to the extent the former fails to achieve offtake estimates, Kuwait would acquire most of the alternative outlet." And the *Forecast* for 1967 states, "Kuwait's growth would be retarded because major offtakers of that crude are developing new production in Africa and elsewhere."

Chart 5-3 confirms the expectation that the growth rates for Iran and Saudi Arabia have in fact been virtually identical, as well as the fact that the growth rate of Iraq was indeed kept "down" to less than half that of the two larger countries. In addition, the chart reflects the efforts of the majors to "make room" during the late 1960's for the rapid increase taking place in Libyan production. Between 1965 and 1970, actual production fell below the historical growth rate for five years in the case of Iran and Saudi Arabia and for four years in the case of Kuwait. But after 1970, Libyan production turned sharply downward, and thereafter output in both Iran and Saudi Arabia rose to levels at or above their growth rates.

This control system has been applied of course only to countries actually engaged in production. It has been supplemented to an unknown extent and for unknown durations by the withholding of newly discovered sources of supply. Page of Exxon recounted the dismay occasioned by the discovery of a potential new source in Oman:

> Just at this time, the producing department brought in their geologist who had just come back from Oman, and he stated, "I am

CHART 5-3
Crude Oil Production: Actual Versus Estimated Growth Rate, 1958–72

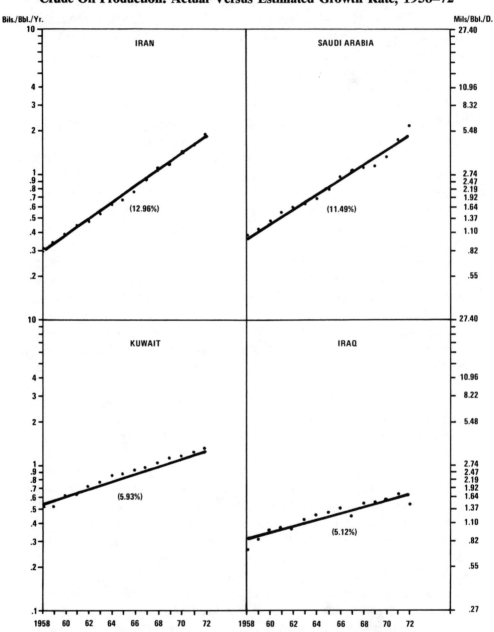

Source: Derived from Organization of Petroleum Exporting Countries, Statistical Bulletins.

sure there is a 10 billion oil field there"; and I said, "Well, then, I am absolutely sure we don't want to go into it, and that settles it." I might put some money in it if I was sure we weren't going to get some oil, but not if we are going to get oil because we are liable to lose the Aramco concession, our share of the Aramco concession, anyway if we were going to back up any further on it by going into new areas.[26]

THE PRICE-MATCHING SYSTEM

The mechanism used to control output in international oil is not the only system employed by the international oil companies. Just as it has been customary for producers generally to abandon meetings, agreements, and other explicit forms of collusion to control and divide output, so also has it been the practice to evolve complicated pricing systems designed to eliminate differences in delivered prices, regardless of the location of the sellers. While the delivered prices will differ from one location to another, reflecting differences in freight costs, the choice of the seller, insofar as a *given* buyer is concerned, becomes a matter of indifference. Even if overall supply were limited to total demand (at the existing price), the absence of such a price-matching system would lead to uncertainty among the sellers, as no seller could be sure that his failure to secure a buyer's order was not the result of price cutting by a competitor. Only if each seller abstained from cutting the f.o.b. price and absorbed whatever freight was necessary from a governing basing point to the point of delivery could this concern (and potential source of price competition) be eliminated. It is for this reason that industries such as steel, which had long since replaced the "Judge Gary" dinners with the more sophisticated device of price leadership, nonetheless fought tenaciously for years for the right to maintain a basing point system.

From the earliest days of the industry, oil sold in world markets was priced as if it had originated in Texas. As long as Texas was by far the largest producing and exporting area in the world, the use of the "Texas Gulf" system did no great violence to the realities of trade. Problems developed only after the Middle East began to emerge as an important producing area, since the use of the Texas quotation as the "base price" meant that sales of Mideast oil, even to buyers in the Middle East, included "phantom freight" from Texas. It was therefore not surprising that in 1944 His Majesty's Government objected to paying phantom freight from Texas (obliquely referred to as an "origin differential") on fuel oil purchased by the British Navy from a Mideast refinery. In the words of the British Auditor-General:

Before the war the price of oil f.o.b. in the Gulf of Mexico was the generally accepted basis regulating the prices of commercial supplies of oil in the Atlantic area. It also influenced, under competitive conditions, prices in other areas.

In the course of their inquiries the Committee found that in many cases the price of bunker oils charged or proposed to be charged to the Ministry at ports in the Indian Ocean and Middle East included an element described as an origin differential. This differential (which did not represent actual costs incurred by suppliers, and which applied to all oil products, and not solely to bunker fuels) was a means of equating c.i.f. [delivered] prices, whatever the point of production. The general result was that when the source of supply was more distant than the Gulf, the application of the differential would operate to the disadvantage of the supplier and, when it was nearer, to his advantage.

. . . We could no longer accept this origin differential automatically as a proper element in bunker prices in overseas ports, mainly because owing to the vital necessity for getting the utmost possible service out of tanker tonnage it was a matter of policy and principle to draw supplies from the nearest available source. It was no longer a matter of commercial competition. It was a matter of imposed policy that every ton of oil that could be drawn from a near source had to be taken from that source and from none other. . . .[27]

As a result of this British protest, a second basing point was established at the Persian Gulf but at the level of the Texas Gulf price. Although phantom freight to buyers nearer the Middle East was thus eliminated, the system continued to yield identical delivered prices for each destination regardless of source of supply. Because of the lower costs in the Middle East, the British had also sought a lower price but were confronted by a refusal on the part of the U.S. companies to divulge their actual costs of production. A protest also came from the U.S. Navy, which was purchasing oil from Aramco for delivery to the French government under the Lend-Lease Act. As was brought out in a Senate investigation headed by Senator Owen Brewster[28] the Navy negotiators felt the price should reflect the lower costs of Mideast production. Aramco was adamant, however, that the base price for the Middle East should be the same as the Texas Gulf price; ". . . confronted by Aramco's uncompromising 'take it or leave it' attitude, and informed by his superiors the oil was unobtainable elsewhere, the Navy negotiators felt compelled, because of the urgent need, to agree to the company's original quotation."[29]

But the fundamental criticism remained: the price in an area of lower, falling costs was being determined by the price in an area of higher, rising costs. To compound the inequity, prices in the United States were higher not merely because of inherent geological differences, but also because of restrictions[30] deliberately designed to artificially raise the level of U.S. prices. Objecting to the transmission to world markets of the results of such policies, Paul H. Frankel pointed out that not only must "Americans pay more for their gasoline," but that "their fate is shared by people who can afford it still less, say, by the owners of Italian tractors or Chinese trucks. Is there no way of stopping any slight rumbling in Texas or Oklahoma from being amplified until it becomes a thunder resounding all over the world?"[31] If the Americans wished to protect their own high-cost producers, that was their own affair; but, he argued, it was something else again if they burdened the rest of the world with the consequences of such policies: ". . . it is doubtful whether the protection of the high-cost level of American prices can in the long run be achieved just by scaling up the prices from all sources in sympathy with price movements within the United States. No one in another country has the right to interfere with the domestic economic policy of the United States, but if the Americans wish to protect their industry they should do so at their own border and not at sources, as it were, in other people's countries."[32]

A further objection to the pricing system was that it had the perverse effect of causing realized Mideast prices to move in a direction opposite to the change in demand, as reflected by the movement of tanker rates. Professor Helmut J. Frank pointed out that

> the "formula" price . . . contained a perverse mechanism which would have required Persian Gulf prices to go up when markets were depressed (because freight rates then are low) and to go down when markets were strong (because freight rates then are high). . . . The effect of a change in freight rates from the Middle East, if the freight rates were down to, say, 50 percent below the U.S.M.C. rate instead of 35½ percent, would have resulted in an increase in the Middle East price to over $2, about $2.08 my calculations show. Of course, this is a little irrational because normally freight rates are down when the markets are depressed and there is a surplus of tankers and of oil.
>
> On the other hand, if there was a strong demand for tankers and for oil and the freight rates, say, rose to the U.S.M.C. flat, this would have required under the formula the price in the Middle East to fall from $1.75 down to $1.30 and, again, that does not make very much economic sense.[33]

Partly because of these protests and partly because the companies began to realize that their own best interests would be better served by something other than a duplicate base price in the Middle East, a number of modifications were made to move westward the point at which delivered prices from Texas and the Persian Gulf were equalized. Before these modifications, on shipments westward from the Middle East, beyond the mid-Mediterranean the United States had been nearer (freight-wise) to the important and rapidly expanding markets of Western Europe. Thus in selling to Europe, the companies operating in the Middle East were forced to absorb freight and take a lower net price than if shipments had been made from the United States. To open up the markets of Western Europe and later the United States to Mideast oil, the point of equalization between Texas and Mideast delivered prices was changed, first from the mid-Mediterranean to England, and then to the Eastern seaboard of the United States.[34] After the last of these modifications, the price of the Mideast "marker crude" (Arabian light, f.o.b. Ras Tanura) was equalized with Texas crude oil at U.S. Eastern seaboard ports north of Cape Hatteras. This was accomplished by an involved series of additions and subtractions, the starting point of which was the posted price for western Texas crude. To this were added gathering and related costs to a Gulf of Mexico port, plus freight to New York City. Deductions were then made for the U.S. tariff, and for a small quality differential. Freight was then deducted from New York back to the Persian Gulf, giving rise to the appellation "netback" price.

Chart 5-4 shows that the actual behavior of the Persian Gulf posted price accorded closely with the movements to be expected of a price determined under a basing point system. Linked to the sharp advances in the U.S. price upon the termination of OPA price controls, the 1946–47 increases established Mideast prices at a plateau in the vicinity of which they remained for over a decade. Because of their importance in establishing the postwar level of prices, these increases are worth describing in some detail. According to the *International Petroleum Cartel* report:

> The upward spiral in Middle East prices, reflecting these increases in United States Gulf prices, began with an action by Aramco raising its Persian Gulf price for the contract period December 1946–March 1947, from $1.05 to $1.17–$1.23 (depending on gravity) for crude oil sold to the Navy for UNRRA. For a time nonuniform Persian Gulf crude quotations prevailed, as Caltex, Socony-Vacuum and Esso Export raised their Middle East crude oil prices at different times, in a lagging pursuit of the rapidly rising American crude oil price level.
>
> On December 6, 1947, just 5 days after the last 50 cent increase in United States crude prices, Esso Export, a newcomer in the Persian Gulf, raised its Persian Gulf crude prices to a record $2.22

CHART 5-4
United States and Middle East Crude Oil Prices, 1945–60

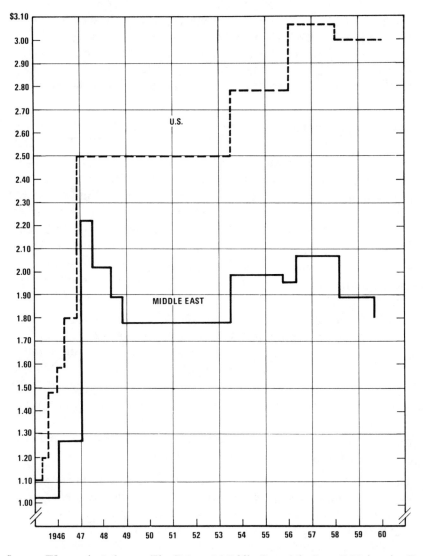

Source: Wayne A. Lehman, *The Price of Middle East Oil,* Cornell University Press, 1962, p. 946.

per barrel on shipments to Italy—93 cents above the previous high of $1.29. Socony followed Esso's lead in February 1948 while Caltex, also initially raising its price to $1.59, did not reach the $2.22 level until March 1948. Before the ECA program was initiated, all major Middle East producers had established a uniform price of $2.22 f.o.b. Ras Tanura, representing an aggregate increase of $1.17 per barrel over the July 1945 Aramco-Navy contract price. This increase was somewhat less than the rise of $1.40 in United States Gulf crude quotations over the same period.[35]

Downward adjustments were then made during the late 1940's with the Persian Gulf posted price stabilized in 1949 at $1.70. Thereafter, its movements paralleled the changes of the U.S. Gulf price in timing and direction, with minor differences in extent. After several years of stability both prices were increased in 1953, the Persian Gulf quotation rising to $1.93. The next increase, associated with the first Suez crisis, took place in 1957, with the Mideast price advancing to $2.08. But, as will be brought out later, price weakness began to develop in the latter 1950's. In February 1959, both prices were reduced, and a further minor reduction in August 1960 brought the Persian Gulf price down to $1.80. Thereafter, a widening divergence developed in world markets between the posted and the actual or "armslength" prices; the international basing point system had broken down.

In 1970, the fact that the price received by one producing country was below the price that should have prevailed under the system became the basis of an important claim against the companies. In 1970, the new revolutionary government of Libya under the leadership of Colonel Qadaffi demanded a price increase of 40 cents a barrel. In the view of James E. Akins, head of the Office of Fuels and Energy of the Department of State, the claim was justified:

> The prices in the world were . . . and still are, and very likely will be for some time to come, set by prices in the Persian Gulf, exactly as they used to be set by Texas for the entire world . . . you take the Persian Gulf price, take the transportation costs to Europe, and then subtract transportation costs to country X, Libya in this case, and you get a value of oil in that particular spot, Libya. . . . Libyan oil by most calculations seemed to be underpriced, at least the Libyans concluded that it was very substantially underpriced. Tanker figures were published, these were available, the Libyans had them. . . .
> I have the same slide rules that the Libyans have . . . we knew how much it cost to ship oil from the Persian Gulf to Rotterdam . . . and then how much from Tripoli or one of the Libyan ports to . . . Northern Europe and you could see exactly how much this oil is worth. . . .[36]

Shortly before or during the momentous events of 1973–74 the sytem was again made operative, with, however, the initiating basing point shifted from Texas to the Persian Gulf. That it is indeed in operation is indicated by the fact that in early 1974 the short-haul Mediterranean countries were forced to reduce their f.o.b. prices in order to equalize their delivered quotations at north European ports with the Persian Gulf countries, whose delivered prices had been lowered by falling tanker rates for the long haul around the Cape of Good Hope. According to *The New York Times,* "The price reductions by Algeria, Libya, Iraq, and Saudi Arabia for oil sold at Mediterranean export terminals are designed to maintain sales in Western Europe and the United States against lower-cost deliveries by big bulk tankers from the Persian Gulf." What precipitated these reductions was the competition that had developed among the independently owned supertankers. Faced with a falling demand resulting not only from the worldwide recession but also from an unusually mild European winter, the owners competed for the declining volume of business by progressively reducing their rates: "Because of declines in freight rates for large tankers, the Persian Gulf oil has been cheaper at delivery terminals than the Mediterranean crude."[37] With the reductions by the Mediterranean countries, the central objective of any basing point system was again realized—the elimination of differences in delivered prices at any given point of destination, regardless of the location (and costs) of the sellers.

*   *   *

Conceivably output could have been controlled and price competition eliminated as a result of explicit collusion, oligopolistic interdependence, or the common use of complex systems. To be the sole or even principal explanation the first would have required a vast number of interminable ad hoc meetings, directed toward securing agreement on innumerable day-to-day issues and problems. The basic condition for the second—an oligopolistic structure—has certainly been present in international oil. In 1972 the four largest firms accounted for 54.9 percent of total production in the Middle East (plus Libya) and 52.9 percent of total output in all OPEC countries; the corresponding figures for the seven largest were 77.6 percent and 77.1 percent.[38] But self-restraint based on an awareness of mutual self-interest could have been the explanation only if there existed, among the majors, a remarkable degree of trust that none would engage in expansionary activities which would increase its share of the market. Obviously, aggressive expansion by any one major would force the others to do likewise simply to maintain their market shares, even though all were fully cognizant of the consequences of their actions on overall supply. Only if each major was confident that the expansion plans of its rivals would do no more than roughly maintain the established market shares could it reasonably be expected to limit its own expansion. The unique value of the production-control and price-matching systems is that they rendered unnecessary most of the cumbersome (and potentially dangerous) meetings involved in day-to-day market control, as well as an excessive reliance on an awareness of mutual self-interest.

Part
TWO

THE CONTROL OF
DOMESTIC OIL

While world attention since 1973 has focused on the Middle East and Africa as sources of oil supply, some three-fifths of U.S. consumption still comes from domestic production. And although domestic output will probably continue a downward trend that began in 1970, the United States is likely to remain its own largest supplier for some time to come. In addition to its sheer volume, the question of control over this vast resource is important for other reasons. The greater the concentration of reserves in the hands of a few companies, the fewer are the options available for public policy. Confronted with a government action which they opposed, a few large owners would be in a position to keep the oil in the ground, secure in the knowledge that over a long-term inflationary period time would be on their side. Moreover, to the extent that control over domestic refining and marketing is in the hand of the same companies that lift the foreign crude, the lower prices that might be secured for the latter would not necessarily mean lower prices for consumers. Even though foreign sources will no doubt supply a steadily increasing proportion of U.S. needs, the question of control over the domestic industry will for these and other reasons continue to be of critical importance to the American consumer.

To the extent that domestic supply is controlled by private means alone, the control has been achieved through a composite of a moderately high concentration of reserves, output, and facilities in the hands of a relatively small number of giant companies, reinforced by an extensive network of intercorporate relationships achieved through joint ventures, intercorporate stockholdings, and interlocking directorates. These private means of control are examined in Chapter 6.

To shore up the private methods of market control, the oil industry has made extensive use of the power of the state to do that which it could not do for itself, inducing the government to provide it with the benefits of restricted domestic output and absolute limitations on imports. These supplementary and reinforcing public means of control are discussed in Chapter 7. Interwoven throughout the domestic control system has been a complex of preferential tax advantages, enjoyed principally by the major integrated companies and not by their principal sources of competition—the independent refiners and marketers. These tax advantages are examined in Chapter 8.

CONCENTRATION IN DOMESTIC OIL

6

FROM ITS EARLIEST DAYS the production of crude oil in the United States has been widely dispersed among numerous producers. Although the concentration of domestic crude production has been rising as the result of mergers and other causes, it still remains well below the levels of oil-producing countries elsewhere. Among the factors that have combined to bring this about is a legal principle not present in most other oil-producing lands: the private ownership of subsoil mineral rights. A philosophic principle that has emerged in the development of Western civilization is the right of the individual to own property, including the ownership not only of the surface land but of what lies below. Where the subsoil mineral rights are the property of the state or the ruler, as in the Middle East, the obtaining of concessions has involved negotiations only with the governing body. But in the United States, the right to withdraw oil must be negotiated with individual private property owners whose number is legion.

Moreover, unlike the Middle East, where most of the output comes from a few large fields, production in the United States is scattered among a large number of small and medium-size fields, each of which has its own independent producers and royalty owners usually tracing back to discovery by independent wildcatters. Although over the years the major oil companies have been able to acquire control over most of their output, the circumstances of their discovery left behind a legacy of individual ownership. In a statement to the Temporary National Economic Committee in 1939, Karl A. Crowley, an attorney of Fort Worth, Texas, testified: "The independent wildcatter must be given credit for practically every major discovery of oil in the United States. It was due to the faith of independents that the great Ranger field was discovered when the world was faced with a shortage of oil during the World War. Independents opened the gigantic Burkburnett pool, Cushing, Seminole, Spindletop, and countless others. The hardy independent has discovered and used new methods for locating oil pools, and time after time he has gone into territory condemned by the majors and unearthed a new store of nature's riches." Of fifteen large oil pools discovered in Oklahoma and West Texas between 1912 and 1926, the majors found only one—Oklahoma's Hewitt field, discovered by the Texas Co.

Crowley went on to describe the discovery of the Great Permian Basin in Winkler County: "There the majors had condemned that entire area as being worthless for oil—said that it was impossible to produce oil from the formations that were to be found there. It was condemned as being so utterly worthless that the fool-hardy wildcatter there was unable to sell any of his leases to the major companies and had to depend upon individual speculators to obtain a few dollars from time to time until he literally worried his well down to production. He and his associates found themselves the possessors of a great well located in a block of nearly 30,000 acres of land that has proved to be immensely rich and productive."[1]

The great East Texas field owed its discovery to the persistence of an impoverished wildcatter, the legendary "Dad" Joiner. Volume from this field quickly rose to about 1 billion barrels a day, or about one-third of the national requirements. In Crowley's words:

> It remained for a true independent, C. M. "Dad" Joiner, to discover the world's largest oil pool and to add billions of new wealth to the State of Texas and an unheard-of supply of cheap oil for the people of the nation. Joiner spent more than a year drilling his well. He often was compelled to shut down operations for lack of money and was only able to finish his well by borrowing money from his friends and selling a few leases to individuals. Not a dollar did he ever get from any major company. Joiner's well came in October 3, 1930; it produced 300 barrels of oil a day and it encouraged others to drill in the area and three months later on December 28, 1930, another independent drilled 15 miles farther north and completed a well with an initial production of 10,000 barrels daily. Approximately one month later, about January 26, 1931, another independent brought in still another well, 15 miles farther and this one came in for 12,000 barrels of oil daily.
>
> With the discovery of the latter two great wells by independents, the majors found themselves with very few leases in the field. They sent their buyers, land men and lawyers to the field by the hundreds, all armed with plenty of money, and entered into an unprecedented buying campaign to acquire the choicest leases, covering land that they had before condemned as being utterly worthless. The independents, however, had secured a toe-hold and even at this time owned half of the leases in that great field.

And so it was that the East Texas field, the greatest oil field in all history, came into existence through the adventuresome spirit, faith, confidence and capability of independent wildcatters.[2]

Although decentralization was thus inherent in the circumstances of crude production, the subsequent stages of refining and transportation offered the potential for centralized control. And John D. Rockefeller was quick to seize the opportunity, gathering into the hands of the old Standard Oil "Trust" control over the great bulk of the nation's refining capacity. When in 1911 the Supreme Court dissolved the trust, the way was opened for the subsequent growth of other major companies. Had it not been for its dissolution the "Trust," through its control of transportation and refining, could have brought concentration in crude production to even further heights by continuing to determine which producers could get their oil transported and refined. Nonetheless, the Court's order was badly flawed in one respect: the assets of the holding company were distributed back to its own stockholders—assets consisting of the stock of the operating companies, which were spread over production, transportation, refining, and marketing.[3] The result of leaving the ownership of the operating companies in the hands of those who had owned the old parent corporation was of course to leave the dominant ownership with the Rockefeller interests. After an investigation eleven years later, the Federal Trade Commission noted: "There is, as is generally known, an interlocking stock ownership in the different organizations [of the Standard Oil group] which has perpetuated the very monopolistic control which the courts sought to terminate."[4]

Not long after the old Standard Oil "Trust" had been broken up in 1911, the newly divided operating companies resumed their growth by merger. As early as 1921, Standard (Ind.) acquired a sizable rival, Midwest Refining, with assets of $85.9 million. Four years later, it absorbed an even larger company, Pan American Petroleum and Transportation, with assets of $179.5 million. In the same year, Standard of N.Y. (Mobil) acquired one of the nation's largest independents, Magnolia Petroleum, with assets of $212.8 million, and in 1926 it purchased General Petroleum ($102 million). Also in 1926, Standard (Calif.) made two important acquisitions, Pacific Oil and Pacific Petroleum ($181 million and $95 million, respectively). These acquisitions formed an important part of the foundation on which the subsequent growth of the Standard companies was based.[5]

While the descendants of the old trust have continued to grow by merger and otherwise, so also have other integrated majors—companies with their own reserves, refining facilities, and retail outlets. Together with the nonintegrated independents, they make up a threeway division of the domestic industry. In years past it was customary to speak of the "20 majors," but a recent Staff Report of the Federal Trade Commission identifies "17 majors." The reduction is the result of mergers: e.g., Richfield with Atlantic, Pure with Union, Sinclair with ARCO and BP. Within this group of seventeen, the ubiquity of their leadership positions at each of the industry's stages suggests that the eight largest companies represent a group clearly separate from and above the other majors, who are usually an important factor only at one stage. For example, the ninth-ranking firm in ownership of reserves and crude production (Getty) ranks sixteenth in refining capacity and was not even among the twenty largest in retail gasoline sales. The ninth largest in retail sales and refining (Sun) ranked eleventh in crude production and fourteenth in ownership of reserves. Unlike the international industry, the domestic industry has evolved, not into a dichotomy ("majors" and "independents"), but into a trichotomy ("the top eight," "lesser majors," and nonintegrated "independents").

Measured by the customary "four-company" concentration ratio, domestic oil is certainly not one of the nation's most concentrated industries, a fact frequently cited by its defenders. Commenting on this line of argument, John W. Wilson has observed:

> Despite its size, conventional concentration ratio measurements indicate that oil is not particularly concentrated in comparison with other major industries . . . while the concentration ratios for the top four or top eight crude oil producers have increased substantially in the last twenty years, the industry still seems to compare favorably with other leading manufacturing industries, such as automobiles, copper, computers, and aluminum. Thus, argue the industry's defenders, right-thinking rational men should direct their antitrust interests toward more critical targets like breakfast cereals and beer, and leave oil alone.[6]

But this reasoning overlooks the joint ventures and communities of interest among the largest companies and, above all, the use of government to supplement and strengthen private methods of control.

THE CONCENTRATION OF DOMESTIC SUPPLY

On July 12, 1973, Senator Henry M. Jackson, chairman of the Permanent Senate Subcommittee on Investigations, made public as a committee print a sixty-two-page document entitled "Preliminary Federal Trade Commission Staff Report on Its Investigation of the Petroleum Industry."[7] This report presents concentration figures in terms of individual companies for each of the four sectors of the industry—reserves, production, refining, and retail marketing.

Nearly all (93.6%) of the nation's proved reserves of crude oil are held by twenty major oil companies. The United States can thus secure domestic oil that "with reasonable certainty" is "recoverable from known reservoirs under existing economic and operating conditions" only to the extent that this small group of companies agrees to its extraction. Any policies on price, taxes, etc., with which these companies disagree can result in their oil simply being left in the ground, where its value will appreciate as demand and price levels continue to rise.

Nearly two-thirds of the reserves are held by the eight largest firms, and over one-third (37.2%) by the four largest, each of which holds about 9 percent of the total. The top eight in the control of reserves were also the top eight in each of the industry's successive stages. As Table 6-1 reveals, their rankings may differ somewhat from stage to stage; but in ownership of reserves, crude production, refining capacity, and retail sales, the top eight invariably consist of Exxon, Texaco, Gulf, SoCal, Standard (Ind.), Atlantic-Richfield (ARCO), Shell, and Mobil. For the top eight as a group, their aggregate share of retail sales (55.0%) is firmly based on a slightly higher percentage of refining

TABLE 6-1

**Eight Top Companies: Shares and Ranking at Successive Stages
of the Petroleum Industry, 1970**

	Domestic Reserves		Crude Production*		Refining Capacity		Retail Gasoline Sales	
	Share	Rank	Share	Rank	Share	Rank	Share	Rank
Exxon	9.9%	1	9.8%	1	8.6%	1	7.4%	3
Texaco	9.3	2	8.5	2	8.1	3	8.1	1
Gulf	9.0	3	6.8	3	5.8	7	7.1	5
SoCal	9.0	4	5.3	5	7.7	5	5.0	8
Standard (Ind.)	8.5	5	5.1	7	8.2	2	7.3	4
ARCO	7.5	6	5.1	6	5.4	8	5.6	7
Shell	5.9	7	6.1	4	8.0	4	7.9	2
Mobil	4.9	8	3.9	8	6.3	6	6.6	6
Top eight	64.0		50.5		58.1		55.0	

* 1969.
Source: 1973 FTC Staff Report, pp. 13–22.

capacity (58.1%), and their share of refining capacity on an even higher proportion of domestic reserves (64.0%). In a period of diminishing supplies, the last will, of course, be the critical determinant.

While it is the *level* of concentration that is associated with differences in an industry's behavior, the direction and rate of change is also of great importance from the point of view of public policy. For economic as well as legal reasons, it is far harder to restore competition than to preserve it. It is by preventing increases in concentration that antitrust has its best opportunity to preserve competitive behavior. Although petroleum has presented an almost ideal opportunity for the preservation of competition through the application of the existing law against mergers, the opportunity has not been seized. Partly as a result, concentration has increased markedly in both the ownership of domestic reserves and the production of crude oil, as can be seen in Table 6-2. From just over a third, the six companies which with BP make up the "seven sisters" increased their share of domestic reserves during 1949–70 to slightly less than a half. Three of the six—Gulf, SoCal, and Shell—nearly doubled their ownership proportions. In terms of crude production, the share held by the six during the more limited period 1960–69 rose from a third to over two-fifths, with by far the largest gain (from 6.5% to 9.8%) being recorded by the industry's largest firm. These increases, it should be noted, took place despite a vast proliferation in the number of producers.[8]

TABLE 6-2

**Six Major Oil Companies: Change in Concentration of
Domestic Proved Reserves and Crude Production**

	Reserves		Production	
	1949	*1970*	*1960*	*1969*
Exxon	11.1%	9.9%	6.5%	9.8%
Texaco	5.4	9.3	8.9	8.5
Gulf	4.6	9.0	5.1	6.8
SoCal	4.6	9.0	4.8	5.3
Shell	2.9	5.9	4.8	6.1
Mobil	5.0	4.9	3.4	3.9
Total	33.6	48.0	33.5	40.4
Top four	25.7	37.2	25.3	30.4

Sources: International Petroleum Cartel, p. 23; 1973 FTC Staff Report, pp. 13, 14.

THE CONCENTRATION OF REFINING CAPACITY

In contrast to production, the capital entrance requirements in refining are high and rising, and the number of refiners is low and falling. Although many older refineries are smaller, the minimum optimal size of a new refinery has been placed at about 150,000 barrels a day, costing $250–$400 million. As would be expected from the higher capital entrance requirements, the level of concentration is higher in refining capacity than in production. Between 1961 and 1972, the number of domestic petroleum refineries fell from 311 to 282, while the number of refining companies dropped from 175 to 129. Accompanying this decline in the number of refineries, concentration moved steadily upward. As can be seen from Table 6-3, the top four increased their share of domestic refining capacity from 28.5 percent in 1960 to 32.9 percent in 1970, while the top eight enlarged their proportion from 46.0 to 58.1 percent. The effective control over refining capacity is undoubtedly even higher. Concerning the concentration ratio for refining, the FTC report noted that: "due to the existence of processing arrangements between major oil companies and independent refiners through which major oil companies supply

TABLE 6-3

**Changes in Concentration of
Domestic Refining Capacity, 1960–70**

	1960	1970
Exxon	—	8.6%
Texaco	—	8.1
Shell	—	8.0
SoCal	—	7.7
Mobil	—	6.3
Gulf	—	5.8
Total	—	44.5
Standard (Ind.)	—	8.2
ARCO	—	5.4
Top four	28.5	32.9
Top eight	46.0	58.1

Source: 1973 FTC Staff Report, p. 18, n. 18.

crude oil in return for refined product, this figure may substantially understate effective refinery concentration."[9]

In any event, the majors' position at the refining stage has enabled them to eliminate excess capacity by the simple expedient of not building new refineries. Because of the large number of crude producers, the limitation of production required government intercession. But in refining, the number of companies is sufficiently limited and the concentration sufficiently high to make possible an effective tailoring of capacity to demand without such intercession. As Chart 6-1 shows, the growth of refining capacity in relation to demand has undergone three distinct stages during the past quarter century. In the first period, 1952–59, capacity and demand rose closely in tandem with each other, with capacity showing a higher average growth rate (3.71%) than demand (2.85%). As a result, refining capacity by 1959 was some 600,000 b/d in excess of demand. Although in the second period, 1959–66, demand continued to rise at nearly the same rate (2.68%), the annual growth rate of capacity was cut back to only 1.28 percent.

TABLE 6-4

Average Annual Growth Rate for Domestic Refining Capacity and Demand, Selected Periods

From		To 1959	1966	1972
1952	Capacity	3.71% ——	2.51%	2.59%
	Demand	2.85	2.39	3.04
1959	Capacity		1.28	2.45
	Demand		2.68	3.76
1966	Capacity			4.22
	Demand			4.68

Sources: Bureau of Mines and American Petroleum Institute. To secure comparability with the series for refining capacity, the measure used for domestic demand is the production of domestic refineries plus that of natural gas liquid plants (whose output is largely for sale) minus imports.

During 1959–66, average net additions to distillation capacity fell from an annual level of 330,000 to 170,000 barrels a day.[10] Thus, by 1966 the former relationship had been reversed, with capacity falling some 500,000 b/d below demand. During the third period, the expansion of capacity went forward at a more rapid rate (4.22%), but this

CHART 6-1
Domestic Demand* and Refining Capacity, 1950–72

Millions of Bbls.

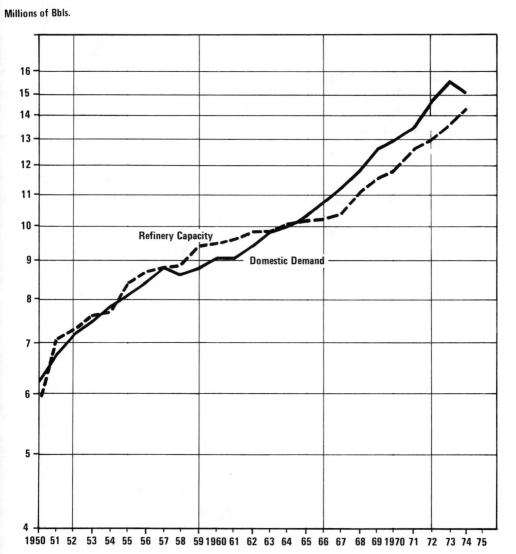

* Primary supply minus production of natural gas liquid plants minus exports and crude losses.
Sources: Bureau of Mines and American Petroleum Institute.

was not sufficient to enable supply to catch up with demand, since the latter was rising at the still more rapid rate of 4.68 percent. Capital expenditures on petroleum refineries were reduced from $825 million in 1957 to $350 million in 1959, near which level they remained for the next five years. Some of the largest companies reduced not only their financial outlays for expansion but their actual capacity as well. Exxon's refining capacity in Texas, Louisiana, and the Gulf Coast was lowered from 919,040 b/d in 1956 to 879,000 b/d in 1964; Gulf's from 477,490 to 457,000 b/d; and Sun's from 160,000 to 155,000. Others in the face of rising demand kept their capacity unchanged, e.g., Atlantic-Richfield at 210,000 b/d and Cities Service at 199,300 b/d.[11]

The retrenchment in refinery construction can hardly be attributed to an inability to obtain the necessary capital since at the very time the oil companies were reducing their investments in refineries at home, they were greatly expanding their refining capacity abroad. According to the Office of Oil and Gas of the Interior Department, some 1,720,000 b/d of refining capacity was "exported" by American oil firms to foreign locations.[12] Moreover, the majors were also embarked on a vigorous invasion into the U.S. chemical industry. Chart 6-2 indicates that the halving of their capital outlays on petroleum refineries was accompanied by a tripling of their investments in chemical plants, with the result that in the first half of the 1960's their expenditures in new chemicals closely approximated outlays in their primary field. By 1967, their investments in chemicals had exceeded their outlays in petroleum by some $50 million. As a consequence, no fewer than eleven of the thirty top sellers of chemicals had by 1968 become petroleum companies; the leaders were Standard (N.J.) which ranked sixth in chemical sales, Occidental (eleventh), Shell (thirteenth), Phillips (seventeenth), and Mobil (nineteenth).[13]

Nor can the industry's failure to expand capacity during the 1960's be traced to environmental objections. The widespread concern with protecting the environment from oil dates from the Santa Barbara oil spill, which did not occur until 1969. In a survey conducted in 1973 by the Senate Commerce Committee, each major oil company was asked how many refineries it had specifically proposed in the continental United States since 1958 that were *not* built because of citizens' law suits based upon environmental issues. Of the ten majors responding, not one stated that it had failed to build a refinery because of environmentally based civil law suits.[14] The most logical explanation, occasionally alluded to in the trade press, is of course the most obvious one. In the words of the *Oil and Gas Journal*, "the conviction of many refiners—who point to widespread price-warring and dis-

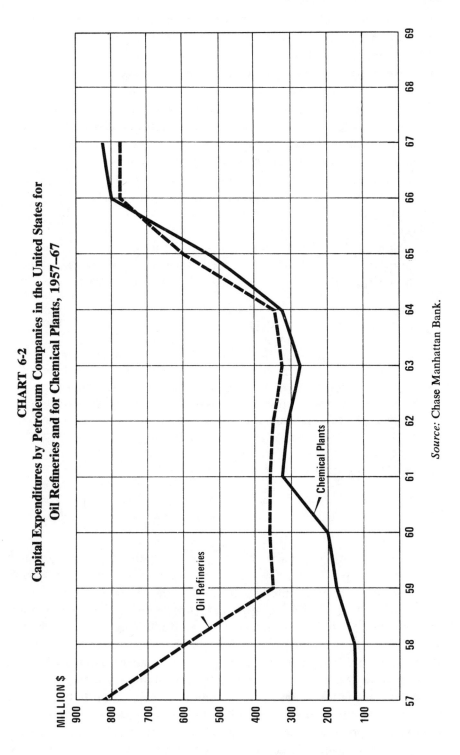

CHART 6-2

Capital Expenditures by Petroleum Companies in the United States for Oil Refineries and for Chemical Plants, 1957–67

Source: Chase Manhattan Bank.

tressed gasoline—is that a lull in construction is needed to let demand catch up a bit."[15] By 1972 that objective had been largely achieved.

INTERCORPORATE RELATIONSHIPS

The analysis of market concentration presented above has presumed the leading companies to be separate and independent, free from any influence through intercorporate relationships that would affect their competitive behavior. In the case of the petroleum industry, such an assumption is a fiction. Through interlocking corporate relationships and joint ventures of every conceivable form, the opportunities for substituting collective for independent judgment are legion. Indeed, it is the view of John W. Wilson (former chief of the Division of Economic Studies, Federal Power Commission) that the effect of bringing "horizontally and vertically juxtaposed firms into close working relationships with each other" is to make cooperation a necessity:

> They *must* work together to further their joint interests. Consequently, each becomes familiar with the others and with each other's operations. Men in such close working relationships learn to consider one another's interests. This process of learning to live together is, of course, quite laudable in certain social and political contexts. The success of our Nation's international relations, for example, depends greatly upon this process. But it is, most assuredly, not the kind of institutional setting within which a free market economy can be expected to function efficiently. Real economic competition is made of tougher stuff. . . . In order to function both efficiently and in the public interest, free markets *must be competitive*. This means that the participants must be structurally and behaviorally independent of each other. That precondition, quite apparently does not apply to the petroleum industry.[16]

Among the many ways in which rival companies are brought together is the joint venture, which for its specific purpose necessarily subordinates individual interests to a concern for the common good. No other industry begins to approach petroleum in the number and importance of jointly owned enterprises. While found in practically every stage of the industry, they have been particularly important with respect to foreign oil reserves, pipelines, and offshore oil leases. Among vertically integrated companies, the conduct of such a series of successive activities through joint ventures has a cumulative effect, progressively narrowing the area in which independent rivalrous conduct is even possible. The joint venture's inhibiting effect on competition is obvious where a company is confronted with the alternative either of embarking on a potentially rewarding (and potentially dangerous) course of independent competitive behavior or of avoiding the competitive struggle by forming a common enterprise with its rivals.

JOINT OWNERSHIP OF PIPELINES. By its very nature the pipeline is a bottleneck, invariably owned and controlled by the majors but of critical importance to the independents. Without the services of a gathering line, the independent producer cannot get his product to a refinery. And without the continuous, assured supply provided by a pipeline, a refinery, because of its high fixed costs, cannot operate efficiently. Even where his supply is provided by independent producers, the independent refiner using a major-owned pipeline is still not free from the influence of his larger competitors.

The opportunities presented by the pipeline for securing monopoly control have long been recognized. When first incorporated in 1870, the Standard Oil Co. controlled only about 10 percent of the nation's petroleum refining capacity. Three years later, it began to gather and transport crude bought from others through pipelines. By 1879, less than a decade after the original incorporation, it had increased its control over refining capacity to 90 percent. This astonishing increase was achieved in large part through control over transportation—both pipelines and railroads.[17]

Today, approximately 75 percent of the crude produced in the United States flows to the refinery by pipeline, 17 percent by tanker and 8 percent by truck.[18] Pipelines transporting crude oil across state lines are common carriers, subject to regulation by the Interstate Commerce Commission, and the egregious tactics employed by the old Standard Oil "Trust" are unlawful. In its recent investigation, however, the FTC Staff found that much the same objectives can be accomplished by more subtle means. The flow of crude to independent refiners can be stopped or limited by: "(1) requiring shipments of minimum size, (2) granting independents irregular shipping dates, (3) limiting available storage at the pipeline terminals, (4) imposing unreasonable product standards upon independent customers of pipelines, and (5) employing other harassing or delaying tactics."[19] Although pipeline owners must obtain ICC approval for rates providing a fair return on their pipeline investment, the rates approved may be well above the competitive cost of transporting oil. For the vertically integrated firm, this merely increases the profitability of its pipeline operation and decreases that of its refinery. For the nonintegrated refiner, an excessive pipeline charge is a real cost not transferrable to any other department.[20]

Whether because of their potential for monopoly control or their formidable capital costs, or both, nearly all petroleum pipelines throughout the world have long been owned and controlled by the major oil companies, usually as joint ventures. In 1952 it was found that outside the United States, ". . . every important pipeline in existence or even proposed is controlled by the seven principal international oil companies, individually or jointly."[21] These included such important arteries as the Trans Arabian Pipeline (Tapline), from Qaisuma, Saudi Arabia, to the Mediterranean, a distance of 753 miles, owned by Exxon, SoCal, Texaco, and Mobil; the Interprovincial Pipeline from Edmonton, Canada, to Superior, Wisconsin, a distance of 1,100 miles, owned by Exxon; a 143-mile line running from Lake Maracaibo in Venezuela to Amsay Bay on the Caribbean, owned by Exxon and other international majors; as well as the complex system of pipelines serving Iran, Iraq, and Bahrein.[22]

That the largest oil companies continue as the principal owners is apparent from data relating to U.S. pipelines presented by Wilson to the Senate Antitrust Subcommittee. Table 6-5 presents the ownership share held by the top eight domestic producers for seven domestic lines (with assets of more than $20 million). In each case companies among the top eight held a majority position. The line with the largest number of companies required to achieve majority control is Dixie, where majority control takes five firms. For the group as a whole, it takes an average of only 3 companies among the country's top eight to hold majority stock ownership.

JOINT OWNERSHIP OF OFFSHORE LEASES. The major oil companies have also joined together in the ownership of, and bidding for, producing leases on offshore lands. Embracing some 16 million acres, of which 80 percent consists of undisputed federal area, the outer continental shelf area off Louisiana (though not off Texas) has proved to contain a large reservoir of oil.[23] The granting of leases to these federal lands is under the jurisdiction of the Department of Interior, whose policies have been criticized as unduly favoring the major oil companies on two grounds.

In the first place, permitting competing companies to join together and submit one bid on their collective behalf contravenes the spirit and objective of the antitrust laws. If in the normal course of business the same group of companies were to meet together privately and agree on the price, who was to get the business, and how the costs and benefits were to be divided, they would be in obvious violation of Section 1 of the Sherman Act. As Walter J. Mead has put it:

> In any given sale, it is obvious that when four firms, each able to bid independently, combine to submit a single bid, three interested, potential bidders have been eliminated; i.e., the combination has restrained trade. This situation does not differ materially

TABLE 6-5

Company Shares of Top Eight in Selected Pipelines

	Colonial	Plantation	Dixie	Laurel	Texas-N. Mex.	Wolverine	Four Corners
Exxon	11.5%	48.8%	11.1%				
Mobil	11.5%		5.0			26.0%	
Texaco	14.3		5.0	33.9%	45.0%	17.0	
SoCal							25.0%
Shell		24.0	5.5				25.0
Gulf	16.8		18.2	49.1		7.0	20.0
Standard (Ind.)	14.3		12.1				
ARCO	1.6		7.4		35.0	25.0	10.0
Total	58.5	72.8	64.3	83.0	80.0	75.0	80.0
Assets ($ million)	$480.2	$176.2	$46.4	$35.9	$30.5	$21.8	$20.9

Source: Compiled from Testimony by John W. Wilson before the Senate Subcommittee on Antitrust and Monopoly, *Hearings on the Natural Gas Industry,* Pt. 1, pp. 456 ff.

from one of explicit collusion in which four firms meet in advance of a given sale and decide who among them should bid (which three should refrain from bidding) for specific leases and, instead of competing among themselves, attempt to rotate the winning bids. The principal difference is that explicit collusion is illegal.[24]

The second criticism goes to the method of bidding; i.e., the practice of "bonus bidding" under which the Department, after requiring a flat one-sixth royalty from all bidders, makes its award on the basis of the cash bonus bid (above a minimal per-acre figure). With individual bids exceeding $100 million per lease, it is difficult to conceive of a bidding procedure more favorable to the largest firms and more disadvantageous to the independents. Even if any independent, or group of them, were able to outbid the majors, the cost of the bid itself would absorb cash capital better devoted to undertaking an adequate drilling program. In place of bonus bidding the present procedure could, without change in the law, be simply reversed. Under a proposal originally advanced by E. Wayles Browne, a flat dollar amount per acre would be fixed; the variable would be the royalty percentage, with the award going to the bidder who offered the government the greatest share. Under such a "royalty" bidding procedure, any independent company that is able to contract for an offshore well could enter the bidding, with some possibility of success. Without having to tie up its funds for a lease bonus, substantially all of its working capital would be available for use in geological and geophysical work and in drilling. Moreover, during the foreseeable years of apparently continuing inflation, such a procedure would have the very real advantage of yielding payments to the government in dollars of constant purchasing power. Until such an alternative is adopted, the present "bonus" system will bar even sizable independents from access to these government-owned resources. Testimony to this effect was cited by Wilson:

> As the president of an established oil company with annual revenues of over $100 billion recently testified in an FPC hearing, it would now take a consortium of 15 or more firms like his to surmount the offshore entry barriers which have been erected under Interior's watchful eye. Consequently, his company and others like it have been effectively precluded from entering these producing areas except by obtaining limited farmouts of unwanted acreage from the dominant majors or perhaps by joining one of the established combines as a junior partner.[25]

As an experiment, the Interior Department in October 1974 put up several plots for royalty bidding. The refusal by several of the largest companies even to offer bids was taken by the Department as evidence of the procedure's unworkability. To the majors royalty bidding meant not only greater competition but a lessening of immediate tax benefits. If, under bonus bidding, the lease turns out to yield dry holes or is abandoned for other reasons, half of the bonus can be deducted immediately as a business expense. If the property is income-producing, the company can reclaim half the bonus in equal installments over five years.

As might be surmised from this governmentally imposed barrier to entry, concentration in production from offshore areas is even higher than in the industry's other stages. To measure the concentration of ownership, Walter S. Measday of the Senate Antitrust Subcommittee examined sixty-four fields accounting for 94 percent of all production on federal lands in the Louisiana Outer Continental Shelf (OCS), the results of which are shown in Table 6-6.[26] In comparison with their share of 50.5 percent for total domestic crude production, the top

TABLE 6-6

Company Shares of Sales of Crude and Condensate,
Federal Gulf of Mexico, Louisiana
Outer Continental Shelf, 1974

Top Eight	Thousands of Barrels	Percent
Shell	60,807	18.8%
Exxon	44,828	13.9
SoCal	36,467	11.3
Gulf	21,610	6.7
ARCO	16,380	5.1
Texaco	11,701	3.6
Mobil	9,026	2.8
Standard (Indiana)	7,801	2.4
Top 8	208,620	64.5
Lesser Majors	65,190	20.3
Others	49,217	15.2
Total	323,027	100.0

Source: 94th Cong., 1st Sess., Senate Subcommittee on Antitrust and Monopoly, *Hearings on S. 2387 and Related Bills,* Pt. 1, pp. 51–70 (Statement of Walter S. Measday), September 23, 1975.

eight accounted for 64.5 percent of the output from the offshore area. Nearly half came from just three of the top eight—Shell, Exxon, and SoCal.

Much of the offshore output is produced by joint ventures, thus affording the majors still another opportunity for the development of commonalities of interest. Exxon shares ownership of federal offshore leases with Gulf and Mobil; Shell shares ownership with SoCal; Gulf with Mobil, SoCal with Mobil and ARCO; and Standard (Ind.) with Texaco and Mobil.[27] But an analysis of the data reveals something else. By and large, the companies with the greatest financial resources, (e.g., Exxon, Gulf, Shell, and SoCal) have little need to spread the costs or share the risks. Hence, it is not surprising to find that most of the leases held by these companies are individually owned, without participation by other firms. Forty-three out of 52 leases held by Exxon are individually owned; 64 of 68 held by Shell Oil, 34 of 51 held by Gulf, and 86 of 105 held by SoCal are individually owned. In contrast, the lesser majors rely heavily on participations with other companies. All but 1 of Continental's 119 and of Cities Service's 101 leases are joint ventures; the same is true of all but 2 of Getty's 100 leases. All of the leases of Amerada Hess (15), Marathon (18), and Sun (19) are joint ventures. For companies of this intermediate size, offerings under the bonus bidding procedure appear to be possible only if the cost is shared. But while the joint venture makes participation possible, it also lessens the value to the lessee of any possible discovery.

The present bidding procedure thus has several strategic advantages for the largest companies: it virtually excludes the independents; it dilutes the value of a discovery to any potential maverick by forcing the "lesser majors" into joint offerings; and it gives to the largest firms the option of either spreading the cost through a joint offering or reaping the full benefit through an independent offering. With good reason Wilson has criticized the offshore leasing program as "one of the most onerous anticompetitive cartelization devices at work . . ."[28]

INTERLOCKING DIRECTORATES. In 1914, Congress addressed itself for the first and last time to the problem of interlocking directorates. The occasion was the consideration of what became known as the Clayton Act, a keystone of President Wilson's New Freedoms. In a message to Congress on January 20, 1914, the President called for the enactment of "laws which will effectively prohibit and prevent such interlockings of the personnel of the directorates of great corporations—banks and railroads, industrial, commercial, and public service bodies—and in effect result in making those who borrow and those who lend practically one and the same, those who sell and those who buy but the same persons trading with another under different names and in different combinations, and those who affect to compete in fact partners and masters of some whole field of business."[29] In their reports accompanying the measure, the House and Senate Committees likewise showed their concern with the general problem of concentrated economic power: "The concentration of wealth, money and property in the United States under the control and in the hands of a few individuals or great corporations has grown to such an enormous extent that unless checked it will ultimately threaten the perpetuity of our institutions. The idea that there are only a few men in any of our great corporations and industries who are capable of handling the affairs of the same is contrary to the spirit of our institutions."[30]

As finally enacted, however, the provision dealing with interlocking directorates (Section 8) was based not on any broad standard directed to the concentration of economic power* but on a much narrower test.[31] Specifically, it provided that no person could be a director of two or more industrial or commercial enterprises (with capital, surplus, and undivided profits of more than $1 million), if the concerns were, or are, competitors, "so that the elimination of competition by agreement between them would constitute a violation of any of the provisions of any of the antitrust laws."† The principal weakness of the law, although not its only deficiency,‡ is its failure to reach indirect interlocks—the coming together of directors of two or more competing companies as directors of another concern, particularly a financial institution.[32] This loophole has certainly not been overlooked by the major oil companies. In a study of interlocking directorates as of 1946, the Federal Trade Commission found that:

* The concern with the concentration of economic power in the hands of financial institutions was exemplified by the remarks of Rep. Helbering, who stressed their importance as the focal point from which directorates radiated out to every sector of the economy. Citing cases described in the Report of the Pujo Committee, he called attention to the fact that members of the board of the First National Bank were also directors of forty-nine other corporations, with aggregate resources of $11,542 million; members of J. P. Morgan and Co. "held 72 directorships in 47 of the country's largest companies." All told, members of J. P. Morgan and Co. and the directors of their controlled trust companies and of the First National and National City Bank held "341 directorships in 112 corporations having aggregate resources or capitalization of $22,245,000,000" (63rd Cong., 2nd Sess., *Congressional Record*, May 23, 1914, p. 9,186).

† Within its limited scope of preventing *direct* interlocks between competing firms, the law appears to have been surprisingly effective. In a study of 1,146 interlocks held by directors of industrial and merchandising corporations, Peter C. Dooley found that only 133, or 12%, were with competitors. Allowing for possible nonparticipation in the same geographic market or the occasional excessive breadth of the Census product classes used in the analysis, even this appears to be an overestimate (Peter C. Dooley, "The Interlocking Directorate," *American Economic Review*, June 1969, pp. 314–323).

‡ The statute applies only to directors and not officers; it prohibits only interlocks with competitors, not customers or suppliers.

The third, fourth, fifth, sixth, and eighth and ninth largest of the oil companies were linked with one another through three banks. Standard of Indiana, Standard of California, Gulf Oil and Continental Oil all had directors who were on the board of the Chase National Bank. Standard of Indiana and Texas Co. were linked through Continental Illinois National Bank and Trust Co., while Texas Co., Shell Union Oil and Tidewater Oil were linked through Central Hanover Bank and Trust Company.[33]

Somewhat to its surprise, the Commission also found a number of direct interlocks which would appear to have represented outright violations of the law: "While there were no direct interlocks among the top six oil companies, several of the medium-sized companies did have such ties. Thus, Sinclair had three directors in common with Richfield, which in turn had three directors in common with Empire."[34] "Conspicuous by their absence" among companies with interlocks —direct or indirect—were Standard of New Jersey and Socony-Vacuum.[35] The Commission noted, however, that ". . . these two companies had a series of ties with each other and with other petroleum companies through joint stock ownership in third companies."[36] In fact, the Commission emphasized the importance in the petroleum industry of "other types of close relationships":

> Opportunities for joint action occur, for example, when two or more petroleum companies own affiliated domestic petroleum companies, foreign or domestic companies which produce or market petroleum in foreign countries, domestic natural gas pipeline companies, domestic crude oil pipeline companies, foreign crude oil pipeline companies, domestic gasoline pipeline companies, and various other interests. If the directors or operating executives of major oil companies jointly work out problems in connection with affiliated companies, the consequence may be much the same as if they are linked by interlocking directorates.[37]

Since the time of the FTC study, the frequency with which directors of the major oil companies come together on the boards of the largest banks seems, if anything, to have increased. Chart 6-3 shows the indirect interlocks among thirteen major oil companies whose directors met together in 1972 on the boards of eight of the nation's largest commercial banks.[38] At the top left are seven of the top eight companies; below are six other majors who are linked with each other or with the top eight through indirect interlocks with the eight commercial banks.

With the exception of Gulf and SoCal, all of the eight largest oil companies were interlocked in 1972 through large commercial banks with at least one other member of the top group. Exxon had four such

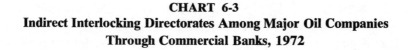

CHART 6-3
Indirect Interlocking Directorates Among Major Oil Companies
Through Commercial Banks, 1972

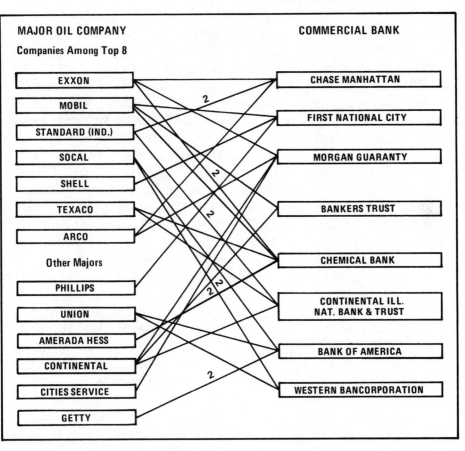

Source: Compiled from Stanley H. Ruttenberg and Associates, *The American Oil Industry—A Failure of Antitrust Policy,* Washington, D.C., 1974, pp. 83, 147–60.

interlocks—with Mobil, Standard (Ind.), Texaco, and ARCO. Mobil had three (with Exxon, Shell, and Texaco), as did Standard of Indiana (with Exxon, Texaco, and ARCO), as well as Texaco (with Exxon, Mobil, and Standard of Ind.). ARCO was interlocked with Exxon, and Standard (Ind.), and Shell with Mobil. Whenever all of the six commercial banks shown in the chart (exclusive of Bank of America and Western Bancorporation) hold their board meetings, directors of the top eight (excluding Gulf and SoCal) meet with directors of, on the average, 3.2 of their largest competitors.

Since the 1946 FTC study, the most notable change has been the abandonment by Exxon and Mobil (formerly Socony-Vacuum) of their earlier reticence. By 1972, Exxon had become indirectly interlocked with Standard (Ind.) and ARCO (through Chase Manhattan), with ARCO, Continental, and Cities Service (through Morgan Guaranty), and with Mobil, Texaco, and Amerada Hess (through Chemical Bank). In addition to its ties with Exxon, Mobil had forged links with Shell and Phillips (through First National City Bank), with Continental (through Bankers Trust), and with Texaco and Amerada Hess (through Chemical Bank). These two companies, which had no indirect interlocks in 1946, had by 1972 established such interlocks through five large commercial banks with each other and with eight other major oil companies. The interesting question is why the increase, particularly if the interlocks are without competitive significance? One possible explanation is that in 1946 the oil companies must have had fresh in their minds the investigations of the Temporary National Economic Committee, in which they had been a prime target, whereas by 1972 antitrust activity against the oil industry had been quiescent for over a decade and a half.

The information on interlocking directorates also bears a number of interesting regional implications. When the Bank of America holds its board meetings, for example, directors of the three leading oil producers in the Far West (SoCal, Union, and Getty) sit down together. Further cohesiveness is provided by Western Bancorporation, whose board meetings provide a handy occasion for directors of SoCal and Union to meet together. In the Midwest, the leader (Standard of Ind.) and the sixth largest refiner (Texaco) sit on the board of Continental Illinois Bank and Trust. The area's fifth and eighth largest refiners (Shell and Mobil) meet on the board of First National City Bank. And the third and seventh largest refiners (Standard of Ohio and Marathon) are indirectly interlocked.[39]

Because the necessary information is available, establishing the fact of interlocking directorates is a feasible, though tedious, undertaking. Because the information is conspicuously not available, determining their real significance is quite another matter.[40] At the very least, meeting together presents directors of competing companies with potential conflicts of interest:

> A director, whether direct or indirect, of two competing corporations cannot in good conscience recommend that either shall undertake a type of competition which is likely to injure the other. . . .
>
> A director on the board of an oil company and a financial institution would find it hard in good conscience to encourage his bank to finance expansion by competitors of his oil company thereby jeopardizing its prosperity. Nor can he in good conscience encourage the oil company to obtain its credit through other channels.
>
> If a person is a director of an oil company and a bank in which the latter is the caretaker and advisor of a pension trust fund of the former, he would feel it incumbent upon himself as a director of the bank to influence the trust department to vote those common stock holdings in favor of management of the oil company of which he is a part. Other directors on the bank board would feel it incumbent upon themselves, in order to retain the business of the oil company, to be mindful of the pressures which are brought by the director serving both companies to keep an eye out for the interest of those two companies.[41]

A potentially adverse effect on competition can arise when a medium-size company and a large firm are represented on the board of a bank which supplies funds to both. If the lesser firm wishes to obtain additional credit to finance a course of competitive conduct that will adversely affect the larger firm, the probable reaction of the bank is not hard to envision. Yet in the oil industry indirect interlocks between the largest firms and other majors are a commonplace. Thus, through First National City Bank, Phillips is interlocked with Shell and Mobil; through the Chemical Bank, Amerada Hess is interlocked with Exxon, Mobil, and Texaco; through Morgan Guaranty, Cities Service is connected with Exxon and ARCO. But by far the most widely represented among the second tier of companies is Continental Oil, which through Bankers Trust is related to Mobil, through Continental Illinois National Bank and Trust to Standard (Ind.) and Texaco, and through Morgan Guaranty to Exxon and ARCO. Such relationships pose an inherent conflict of interest to the banks on whose board the oil companies meet.

THE "ROCKEFELLER" COMPANIES: AN INNER COMMUNITY? Do the "Rockefeller" companies constitute a tight, cohesive grouping within the larger community of the major oil companies?

This is a question that has long intrigued students of the petroleum industry. The successors to the old Standard Oil Trust, broken up in 1911—Exxon, Mobil, Standard (Ind.), and SoCal—own 32.2 percent of domestic reserves, hold 30.8 percent of domestic refining capacity, and make 26.3 percent of all retail gasoline sales.

Although the managers of the operating companies and the Rockefeller interests have undoubtedly seen eye to eye on most issues, at least one open conflict over the locus of power did take place. The controversy involved control over Standard of Indiana:

> . . . the most striking illustration of this fight for control was presented by the open warfare between Mr. John D. Rockefeller, Jr., and the management of the Standard Oil Company of Indiana. Mr. Rockefeller actually held 14.9 percent of the voting stock. He had been in substantial control of the company for years. Colonel Stewart, the chairman of the board of directors and undeniably the driving force behind much of that company's activity, displeased Mr. Rockefeller in connection with certain transactions which were the subject of discussion during the administration of President Harding. He asked Colonel Stewart to resign; Stewart refused and did not grant to Mr. Rockefeller the use of the proxy machinery at the following annual election of directors. Thereupon Mr. Rockefeller waged a most dramatic proxy battle against him. He circularized the stockholders at considerable expense, asking for proxies. He engaged the most eminent legal talent to guard against any "technical mistakes." He brought to bear the tremendous influence of his standing in the community. The *Wall Street Journal* pointed out at the time that the fight marked the first time the Rockefeller domination in a large Standard Oil unit "had been really in question." In opposition, Colonel Stewart obtained the full support of the existing board of directors and sought the support of the 16,000 employees who were stockholders. At this most opportune moment the company declared a 50 percent stock dividend. The issue was for long in grave doubt. Four days previous to the election both sides are reported to have claimed the support of a majority, the one of votes and the other of stockholders. In the final election of directors, Mr. Rockefeller won 50 percent of the votes outstanding or 65 percent of the votes cast being in favor of his candidates. Control may be said to have remained in his hands. Colonel Stewart's connection with the company was brought to a close.[42]

Since managers can readily comprehend the probable personal repercussions of losing in a fight with an important stock-owning group, such episodes are a rarity. And this understandable reticence also extends to the making of competitive moves against a rival corporation whose stock is significantly held by the same owning group. In this way competition can be lessened without either directions to management or meetings, and certainly without publicly aired controversies.

The one and only occasion when ownership of the largest corporation has been traced back through the "owners of record" to the real or "beneficial" owners was a study by the Securities and Exchange Commission for the Temporary National Economic Committee, entitled *The Distribution of Ownership in the 200 Largest Nonfinancial Corporations.* For the four "Standard" companies, the holdings in 1938 of the Rockefeller family as individuals, through trusts and estates, foundations and other "Rockefeller-dominated corporations," were as follows:

TABLE 6-7

Holdings of the Rockefeller Family in Equity Securities of Four "Standard" Oil Companies, 1938
(percent of total stock outstanding)

Company	Individuals	Trusts & Estates	Foundations	Rockefeller-Dominated Corps.	Total
Exxon	6.45%	2.24%	4.82%	6.69%*	20.20%
Mobil	8.64	7.70			16.34
Standard Oil (Ind.)	2.44	4.39	4.53		11.36
SoCal	7.37	4.49	.46		12.32

* Through Standard Oil Co. (Ind.).
Source: 76th Cong., 3rd Sess., Temporary National Economic Committee, Monograph 29, *The Distribution of Ownership in the 200 Largest Nonfinancial Corporations,* 1940, p. 127.

Since in each case the remainder of the stock was widely dispersed, these holdings were considered sufficient by the Securities and Exchange Commission to give the Rockefeller family control over the corporations. Of Exxon, the Commission stated: "The combined block aggregating 13.5% of the common stock represented by far the largest holding and in view of the wide distribution of the majority of the stock should carry with it an amount of influence equivalent to working control. Furthermore, Standard Oil Co. (Indiana) owned 6.7 percent of the Standard Oil Co. (New Jersey), bringing direct and indirect holdings of the Rockefeller family to 20.2 percent." For Mobil (Socony-Vacuum): "Members of the family owned 16.3 percent of the common stock. . . . As this was by far the largest single block and most of the stock was widely distributed the Rockefeller interests seemed to have safe working control. . . ." Of Standard (Ind.), it was stated, "Members of the family owned 6.8 percent and family foundations 4.5 percent of the common stock. . . . The combined holdings of 11.4 percent appear to carry working control. . . ." And for SoCal (Standard of Calif.), "The Rockefeller family owned 11.9 percent of the common stock . . . and family foundations held another 0.5 percent. The block appeared to carry working control. . . ."[43]

As a result of the vast growth of these companies, the "dilution" of existing holdings resulting from the flotation of new issues, and the emergence of important new stock-owning institutions (mutual funds, pension funds), the relative importance of the Rockefeller holdings since the T.N.E.C. investigation has probably diminished. But has it fallen below the level required for working control? R. H. Larner has used as his standard of the proportion of stock required for control the ownership by a stockholder group of 10 percent.[44] Jean-Marie Chevalier, however, maintains that this is too high, contending that large corporations can be subject to effective minority control if a group owns 5 percent of the stock and is represented on the board of directors.[45] In addition to stock ownership, there is the linkage through interlocking directorates. Directors of Exxon and Standard (Ind.) come together as directors of Chase Manhattan, long identified as the "Rockefeller" bank. Directors of Exxon and Mobil meet together on the Chemical Bank. And, of course, there are the additional linkages among the companies through numerous joint ventures, some of which have been noted above.

Finally, there is the matter of the geographic division of markets. Years ago it was contended that each of the Standard companies tended to confine its operations to one or two contiguous regions, that in these areas it was usually the leading seller, and that as a result the individual Standard companies were able to dominate particular markets without encountering substantial competition from other Standard companies. Considering their resources and marketing abilities, such an orderly division of markets would be unlikely to take place without some coordinating influence. Some credence to this line of argument is lent by current data on retail gasoline market shares.[46] In 1972, Standard (Ind.) was the leading seller in thirteen states—all in the Midwest and Great Plains areas; in only one was Exxon among the four largest sellers. Conversely, Exxon was the leader in twelve other states—all along the Eastern seaboard or in the South; in nine, Standard (Ind.) was not among the four largest. Mobil was the leading seller in four states—New York and three New England states; in none was Standard (Ind.) among the four largest. Moreover, SoCal was the leader in eleven states—six in its historical region of the Far West and five in the South, the latter acquired in its absorption of Standard of Kentucky. In none of these eleven was Exxon among the four largest sellers, and in only two was Standard (Ind.) among the four largest.

*   *   *

On their face the concentration ratios would place the industry in what has been referred to as the "moderately-concentrated" category, whose behavior has usually been found to lie between that of the "concentrated" sector (industries with concentration ratios of 50% or more) and the "unconcentrated" category (those with ratios of less than 25%). If concentration ratios were all that mattered, the behavior of the petroleum industry would presumably be more competitive than that usually associated with oligopolistic industries. But there are other factors to be considered. Concentration in this industry is supplemented by a complex of intercorporate relationships imparting to separate companies a cohesiveness and commonality not approached in any other industry. As Wilson has put it, "The key structural feature of the petroleum industry is that virtually all of its corporate entities are extensively tied together through a very large number of joint venture arrangements and other types of intercorporate interlocks. Consequently, these firms cannot be viewed in parallel with independent unrelated market rivals in other industries."[47] Moreover, competition has been further lessened by the control of the market achieved through the artful use of government—the subject of Chapter 7. Petroleum thus represents the case, *par exemple*, where concentration is simply one of a series of interlocking building blocks on which an effective control of the market has been erected.

7

THE DOMESTIC CONTROL MECHANISM

IN THE PAST, the control over petroleum markets achieved by private means has not always been adequate to prevent the outbreak of competition in the most vigorous—or in the industry's term, "ruinous"—form. The control of reserves, production, capacity, and sales held by the largest firms, even though reinforced by intercorporate relationships, has simply not been sufficient to prevent the sporadic appearance of "distressed" oil. Confronted with this unpleasant reality, the petroleum industry, probably more than any other field of business activity, has been remarkably successful in inducing the state to shore up the private means of control with the mandatory powers of government. The principal forms of government intervention have been directed toward the limitation of domestic production and the restriction of imports. The former was achieved through an intricate production-control mechanism, the heart of which was "prorationing" by the various oil-producing states; the latter was authorized by Congress through a little-noted amendment to a "Trade Expansion" act and made operational by a presidential directive.

The restriction of domestic oil production imposed by government authority has taken two different forms, with differing objectives, each of which can be achieved by different means. The objective of the one is the prevention of physical waste, i.e., waste of the physical substance of petroleum "through evaporation, seepage, fire and especially through avoidable loss of gas in the reservoir that renders unproducible the oil left in the reservoir." The objective of the other is the prevention of what has been termed "economic waste," i.e., waste in the form of "pecuniary losses caused by unduly depressed prices," which in turn stems from an excess of production over what can be consumed at an existent price.[1] The term most widely used to refer to the prevention of physical waste is "conservation," though industry spokesmen have frequently stretched "conservation" to encompass the prevention of economic waste as well.

152

Although any restriction of output will of course tend to strengthen the market, the conceptual distinction becomes evident when the curtailment of output to maintain the price is greater than that required to prevent physical waste. A simple example was provided by the case of the State of Louisiana. Testifying in 1969 before the Senate Antitrust Subcommittee, J. M. Menefee, Commissioner of the Louisiana Department of Conservation, compared the state's current production of 2 million barrels a day with a potential "in the neighborhood of 2,900,000, up to 3 million barrels *with conservatively taking care of the reservoirs*. . . . Conservatively speaking . . . we can produce it prudently where it is not going to, in effect, hurt the reservoirs as far as other recovery is concerned. Now that doesn't mean that we can't open them wide open and produce a lot more oil than that."[2] Thus there are three levels of output: unrestricted production, amounting in this case to "a lot more" than 3,000,000 b/d; a lower level of 3,000,000 b/d, which would not "hurt the reservoirs" but would weaken the price; and an even lower (actual) level of 2,000,000 b/d, which would neither hurt the reservoirs nor weaken the price.

Concern over physical waste traces back to the turn of the century, while interest in preventing "unduly depressed prices" did not become widespread until the Great Depression. At the present time, no state is limiting production for the explicit purpose of maintaining the price; but the method employed in the nation's largest producing state not only depleted the reservoirs at an unduly rapid rate but left behind a maze of legal rights that tends to block the adoption of advanced methods of increasing the recoverable supply.

THE ORIGINS OF THE CONSERVATION MOVEMENT

As an example of the physical waste of uncontrolled production, the Department of Interior in 1929 pointed to the ". . . record of two wells (on federal leases) in California which have already turned into the pipe lines nearly $5,000,000 worth of oil and gas but from which gas and gasoline vapor worth more than $10,000,000 have gone up into the air—a total loss to present and future citizens of that State."[3] Although there are other sources of waste, the most important in oil production is the loss of gas in the oil sands: "Dissolved in the oil, gas makes the oil flow more freely to the well and there forces it upward, and the longer the gas is retained in solution the larger is the recovery of oil. Waste of gas is therefore a double waste, and the impairment of the gas pressure in the oil sand by one owner may prevent his neighbors from recovering any of the oil beneath their land and himself securing more than a small part of the oil underlying his land."[4]

The central objective of conservationists therefore became to maintain the natural gas and hydrostatic pressures needed to ensure the maximum total recovery of oil over the productive life of an oil field. Legislation designed to accomplish this objective dates back to the last century: "In 1899, the Texas Legislature passed an act designed to stop the worst forms of waste as then understood. Water was to be cased off, abandoned wells were to be plugged, gas was not to be burned in flambeau lights, and gas from a gas well was not to be allowed to escape."[5] This statute was followed by later enactments in 1919 and 1929 which were specifically limited to the prevention of physical waste.

The need for such legislation was intensified by the two legal principles that have had a profound influence in shaping the domestic oil industry: the ownership of subsoil mineral rights by the owner of the surface land,[6] and the "rule of capture." The former led to a proliferation of owners, each of whom quite naturally tended to place his short-run gain over the long-run interest of resource conservation. Under the rule of capture, moreover, oil belongs to whoever extracts it, even though drained from another's property. As John Ise put it, "when the problem of legal title to oil deposits first came up, the courts decided that the oil was like 'wild animals' and subject to the rule of capture—that it belonged to the one who could get it out first. It was the application of this principle which brought the frenzied haste, and until recently [1940] the great waste of oil, capital and energy which have characterized the exploitation of most oil pools."[7] Because of the private ownership of subsoil mineral rights, oil fields in the United States have usually had multiple owners. And because of the rule of capture, each of those owners has had good reason to extract his share as quickly as possible—if for no other reason than to prevent it from being drained away by his neighbors. Alfred E. Kahn has drawn the analogy of placing an ice-cream soda with several straws before a group of small boys. In such a legal environment the state of the industry approached utter chaos:

> . . . oil operators were merrily going ahead with their traditional procedures of oil production, each drilling and producing as he pleased, trying to protect his own land against adverse drainage, and at the same time trying to drain oil and gas from his neighbors' lands, each operator relying on self-help to protect his property. Waste and violation of property rights went hand in hand. Reservoirs were ruined, with four-fifths and more of their oil unproduced; labor and steel were wasted on unnecessary and even harmful wells; oil was produced for which there was no market— untold millions of barrels running down the creeks and streams —or was lost in part when put in storage, often in earthen pits,

as the result of fire, leakage, and evaporation; gas was flared or vented by the billions and even trillions of cubic feet. The strong rode roughshod over the rights of his weaker neighbor.[8]

If anyone can be credited for bringing about an awareness at the highest levels of government of this appalling waste, it was Henry L. Doherty, architect and power behind the Cities Service empire. As a high government official during World War I, he had become aware of the savings achieved by "rationalization" in railroads and other fields. Although research into reservoir behavior was then in its infancy, he recognized that waste in oil would continue until rationalization was applied to entire fields. Later referred to as "unitization," his solution was the operation of each field as a unit under some centralized administrative control, with the various owners of the field's mineral rights receiving *pro rata* shares of its total income. The case for unitization has never been put more cogently than in this statement by the Federal Oil Conservation Board:

> Man may draw property lines on the surface, making a checkerboard for title searchers and lease lawyers to play on, but nature has fixed a boundary line around the underground deposit for geologists to discover and engineers to use in the development of the hidden resource. The unit-operation plan is a "back to nature" movement. Code of laws and judicial decisions relating to oil deposits have accorded to the surface checkerboard a sanctity quite beyond its deserts, while the facts of nature as now known have received little attention and have commanded less respect.
>
> Fences, walls, and other land lines serve effectively as property boundaries where the property is fixed in character and position, whether it is valuable as tillable soil or as a structural foundation. These same lines may be extended downward as vertical planes and serve no less acceptably to define property rights in the ores we mine. The essential part of the property-line is our faith in the continuing relation of the line to the fixed property. It serves best of all when by triangulation we tie our private land corners to the geodetic constants; then the hand of man cannot erase beyond recovery the boundaries of our estate. Quite different, however, is the relation of any land lines to property rights in the winds that blow and the waters that flow across these man-marked boundaries. The mobile and fugitive nature of air and water makes our rights to their possession and use related to the rights of our neighbors, so that some coordination is required, lest the use by one interfere with that by others.
>
> Self-regulation in handling of an oil pool means both efficiency in development and operation and the determination of equities among the owners, and this can best be accomplished by unit

operation. By this plan only can each and every owner secure full economic benefits. By this plan only can the public be assured of the largest possible supply of oil and gas from a particular field, won from the ground at lowest cost, and over a period measured by market demand rather than fixed by individualistic greed.[9]

In late 1924, Doherty urged President Coolidge to introduce legislation for compulsory unitization, which, he contended, would double or triple the recovery of oil. Partly in response, the President in December 1924 created the Federal Oil Conservation Board (composed of the Secretaries of Interior, War, Navy, and Commerce). But he stopped short of proposing unitization, while the Board contented itself, first, with issuing reports and later with operating as one of the arms of the major oil companies in government.[10]

THE CHANGING ATTITUDE OF THE MAJORS

Until the late 1920's, the attitude of the majors toward conservation ranged from indifference to outright hostility. Although a director of the American Petroleum Institute, Doherty was refused permission to submit his ideas to its Board of Directors in 1923, in 1924, and again in 1925. In 1926 Charles Evans Hughes, then counsel for the API and later Chief Justice of the Supreme Court, vigorously attacked the conservation movement, contending that mineral extraction was not "commerce" and that no conservation restraint could be imposed by a majority on a minority. By equating "conservation" with "economical use" he defined the problem away, his only recommendation being the now familiar one that agreements to curtail production be exempted from the antitrust laws.[11]

But this intransigence was soon to give way to a recognition that the cause of conservation could be put to the use of market stabilization. During the late twenties, industry leaders were beginning to realize that the nature of the problem was radically altering. Fears bred during World War I that the country was "running out of oil" were giving way to concern with overproduction. Production in this country was in the process of expanding from 355.9 million barrels in 1918 to 732.4 million in 1923 and to 1,007.3 million in 1929. Concerned over the "too rapid development" of oil fields, the American Petroleum Institute in early 1928 appointed a Committee on World Production and Consumption of Petroleum and Its Products, which on March 15, 1929, recommended a simple and drastic plan to restrict production: "The Committee recommended that 1928 production of crude oil in the United States should be considered as peak requirements for 1929 *and subsequent years*, proposing in effect that average production in future years be held to the *1928 level*."[12] This recommendation for the United States, it should be noted, was virtually identical to the first principle of the Achnacarry "As Is" Agreement adopted on September 17, 1928, by Exxon, Shell, and British Petroleum.

The API's committee proposal was formally approved by the full Institute on March 29, 1929, and then accepted and put forward by the Federal Oil Conservation Board, only to be jettisoned by the Attorney-General. Congress, he said, "had not given the Board any power to grant to any persons immunity from the antitrust laws, and the Board had 'no authority to approve any action which is contrary to an Act of Congress or to the antitrust laws of any State.' "[13] In notifying the American Petroleum Institute of the Attorney-General's decision, Chairman Wilbur of the Oil Conservation Board on April 8, 1929, proposed a more roundabout approach to accomplish the same objective. He suggested discussions "with the State authorities of the three or four principal oil-producing states, particularly to learn if it is not possible for them to enter upon an interstate compact under the provision of the Constitution authorizing such compacts to which the Federal Government, through Congressional action, would be a party."[14]

In an ensuing report the Board developed this ingenious approach in greater detail, describing with unusual candor the real reasons behind it, namely that foreign producers could not be expected to observe international agreements unless U.S. production was also curtailed: "If international markets are to be *fairly allocated* and our foreign markets protected, the allocation requires reciprocal *agreements on international production quotas*." But the report went on to point out that the division of powers between the federal government and the states posed a problem: "Under our Constitutional system the consummation of such agreements is a federal prerogative, but the enforcement of them is the State's, whose police power is essential to such enforcement." The solution lay in the establishment of a new institution: "An interstate compact would enable the states, through their interstate body, to assist the federal representatives in negotiating agreements which the compacting states could enforce as their municipal laws."[15]

In the eyes of the Board the need was for ways and means, first of determining the magnitude of total demand, then of dividing up the needed production among the states, and finally, of allocating allowed production ("allowables") to each state's individual producers. Armed with forecasts of demand, and taking into account exports, imports, and stocks on hand, a governmental body[16] (which turned out to be the Interstate Compact Commission) could certify to member states "the respective State production quotas." Each state was then to make its quota effective; but each state must necessarily be free to do so by such legal machinery as it saw fit, and solely under its own laws.

THE RELATIONSHIP TO THE "AS IS" AGREEMENT

Before World War II, Rumania was Europe's principal oil-producing country. Made up of both the international majors and independent producers, the latter were a constant thorn in the side of the majors.[17] In 1929, efforts were made to bring the Rumanian operation into line with the principles of the Achnacarry or "As Is" Agreement reached a year earlier by Exxon, Shell, and British Petroleum. Early in December of that year it was announced that practically all the Rumanian operators had signed an agreement to limit production and fix prices. In less than a year this settlement collapsed, owing in good part to the Rumanians' insistence on protection from competitive inroads by American independents. After prolonged negotiations a new agreement was entered into in 1932, which the Rumanian independents signed only on the condition that they be given a larger production quota than would have been allowed on the basis of their 1928 output (the base year of the "As Is" Agreement).[18] A key provision gave the Rumanians the right to withdraw if U.S. production was not limited to 2 million barrels daily. But with the discovery of the East Texas field, such a limitation proved impossible. With independent American producers flooding the market, the majors retaliated by posting prices as low as 10 cents per barrel for the East Texas field and 30 cents per barrel for export from Gulf ports. The purpose of these extreme price cuts was described at the time by *The Petroleum Times* of London:

> Disturbing news from East Texas where the increase in production alone in the past few days is many times greater than the total output in Rumania, and this formidable increase in production has been met by the international group posting crude prices down to 10 cents per barrel *in order to kill the efforts of the independents.*[19]

The reaction of the Rumanians was predictable: "The disgusted Rumanian Association of Petroleum Industrialists thereupon unanimously agreed not to follow the restrictions on output imposed by the Paris agreement."[20] Shipping a few cargoes as far as Canada and Australia, the Rumanians increased their exports in the following year by 20 percent: ". . . the existence of a fringe of uncontrolled producers proved to be just as troublesome in the early thirties to the new strategy of setting up local agreements as it had been to the previous effort to establish a comprehensive cartel."[21] There was, however, one important difference between the Achnacarry Agreement and the recommendations of the American Petroleum Institute:

> . . . the conservation recommendation for the United States would permit no increased production over that of 1928, whereas the Achnacarry Agreement contemplated increases in production to cover increased world consumption. If United States production could be held rigidly to the 1928 level there would of course be no "surplus" production available to trouble the cartel. Thus the proposed American conservation control plan would have had the effect of plugging the loophole which, for legal reasons, had been left in the cartel agreement by the deliberate exclusion of the domestic market of the United States and imports into the United States.[22]

Commenting in 1946 on the connection between what the industry increasingly referred to as the "conservation" program in the United States and the cartel's efforts to stabilize world production and prices, Paul H. Frankel observed, "There can be little doubt that the American counterparts of this international set-up were 'conservation' and 'proration' as we knew them in the thirties. . . . What mattered most, apart from the aspect of technology, where sound argument seemed to support it, was the fact that only with a certain degree of production control could the United States be fitted into the world-wide structure of the oil industry. Conservation was the missing link which had to be forged."[23]

THE CONTROL OF DOMESTIC PRODUCTION

By the mid-thirties a complex mechanism of limiting production to market demand, closely modeled after the Federal Oil Conservation Board's blueprint, had been constructed and put into operation. It is a tribute to the oil industry's bipartisan way of doing things that the recommendations were originated during the administration of one political party and implemented during the administration of the other.

MARKET DEMAND PRORATIONING. No matter what its nature, any government effort to bring output down to "market demand" hinged upon acceptance by the State of Texas. In the light of later history, it is surprising to find that initially the Texas legislature was not only uncooperative but actually hostile: "The mere mention of stability or stabilization or of any effect on prices was sufficient to arouse the suspicion that the waste-preventing conservational features of the scheme were mere window-dressing, camouflage to hide the real objectives of the regulatory measures—stable, preferably higher prices."[24] The sentiment was so strong as to find expression in state statutes, restricting the authority of the state agency which performed the function of limiting oil production, the Texas Railroad Commission. When the Conservation Act of 1919 was amended in 1929, a specific proviso was inserted to the effect that prohibitable waste "shall not be construed to mean economic waste." And on August 12, 1931, the legislature in what became known as the "Anti-Market Demand Act" not only annulled all outstanding orders of the Texas Railroad Commission but prohibited the issuance of new orders without formal notice and hearings.[25]

Resistance to market demand prorationing, however, was overwhelmed by the way in which the majors exploited the vast flood of oil coming from the newly discovered East Texas field. The volume from this field, which quickly rose to about 1 million barrels a day or about one-third of the national requirements, was so "tremendous that it could singlehandedly defeat all attempts at regulation made elsewhere."[26] Coming at a time of worsening economic activity, this huge increment to supply had the inevitable effect of further depressing oil prices. Among other things it frustrated all efforts to implement the Achnacarry Agreement, since the Rumanian producers, angered by cut-rate sales of Texas crude in world markets, ended their cooperation with the cartel. In Texas the economic distress resulting from the natural play of economic forces was severely aggravated, as the majors adroitly used the occasion to force the acceptance of market demand prorationing. The circumstances were described by Karl Crowley as follows:

> In order to restrict production the major companies first prevailed upon the then Governor of Texas to proclaim martial law in the East Texas oil field. Officers of major companies were likewise officers of the National Guard in control over the oil field. Federal courts held that the Governor was without authority to do this. The major companies began building pipe lines from the field to tidewater, and independent refineries began building in the field. Oil was selling then in the field at 50 cents a barrel, but on April 24, 1933, the majors dropped the posted price to ten cents a barrel as the first move to enlist the aid of independents themselves in securing the drastic proration laws Texas now has.
>
> The majors said in effect, "Cut production in East Texas to

what we think it ought to be and we will pay you $1.00 a barrel for oil. If you do not, we will ruin you with low prices."

Using the club of ruinous prices, the integrated companies went before the Texas Legislature and demanded that they be given the right to prorate oil according to their demands. As a club to enlist the support of the Railroad Commission, which has jurisdiction to regulate oil production, they even had introduced a bill which passed the House to create a new Commission to administer oil. The Austin *Dispatch* in an editorial said:

"There is only one reason for such a measure; to oust the regulators who fail to do the major oil companies' bidding and to put in others who will. East Texas is one of the few oil fields where the landowner, wildcatter and true independent got a handhold and the octopus means to break that hold by whatever means are found necessary."

The means were found. The means were the ruinous prices paid for oil by the majors in the East Texas field. They determined to speak their piece with prices and sandbag the Legislature into passing their so-called conservation bills. . . .

The rapid price changes posted in the East Texas field almost tell a story of their own. The first posted price was 68 cents per barrel which was from August to November 1st, 1931. When the fight came on for the enactment of the proration laws in December, 1932, the price was from 75 cents to 98 cents a barrel. While the major integrated companies had the State Capitol at Austin full of lobbyists, they began to put on the pressure through the price squeeze. On January 18th, the 75–98 cent price was cut to 25, then to the ridiculous price of ten cents, and it was not until September 29, 1933 that the price ever again reached $1.00 a barrel. During this time the major companies not only got enacted the proration law, but they bought tens of millions of barrels of oil at prices ranging from ten cents to 50 cents a barrel.[27]

On November 12, 1932, the Texas State Legislature passed what became known as the Market Demand Act. Not only did the new law omit the earlier prohibitions against considering economic waste or reasonable market demand; it explicitly included production in excess of market demand in the definition of "prohibitable waste." Restricting production to maintain price had been inserted under the protective blanket of "conservation." Protests against the co-mingling of the two, such as the objection voiced by Senator Joe L. Hill of the state legislature, were unavailing: "It is the rankest hypocrisy for a man to stand on this floor and say that the purpose of proration is anything other than price-fixing. I sit here in utter amazement and see men get up and blandly talk about market demand as an abstract proposition, and contending that it has got no relation to price-fixing."[28] With a brake thus attached to the pivotal Texas "balance wheel," work could proceed in fashioning the other components of the domestic control mechanism, as originally designed by the Federal Oil Conservation Board.

FORECASTS OF DEMAND. What set the control mechanism in operation have been monthly forecasts of demand issued by the Bureau of Mines. Although the organic act establishing the Bureau contains no explicit legal authorization for the preparation of forecasts, the program was put into effect on March 10, 1930, by Secretary of the Interior Ray Lyman Wilbur, at the request of the American Petroleum Institute. Since that time, the Bureau has issued each month a forecast of the total quantity of domestic crude oil which, when added to expected imports, will supply the quantity of crude oil and petroleum products estimated to be needed during the ensuing month.

During the Hearings of the Temporary National Economic Committee, these forecasts were described in considerable detail by Dr. Joseph E. Pogue, then vice-president of the Chase National Bank, who in his previous capacity as director of the Bureau of Mines "drew up the first estimates of market demand."[29] Fred E. Berquist, special assistant to the Attorney-General, asked whether the making of a demand forecast did not necessarily assume some level of price. After pointing out that demand for gasoline is "very inelastic," Pogue replied, "In other words this quota system involves estimating demand a month ahead and then the estimators of demand *never consider price* because the price fluctuations that take place within that period are so mild that we don't know the effect they have on demand, if indeed they have any effect, so as a practical matter that doesn't enter in."[30] To this, Berquist observed that the fluctuations are mild precisely "because a pretty good job was being made of keeping back the supply, so that your demand was adequate to keep the price at that level."[31] When Dr. Pogue objected that a hypothetical price of $1.50 a gallon was an "unnatural" assumption, Hugh B. Cox of the Department of Justice raised a question of considerable import today: Just how inelastic is the demand for gasoline when there occurs a change in price well beyond the range of past experience? Referring to the supply forecast, Dr. Pogue responded, "I have made up hundreds of those myself and I don't know what runs through anybody else's mind, but I know I wouldn't waste any time on thinking about a price if I were drawing the thing up."[32]

THE INTERSTATE OIL AND GAS COMPACT COMMISSION. Since oil is produced in some thirty states, the Oil Conservation Board had recommended that an "interstate compact" be established, which would certify to the oil-producing states "the respective state production quotas." In setting up such a compact the initiative was taken by Ernest W. Marland, a prominent oil man and newly elected governor of Oklahoma, who in late 1934 and early 1935 called a series of meetings of oil-state governors. At these meetings a sharp conflict developed between Marland and Governor Allred of Texas, with the latter's representative denouncing ". . . monopoly and regimentation and unalterably opposing anything that suggested price fixing, even market demand restriction unless proved necessary to prevent physical waste." In contrast, Marland ". . . hoped to set up an organization that would allocate the Bureau of Mines estimates of market demand to the different oil-producing states with power to enforce production in accordance with this quota allocation."[33] Under the resulting compromise, signed into law by President Roosevelt on August 27, 1935, an Interstate Compact to Conserve Oil and Gas was established and thereafter has been regularly renewed by the Congress, usually without debate. Though lacking power to enforce its quotas, it disseminates information, holds meetings and discussions, and in other informal ways "promotes harmony among heterogeneous elements, and creates a favorable environment for understanding and collaboration."[34] Its success is attested by the rare occasion when domestic oil has been produced in sufficient quantity to bring about a price reduction.

THE CONNALLY "HOT OIL" ACT. Implicit in the blueprint for control was of course the assumption that the amount of oil actually produced in a given state would not be in excess of its quota. In point of fact, actual output was frequently well in excess of its permissible quantity. For example, the East Texas field in May 1933 was producing nearly a million barrels of oil a day, of which at least 150,000 barrels were produced in excess of the "allowable" set for this field.[35] The problem stemmed from the absence of state jurisdiction over oil moving in interstate commerce. As described by Russell Brown, general counsel of the Independent Petroleum Association of America: ". . . after most of the States had adopted some form of conservation law, we found that their ability to enforce these laws was somewhat interfered with, because under our interstate commerce laws the transportation systems are required to take commodities presented to them, and a man might drill into a field in the State of Texas, for example, and produce more than the State allowed. The State laws would probably not permit that to move into intrastate commerce, but there was no power to prevent it from moving in interstate commerce."[36] Once again, the powers of the federal government were used to meet the problem. On February 22, 1935, the Connally Act (named after Senator Tom Connally of Texas) became law, prohibiting shipments in interstate commerce of oil produced in excess of state laws, variously referred to as "hot" or "contraband oil."

With the plugging of the "hot oil" loophole, all the components of the domestic control mechanism were now in place and functioning. Reflecting admiration for its efficiency though not its purposes, a report of the Senate Small Business Committee stated:

> There is a mechanism controlling the production of crude oil to market demand (or below) that operates as smoothly and effectively as the finest watch. During the year and a half the committee has been investigating the oil industry, there never has been a real overall shortage of petroleum. Price increases on crude oil have been frequent and substantial, going from $1.25 per barrel at the end of 1945 to $2.65 per barrel in the spring of 1947, with several companies posting $3 per barrel as this report is written. At the time the consumers were feeling the greatest pinch in January and February, 1947, there were 220,000,000 barrels of crude oil in storage, mainly controlled by the larger units, which could have been distributed among independent refiners who were running under capacity. But the controlled economy existing in the oil industry needs an absolute balance of supply and demand because it does not contemplate drawing on stocks. When the Bureau of Mines through their monthly forecast of demand underestimated the demand by close to 2 percent for each of the years 1946 and 1947, the spot shortages followed as night the day. The mechanism was wound too tight. Independent refiners could not take more oil out of their own wells because of state proration laws, and the integrated companies would not allow them to take their crude oil except by a processing or tied-in sales agreement. Those cut off of supply by independent refiners or by integrated units desiring to favor one customer over another were suffering, and in turn their consumer accounts were without oil. A truly competitive system based only on real conservation practices, could not possibly have held the flow of oil so close to market demand.
>
> The oil-control policies in effect in the United States consist of a series of State and Federal statutes, recommendations of committees made up of integrated-oil-company economists and recommendations as to market demand made by the Bureau of Mines of the Department of the Interior. No single item is in itself controlling; taken together they form a perfect pattern of monopolistic control over oil production and the distribution thereof among refiners and distributors, and ultimately the price paid by the public.[37]

THE EFFECTS OF PRORATIONING

The pivotal component of the control mechanism, market demand prorationing, is doubly objectionable in that it inflates both prices and costs. Prices are inflated by restricting production to (or below) demand; costs are inflated by reducing the output of the more efficient, low-cost wells and keeping in operation inefficient, high-cost wells. Alfred E. Kahn illustrated the direct effect on price by recounting the actions of the Texas Railroad Commission during the late fifties and early sixties: the number of days of permitted production, which had reached 261 in 1952, "during the mild recession year of 1954 . . . were cut to only 194 days; by 1958, the first full year after the reopening of the Suez Canal, they were down to 122, and in 1962, the low point, production was permitted only 97 days in the entire year. That was 8 days a month. . . ."

It is, of course, difficult to measure the extent to which costs have been inflated by the artificial restrictions of prorationing. But the restraints have obviously fallen with particular severity on the large-volume, low-cost wells which in a free market would have enjoyed the highest rates of operation, since the marginal "stripper" wells (i.e., those producing less than ten barrels a day) have been completely exempt from prorationing. In Kahn's words: "The cutting back of output of the lower cost wells, imposing on them the vastly disproportionate burden of excess capacity, is the way in which price is sustained at its noncompetitive level and costs are equated—upward— to that cartel-sustained price."[38]

That efficient producers have been forced to operate far below capacity can be illustrated by the performance of low-cost wells between May and August 1967. This was the period of the second Suez crisis, when to achieve greater domestic supplies, U.S. wells were partially released from the restraints of market demand prorationing. From records of the Department of Interior offices in Louisiana, E. Wayles Browne selected five wells in each of six leases which appeared to be typical of the more efficient offshore producers.[39] It was found that in only four months, these thirty wells increased their average production by more than two-thirds. The average increases among the six leases ranged from a low of just over 50 percent to a high of nearly 100 percent.

The effectiveness of prorationing can best be seen during periods of declining economic activity. Had output not been effectively curtailed, more oil would have been produced than the market could absorb, thereby resulting in a lower price. That prorationing was successful in preventing such a development during the recessions of both 1953–54 and 1957–58 is apparent from Chart 7-1.

During 1953, the price was raised on two occasions: 2.5 percent between January and February and 8.4 percent between May and June. Thereafter, it remained almost completely stable through the end of 1954. In the face of the worsening recession, the maintenance of price at this higher level was made possible by reductions in output. Between September and October 1953, production was reduced 4.5 percent. In the early months of 1954, it rose slightly above the peak of the preceding year, only to fall again in the late spring and summer; by September it was 7.7 percent below the April level. Actions by state proration authorities had brought about the decline in output: the Texas Railroad Commission reduced the number of days which wells subject to its jurisdiction were permitted to operate from 261 in 1952 to 194 days in 1954, or slightly more than half the days of the year.[40]

During the more severe recession of 1957–58, there was only one increase in price, and the curtailments in output were more pronounced. Again a price advance took place at the beginning of the period, the price rising 6.7 percent between January and February 1957. And again, the subsequent pattern was one of almost complete price stability through the end of the recession. Beginning in the spring of 1957, production was steadily reduced. Further curtailments were made in early 1958. By May, output was 11.6 percent below and price 6.5 percent above their levels of January 1957. Once more curtailments ordered by state proration authorities bore the major responsibility, the Texas Railroad Commission having permitted wells subject to prorationing to operate for only 122 days—down to one-third the days of the year.

The changes in price and production during the recession of 1970–71 followed a somewhat different sequence. During the latter half of 1970, the general rate of economic activity was declining; but paradoxically oil production was steadily rising. In December, which marked the bottom of the recession, the price was raised 8 percent. Although economic conditions began to improve in 1971, the general increase in demand was apparently not sufficient to support both price and production at the higher levels reached at the end of 1970. Accordingly, production was slowly but progressively reduced throughout most of 1971, with the result that by October output was 8.3 percent below the end of the previous year. This curtailment in supply proved adequate to validate the earlier price increase, as the price remained stable for the remainder of the year.

CHART 7-1

Trends of Domestic Crude Oil Prices and Production (Three Recessions)

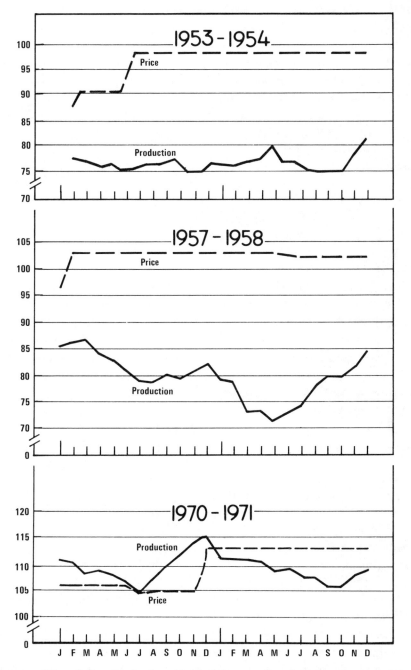

Sources: Oil and Gas Production, Federal Reserve Board; Price, Bureau of Labor Statistics.

PRORATIONING AND ADVANCED
RECOVERY METHODS

Because it has served as an alternative to unitization, prorationing has had the effect of impeding the adoption of advanced recovery methods. Unitization, in Zimmerman's words, "is an irreducible *sine qua non* for secondary recovery."[41] Of twenty-eight oil-producing states, only Texas and New Mexico have no compulsory unitization statutes. To the natural ebb and flow of oil within a reservoir, modern recovery methods necessarily add further mobility, destroying all vestiges of relationships between ownership of surface acreage and rights to subsoil minerals. Essentially 100 percent of the royalty and working-interest owners have to agree on the need for the project and on their share of the unit in order to bring a field under unification. The chairman of the Texas Railroad Commission, William J. Murray, Jr., illustrated the difficulties of securing unification on a voluntary basis by citing the case of the Scurry Reef field of West Texas. Through secondary recovery methods the ultimate recovery from a portion of this one field could have been increased from 457 million to 1,180 million barrels, or by nearly *three-quarters of a billion barrels*. Yet within the area there were 70 operators with 363 working interests and over 3,000 separate royalty owners. As Murray put it: "The difficulty of getting all of these operators, working interests, and royalty owners to agree on a basis of participation in the proceeds from the unit should be apparent."[42] The problem extends even to small fields. On May 24, 1971, a petroleum geologist, Stephen W. Schneider, wrote to Texas legislators: "A few years back along with partners we found a nice small oil field in the two-to-three million barrel class. An evaluation by one of the best petroleum engineering firms in the United States said that a secondary recovery program would probably double the oil to be taken from this reservoir. . . . I jumped into the project of getting this field unitized. I worked at it for over two years . . . a unitization plan was worked out—except that one large independent with less than 3% interest in the proposed unit would not go along. The whole thing went down the tube . . . two to three million barrels will never come out of the ground."

In some cases, the refusal to cooperate is due to lack of knowledge or downright intransigence. In others, there exists at least some basis in self-interest. As one industry observer put it, "As a field is depleted it is usually the outlying wells that dry up first while those in the center of the reservoir usually produce over a much longer period. The fortunate owners of the producing wells frequently are unwilling to share with the owners of wells less fortunately situated." Moreover, obstructionism often has a nuisance value. According to an article in *Oil Daily*, "Unfortunately, there are always a few in any large group who will realize the nuisance value of holding out, particularly if their interest is small and they do not have much to lose. By holding out, they can be important and exact a high toll for their concurrence."[43] As a result of the near-impossibility of securing unanimity, only 10 percent of the Texas fields have been brought under unitization, while the number of secondary recovery units formed fell from over sixty in 1970 to less than a third that number in 1971: "Unification of the easy fields has been done. Most of those that remain to be unitized represent such an insurmountable problem under existing rules that there is not enough incentive to try."[44]

In 1972, a vigorous drive was launched in Texas to secure enactment of a compulsory unitization measure. Under the proposed bill, unitization proposals would be submitted to the Texas Railroad Commission, which would determine whether they would result in the recovery of additional oil and gas. Although some states require lesser proportions, the Texas bill would require approval by 75 percent of the field's ownership. Owners would share equitably in the oil and gas yielded by the field, while costs would be borne by the operators with no expense to the royalty owners. Supported by major oil companies, by the Texas Independent Producers and Royalty Owners Association, the governor, the Texas press, and leading liberal and conservative legislators, the bill (H.B. No. 311) was passed in 1973 by the House of Representatives without any open opposition, but inexplicably died in the Senate, its proponents losing in a vote simply to bring it up on the Senate floor.

THE ORIGINS OF THE IMPORT QUOTA*

As early as 1932, the Federal Oil Conservation Board had recognized that restrictions on imports would inevitably be an essential component of any effective control mechanism: "Assuming that a scientific forecast has been made of the quantity needed, there are two general methods of restricting imports to that figure—a flexible tariff and proration. The Federal statutes which authorize the compact or ratify it should therefore implement the compact by one method or the other."[45] But with the discovery of new fields in the early 1930's, the United

---

* In preparing this section, considerable use has been made of "A History of Federal Cooperation with the Petroleum Industry," by Walter S. Measday (*Hearings on Governmental Intervention*, Pt. 1, pp. 578–599).

States soon led the world in low-cost production, exporting more than it imported. The issue of import controls thus remained moot for over two decades.

In the early 1950's, however, the availability of low-cost resources abroad combined with restricted production at home constituted a powerful incentive for the "lesser majors" and larger independents to seek supplies outside the United States. Once having made discoveries, the most attractive market was of course the United States, where prices were artificially enhanced by the very restraints that had impelled the companies to look abroad in the first place. In the words of Alfred E. Kahn:

> But artificial restrictions on competition, once imposed, almost always have a tendency to intensify and to spread. We already have seen how the production controls had to be drawn tighter and tighter until around 1963. Sooner or later controls would have to be extended to imports as well. Inflated domestic prices and costs of production greatly increased the incentive of American companies to look abroad—American-owned production abroad soared, and American refiners brought in increasing quantities of foreign oil. So while the domestic price was being maintained by intensified production cutbacks in 1954, imports increased sharply and so-called voluntary controls were instituted. When the same thing happened at the higher price level of 1957–58, while prices abroad were dropping under the impact of growing supplies in weakening hands, the pretense of voluntary controls had finally to be dropped, and mandatory controls instituted.[46]

By the mid-fifties, oil from abroad had overcome the transportation costs plus the modest import duty of 10 cents a barrel and was underselling U.S. oil not only on the Eastern seaboard but as far inland as western Pennsylvania. Compared to their 1953–56 average, the rates of return for the leading sellers in the Eastern part of the country had by 1957 begun to fall; and by 1958, they had dropped 45 percent in the case of Mobil and Shell, 43 percent for Exxon, and 33 percent for ARCO. Inasmuch as 1958 was a recession year, not all of this deterioration can be attributed to the inroads of foreign imports, but the change in the general rate of business activity would not explain the fact that these profit rates remained relatively depressed during the recovery year of 1959. Moreover, the decline in profit rates was far more severe during 1957–58 than in other postwar recessions.[47] Once again the vulnerability of oil prices to even a relatively small amount of uncontrolled supply had been demonstrated, and once again the stage had been set for intervention by government to stabilize the market.

THE VOLUNTARY PROGRAM

Confronted with any troublesome economic problem, the standard operating procedure for government is first to invoke cooperation through exhortation; when this fails, a program of "voluntary" measures is announced, which, because of the customary intransigence of some parties, in turn gives way to mandatory controls. The sequence is invariably the same, regardless of whether the objective is the protection of the public interest or, as in this case, its exploitation.

In this case, the hortatory stage took the form of pleas by Dr. Arthur Fleming, director of the Office of Civilian Defense Mobilization, that imports be cut back. But it took more than "hold-the-line" entreaties to persuade the importing firms to give up the bonanza profits available in the U.S. market. The next step was a formal but still voluntary program instituted on July 1, 1957. Existing importers "voluntarily" agreed to accept quotas established by the Oil Import Administration, while newcomers were directed to apply six months in advance for permission to bring in foreign crude. What the penalty would be for non-compliance was never very clear. It was hinted that government purchasing agencies might boycott uncooperative firms, but such threats were never carried out. Actuallly, the imports of crude oil did stop rising, but the imports of petroleum products continued to increase as importers merely changed the nature of the product that was brought in. The voluntary program contained no restrictions relating either to unfinished (semi-processed) oils or to finished products. Importers were quick to take advantage of this loophole, and by mid-1958 imports of unfinished oils had risen more than a hundredfold over the first half of 1957, while imports of gasoline and other finished products had increased by 143 percent. The addition of unfinished oils to crude raised imports in 1958 from slightly over 700,000 to just under 900,000 barrels a day.

THE MANDATORY PROGRAM

With the inevitable collapse of the voluntary effort, a mandatory program was instituted on March 11, 1959, which was to remain in effect for fourteen years; its result was to raise the price to American buyers and seriously deplete the U.S. reserves.

Ironically enough, the legislative basis for the mandatory quota was an amendment tacked onto a bill designed to expand trade—the Trade Agreements Act of 1958. This is one of the few legislative enactments for which there are available not only the formal legislative history—

consisting of executive reports, recommendations, congressional hearings, reports, and floor debates—but also a detailed and responsible "behind-the-scenes" account of what actually took place. What makes this episode even more remarkable is the lack of substance of the former and the lack of attention accorded the latter.

In reviewing the documents making up its official legislative history, the Cabinet Task Force on Oil Import Control set up in 1969 by President Nixon held that the amendment's purpose of protecting "national security" had two "senses": "(a) the protection of military and essential civilian demand against reasonably possible foreign supply interruptions that could not be overcome by feasible replacement steps in an emergency; and (b) the prevention of damage to domestic industry from excessive imports that would so weaken the national economy as to impair the national security."[48] In imputing such clarity of purpose the Task Force's interpretation can only be regarded as charitable, since a reading of the history itself reveals little as to purpose other than a desire to stop imports on the grounds that they were injuring "national security." Referring to the basic issues involved, Professor M. A. Adelman testified: "They have never been seriously discussed and debated (least of all by the Cabinet Committees of the 1950's)."[49] This remark provoked Senator Hruska into listing the documents that make up the legislative history:

SEN. HRUSKA: Are all of these printed pages and these laws and all of these actions subjects that have never been seriously discussed and debated?

DR. ADELMAN: I think I would have to say that I have most of those hearings in my office and that is one reason why I have a space problem there, and that I looked at them before I wrote that sentence, Senator. Sometimes the truth is inadvertently painful but I think I have to stand on that, that all of these voluminous writings and hearings were concerned with the preservation of one or another interest, special interests usually. . . .

SEN. HRUSKA: Well, the Act of 1954 as amended by the Extension Act of 1955 was the basis for the President's mandatory oil import program.

DR. ADELMAN: Yes, sir.

SEN. HRUSKA: And the thrust of those acts is national security.

DR. ADELMAN: Those are the words.

SEN. HRUSKA: Not individual investments, not individual industries, not even the economics of the thing. The thrust was national security.

Now, do you mean to tell me that all of this legislation and all of these things taken on behalf of preserving our national security is not a serious discussion and debate and effort?

DR. ADELMAN: The tone is a serious one, Senator, but the substance, I am afraid, was frivolous.

SEN. HRUSKA: Was what?

DR. ADELMAN: Frivolous, light-minded, not concerned with the basic facts, and I must say that reading—and I have spent many more hours than I like to recollect reading them—was like hearing the same scratchy record played over and over again.[50]

It is difficult to believe that the constant repetition of the words "national security" would have been enough, in itself, to bring about such a far-reaching change in national policy, even to benefit a special interest as powerful as the oil industry. That there was indeed something else to the matter was brought out in a brilliant journalistic exposé by Bernard Nossiter of the *Washington Post*.[51]

The central figure of the Nossiter story, Robert B. Anderson, had been Secretary of the Navy (a post which because of the Navy's large oil holdings has been often occupied by Texans), Assistant Secretary of Defense, and after a sojourn in private industry, President Eisenhower's Secretary of the Treasury. In the latter capacity he served as a member and leading figure of the Cabinet Committee that recommended the adoption of the mandatory quota. According to Nossiter, "Just before he became Treasury Secretary in 1957 and a central figure in policy-making to protect oil prices, Robert B. Anderson completed a deal with some oil men to pay him nearly $1 million. Of this amount $270,000 was scheduled to be paid during his term in office. His chances of receiving some $450,000 of the rest depended in part on the price of oil." Involved in the account are such well-known figures and enterprises as the legendary Texas oil men, Sid Richardson and Clint Murchison, Standard Oil of Indiana and the Rockefeller-owned International Basic Economy Corporation (IBEC). Excerpts from the story follow.

> The documents—leases, transfers, assignments, corporate charters, applications for drilling permits—tell a complex story in which mineral interests apparently passed through several hands and ultimately came back to Richardson's heir.
>
> The mineral rights Anderson received and sold before he took office are in two tracts in West Texas and three in Acadia Parish, La. The Texas rights were valued at 19 times those in Louisiana, and so it is the Texas documents that demand the most attention.
>
> Those on file at the Winkler County Courthouse and at the Texas Railroad Commission, the state's oil regulating board, were

recently compiled by a former district attorney from Monahans, Texas, A. Rado Archer. Anderson's office supplied three un-recorded agreements. Together, these papers describe the following chain.

In 1955, Stanolind Oil and Gas Co., the Indiana Standard subsidiary, held leases embracing two tracts in the west half of Section 22, Block B-11, Public School Lands, Winkler County.

On Aug. 19, papers supplied by Anderson's office show Stano-lind gave a farmout in the property's mineral rights to Frederick Jay Adams. He was a retired Gulf Oil executive, a friend of Ander-son and Richardson. He was to benefit only if he got a well drilled on the property.

Eleven days later, Adams dealt off about half of his farmout to a Richardson concern that agreed to do the drilling. That same day, Adams gave roughly the other half to Anderson. Less than two years later, Anderson was able to sell it for what he hoped would be $900,000. The papers indicate that Adams received about $40,000 for his part in the deal.

On Sept. 8, the Richardson company applied to the Texas Railroad Commission to drill the first well. It began on Sept. 21 and finished the drilling on March 8, 1956. The well was a good one: the initial test production was 447.15 barrels a day.

Now that oil was struck, brokers Adams and Anderson could begin to get paid. In oil parlance, their farmouts were converted into oil lease assignments. The assignment to Anderson is dated March 5, 1956. But it was not filed in the Winkler Courthouse until a full year later, March 14, 1957.

Anderson was nominated to be Treasury Secretary on May 29, 1957. Three weeks later, he sold his interest both in the Texas properties and the much less valuable Louisiana properties. The buyer was a new entrant on the scene, the Dalada Corp.

At birth, Dalada was called the Royal Gorge Co. and was incorporated in Nevada. One of the original directors was a son of Clint Murchison. Another of the Texas super-rich, Murchison Sr. was a crony and frequent partner of Richardson.

On May 16, 1957, Royal Gorge changed its name to Dalada, listed its capital stock at $6,000 and displayed as an officer an associate of still another Texas oil operator, Toddie Lee Wynne. Five days later, Dalada's capital was increased 160 times to $1 million. Four weeks later, it bought out Anderson.

The method of payment deserves special attention. Anderson was to receive $450,000 in six installments evidenced by promis-sory notes. A first payment of $50,000 was due on Jan. 15, 1958; the last of $90,000 on June 15, 1962.

Another $450,000 was to come out of what the wells produced. It is this contingent payment that gave Anderson his direct interest in oil prices during his tenure as Treasury Secretary. He had sold producing oil rights; how much he was paid hung on the revenues they produced.

But the story does not end here. Dalada was dissolved on Sept. 25, 1963. In its dying days, it sold out its interests—and its liability to Anderson—to Bass Brothers Enterprises, Inc., for $137,000. The president of Bass Brothers Enterprises is Perry R. Bass, the nephew and heir of the bachelor Sid W. Richardson. In brief, the oil interests had come full circle. They ended up with the heir of the man who drilled them.

Some help was afforded by the Rockefeller concern involved, the International Basic Economy Corporation or IBEC.

IBEC is closely held by the family and was started by Nelson Rockefeller, its first president, to promote development in poorer countries. The corporation is chartered to demonstrate the virtues of modern management and private enterprise by operating firms abroad, largely in Latin America. The companies are supposed to make profits but "social development" is the ruling motif.

IBEC's records show that in the fall of 1957, when Nelson Rockefeller was still president and Anderson the new Treasury chief, the company made a "commitment" to buy into Dalada. Dalada is the concern that bought out Anderson and owed him $900,000.

In 1958, IBEC paid $150,000 for a half interest in Dalada, 1,500 shares. IBEC's vice president for public affairs, Harvey L. Schwartz, said that his company's records indicate no dividends were ever paid by Dalada. This is presumably because of the liability to Anderson. When Dalada dissolved in 1963, its assets brought $137,000. The Rockefeller company received half this amount and thereby lost $81,250 on the deal.

During the few months that Anderson held the properties in his own name, before the sale to Dalada, he received about $15,000 in payments for his share of the oil revenues. It is this plus the $275,000 he got on the notes that accounts for the *Washington Post* estimate of a total Anderson take of $290,000 through 1963.

OPERATIONS. Once the mandatory program had been put into effect, an overall ceiling for crude and products was set at 9 percent of forecast demand (equivalent to about 10% of production). The "unfinished oils" loophole was closed by a provision that no company could import more than 10 percent of its quota in the form of unfinished oils. Within the overall limitation a separate, relatively small quantity was established for finished products, nearly half of which was reserved for the Department of Defense (and never utilized),

As can be seen in Chart 7-2, the new program brought about a drastic reduction in unauthorized imports from overseas. From the last half of 1959 through 1962, the permissible level of crude and unfinished overseas imports averaged 695,000 barrels a day, a reduction of nearly 200,000 or 22 percent from the 885,000 during the latter part of the voluntary program.

But the reduction in the flow of foreign oil was more apparent than real. The ceiling applied only to imports brought in over water; imports from Canada and Mexico were exempt on the grounds that, by contrast to waterborne shipments, overland movement posed no danger to national security. Again, importers were quick to take advantage of a loophole. Between the last halves of 1959 and 1962, exempt overland imports rose by nearly 100,000 barrels a day. Imports from Canada were coming in at the rate of 121,000 barrels. And an additional 30,000 of Mexican crude was entering through the bizarre "Brownsville turnaround" scheme, by which imports were brought via tanker from Mexico and unloaded into trucks at Brownsville, Texas. The trucks would then transport the oil under bond 10 miles south across the Mexican border, where they would immediately turn around and reenter the United States carrying what was now transformed into "exempt overland imports." Since the import ceiling was calculated on the basis of demand, the rapidly rising overland imports displaced an equivalent amount of domestic production. Paul T. Homan observed that the entry of the overland imports: "permitted an unregulated growth of total imports due to an increasing rate of imports from Canada. The 9 percent of demand formula also permitted the level of imports to grow more rapidly than domestic production because the base was inflated by a rapidly growing rate of residual fuel oil imports. The domestic industry strongly supported an alternative formula that would get rid of both these distasteful features."[52]

On January 1, 1963, the program was revised to meet these problems. As under the voluntary program, the import ceiling was to be calculated on the basis of domestic production (12.2%) rather than demand, thereby eliminating one source of inflationary bias. Another restrictive change was to bring the exempt overland imports within the ceiling. Although free of any licensing and company allocation requirements, these imports were now to be taken "off the top"; what remained after their deduction from the overall ceiling represented what could be imported from all other areas. How much could be imported as overland shipments was to be determined by negotiations between the U.S. and Canadian governments (the Mexican imports remaining unchanged). As can be seen in Chart 7-1, the result of these diplomatic negotiations was a steady and pronounced increase in au-

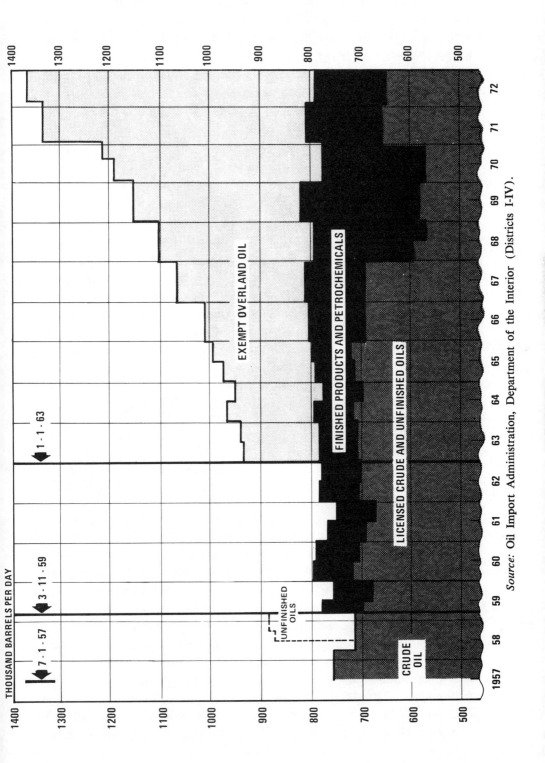

THOUSAND BARRELS PER DAY

7 - 1 - 57

3 - 11 - 59

1 - 1 - 63

EXEMPT OVERLAND OIL

FINISHED PRODUCTS AND PETROCHEMICALS

LICENSED CRUDE AND UNFINISHED OILS

UNFINISHED OILS

CRUDE OIL

Source: Oil Import Administration, Department of the Interior (Districts I-IV).

thorized imports from Canada, which rose from 120,000 barrels in 1963 to 280,000 in 1968.[53] While extremely helpful to U.S. refiners in the Northern tier of states served by pipelines from Canada, the growth in these imports preempted most of the increase permitted by applying 12.2 percent to an expanding volume of production.

EXEMPTIONS. The history of the quota's administration, however, is not merely one of a rising supply for the Canadian-served refineries and of stable supply for everyone else. The latter, as a result of special allotments for a favored few, actually declined. As can be seen in Chart 7-2, imports of licensed crude (other than exempt overland) fell from over 700,000 barrels per day in 1963 to roughly 580,000 in late 1968 and 1969. This came about as a consequence of special-interest regulations on behalf of three fortunate beneficiaries: Amerada Hess, Phillips, and Commonwealth Refining. From a new Virgin Islands refinery, Amerada Hess was permitted to bring into the United States 15,000 barrels per day of finished products. The rationale was the need for heating oil in the Northeast where the company was a major fuel oil dealer. From a new petrochemical plant in Puerto Rico (which in the process of making petrochemical products inevitably produced a sizable quantity of petroleum products), Phillips was permitted to import into the East Coast 24,500 barrels per day. Here the rationale was to help the struggling economy of Puerto Rico, referred to by Professor Adelman as "Secretary Udall's favorite charity." The same arrangement (with the same rationale) was extended to Commonwealth Oil's Puerto Rican petrochemical plant, which was allowed to bring in 10,000 barrels per day. Not only did these favored imports displace an equivalent amount of imports available to other refiners; the Department of Interior took pains to prevent them from disturbing domestic markets. Hence, when the original buyer of Commonwealth's gasoline, an independent West Coast marketer, began to use this supply to reduce prices both in its own service stations and to other retail operators, Commonwealth was permitted by Interior to shift its market from the West Coast to the East Coast, thereby eliminating a troublesome source of competition and saving Commonwealth $1 million a year in transportation charges.[54]

Another allocation with a somewhat more plausible rationale was for petrochemical feedstock. The slowing down in the growth of their principal raw material, natural gas, coupled with the enormous increase in demand for synthetic fibers, plastics, fiberglass, and other petrochemical products, had put the U.S. chemical companies in a bind. An alternative raw material was a petroleum product, naphtha, which cost a third more when purchased in the United States than when purchased abroad. Since chemicals led all U.S. manufacturing industries in foreign sales, anything that impeded the chemical industry's ability to compete in world markets had a serious adverse effect on the country's balance of trade. Moreover, there was nothing in Interior's regulations to prevent oil companies such as Exxon, Mobil, Shell, and others from using refinery crude allocations, based in part on the production of petrochemical feedstocks, for their own large and rapidly growing chemical operations. These considerations were forcibly brought home by an effective Washington lobbying organization, "Chemco," which was set up by the leading chemical firms, with the result that the Department of Interior set aside a special allocation of 72,000 barrels per day—with of course an equivalent deduction from the amount available for everyone else.

In defense of the quota's administration, much has been made of the fact that the allocations were on a graduated basis; the smaller the refinery, the larger the allocation. The program, it has been argued, helped to preserve independent business and promote competition. While valid as far as it goes, this overlooks the fact that as a result of these various exemptions and set-asides, the total to which an independent refiner could apply his graduated percentage was steadily reduced until it was little more than half the 12.2 percent ceiling. This can be seen in Table 7-1, which shows the allocations under the program for the second half of 1968.

The effect of the overland exemption was to reduce the supply available for others from 12.2 to 8.8 percent of domestic production. A further reduction to 7.6 percent resulted from the allocations for finished products. And the petrochemical set-aside plus a few minor adjustments reduced it further to 6.2 percent—or 51 percent of the overall ceiling. In other words, if an independent refiner was not located in the Northern tier served by Canadian oil, if he was not one of the favored few importers of finished products, if he was not a petrochemical producer, the amount of available imported crude that he would have to share with other refiners was only 6.2 instead of 12.2 percent of U.S. production. Moreover, nearly two-thirds of this went to the major oil companies.[55] In 1968, nineteen major oil companies received 65.1 percent of the allotments granted as refinery quotas (which include the so-called historical quotas). In addition to the refinery allocations, the majors received 74.7 percent of the quotas for finished products, 57.3 percent of the exempt overland shipments from Canada and Mexico, and even 34.3 percent of the petrochemical set-aside presumably allocated to assist the chemical companies. Of the total allocations of all types for imported oil, the major oil companies received 61.4 percent. The amount of low-cost foreign oil that inde-

TABLE 7-1

Allocations Under Oil Import Control Programs, Second Half of 1968
(1,000 barrels per day)

	Actual	Cumul.	Percent of U.S. Production
1968 production forecast	9,028.0		
Overall ceiling, 12.2 percent of production	1,101.4		12.2%
Less exempt overland oil:			
Canada	280.0		
Mexico	30.0		
Total	(310.0)	791.4	8.8
Less finished products:			
Historic importers	54.6		
OIAB set-aside	7.0		
Hess, Virgin Islands	15.0		
Phillips, P.R.	20.8		
Commonwealth, P.R.	10.0		
Total	(107.4)	684.0	7.6
Balance, non-exempt crude and unfinished	684.0		
Less 1967 carryover under 1968 ceiling (Allocated)	(35.7)	648.3	7.2
Less petrochemical	72.2		
Newcomer set-aside	6.8		
Total	(79.0)	569.3	6.3
Less Other	(9.1)	560.2	6.2
Balance, allocated as of July 9, 1968	560.2		

Source: Compiled from Walter S. Measday, *Hearings on Governmental Intervention,* Pt. 1, p. 596. Based on Department of Interior press release, July 9 and July 24, 1968.

pendent refiners could possibly use to disturb domestic markets had thus been reduced to *de minimis* proportions.

ALLOTMENTS TO INLAND REFINERS. There was one especially interesting difference between the voluntary and the mandatory programs. Under the voluntary program, allocations had been made only to those refiners who could actually utilize foreign crude (in terms of their geographical locations and refinery design). Under the mandatory program, allocations or "tickets" went to *all* companies with refining capacity, regardless of whether they could actually make use of foreign oil. The result was the emergence of a complicated exchange system between inland refiners who received tickets they could not use and coastal refiners who needed tickets they did not have. Presumably reflecting the difference in the laid-down price between foreign and domestic oil, the value of these tickets became stabilized at around $1.25 a barrel. Although it would have been far simpler for the coastal refiners to have purchased allotments from the inland refiners, this might have given rise to the criticism that private parties were being permitted to sell for profit something whose value was a creation of government. Inasmuch as the criticism was seldom raised against the "exchange" system, this transparent subterfuge apparently served its purpose.

An examination of the purchases of quotas by the largest "net buyers" and the sales by the nine largest "net sellers" in 1968 shows that the amounts involved were not inconsiderable.[56] The terms "net buyers" and "net sellers" refer respectively to those firms which, through exchange agreements, secured from other companies the largest quantity of import tickets and those that dispensed to others the largest quantity of tickets. The group of buyers (all with coastal refineries) purchased 136,485,000 barrels, which after deducting their sales of 37,751,000 barrels left them with net purchases of 98,734,000 barrels. At a cost of $1.25 per barrel, these purchases amounted to $123,417,-000, or 3 percent of their entire net income. The group of sellers (all with inland refineries) sold 41,901,000 barrels, which after deducting their purchases of 12,906,000 barrels left them with net sales of 28,994,000 barrels, with a value of $36,242,000 or 2.6 percent of their net income. If the 1968 experience is at all representative, the aggregate value of net purchases of allotments for the fourteen-year period must have been in excess of $1 billion, most of which was received by inland refiners who for fourteen years were the willing beneficiaries of this unique government welfare program.

THE EFFECTS OF THE QUOTA

Not only did the quota have the long-range effect of seriously depleting the nation's reserves; it imposed an immediate, substantial burden on consumers, estimated by Adelman to amount in the early sixties to $4 billion a year.* At the higher consumption figure for 1968 of 11.8 billion b/d, Adelman's method yielded a cost burden of $5.0 billion;

---

* From domestic consumption of crude oil, residual oil (not covered by the quota) was deducted (leaving 9.4 million barrels a day). From the difference between foreign and domestic oil prices (assumed to be the generally used cost of an import ticket of $1.25), there was deducted an allowance for pipeline costs to move the oil inland. A penetration of 450 miles, it was assumed, would give foreign crude half the domestic market. Multiplying the resultant $1.16 times consumption yielded an estimate cost of the quota to consumers in 1962 of $4.0 billion. (M. A. Adelman, "Efficiency in Resource Use in Crude Petroleum," *Southern Economic Journal,* October 1964, Appendix 1.)

a straight-line extrapolation between his values for 1962 and 1968 would place the total cost of the import quota between 1959 and 1969 at slightly over $50 billion, probably the largest subsidy to any single industry in U.S. history.

Had the quota not been in existence consumers would have enjoyed savings of around 4 cents a gallon for gasoline, kerosene, and other light distillates, 3 cents for middle distillates, as well as 75 cents a barrel for residual oil.[57]

The quota also had the effect of imposing serious hardship on particular industries and regions. Denied entry to the world's largest market, low-cost foreign oil flowed to Europe and Japan, with attendant benefits to their industrial users as well as their consumers. Testifying in 1969, Wayne A. Leeman observed: "At present oil kept out of the United States is, at least in part, pushed into other countries. . . . Manufacturers in Japan and Western Europe buy energy, industrial heat, and petrochemical feedstocks at prices which give them a competitive advantage over U.S. producers. And they have this competitive advantage partly because import quotas give U.S. firms only limited access to cheap foreign oil and partly because oil shut out of the United States depresses the prices they pay."[58]

The differential disadvantage was particularly serious for those American industries which are either large energy users or utilize petroleum products as their raw materials. Principal among the latter is the petrochemical industry, whose problems were summarized by Professor Walter Adams: "Major American chemical companies . . . have estimated that domestic oil prices on the East Coast average $1.25 per barrel more than elsewhere in the world; this amounts to 3 cents a gallon, or 60 percent above the world price. This quota-protected price differential, they point out, can be critical, if not fatal, in petrochemical production, where in many cases raw material costs account for more than 50 percent of the cost of basic products."[59] The loss to the economy in the form of capital expenditures was described by Kenneth E. Hannan, vice-chairman of the Board, Union Carbide Co.:

DR. BLAIR: And how many petrochemical facilities do you think would be constructed by the companies in the Chemco group if you did have unlimited access [to foreign oil]?

MR. HANNAN: We are growing at quite a rate. We have in being now some, let us say $23 billion of plant and equipment. If we grow at 10 percent a year, we would be investing about $2½ billion a year. Last year we invested two billion eight. If you use an average of, let us say, $250 million, which is on the high side, for each plant, that is four plants per billion, or 10—the equivalent of 10 plants a year. Ten petrochemical complexes a year could be built, or their equivalent in new facilities.[60]

The quota also worked severe hardships on those geographic areas most distantly located from domestic sources and most advantageously located to receive and use foreign oil. Particularly hard hit was New England,[61] for which the quota, according to Professor Joel Dirlam, imposed an excess cost of some $300 million a year: "New Englanders, and to a somewhat lesser extent, those in the Middle Atlantic States, differ from energy consumers elsewhere because of their heavy dependence on middle distillate oil for home heating, and on residual fuel for industrial and commercial heating and electric power generation. In New England, 76 percent of the residential-commercial energy demand is currently met by oil, compared with 33 percent for the Nation as a whole. Per capita consumption of distillate and residual fuel oil in New England was 12.7 barrels per capita. The U.S. average was 3.8 barrels."[62] A situation which the New England representatives found "particularly annoying" was the movement of foreign oil by pipeline (under bond) from Portland, Maine to Montreal, Canada, where it was sold several cents below the Boston price.[63] Had New England consumers been able to purchase heating oil at the Montreal price, they would have saved, according to Governor Curtis of Maine, some $143 million a year.[64] Another source of annoyance was the inconsistency, on the one hand, of granting quotas "to inland refiners despite their inability to use foreign oil,"[65] and on the other of denying them to New England despite the fact that "imported oil coming from the Mediterranean travels a shorter distance to New England ports than to other American ports."[66]

THE DENOUEMENT

Toward the end of the 1960's it appeared that the days of the quota were numbered. Opposition had developed not only in such traditional sources as the chemical industry and the New England interests, but in a miscellany of other trade and governmental bodies, including independent terminal operators,[67] independent fuel distributors,[68] independent oil and gas associations,[69] private-brand gasoline marketers,[70] officials of state bodies in North Carolina,[71] South Carolina,[72] Hawaii,[73] and others. Partly in response to this growing opposition, the Senate Subcommittee on Antitrust and Monopoly announced in its program for 1968 an intention to explore the ways in which competition could be lessened by "governmental intervention in the market." Because of the late session of Congress in 1968, those hearings did not get under way until the spring of the following year. On March 25, 1969, the Subcommittee began its inquiry into the use of government to suppress competition with hearings on the petroleum industry. Two weeks after the Subcommittee had started its hearings, President Nixon established a Cabinet Task Force on Oil Import Control, naming Secretary of Labor George Shultz as its chairman.

On its part, the Subcommittee conducted a four-volume set of hearings,* while the Cabinet Task Force solicited and received great reams of unsystematic and uncoordinated materials on every aspect of the petroleum industry from nearly every industry, every region, every type of user and indeed virtually every interested party. On the basis of this mass of documents and other information, the Task Force issued a highly structured, formalized report (with every paragraph numbered!), containing majority and minority recommendations. The position of the majority was summarized before the Antitrust Subcommittee by the chairman of the Task Force, Secretary Shultz:

> To replace the present method and level of import restrictions, the report recommends phased-in adoption of a preferential tariff system that would draw the bulk of future imports from secure Western Hemisphere sources. A ceiling would be placed on imports from the Eastern Hemisphere. These would not be allowed to exceed 10 percent of U.S. demand.
>
> The tariff system would restore a measure of market competition to the domestic industry and get the Government, after a 3-to-5 year transition period, out of the unsatisfactory business of allocating highly valuable import rights among industry claimants. Tariffs also would eliminate the rigid price structure maintained by the present import quotas.[74]

Although widely hailed as a far-reaching, liberalizing proposal, the Task Force report contained a little-noted restriction which would have largely vitiated the effectiveness of its recommendations. This was the provision that imports from Eastern Hemisphere countries would not be allowed to exceed 10 percent of U.S. demand.[75] Since most of the lower-priced oil moving in world markets came from the Eastern Hemisphere, this restriction—which would have limited the proposed

---

*While M. A. Wright, vice-president of Standard (N.J.), did appear, leaders of five other major oil companies declined the Subcommittee's invitation to testify. Albert Nickerson of Mobil declined on the grounds that "I have been out of the country for the past month and have just returned to my office"; J. E. Swearingen of Standard (Ind.) could not attend because "My own plans involve a foreign trip. . . ." E. D. Brockett of Gulf and O. N. Miller of SoCal were certain that their testimony would be, respectively, "cumulative" and "repetitive." And J. Howard Rambin, Jr., of Texaco gave as his reason the fact that the American Petroleum Institute was arranging a "comprehensive and organized presentation." (*Hearings on Governmental Intervention*, Pt. 2, pp. 607–609.)

liberalization's benefits largely to Venezuela—was of no small moment:

DR. BLAIR: . . . if Eastern Hemisphere imports are kept down to 10 percent of demand, and if oil production in Venezuela is extremely concentrated, from where is it reasonable to expect that competitors interested in obtaining a larger share of the U.S. market by reducing price, resulting in benefits to the consumer—from where are they to come? . . . Why is there such a severe limitation on the amount that can be brought in by companies operating in North Africa or Nigeria which are not much farther away from the eastern seaboard than Venezuela?

SECRETARY SHULTZ: As to the reasons for having different tariff rates for Canada, Latin America, and others, that does reflect a judgment about the relative security of these sources of crude. And since the national security is what the program is all about, we felt that that was an appropriate thing to do.[76]

Even though they would have had, at best, only a marginal effect on U.S. prices, the recommendations by the Task Force of his own Cabinet apparently went too far for President Nixon. On February 20, 1970, a press conference was held at the White House to discuss the recently submitted Task Force report. The spokesman for the White House was Peter M. Flanigan, Assistant to the President. In the conference, the following exchange took place:

QUESTION: Is it correct to assume, then, from the tenor of the President's statement, that what we are going to do pending completion of these studies, pending completion of discussions with our allies, pending completion of negotiations with the Canadians, Mexicans, Venezuelans, and the Latin Americans is that we are going to retain the present quota system as it now stands for a while?

MR. FLANIGAN: That is correct.*

*   *   *

Evaluating the effect of prorationing on supply depends on what it is compared against. Compared against no controls whatever, prorationing, by keeping more oil in the ground than would otherwise have been the case, had the effect of conserving the supply. But if compared against the preferable method of accomplishing the same objective, prorationing has tended to accelerate the depletion of re-

---

* Reprinted in *Hearings on Governmental Intervention*, Pt. 4, p. 1,774. President Nixon did not even accept the minority recommendations which, while rejecting the replacement of the quota with a tariff, included a proposal that the "unrestricted entry of residual fuel into District I be extended to other districts," and that government policy should "provide petrochemical producers with a growing volume of imported oil" (*ibid.*, pp. 1,751–1,755).

serves in two ways: (a) by leading to the drilling of an excessive number of duplicate wells, resulting in the needless waste of invaluable gas pressures; and (b) by leaving as a legacy a maze of individual property rights that tends to impede the adoption of secondary and tertiary recovery. Concerning the former, Robert E. Hardwicke wrote more than two decades ago: "The problem of unnecessary wells is a serious one, and the economic waste (money, labor and materials) resulting from drilling, equipping and operating unnecessary wells in Texas is tremendous, amounting as an average to much more than $100,000,000 each year of the last five and one half years. The figure is a conservative one."[77] Although the Texas Railroad Commission has ended or reduced some of the more extreme forms of physical waste, the Commission has followed the practice of granting wholesale exemptions from its own oil-well spacing regulations. According to Zimmerman (on most matters a sympathetic observer), ". . . the current unnecessary expenditure because of faulty well-spacing regulations is appalling . . . the Railroad Commission stands ready to grant exceptions to the general spacing rule or any special spacing rule worked out for a particular pool, under conditions which usually are so favorable that there is not the least incentive to voluntary pooling."[78] Behind the granting of exceptions is a lower court ruling rendered in favor of Exxon's subsidiary, Humble Oil and Refining: ". . . unless a voluntary division has been made in face of the rule, the owner of a tract is entitled to at least one well *and to an allowable so that he can make a profit*."[79] Forty years of prorationing have left the State of Texas with a vast number of excess wells, each with its own individual rights. Without compulsory unitization powers, their very existence makes it exceedingly difficult for the state to increase its recoverable supply through modern recovery methods.

By sharply limiting the use of foreign oil for fourteen years, the import quota obviously hastened the depletion of domestic reserves, though the extent is probably incalculable. It is known that before the quota was introduced foreign oil had penetrated as far as western Pennsylvania. What is not known, however, is how much of the Eastern seaboard market would have come to be supplied by foreign oil, which in turn would have depended on whether the Texas Gulf price would have been lowered to meet (or beat) the foreign competition, on the changes in tanker rates, on changes in pipeline charges, and on other uncertain variables. That the drain on U.S. reserves must have been of sizable proportions is evident from the fact that for nearly a decade and a half 88 percent of the world's largest market was reserved for domestic production.

PREFERENTIAL
TAXATION

8

OVER A LONG PERIOD of years, nothing has contributed more to the evolving structure of the oil industry than the preferential tax advantages bestowed on it by the Congress. Their importance is apparent from the fact that, in the face of a corporate tax rate of 48 percent, the federal income taxes paid in 1974 by the nineteen largest oil companies amounted to only 7.6 percent of their income before taxes.[1] Recognizable only to those trained in the arcane art of translating the almost undecipherable prose of tax statutes, the proliferation of preferential provisions is a tribute to the ingenuity and thoroughness with which the industry's tax lawyers (and their Congressional allies) have gone about their work. Of the preferential provisions, three have been by far the most important—percentage depletion, the expensing of intangible drilling costs, and the foreign tax credit.

In the past, criticism of these tax preferences has focused largely on the loss of revenue and the lack of equity. Concerning the former, the staffs of the Treasury Department and the Joint Committee on Internal Revenue Taxation placed the combined tax loss in 1972 from percentage depletion and the expensing of exploration and development costs at $2.35 billion.[2] With respect to equity, the point has repeatedly been made that the tax preferences have had the effect of shifting to individual taxpayers, as well as to other industries, a sizable tax burden that the oil companies would otherwise have to pay. For example, the three "defense-related" industries—petroleum, motor vehicles, and aircraft and missiles—had in 1965–66 total assets of $96,778 million and paid U.S. income taxes of $3,185 million. Of these totals, petroleum companies held 59.7 percent of the assets but paid only 9.3 percent of the taxes. In contrast, motor vehicle companies accounted for 31.7 percent of the assets but paid 79.2 percent of the taxes. And companies in the aircraft and missiles industry held 8.6 percent of the assets but paid 11.5 percent of the taxes.[3]

Less well recognized than the revenue and equity criticisms is the

187

fact that the particular forms of tax favoritism employed by the oil industry have been such as to give a powerful discriminatory advantage to integrated companies over the nonintegrated refiners and marketers. This results from the fact that two of the three principal tax advantages—percentage depletion and expensing of exploration costs —are available only to firms engaged in crude production, and the foreign tax credit is likely to be more valuable to them. The international majors have been doubly blessed: not only have they been permitted to operate as virtually tax-free enterprises, but the very provisions of law that have made this possible are not available to their principal sources of competition.

The combination of rapidly rising prices and profits (otherwise subject to high personal and corporate tax rates), with the attractiveness of percentage depletion and the expensing privilege, touched off an explosion in the number of domestic oil producers in the years following World War II. As Alfred E. Kahn has put it,

> . . . the rise in the corporation tax rate from 19 percent in 1939 to 52 percent after the war (with excess profits tax rates even higher) made these arrangements far more attractive to the oil industry than they had been before. Similarly, when the highest income surtax rate was up at 91 percent, it meant that when anyone in that bracket spent a dollar to drill a dry hole it cost him only 9 cents; the government paid the other 91 cents.
>
> The result . . . was an enormous increase in well-drilling activity; total exploratory wells drilled rose from 5,600 in 1945 to 10,000 in 1950 and 16,200 in 1956. The drilling of developmental wells increased from 19,000 to 41,000 over the same 11-year span.[4]

The interaction of tax privileges with supply control measures has constituted a striking example of synergism—the effects of different elements, when combined, being greater than their effects taken separately. Thus, in the years following World War II the tax privileges led to a vast expansion in well-drilling activity. To prevent the appearance of "distressed oil," severe limitations on production had to be imposed through the domestic control mechanism. But new entrants continued to be attracted by the resultant stabilization of price, thereby creating the need for even more stringent production cutbacks. So greatly had their domestic output been restricted and so profitable had foreign production become (thanks in good part to the foreign tax credit) that some of the lesser majors and larger independents sought, and obtained, concessions abroad. Their rapid success in bringing low-cost foreign oil to the United States inevitably gave rise to still another form of control—the import quota. This complex of tax preferences and supply controls artificially raised and maintained prices, increased the after-tax profitability of oil production, shifted to other taxpayers the burden that would have been borne by the oil industry, and resulted in a vast waste of economic resources. It also had the effect, little noted at the time, of hastening the day when the United States would run out of oil.

PERCENTAGE DEPLETION

For tax purposes, the right to base a deduction not on cost but on selling price is one of the two features that generally differentiate percentage depletion from depreciation. The other is the fact that the depletion allowance continues as long as the property is yielding income, whereas under depreciation, deductions can no longer be made after the cost of the property has been fully amortized. Studies have indicated that percentage depletion allowances have provided deductions that over the life of a productive property recover from ten to twenty times its cost.

A variation of the privilege known as "percentage depletion" traces back to the original income tax law, which allowed a depletion deduction of up to 5 percent, limited to the overall original cost of the property *or* its market value. A tax on value accruing before March 1, 1913, would have taxed income before the income tax became constitutional. Recognizing the inequity of basing depletion on cost for oil discovered before that date but on value for oil discovered thereafter, Congress in 1918 expanded the original provisions by applying depletion to the value of *all new* discoveries, which became known as "discovery value depletion." In its report on the Revenue Act of 1918, the Senate Finance Committee stated, "the prospector for mines or oil and gas frequently expends many years and much money in fruitless search. When he does locate a productive property and comes to settle, it seems unwise and unfair that his profit be taxed at the maximum rate as if it were ordinary income attributable to the normal activities of a single year."[5] According to a staff report of the Joint Committee on Internal Revenue, "the stated purpose to 'stimulate prospecting and exploration' was . . . applicable to the allowance of discovery depletion."[6] In floor debate, Senator La Follette objected on the grounds that discovery depletion would permit oil producers to take depletion allowances far in excess of costs; a property which had cost only $100,000 might have its "fair market value" placed at $1,000,000.[7] An amendment that he introduced, which would have limited depletion to the cost of the property or to its value on March 1, 1913 (when the price of oil was far lower), was defeated.[8]

It soon became apparent that the determination of "fair market value" was subjective and arbitrary in the extreme. As a Senate Investigating Committee put it: "analytic appraisals, which determine values to be depleted by discounting estimated expected profits, are too elastic and leave too much to the judgment of individual engineers to be suitable for taxation purposes."[9] It also became apparent that the "discovery depletion" privilege was being extended to wells with only the most remote resemblance to true discoveries. Professor Thomas S. Adams pointed out that it was even extended to wells drilled to *reduce* the value of a true discovery: "If I own a tract of land and somebody discovers an oil well on an adjoining tract and I immediately sink an offsetting well in order to prevent the discoverer from draining the pool which we are both tapping, I am entitled to depletion for discovery value based upon the market value of my offsetting well. . . . Discovery depletion is granted to 3 offsetting wells and perhaps 10 where it is granted to 1 true discovery well."[10]

The intent of Congress to limit the privilege was thus largely nullified by laxity in enforcement. According to Ronnie Dugger:

> The 1918 law was only three years old when a treasury tax official who had been working in the minerals section attacked discovery depletion as "an enormous privilege," "really a gift in the form of tax-free income." He explained how, under an artificial definition of what a "proven field" was, thousands of wells were qualifying, making this "unquestionably one of the greatest loopholes of escape from taxation to be found in the entire statute." With the deduction often exceeding the entire income from a well, Congress in 1921 limited it to 100 percent of profit, but again in 1924 a Missouri congressman warned of "a great leak" in the tax laws because of the way a proven field had been defined, letting every well drilled in six square miles get "discovery" depletion. The deduction was limited to 50 percent of profit that year, but just about every well was still getting it.[11]

As evidence of abuse mounted, the Senate appointed a Select Committee on Investigation of the Bureau of Internal Revenue, headed by Senator Cousins of Michigan, which conducted extensive hearings on the administration of discovery depletion. In its report, the Committee contrasted the original intent of Congress with actual performance: ". . . a minor part of this [depletion] exemption is received by the wildcatter or prospector for whose benefit it was intended. The major portion of this exemption goes to the large oil-producing companies, which also deduct the prospecting and developing expense, intended to be offset by discovery depletion, from income as operating expense. The regulations governing discovery depletion do not confine this exemption to the discovery of new deposits, but permit the blanketing of known pools of oil with discovery values, to be depleted, free of tax."[12]

Taking up the argument that depletion is justified because of the "great risk" assumed in oil drilling and prospecting, the Committee noted that "discovery depletion is allowed to the lessor who sits idly by and risks nothing that is not risked by every investor in real estate." Most of the privilege was found to have gone to those whose risk is minimal: ". . . the greater part of the allowances for discovery depletion are made to those who drill in proven ground, where the finding of oil is practically certain." Further, the Committee pointed out, the assumption of risk is not peculiar to oil alone: ". . . every investor in speculative stocks, particularly those who invest in new enterprises, organized to manufacture new inventions assume great risks of loss. Except in the case of mines and oil and gas wells, no investor is permitted to set up the value of his business, after its success has been demonstrated, as a deduction from the profit to be derived from that business for the purpose of determining his net taxable income."[13]

As evidence that most discovery depletion allowances had been granted to large companies and not to wildcatters, the Cousins Committee reported that out of 13,671 cases in which discovery depletion was claimed, only 35 were actual discoveries of new oil deposits. The former chief of the natural resources division of the Income Tax Unit estimated that only 3.5 percent of discovery depletion deductions went to wildcatters. Typical of the many specific examples cited by the Committee was the Texas Gulf Sulphur Company, which had been given a discovery value of $38,920,000 on property it had purchased in 1909 for $250,000.[14] In the words of the report, "Discovery depletion . . . is a discrimination against every other taxpayer and every other industry."[15]

Congress reacted to these revelations by replacing the subjective and variable standard of "fair market value" with an objective but exceedingly generous standard. In place of the troublesome yardstick of "fair market value," Congress in 1925 adopted a specific figure, 27.5 percent, as a percentage of gross income from oil production that would be free from tax. In addition, there was no longer any limit on the amount of depletion deductions.

According to Dugger, this percentage had its origin in a recommendation by the president of the Mid-Continent Oil and Gas Association that 25 percent of gross income be exempted from taxation. The Senate narrowly escaped the ignominy of being considerably more generous, rejecting a proposal for a 35 percent deduction by only one vote; the final figure of 27.5 percent was a compromise between a Senate-passed bill providing for 30 percent and the House measure of 25 percent. Congress also widened the depletion privilege by explicitly extending it in 1926 to oil produced from *all* wells, old as well as new. Abandoning any attempt to link the monetary reward to new discoveries, Congress in effect accepted the argument that the best way to promote the cause of the independent wildcatter was to permit *all* enterprises and individuals to retain more of their profits from oil.*

The percentage depletion rate remained for over four decades at 27.5 percent until it was reduced to 22 percent upon the courageous motion of a member of Congress from an important oil-producing state, the late majority leader, Representative Hale Boggs of Louisiana.

EXPENSING INTANGIBLE DRILLING COSTS

In addition to receiving tax-free treatment, in the words of Senator Paul Douglas, for "27½ % of gross income up to 50% of net income, world without end, amen," oil companies have been allowed large and immediate tax deductions for their "intangible drilling expenses." In a typical drilling operation, from one-tenth to one-quarter of the total outlay pays for the derrick, pipe in the ground, and other immovable material and equipment, while the other nine-tenths to three-fourths (the "intangible drilling expenses") goes for wages and salaries, fuel, machine and tool rental—costs without salvage values. In any other industry, the latter would be regarded as part of the cost of developing an income-producing property, and together with the original outlay would constitute a capital cost, to be amortized gradually over the "useful life" of the property. But in the oil industry, the "intangible drilling expenses" may be deducted in the year in which they are incurred. The result of this extraordinarily rapid amortization is a huge first-year deduction which can be used to shelter an equivalent amount of taxable income from other sources.

Through the combination of this provision with percentage depletion, the Treasury Department loses in two ways. First, it loses the taxes on the other income which are offset by the amount invested in a drilling operation, which *immediately* becomes a deductible "intangible drilling expense." The taxes on the other income are lost regardless of whether the venture ends up with a "dry hole" or a producing well. And secondly, since percentage depletion is not limited to

---

* Operating on the basis of the premise that what has been so beneficial to oil interests should not be denied to others profiting from the exploitation of natural deposits, Congress has granted percentage depletion to most other minerals, excluding only "soil, sod, turf, water or mosses or minerals from sea water, the air or similar inexhaustible sources." There have, however, been two important differences: (a) none has been given as high a rate as 27½ percent, and (b) the rate allowed for the extraction of minerals abroad is lower than for U.S. deposits. At present twenty-four metals and minerals, ranging from antimony to zinc and including such important materials as lead, manganese, and bauxite, enjoy a depletion rate of 22 percent (previously 23 percent) in the U.S. but only 14 percent (previously 15 percent) elsewhere. For asbestos the U.S. rate is 22 percent (previously 23 percent) but only 10 percent elsewhere.

cost if the drilling is successful, the Treasury never recoups the intangible drilling expenses previously written off. Thus, this cost is in effect written off twice: once, in the form of intangible expenses, and again, through percentage depletion which is not reduced because this part of the cost has previously been written off.

It is the combination of the rapid write-off for intangible drilling expenses with percentage depletion which, in the words of Alfred E. Kahn, "grossly inflate[s] the tendency of the latter to permit companies to recover more than original investment cost free of tax; when the major costs have already been charged against income, the option thereafter to take depletion as a percentage of revenue without regard to costs becomes correspondingly attractive." The "intangibles" provision, "like any accelerated amortization, would permit an alteration only in the timing of the tax, amounting to an interest free loan to the taxpayer." But combining it with percentage depletion "tears up the promissory note."[16] The fact that in 1957, for example, corporations taking depletion deductions of $678 million also took $471 million of "intangible" deductions indicates that in practice the two provisions go in tandem.[17]

Like percentage depletion, this privilege has been fully applicable to operations by U.S. oil companies abroad as well as at home. But unlike percentage depletion, the "intangibles" provision originated not with Congress but with the administrative branch of government—specifically, a ruling issued in 1916 by the Internal Revenue Service. In 1945, a Circuit Court of Appeals whose jurisdiction, *mirabile dictu,* included Texas ruled that the agency lacked the power to transform by edict capital outlays into expenses. Thereupon, Congress "promptly adopted a resolution affirming Internal Revenue's power to grant the more favorable treatment to the 'intangible' expenses. In 1954, to end all doubt, Congress *directed* Internal Revenue, by statute, to issue such a ruling."[18]

The loss in tax revenue from this provision has averaged over half a billion dollars a year. For 1972, the staffs of the Treasury Department and the Joint Committee on Internal Revenue Taxation estimated the tax loss from the expensing of exploration and development costs at $650 million. Together with the $1.7 billion loss from percentage depletion, these two privileges yielded a tax subsidy of $2.35 billion.[19]

FOREIGN TAX CREDIT

Important as the foregoing provisions have been in the past, they have been overshadowed by the foreign tax credit—i.e., the right of companies operating internationally to use the taxes paid to one country as direct offsets against taxes owed to another. As credits, they are "dollar-for-dollar" offsets, whereas as royalties they would be worth only 48 cents on the dollar. The country of *source* taxes in the first instance, with the country of *nationality* then imposing its tax only to the extent that its own corporate tax rate exceeds that of the source country. Where the tax rate in the country of source is higher than in the country of nationality, an "excess credit" is created, which can offset taxes less than U.S. taxes on other foreign income. Under carry-forward and carry-back provisions the "excess credit" can often be applied against future or past income. For over two decades, the greater part of the payments made by U.S. oil companies producing abroad have been in the form of taxes rather than royalties to the host government. For these companies, though not for domestic producers, percentage depletion thus became an expendable loophole. In the words of Glenn P. Jenkins:

> While this provision [percentage depletion] is an important device for decreasing the tax liability in domestic petroleum production, we find that at the present time it is relatively worthless to the American corporations producing abroad. This is the case because each year there exist very large amounts of excess foreign tax credits. Since at least 1966 the annual excess of foreign tax credits has been greater than the increase in the United States tax liability that would be created by the complete elimination of the percentage depletion allowance for foreign petroleum production. . . .
> Using data for 1971 I find that over forty percent of the foreign tax credits would have to be eliminated before the percentage depletion allowance would begin to be effective.[20]

Although rationalized as necessary to secure equitable treatment for a multinational corporation operating in different countries with differing tax laws,[21] the foreign tax credit can itself be a source of an extreme inequity where a fundamental difference exists in the legal status of the recipients of payments. In petroleum the difference is in the legal status of the owners of subsoil mineral rights. As we have seen, the right to own private property, including everything below (and in theory everything above) the surface area itself, means that payment in the Western world for such activities as the extraction of petroleum must be made to the private owners, customarily in the form of royalties. Elsewhere, the payments can be made either as royalties or as taxes, the form usually being a matter of profound indifference to the recipient. Where the corporation benefits by making its payments in the form of taxes, a gross inequity is obviously visited on the private landowners (and on their country) by virtue of the fact that their compensation is necessarily limited to royalties.

LEGISLATIVE HISTORY. The foreign tax credit had been on the statute books since the Revenue Act of 1918, although it was not used by the oil companies until the early 1950's. Originally, it contained no limitations on the amount which could be credited against U.S. taxes. At the time, the U.S. corporate tax rate was 12 percent while the British rate was 27 percent. Hence U.S. companies with operations in the United Kingdom could apply more than half of their British income tax against taxes due the U.S. government on income earned within the United States itself. In 1921, the privilege was narrowed by a provision based on the principle that the ratio of foreign tax credit to U.S. tax liability on income from all sources may not exceed the proportion of foreign source income to income from all sources. But while this was a reasonable and significant constraint on most U.S. firms doing business abroad, the international majors have so arranged their affairs that most of their taxable income (which is vastly different from income reported in financial statements) is derived from foreign sources. This is indicated by the only data available—an IRS publication covering the 1961 tax year for those companies claiming foreign tax credits: more than 85 percent of the oil companies' taxable income was made up of foreign source income.[22]

The revision of the 1921 Revenue Act establishing the general principle of a proportional limitation did so by specifying that the limitation would be computed on an *overall* basis only. The alternative employed in later years is the *per country* basis. The overall limitation provides the more generous credit whenever a company does business in some foreign countries with effective tax rates higher than that in the United States. The advantage of the per-country limitation comes into play when the U.S. company incurs losses in certain foreign operations. Under the overall limitation, foreign source losses are balanced against foreign source profits, so that overall foreign source income—and hence the allowance tax credit—is a smaller fraction of total income than it otherwise would be. With the per-country limitation, losses in one foreign country are effectively offset against U.S. earnings rather than against *other foreign* source earnings; the ratio of earnings from profitable foreign sources (and the maximum tax credit) to total earnings is thus larger than it would otherwise be.

From 1921 to 1932, the foreign tax credit could be computed on the overall basis only. But the onset of the Great Depression led to considerable criticism of the foreign tax credit, culminating in a serious drive to eliminate it. To keep the credit, its supporters agreed to a compromise under which companies were required to compute the allowable credit both on an overall and a per-country basis and use the *lesser* of the two. The law remained in this form throughout the remainder of the Depression, World War II, and the immediate post-war years. The Revenue Act of 1954, however, specified that *only* the per-country limitation could be used. But six years later, Congress in the Revenue Act of 1960 approved the most generous provisions authorized since the foreign credit limitation had first been adopted.[23] The taxpayer was permitted to use either the overall or the per-country limitation, whichever was *greater*.[24]

INSTITUTION BY THE OIL COMPANIES. In testimony before the Senate Subcommittee on Multinational Corporations, George McGhee, who at the time had been Assistant Secretary of State for Near Eastern, South Asian, and Africa (and also, incidentally, a former vice-president of Mobil), recounted the bizarre circumstances under which the hitherto little-noted provision of law was transformed almost overnight into one of the nation's leading tax loopholes. Recalling the political conditions in the Middle East during the late 1940's, McGhee observed:

> At that time, the Middle East was perhaps the most critical area in the world in the contest between ourselves and the Soviets. The governments in the area were very unstable. We had no security pact covering this area. The Soviets had threatened Greece, Turkey and Iran. . . .
>
> The Arab States were very hostile to us because of our involvement in the Israeli affair[s], as we know. Saudi Arabia which is, I assume, the key country we will be discussing, was more tolerant than the others. King Ibn Saud always seemed a little less affected by Israel in his relations with us than the other Arab States. There were, however, threats of strikes against us in Saudi Arabia. Always in the background there was the possibility of some nationalist leader, particularly in the countries where there were kings and sheiks, who might seize power as Nasser did later.
>
> I think, in retrospect, this was always a greater danger in the Arab States than communism itself, which didn't find fertile ground among the Arabs. It was only later through Egypt that the Soviets obtained access to the Arab States.
>
> At this time, the principal threat to the Middle East lay in the possibility of nationalist leaders moving to upset regimes which were relatively inept and corrupt, and not attuned to the modern world.[25]

King Ibn Saud's displeasure with his royalty rate (12%) became even more intense when he learned that Venezuela had entered into a new agreement under which its share would be 50 percent. And, according to McGhee, ". . . the people in the Middle East who produced oil were aware of it. Venezuela had . . . sent a mission to the

Middle East to propagandize the 50-50 concept." A particularly sharp thorn in the side of the U.S. was Saudi Arabia's Finance Minister: "Abdullah [Sumay] Sulaiman . . . proved very difficult to deal with. He was always pressing to shut down the oil fields unless the Saudis got more money. . . ." It was obvious to McGhee that the existing arrangement could not long continue: "Taking into account everything I have said, both the Aramco officials and the [State] Department had independently reached the conclusion that something had to give. Some greater sharing of profits with Saudi Arabia must take place, otherwise there would be an increasing threat to the regime and to Aramco's ability to maintain its concessions."[26]

Although "quite happy with their existing profit split" ($.91 out of $1.34!), the officials of Aramco, in McGhee's words, "had reached the conclusion that they should offer the 50-50 split." These were the officials directly responsible for operations in Saudi Arabia: "They had spent a great deal of time in Saudi Arabia and understood the local problems. They had been under constant pressure in Saudi Arabia to give more money. . . ." But the need for such an upward revision was not shared by the officials of the parent companies—Exxon, Mobil, Standard of California, and Texaco. According to Ambassador McGhee, "The Aramco officials brought the officials of their parent companies down to the Department, I think, in order to help educate them as to the situation in Saudi Arabia. In this meeting, where all of the parents of Aramco were represented, the Aramco officials presented their judgment that they should offer the 50-50. The parents then said that they weren't quite convinced. They didn't think they needed to go so far."[27]

The problem thus became one of devising a way "to give more money" to Ibn Saud which would be acceptable to the parent companies. The simplest approach, raising the royalty rate from 12 to 50 percent, was not likely to have met the latter requirement, since it would have reduced Aramco's profit margin by two-fifths. Almost a conditioned reflex, the solicitude demonstrated by the State Department for the financial well-being of U.S. corporations seems in this instance a little strained, since Aramco's profits at the time were running at the astonishing rate of around 50 percent on its total investment. Meeting Saud's monetary requirements by raising the posted price would not have met his demand for at least the same participation share that had been obtained by the Venezuelans. And it would have resulted in a Mideast price far above the level determined by the "netback" international basing point system, thus foreclosing Mideast oil from most of the world's consuming markets. Under all the circumstances involved, the devising of a solution that would give Ibn Saud his fifty-fifty participation without reducing Aramco's profit margin must be regarded as an act of pure genius. Generally attributed to a Treasury official, the essence of the solution was that the difference between 12 and 50 percent be made up of taxes paid to Saudi Arabia. Under the foreign tax credit, such payments could then be used in their entirety to offset taxes on other foreign income owed by the oil companies to the U.S. Treasury. Were the payments to be made in the form of royalties, they would be classified as business expenses worth, at a corporate tax rate of 50 percent, only 50 cents on the dollar.

The nature of the change was clearly delineated in a colloquy between Senator Church and Ambassador McGhee:

SENATOR CHURCH: If an oil company were doing business within the United States and had to pay a royalty to the owner of the land on which the wells were located and had to pay taxes to the state in which the lands were situated, both the royalty and the taxes paid to the state government would be treated, if I understand the law correctly, as regular business expenses and deducted as regular business expenses in determining the profit on which the company would have to pay income tax to the Federal Government.

But upon the recommendation of the National Security Council, the Treasury made the decision to permit Aramco to treat royalties paid to Saudi Arabia as though they were taxes paid to the Arabian Government. The effect was dramatically different from the U.S. example because instead of deducting those royalties as regular business expenses, in determining the net profit, Aramco was permitted to credit those royalties directly against any tax otherwise due the Government of the United States.

So that, first of all, the impact on the national treasury was direct and dramatic and resulted, I am told, in a loss in the first year after the decision of over $50 million in tax revenues from operations of Aramco in Arabia.

Isn't that true?

AMBASSADOR MCGHEE: Yes. I might elaborate a little. I find in my records that I pointed out at the time, that the U.S. Treasury would in a sense be financing this change, and I didn't make the decision to give the tax credit. . . .

SENATOR CHURCH: However, even then the effect of the decision was to transfer $50 million out of the U.S. Treasury and into the Arabian treasury. That was the way it was decided to give Arabia more money and to do it by the tax route. Isn't that correct?

AMBASSADOR MCGHEE: Yes, that is one way of looking at it. . . .

SENATOR CHURCH: In this case the reason that I think it is so intriguing is because the companies had been paying a royalty that received one tax. Then a decision was made in our Government to treat that royalty differently so it would have the status of a tax credit with the effect that $50 million in the next year was transferred out of our Treasury into the treasury of Saudi Arabia.

AMBASSADOR MCGHEE: That is right.[28]

Shortly thereafter, a team of tax lawyers drawn from the oil companies and Treasury was dispatched to Saudi Arabia to draw up a corporate income tax for a land virtually devoid of corporations. Appropriate action by Saudi Arabia, and soon followed by other Mideast states, was not long in coming. In an agreement of December 30, 1950, Aramco "submitted" to the principle of taxation, with the government agreeing that the total of income taxes "and all other taxes, royalties, rentals and exactions of the Government for any year would not exceed fifty percent of the net operating profits of the company, these profits to be calculated after the payment of foreign income taxes." In December 1951, the Kuwait concession was revised along the same lines. Likewise the taxation principle was incorporated into the Iranian-Consortium Agreement of October 29, 1954, which in Article 28 recognized the income tax liability of the trading and operating companies. Moreover, this principle of taxation was also applied to the transit conventions. In 1952–53, it was proposed in Lebanon that the Trans-Arabian Pipeline Company and the Iraq Petroleum Company be subjected to income taxes, with the Lebanese Parliament on June 29, 1956, passing a law imposing income taxes on all concessionary companies operating in Lebanon.

COMPARATIVE COST BREAKDOWNS. For the benefit of Senators who found themselves perplexed by this financial legerdemain, Ambassador McGhee went through the steps of the calculation:

> In the Persian Gulf they were selling the oil for $1.75. At times there were discounts. The cost of production was about 20 cents a barrel. That left $1.55. The royalty was 21 cents. That left $1.34. That was the net that the companies got at that time. I am told that the average tax was 25 cents. That would leave them after that tax a little over $1. After they offered the 50-50 the royalty remained the same as did the cost of production. The profit was still $1.34. The Saudis now get half, 67 cents, and the company gets 67 cents.
>
> The company now pays no tax and indeed including depletion has a credit arising out of the operation which is transferable to another operation. That is how the companies get back to about the same profit level they had before, about a dollar a barrel. It can't be simplified. It is a complicated affair.[29]

Using the figures cited by McGhee,* Aramco's existing unit cost breakdown (Col. A) can be compared to what would have been the case had the royalty been raised to 50 percent (Col. B) and also to what was actually adopted: a total Saudi Arabia "take" of 50 percent, made up of the existing royalty plus a new Saudi corporate tax (Col. C).

As Table 8-1 shows, the figures used for price and operating expenses remain the same: $1.75 and $.20 per barrel, respectively. Under the then existing royalty arrangement, the deduction of the operating expenses and the royalty (at 12%) yields the $1.34 cited by McGhee. To derive the U.S. income tax, it is necessary first to subtract the allowance for percentage depletion (27.5%) and then to divide the residual by half (assuming a U.S. corporate tax rate of 50%). The deduction of this latter amount ($.43) from $1.34 yields a net income after taxes of $.91.

All of the differences between Columns A and B stem from the higher royalty ($.88) which reduces the net income before taxes to $.67. Because percentage depletion cannot exceed 50 percent of net income, half of this figure is then deducted, with the residual again being reduced by half. The deduction of the U.S. tax ($.17) yields a net income after taxes of $.50—or 44 percent below the net income at a royalty rate of 12 percent.

Under Column C, the royalty remains at 12 percent but a new corporate tax imposed by Saudi Arabia is assumed; this is the amount ($.67) which when added to the royalty ($.21) gives that country 50 percent of the gross income (or price). The U.S. corporate tax of $.43, derived in the same way as before the change, is less than the new Saudi tax. Not only would it not have to be paid, but the difference ($.25) would be an excess tax credit that could be used to directly offset taxes owed on other foreign income. The addition of the excess credit brings the net income after tax up to $.91, or precisely the same level as before the change was made. In this way the companies, as McGhee put it, "came out of this thing just about where they entered."

THE CURIOUS APATHY OF TREASURY. The loss of U.S. tax revenue was immediate and substantial. Between 1950 and 1951, Aramco's payment to Saudi Arabia rose from $66 million to $110 million, while its payment to the U.S. Treasury fell from $50 million

---

* There is one exception to the figures cited by McGhee—the tax paid to the U.S. before the change which, McGhee states, "I am told . . . was 25 cents." On the basis of other data this figure, given the existing tax laws, should apparently have been somewhat higher—approximately 43 cents. The difference, however, is not of sufficient magnitude to affect the comparison for illustrative purposes.

TABLE 8-1

**Aramco: Comparison of Net Income on Alternative Royalty
and Tax Credit Bases
(per barrel)**

		12% Royalty Rate (A)	50-50 on Basis of Royalty (B)	50-50 on Basis of Tax Credit (C)
1.	Price	$1.75[a]	$1.75[a]	$1.75[a]
2.	Expenses			
	(a) operating	.20	.20	.20
	(b) royalty	.21[b]	.88[c]	.21[b]
	(c) subtotal	.41	1.08	.41
3.	Net income before taxes (1 − 2c)	1.34	.67	1.34
4.	Taxes			
	(a) Saudi Arabia	—	—	.67
	(b) U.S.	.43	.17	(.43)
	(c) subtotal	.43	.17	.67
5.	Net income after taxes (3 − 4c)	.91	.50	.67
6.	Gross margin			
	(a) Price (1)	1.75	1.75	1.75
	(b) Tax paid cost (2c + 4c)	.84	1.25	1.08
	(c) Margin (6a − 6b)	.91	.50	.67
	(d) Excess tax credit (4a − 4b)	—	—	.24
	(e) Margin plus excess tax credit (4c + 4d)	.91	.50	.91
Computation of Tax				
7.	Price (1)	1.75	1.75	1.75
8.	Operating expenses & royalty (2c)	.41	1.08	.41
9.	Net income before taxes (7 − 8)	1.34	.67	1.34
10.	Percentage depletion (1 × 27.5%)	.48	.33[d]	.48
11.	Net income after depletion before income tax (9 − 10)	.86	.34	.86
12.	U.S. income tax (11 × 50%)	.43	.17	.43

[a] Posted price.
[b] Royalty at 12%.
[c] Royalty at 50%.
[d] At maximum level of 50% of net income.

to $6 million.[30] The only loser was the American taxpayer, who had
to make up the loss in U.S. tax revenues. By 1955, the annual loss to
the U.S. Treasury from Aramco had tripled, rising to $154 million.[31]
Comparing the company's actual income statement with what would
have been the case had it been a domestic U.S. producer, assuming
the other entries to have been the same, Aramco, as a domestic concern, would have returned $154,867,000 in taxes to the federal gov-
ernment plus $42,030,000 to state and local governments. Instead,
$192,743,000 was paid in the form of corporate income taxes to the
Saudi Arabian government.[32]

That the Treasury Department would accept with equanimity such
a loss of revenue (which over the years has grown into multi-billion-
dollar proportions) struck the Senators as slightly incredible:

SENATOR PERCY: You would think there would be screams from the
Treasury that is always looking for revenue. Every time we put an
amendment on the floor that is going to cost the Treasury something
someone objects that it is going to throw the budget out of balance.
How much protest was there from the Treasury and where did it come
from and who resolved the difference and the difficulty then?

AMBASSADOR MCGHEE: Frankly, I don't know—

SENATOR PERCY: Those officials who were screaming about it?

AMBASSADOR MCGHEE: I frankly don't know, Senator. I hate to say
that this was somebody else's business. But, not being a tax man, I
didn't feel myself competent. Having made my recommendation about
the political and strategic aspects of the question I frankly left it to
Treasury to make this decision. But the impression I had then was
that no one objected to it. Everyone thought it was reasonable under
the circumstances.[33]

The value of the tax credit was enhanced by the use in its deriva-
tions of the inflated "posted" price which by the latter 1960's had
become an artificial construct as a result of the decline in the true
or "armslength" price. As described by Edith Penrose:

Socony-Mobil was the first company to announce the price at
which it would sell oil from the Middle East, and thus in 1951
began the institution of "posted prices.". . .
    These are the prices which are now called "tax reference prices,"
because they bear no relation to any price at which oil actually
moves. They are the prices which are used to impute profits to
crude oil for taxation purposes in the producing countries, but
since integrated transactions dominated world trade in crude oil,
there was no effective free market for crude and, therefore, the
posted prices could not in any meaningful economic sense be

called market prices. Hence, it developed that the income of the governments of the crude oil producing countries, as well as their national income became dependent on a price which was soon seen to be determined not by the marketplace but by the companies. Clearly the seeds of severe trouble were sown when this arrangement was made.[34]

As a result of discounts and concessions, the actual armslength prices as early as 1956 were some 15 percent below the posted prices; ten years later, the difference had widened to about 30 percent.[35] To the extent that such a difference existed, the application against U.S. taxes of a tax credit calculated on the basis of posted prices created a spurious tax saving. According to Stanford G. Ross, the Internal Revenue Service has on occasion questioned this use of posted prices, and on the basis of compromises reached with the oil companies, "substantial payments were made to the Treasury." But, he noted, "Public information on these audits is not available."[36]

RECENT LEGISLATIVE ACTION

In the Tax Reduction Act of 1975 Congress made a clear beginning toward reversing the long process of widening the oil industry's tax loopholes. Fifty years after it was added to the tax law (and fifty-seven years after "discovery value depletion"), percentage depletion was repealed for the major oil companies; limits were imposed on the amount which smaller companies could claim and the depletion rate was gradually phased down to 15 percent. At the same time, other changes were adopted that will prevent intangible drilling expenses incurred abroad from being offset against domestic income for tax purposes. Finally, the value of the foreign tax credit was reduced.

Specifically, percentage depletion was repealed completely (effective as of December 31, 1974) for oil and gas production by taxpayers where they (or related parties) sell any at retail or refine more than 50,000 barrels a day. For smaller producers, percentage depletion is limited to an average daily production in 1975 of no more than 2,000 barrels[37] and is reduced by 200 barrels in each subsequent year until it reaches 1,000 barrels of oil in 1980. The rate of percentage depletion remains at 22 percent through 1980, but goes down to 20 percent in 1981, 18 percent in 1982, 16 percent in 1983, and 15 percent in 1984 and subsequent years. To spur the adoption by smaller companies of modern recovery methods, the rate remains until 1984 at 22 percent for oil extracted through secondary or tertiary processes.[38]

With respect to the expensing of intangible drilling costs, two new provisions make it virtually impossible to claim foreign intangible drilling expenses against U.S. income; i.e., they cannot be claimed against U.S. income when there is oil-related income from *any* foreign country, and even if there is no such foreign income currently, the foreign losses will ultimately be offset against any oil-related income earned in future years. The new statute withdrew the former privilege of computing the foreign tax credit on a per-country basis. Thus, if a company incurs losses from intangible drilling expenditures in one foreign country while making income from oil operations in another, the losses cannot be offset against domestic income, lowering the U.S. tax on this domestic income (Section 601). Moreover, where aggregate foreign oil-related losses are offset against domestic income, either because there is no foreign oil-related income or the foreign income is less than the foreign losses, the U.S. taxes forgone are to be recaptured to the extent of the subsequent foreign income (Section 601).

The value of the foreign tax credit was also lessened by phasing down the maximum amount of foreign tax credits allowed for oil and gas extractive income. For 1977 and later years, it cannot be more than 2 percentage points above the U.S. tax on this income, or 50 percent, given the present 48 percent U.S. tax rate.[39] While this will still permit the offsetting of the entire tentative U.S. tax on the oil and gas extractive income, any usable excess foreign tax credits will be limited to the difference between the 48 percent rate and the 50 percent limit. In addition, the limited excess credits generated in this manner may be offset for crediting purposes only against income from the extraction, transportation, marketing, and financing of *oil and gas* and their related products (Section 601).

*   *   *

The most important of the recent changes is, of course, the elimination of percentage depletion for large companies. Moreover, as purchases by the international majors of "participation" crude increasingly replace taxes on "equity" crude in payment for foreign oil, the importance of the foreign tax credit should tend to decline, and to the extent that the foreign tax credit no longer offsets taxes owed on other foreign income, the loss of percentage depletion will become a matter of increasing importance. The day of reckoning will be delayed by the existence of accumulated excess foreign tax credits, which however can be carried forward only for five years. But, as will be shown later, the combined effect of (a) the declining importance of the foreign tax credit and (b) the loss of percentage depletion appears to have been more than offset by the increase in the after-tax profit margin resulting from the sharp rise in prices.

Part
THREE

EROSION AND
EXPLOSION

For most of the two decades between the end of World War II and the mid-1960's, the international and domestic market control mechanisms of the oil industry achieved their objectives with exemplary precision. Internationally, overall output was limited with remarkable exactitude to a predetermined growth rate, while price changes initiated in the United States were immediately transmitted throughout the world by the international basing point system. Within the United States, production was similarly limited to predicted levels of demand by the state proration authorities, operating through the Interstate Oil Compact Commission.

But during the mid-1960's, sources of competition outside the mechanisms' control began to disturb the stabilized price structure. Both abroad and at home, streams of oil began to flow around the control of the majors. In international markets, competition was introduced by medium-size companies that had recently won valuable concessions in Libya. Faced with the necessity of finding outlets, they began to force their way into world markets by offering lower and lower prices. Moreover, if world output was not to exceed the predetermined growth rate, the majors were faced with the painful necessity of offsetting the Libyan expansion with corresponding reductions in the Middle East, thereby imperiling their invaluable concessions in that area. In the domestic market, competition came from the private brand operators. Selling at discounts of 4 to 6 cents a gallon, they were rapidly increasing their market shares at the expense of the majors, and with the spread of self-service operations their prospects appeared even brighter.

As compared to the late sixties, the profit rates of the majors had by 1971 fallen approximately a fifth. It was becoming increasingly evident that the intricate mechanisms of the past were no longer adequate to control the market. There seemed to be no way by which the international majors could prevent the Libyan independents from selling their superior crude at lower prices. Nor did there seem to be any way by which they could keep the efficient "frill-less" private branders, supplied by independent refiners or the "lesser majors," from gaining increasing shares of retail gasoline sales. If the downward trend in profitability was to be arrested, these problems would have to be resolved.

In addition to the existing difficulties, two other problems loomed on the horizon. The future of the concession system was endangered by the rising tide of nationalism throughout the Third World, including the oil-producing countries. Demands by OPEC leaders for "control" over their nations' oil wealth were now being achieved through participation and nationalization programs. Even though the majors might be satisfied with the "buy-back" prices at which they were beginning to purchase oil, and even though given exclusive purchase rights, the participation and nationalization actions worked powerfully against the companies in one vital respect: payments to a country for oil not produced by a lessee holding a concession were purchases, not royalties disguised as taxes; and as purchases, they could not conceptually qualify as dollar-for-dollar credits against taxes owed the U.S. Treasury on foreign income. Further, opposition to both the foreign tax credit and the percentage depletion allowance was mounting in the U.S. Congress.

Common logic dictated a recasting of the companies' profit-making structures. The time-honored practice of maximizing the value of the preferential tax advantages by making after-tax profits primarily at the stage of crude production, and using refining and marketing merely as necessary conduits for the disposal of crude, needed to be replaced. What was required was a new cost-price structure that placed less emphasis on production and more on these later stages which, as profit centers, were impervious to the loss of the preferential tax advantages.

To corporate management, the other emerging problem was

the adequacy of the companies' profit rates. In order to finance their expansion needs, the majors had long relied very largely on internal savings; but during the 1960's, they began to turn for supplementary financing to the capital market. According to later testimony, their officials professed increasing concern with the question of whether existing profit rates were sufficient to attract the capital needed for future expansion. In their eyes the obvious solution was to set and meet a new, higher "target" rate of return.

Within a short span of about five years, the majors had achieved solutions for the existing and the emerging problems. What follows is an analysis of how competition in both the international and domestic markets was brought under control, the locus of profit-making was restructured, and new and higher target rates of return were established and met.

THE EVISCERATION OF THE LIBYAN INDEPENDENTS
9

OIL PRODUCTION IN LIBYA has been unusual in two important respects: the rapidity of its growth up to 1970 and the prominence of independent companies. In less than a decade, output increased nearly twenty-fold, soaring from 182,000 barrels a day in 1962 to 3,318,000 in 1970. By 1970, Libya had become the fourth largest producer among the OPEC countries, ranking only slightly below such long-established producers as Saudi Arabia, Iran, and Venezuela.[1] This remarkable performance was immeasurably aided by two circumstances. The sulphur content of Libyan crude was among the lowest in the world—an important consideration to consuming countries that were beginning to become pollution-conscious. And its geographical proximity to European markets gave Libya (a "short-haul" country) an important freight advantage over the "long-haul" Persian Gulf countries.

THE STRUCTURE OF THE LIBYAN OIL INDUSTRY

From its earliest emergence as an important source of world supply, an unusually large proportion of Libyan output has been produced by newcomers to the world of international oil. This was the result of a deliberate policy of the former régime of King Idris, overthrown in 1969 by a revolutionary movement headed by Colonel Qadaffi. 'According to testimony in a private civil suit by King Idris's Prime Minister, Mustaba Halim, concessions were awarded in such a way as to avoid making the country overly dependent on the "seven sisters," who might subordinate the promotion of Libyan output to their much larger interests in the Persian Gulf and to the avoidance of a surplus in world markets: "I did not want Libya to begin as Iraq or as Saudi Arabia or as Kuwait. I didn't want my country to be in the hands of one oil company."[2] Instead, special consideration was given to inde-

211

pendent companies which, lacking concessions elsewhere, would stand or fall by their success in Libya: "We wanted to discover oil quickly. This was why we preferred independents in the first stage, because they had very little interests in the Eastern hemisphere outside Libya."[3] In order to benefit from their established market "positions," concessions were also awarded to the majors. But the concessions of the independents and the majors were deliberately interspersed. As Halim explained, "Well, if on an average I found an independent who had spent more energy and discovered oil, this would permit me to talk to his neighbor and tell him, 'Look here, your neighbor has discovered oil, you are almost in the same structure, come on now; try to drill.' "[4] As a result, Libya led all other OPEC countries in the proportion of its output produced by independents (i.e., companies other than the seven majors, CFP, and state-owned national enterprises). In 1970, independents produced 55 percent of Libya's output, compared to an average of 15 percent for all OPEC countries.

The contrast between the prominence of the independents in Libya and their virtual nonexistence in the Middle East became the subject of a colloquy between Senator Church and Mr. George Henry Schuler of the Bunker Hunt Oil Company:

SENATOR CHURCH: In other words, in the Persian Gulf, the big companies, the majors, the 7 sisters, had tied up the oil in various consortium arrangements?

MR. SCHULER: Yes, sir.

SENATOR CHURCH: But in Libya some of the smaller companies had found a source, and some smaller companies, the so-called independents, were represented in Libya along with the majors, while out in the Persian Gulf it was the majors who were involved?

MR. SCHULER: I think this is certainly in part a function of the fact that the . . . interest in Libya arose in the early 1950's, and the concessionary pattern was established by the petroleum law of 1955. . . .

SENATOR CHURCH: But when oil was discovered in Libya, it was such as to permit the independents to come in, and they did come in. . . .

MR. SCHULER: Yes indeed, it is a fact. The acreage, particularly that which the Oasis group [Continental, Marathon, and Amerada] as well as Bunker Hunt and others obtained, turned out to be very good acreage . . . in fact the independents have a large position in Libya.[5]

The rapidity with which the independents moved to bring their product to the market is well illustrated by the case of Occidental. Within one year after discovering oil in 1967, Occidental had built pumping facilities deep in the desert, as well as a pipeline and a seaport, and was delivering oil into tankers 130 miles away.[6]

THE OUTBREAK OF PRICE COMPETITION

What made the appearance of the Libyan independents a matter of such serious concern to the majors was not only the rapid growth in their market share but their virtual destruction of an already-weakening price structure. As in the United States, the central objective of the majors' price policy abroad had been to try to "hold the line" at the unprecedented levels attained after World War II. Under the basing point system, the Mideast posted price had soared, more or less in tandem with the Texas Gulf price, rising from $1.05 to $1.70–$1.80, in the vicinity of which it remained until 1970. And until the second half of the 1950's, there was apparently little difference between the posted and the real or "armslength" prices.

But by the late 1950's, a divergence between the posted and the real prices had begun to appear—the latter falling from $1.93 in 1956 to $1.60 in 1959. Since the Libyan independents did not become a factor in world markets until the early sixties, this early weakening of the price structure must have resulted from price cutting by independents who had obtained some of the newer Venezuelan concessions, or by the Russians who were increasing their sales in world markets, or perhaps by some of the majors themselves. The very size of the margin between the posted price and operating costs must have offered an almost irresistible temptation for price shading. Further contributing factors were the 1958 recession, which increased the difficulty of finding markets, and the imposition in 1959 of the U.S. import quota, which by foreclosing the world's largest market intensified the competition for European and Japanese markets.

It was in this setting that the independents (Occidental, Continental, Marathon, Amerada, Bunker Hunt) began to put their product on the market. Under strong pressure by the Libyan government to produce, and with no established "market positions," price cutting was their only viable option. And in sales to independent buyers the majors had no alternative but to meet the competition. As a consequence, the "armslength" Mideast prices declined throughout the 1960's. According to data compiled by Walter L. Newton, the net f.o.b. invoice prices paid for Iranian oil by independent Japanese refiners fell steadily during the 1960's, reaching a low of $1.30 in 1967.[7] Even lower quotations have been cited; in 1969 William Summers Johnson, Director of Finance, Honolulu, Hawaii, testified, ". . . while in London I heard reports, which I cannot confirm, of sales of Middle East oil to Japanese buyers at f.o.b. prices as low as $1.20 a barrel."[8] A similar pattern in both trend and level was revealed by prices on government tenders to Latin American countries.[9] Early in 1965,

Argentina had paid nearly $1.60 for Arabian light crude; by the middle of 1967, the price was down to $1.33. At the beginning of 1965, Uruguay paid $1.50 for Iranian light, but by the end of 1968 it had negotiated purchases at $1.35 and $1.29. Information supplied by the Brazilian embassy revealed that by the later 1960's it, too, was purchasing crude from Saudi Arabia, Iraq, and Kuwait (Grades 31–38) at f.o.b. prices of $1.30 a barrel.*

To officials of the major oil companies, the American and the foreign markets during the middle and later sixties were "different worlds." In a colloquy with the Antitrust Subcommittee's chief economist, M. A. Wright, vice-president of Exxon, vividly described the "deterioration" of foreign markets during 1965–68, which he attributed to "people in the producing business for the first time, first time abroad, who have to have an outlet for their crude":

MR. WRIGHT: . . . the competition has been intense during this period of time [1965–68], and there has been a deterioration of crude prices abroad, the degree of which I cannot really tell you, but I understand that to be the situation.

DR. BLAIR: Deterioration as a result of competition?

MR. WRIGHT: As a result of competition. Competition has been intense, particularly in Europe, where you have a considerable number of independent refiners, and you have a substantial number of people in the producing business for the first time, first time abroad, who have to have an outlet for their crude. They have no choice but to sell. So, they are pressed to dispose of their crude which gives a buyer's market and the results have been that there has been deterioration in the crude oil prices in Europe.

DR. BLAIR: We have in the record transaction prices by Esso on sales to Japanese affiliated companies f.o.b. Middle East ports. Your company's quotation for Arabian light to affiliate Japanese companies in early 1965 was $1.63; in 1966 it went down to $1.57; and by late 1968 it was down to $1.46. For Iranian light the decrease was from $1.59 to $1.41, for Iranian heavy from $1.47 down to $1.33—decreases in the vicinity of 10 to 12 percent.

Are we to conclude that at the same time you were raising the price to the American consumer, your company was reducing the price to foreign buyers?

---

* Data on the level of armslength prices paid by independent European buyers were secured from two London oil brokers, an oil industry research organization, and a price-reporting service; this information shows that in late 1968 and early 1969, Arabian and Iranian light crudes were being sold at around $1.30 a barrel and Kuwait crude at about $1.20. (*Hearings on Governmental Intervention*, Pt. 1, p. 75.)

MR. WRIGHT: You are working in two separate worlds when you speak about what you do in the United States compared to what you do abroad, and what you say is exactly right. In the foreign circuit where there has been tremendous competition, the price has gone down. I accept your figures. They sound about right to me. And, of course, the crude price in the United States is a matter of record.

DR. BLAIR: Some of us have difficulty in trying to understand how the national security of the United States is strengthened by a discriminatory pricing practice under which prices paid by American buyers tend to rise while prices paid by European and Japanese competitors are steadily declining. To some of us it would seem that this would weaken rather than strengthen the national security of the United States.[10]

The price competition benefited not only the immediate recipients but the ultimate consumers, as independent European and Japanese refiners who purchased Libyan crude passed along their savings in the form of lower prices for refined products. The wholesale price of gasoline in Rotterdam, for example, fell from 7 cents a gallon during the latter half of 1960 to 5 cents in the first half of 1970[11]—a decrease of nearly 30 percent at a time when price levels generally were rising.

THE EFFECT ON THE MAJORS

From the outset, the attitude of the majors toward Libya was ambivalent. On the one hand, they benefited from the revenues secured from production on their own concessions. On the other, they had good reason to be disturbed over the mounting production of the independents which, if price-weakening surpluses were to be avoided, would have to be offset by corresponding reductions made elsewhere, principally in the Middle East. But as Libyan output continued to rise, the majors became increasingly concerned over whether the Persian Gulf countries would tolerate the necessary compensating reductions in their output and income. And since the majors' production in the Middle East was some twenty times their output in Libya, what they might lose in the former area was far greater than any possible gains in the latter. Yet if they ceased production in Libya, their concessions would probably be turned over to the independents, who would only increase the volume of uncontrolled output.

As early as 1960, Exxon in its internal annual *Forecast* recognized the threat of an expanding Libyan output to Mideast production: "If it were not for the impact of new North African supplies, production in the Middle East could be 1.3 million b/d higher in 1967. The annual growth rate for the Middle East would be 6.4% through 1963 (versus 3.0%) and 4.6% between 1963 and 1967 (versus 2.6%)."* In its 1961 *Forecast*, Exxon anticipated the need for compensating reductions in the Middle East: "During the middle of the 1960–1968 forecast period the advent of large-scale production in Libya and increases in Sahara and other supply sources may restrict the growth of Middle East outlet." In addition to the increases in other areas, Libya between 1963 and 1964 "may get 17% of the total growth in Free Foreign supplies . . . leaving 33% of the growth to the Middle East (compared to 43%) between 1960–1961." For the later 1960's, however, Exxon's 1962 *Forecast* anticipated a slowing down of Libya's growth: "The Middle East is expected to capture 54% of growth in the 1965–1969 period compared to 39% for the 1961–1965 period when the entrance of North African supplies is being felt." But the *Forecast* for 1964 recognized that previous predictions of Libyan production had been too low: "The most significant changes in supply growth will continue to take place in Africa. Rapid growth is expected in Libya, with the terminal year 1.0 million b/d above estimates implicit in the 1963 outlook." A further "upward revision" in African output (offsetting reductions in the Middle East) was noted in the 1967 *Forecast*: ". . . the upward revision previously noted for African production, when coupled with the downward revision in Eastern Hemisphere demands, results in a 600,000 m b/d lower outlook for Persian Gulf crude by 1975 than projected in the 1966 Green Book."

But it was not until 1968 that the panic button was pushed. Not only had the growth in Libyan output outpaced previous estimates, but the independents were proving far more important than had been anticipated:

> Libyan crude oil and NGL production is expected to increase dramatically in the next years achieving a level of 3.5 mm b/d by 1971. This level is sufficient to make Libya the foremost producing country in the Eastern hemisphere in 1971, displacing Iran to second place and Saudi Arabia to third. In contrast with historical ownership patterns in North Africa and the Middle East, *the bulk of the new increments of production will be produced by companies considered "newcomers" to the international oil trade* without established captive outlets and without a significant stake in the Middle East. Since Libyan oil is favorably situated with respect to the major European markets and has desirable low sulfur qualities, *relatively little difficulty in capturing third party markets is expected.*[12]

---

* Exxon's *Forecast of Free World Supply* for 1960. These annual forecasts, which are contained in Exxon's "Green Books," have been supplied to and published by the Senate Subcommittee on Multinational Corporations (*Hearings*, Pt. 8, pp. 591ff.).

Accompanying data (Table 9-1) made it clear that most of the increases in Libyan output were expected to come from independents who lacked other sources of foreign crude or from Amoseas, the joint venture of SoCal and Texaco, both of which were important "crude-long" suppliers to independent refining and marketing companies. Neither SoCal nor Texaco could be expected to absorb the anticipated Libyan increases and still digest their 30 percent shares of the anticipated increase in Aramco's production in Saudi Arabia.

TABLE 9-1

Actual and Anticipated Libyan Crude Oil Production*
(000 b/d)

	1967	1975	Change m b/d	Percent
Occidental	—	1,100	1,100	—
Oasis	630	865	235	37.3%
BP–Hunt	169	200	31	19.0
Total	799	2,165	1,366	170.0
Amoseas (SoCal-Texaco)	129	500	371	287.6
Exxon†	603	525	−78	−12.9
Mobil-Gelsenberg	204	400	196	96.7
Total	807	925	118	14.7
Total	1,744	3,983	2,239	128.4

* Excluding natural gas liquids.
† Esso Libya, Esso Sirte; includes Grace's and Sinclair's share.
Source: Compiled from Exxon's "Green Book" for 1968: *Forecast of Free World Supply.*

Occidental, alone, was expected to account for nearly half (1,100 m b/d) of the predicted total increase of 2,239 m b/d. The joint venture of Continental, Marathon, and Amerada (Oasis) was expected to add another 235 m b/d, while the venture of the crude-long majors, SoCal and Texaco, was expected to contribute 371 m b/d. Interestingly enough, an actual decrease of 78 m b/d was forecast for Exxon, which offset a good part of the increase predicted for Mobil-Gelsenberg. All told, 78 percent of the anticipated total increase was attributed to the independents and to Amoseas. If a collapse in the world price was to be avoided, the message for the Middle East was clear: "The net effect is a 1975 production level [for the Middle East] . . . about 1.0 mm b/d below the 1967 outlook for 1975."

In its 1969 *Forecast,* Exxon faced up squarely to the dilemma. It was not simply a matter of offsetting Libyan increases with corresponding decreases in the Mideast countries; the question was whether the latter would accept the reduction necessary to prevent the appearance of a price-destroying surplus: "No known method of allocating the available growth is likely to simultaneously satisfy each of the four established concessions; i.e., Iraq, Iran, Kuwait and Saudi Arabia." And if it proved impossible "to satisfy" them, the companies could lose their concessions.

A similar pessimistic appraisal appeared in an internal document from Standard Oil of California. In a memorandum dated December 6, 1968, S. E. Watterson, assistant manager of its economics department, warned: ". . . it will become exceedingly difficult, if not impossible, to maintain relatively rapid growth in the high level producing countries of the Middle East and still accommodate reasonable growth of crude production from new as well as old fields in many other countries outside of the Middle East."[13] Anticipated production in 1969 was estimated on three bases: "A," that production would grow "at indicated availability in most countries outside of the Middle East" (i.e., African countries); "B," that it would grow at a moderately lower rate in Africa with a corresponding increase in the Middle East; and "C," that it would rise at a "politically palatable" rate in the Middle East, with a corresponding decrease in Africa. As the summary table below shows, Africa was estimated to have an available capacity that would permit a 35.9 percent rise over 1968. If the growth in the Free World supply were to remain relatively stable at 9 percent,[14] such an increase would require a 2.0 percent *decrease* in Mideast output. If the African potential were reduced by 10 percentage points, Mideast output would rise but only to a rate of 4.9 percent. Obviously, "further adjustments were necessary." Under Assumption "C," Middle East output was raised to an annual growth rate of 6 to 7 percent by further reducing estimated production in Africa.[15]

The memorandum cautioned that the downward revisions in African output might have been excessive. The majors operating in Libya had the incentive to make the necessary reductions, but this was hardly the case for the independents.

> The downward revisions or adjustments of crude production in Libya and Nigeria for 1969 were made on the assumption that major companies with large interests in the Middle East would be required to moderate their liftings from Libya and Nigeria in order to maintain *politically palatable* growth in their liftings from the Middle East. Some companies, however, such as Occidental,

TABLE 9-2

Oil Supply, Demand, and Growth Prospects, 1968–69

	1968 (Actual)	Production (m b/d) 1969: Assumption			Percentage Annual Growth 1968-69		
		A	B	C	A	B	C
Africa: Total	4,031	5,477	5,052	4,952	35.9%	25.3%	22.8%
Libya	2,591	3,355	3,155	3,055	29.5	21.8	17.9
Nigeria	94	530	330	330	100.0+	100.0+	100.0+
Other	1,346	1,592	1,567	1,567	18.3	16.4	16.4
Middle East: Total	11,296	11,064	11,839	12,039	(2.0)	4.9	6.6
Iranian Consortium	2,700	2,700	2,700	2,860	4.7	4.7	9.2
Saudi Arabia	2,800	2,900	2,900	2,970	3.6	3.6	6.1
Other	5,790	5,464	6,239	6,209	(8.2)	5.6	5.6
East. Hemis.: Total	16,683	15,199	18,469	18,569	8.8	10.7	11.3
Free World, ex. the U.S. and Canada	21,732	23,484	23,694	23,794	8.1	9.0	9.5

Source: Derived from Memorandum from S. E. Watterson, Assistant Manager, Economics Dept., to W. K. Morris, Manager of Foreign Operations Staff, Standard Oil Co. of California, December 6, 1968; *Hearings on Multinational Corporations,* Pt. 8, p. 762.

Continental, Marathon and others, without large interests in the Middle East, will be under heavy pressure to expand production rapidly and therefore are not likely to limit their Libyan liftings. Their Libyan oil will be competing vigorously with the majors' oil from the Middle East and Africa.[16]

Although the forecasts are not presented in sufficient detail to make possible a complete match with actual 1969 production figures, it is possible to make such comparisons for leading individual countries:

Comparison of SoCal's Forecast with Actual Production

	1968	1969 Assumption "C"		Actual	
		m b/d	Percent	m b/d	Percent
Libya	2,591	3,055	17.9%	3,169	20.0%
Iranian Consortium	2,700	2,860	5.9	2,945	9.1
Saudi Arabia	2,800*	2,970	6.1	2,992†	6.9
Nigeria	94	330	100.0+	540	100.0+

* Apparently excludes 214 m b/d non-Aramco production.
† Excludes 224 m b/d non-Aramco production.

Exceeding the forecast by slightly more than 2 percentage points, the rise in Libya's actual production was two and a half times that of the increase registered by the Middle East's two principal producers. The actual increase for Iran proved to be roughly in accord with its traditional growth rate. In Saudi Arabia, the actual increase corresponded closely to the predicted rate, though the increase was well below its historical growth rate. The authors' apprehension that they had underestimated the increase in Nigeria proved well founded—and by nearly the exact amount anticipated.

But, *mirabile dictu,* in 1970 the problem which had given rise to such deep concern within Exxon and SoCal (and undoubtedly within the other majors as well) was resolved. Libyan production turned sharply downward, dropping from its peak of 3,318 m b/d in 1970 to 2,761 in 1971, to 2,239 in 1972, and to only 2,100 in 1973. In its 1972 *Forecast,* Exxon promptly revised its Middle East growth rate upward from 4.2 to the historical rate of 10 percent.

THE REVOLUTIONARY GOVERNMENT

On September 1, 1969, the constitutional monarchy of King Idris was overthrown by a group of Libyan army officers. The administration of the government was assumed by a Revolutionary Command Council, headed by Colonel Muammar al-Qadaffi, who prior to the coup had been a captain in the Libyan army. Graduating from the University of Libya in 1963 and the Royal Military Academy in 1965, he had taken advanced military training in both Great Britain and the United States.

The new régime lost no time in precipitating what became the first of a series of confrontations with the oil companies, particularly the independents. On January 29, less than five months after the take-over, Colonel Qadaffi told the representatives of the oil companies that Libyan oil was priced too low in relation to its production cost, its high quality, and its nearness to markets. In addition, he complained that Libyan oil workers were not being treated fairly and warned that Libya could live without oil revenues while it trained its own oil technicians.[17] A number of adjustments were demanded, the most important of which was a price increase of 40 cents a barrel. Although a moderate demand compared to later astronomical increases, it was rejected out of hand by the companies. As has been noted, a principal basis of the demand concerned the price that should have prevailed for Libyan crude under a strict adherence to the industry's international basing point ("netback") system. After allowing for the differences in transportation costs, James E. Akins of the State Department found the difference between what the actual Libyan price was and what it should have been under this formula to be "higher than 40 cents."[18] Coming from a high official of an agency long noted for its sympathy toward the major oil companies and also for its addiction to understatement, Akins's observation approaches a ringing endorsement of the Libyan demand: "I do not think the 40-cent figure was outrageous."[19] To add insult to injury, the companies in dealing with the Libyans discounted the value of low-sulphur content, whereas in dealing with the Venezuelans, whose oil is notoriously high in sulphur, their position was reversed. In Akins's words: "They [the companies] were telling the Libyans, as I recall, that the low-sulfur quality of their oil gave them something on the order of a 10-cent price differential on the gravity side just for sulfur, and at the same time the Venezuelans told us that the companies were telling them that their oil, because of the high-sulfur content, was worth some 50 to 70 cents less than Libyan oil."[20]

Despite these considerations, the companies made a token counteroffer of only 5 cents.[21] The Libyans then sought to take advantage of a split between the majors and the independents that had been widening since the country's tax laws had been changed in 1965. Supported by Exxon but bitterly opposed by the independents, the change required that tax payments be based on posted prices (as in other countries) rather than on the lower market prices. The initial target was the largest of the independents, Occidental Petroleum Co., which was not only completely dependent for its foreign crude on Libya but posed the greatest threat to the majors.[22]

A principal reason cited by the Libyan government for curtailing Occidental's operations was the contention that the company was producing in excess of what was warranted by good conservation practice. But the validity of this contention was questioned by Akins of the State Department:

MR. HENRY: Oil Minister Mabruk said that Occidental had failed to follow good conservative practices in the working of its Idris field?

MR. AKINS: I agree that he made the statement. I do not know if the statement was correct. . . .

. . . the Occidental field in Libya is a very peculiar type of field, it is called a reef structure. It is the closest thing to what is popularly called an oil pool that exists in the world and you can produce it at a very high rate.

The Occidental Co. engineers claimed that they were not overproducing the field, that they could indeed produce from this particular structure as much as they were producing without harming the field. Now, if it were a similar field, a traditional oil field, or even another oil field in Libya or say Saudi Arabia and you were producing as much as Occidental was producing from the same reserves, it would clearly be overproducing.

In the case of Occidental, it is not that clear.[23]

In any event, the Libyan government on June 12, 1970, informed Occidental that its output would be reduced from 800,000 b/d to 500,000 b/d. This was followed on August 19 by a further reduction to 440,000 b/d, lowering Occidental's output to 55 percent of its pre-cut level. Although curtailments were also imposed on other companies, none approached the Occidental cutback in severity.[24] According to the Subcommittee's chief counsel, Jerome Levinson, "Armand Hammer, head of Occidental, in July of 1970, had gone to see Mr. Jamieson, who is the head of Exxon, and told him at that point he could not withstand the Libyan government's demand unless he was assured of an alternative source of crude at cost."[25] Mr. Jamieson was able to resist the plea of a man who was not only a vigorous competitor in international markets but had waged a vigorous and ultimately unsuccessful battle to secure an exemption from the U.S. import quota for a giant refinery in Machiasport, Maine, from which he planned to sell fuel oil at discount prices.[26] Thereupon, Occidental capitulated and signed an agreement with the Libyan government on

September 4, providing for an immediate price increase of 30 cents, rising in five years to 40 cents.[27] In a matter of months the other companies had entered into somewhat similar agreements.

THE ABORTIVE "JOINT APPROACH"

The next series of events involving Libya grew out of efforts by the oil companies—both majors and independents—to confront the OPEC countries with a united front. The companies were galvanized into undertaking this overt joint effort by the fear of "leap-frogging" between Libya and the Middle East. Because of its advantages in terms of location and quality, Libya would be granted a higher price; because of their formidable bargaining power, the Mideast countries would demand and receive a similar increase; because it had been thus deprived of its deserved premiums, Libya would have to be granted a still higher price, which would then have to be extended to the Mideast countries; and so on, *ad infinitum.*

The immediate occasion for action was a set of strongly worded demands drawn up in December 1970 by the Organization of Petroleum Exporting Countries meeting in Caracas, Venezuela. Although imprecisely worded, the message was clear: the governments intended to take over their own oil. The need for a joint approach to counter this danger was described by the companies' counsel, John J. McCloy:

> . . . the necessity for some form of collective bargaining on the part of oil producing companies in the Middle East to meet and contend with the increasing demands of the governments of oil producing nations really came to a head when the Libyan government, with intense pressure put on single companies, accompanied by threats of shutdowns, cutbacks and seizures, forced the acceptance of the Libyan government's sharp demands for an increased "take" in September and October of 1970.
>
> Immediately, the Persian Gulf oil producing countries made similar demands based on the Libyan pattern. The leapfrogging or whipsaw effect came into full play. Yet, I think there was still a reasonable hope that outstanding issues between the companies and the producing governments could be resolved until, in December 1970, a whole new series of demands emanated from an OPEC conference in Caracas in the form of a resolution adopted by the OPEC countries. . . .[28]

In a whirlwind of activity, the following agreements were quickly drafted during late December and early January: a joint communiqué to OPEC, which became known as the "Libyan Producers Agreement"; a provision to supply oil at cost to any company cut off in a reprisal action, which became known as the "Safety Net Agreement"; and a request for clearance by the Antitrust Division, which became known as the "Antitrust Exemption." Signed by the companies on January 15, 1971, the Libyan Producers Agreement stated:

> . . . we have concluded that we cannot further negotiate develop-ment of claims by member countries of OPEC on any other basis than one which reaches a settlement *simultaneously with all pro-ducing governments concerned*. It is, therefore, our proposal that an *all-embracing* negotiation should be commenced between repre-sentatives of ourselves, together with such other oil companies as wish to be associated with this proposal on the one hand, and OPEC, as representing all its member countries on the other hand, under which an *overall and durable* settlement could be achieved.[29]

Insisted upon by the independents, the "Safety Net Agreement" was designed to provide them with insurance. In Schuler's words:

> If a company were cut back or nationalized in Libya and its oil exports seized, the other Libyan companies would bear a per-centage of that prorated according to their production. To share this burden equitably with the Persian Gulf producers, the Libyan group could in turn get oil to meet what they have given to the person who was shut back in Libya; they could get fall-back oil, if you will, from the gulf producing states where there was excess of capacity at that point in time.[30]

Since the agreements obviously involved concerted action which might contravene the antitrust laws, Mr. McCloy sought an advance clearance from the Antitrust Division. On January 13, 1971, he ob-tained a "Business Review" letter stating that on the basis of the facts then before it the Department of Justice did not intend to bring an antitrust action, but reserved the right to do so in the future.* McCloy was at pains to stress that this constituted nothing more than the standardized "boiler-plate" language commonly used for such pur-poses and did not constitute a blanket antitrust exemption which, he emphasized, could be granted only by Congress: "The Department of Justice, in my judgment, does not have the authority to waive the

---

* Signed by the Assistant Attorney-General for the Antitrust Division, Richard W. McLaren, the letter said: "We have reviewed the attached proposed message to OPEC and this is to inform you that the Department does not presently intend to institute any proceedings under the Antitrust laws with respect to this proposed message or the discussions called for thereby.

"In accordance with established policy, we reserve the right to take action in the future if warranted by receipt of additional information or by subsequent develop-ments as set forth in the above cited regulations." (*Hearings on Multinational Corporations*, Pt. 5, p. 260.)

application of the antitrust laws of the United States nor can the Attorney General or the Assistant Attorney General grant exemption from them."[31] Regardless of their precise legal status, however, McCloy considered the letters of sufficient importance to warrant keeping the Antitrust Division aware of changing circumstances through a series of modifications of the original proposal.

The sequence of events during the latter part of January, chronicled by Henry Schuler, may be summarized as follows. On January 16, Under Secretary of State Irwin, newly arrived from the Wall Street firm of Sullivan and Cromwell, went to the Middle East. The purpose of the trip was "to express high level official support for the Message to OPEC and the joint negotiation strategy behind it." Two days later, Irwin met with Iran's Minister of Finance, Dr. Amuzegar, who told him that a collective approach was a "most monumental error" since at an OPEC Conference "moderate" countries like Iran could not restrain more radical governments like Libya and Venezuela. The result would be that the companies would end up with the "highest common denominator." According to a January 19 briefing by Ambassador MacArthur, the Shah had told Irwin that the joint approach smacked of being a "dirty trick" against OPEC, in which case "the entire Gulf would be shut down and no oil would flow." The ambassador recommended to Washington that the joint approach should be abandoned and the companies conduct negotiations with the Middle East and the Libyan governments separately. Apparently his arguments were persuasive, and the Iranians themselves became convinced "that the U.S. government was prepared to abandon OPEC-wide negotiations." Amuzegar was reported to have recommended to Piercy of Exxon, "If you think you have a problem with your governments, I am quite confident they will agree to a regional or Gulf approach." Hardening their opposition, "the Gulf countries gave the companies a 48-hour deadline to agree to 'Gulf only' negotiations."

In reporting on the meetings, the companies' representatives, Piercy and BP's Lord Strathalmond, apparently came to the conclusion that acceptance of Iran's position was inescapable: "It is not easy to advise what should be done. If we commence with Gulf negotiations we must have very firm assurances that stupidities in the Mediterranean will not be reflected here. On the other hand, if we stick firm in the global approach, we cannot but think . . . there will be a complete muddle for many months to come. Somehow we feel the former will in the end be inevitable."[32]

When Piercy arrived in Libya on January 28 with the letter to OPEC, the idea of a joint approach met with the same reception. The Libyan government was understandably opposed to placing itself in the same boat with countries lacking Libya's unique advantages, and like the Iranians, the Libyans saw no reason to replace the leap-frogging process, which was proving so successful, with a "joint approach" deliberately designed to strengthen the hands of those on the other side of the bargaining table. Again the companies capitulated, substituting for the "joint approach" something vaguely described as "separate but necessarily connected" negotiations.

The results of the "separate but necessarily connected" negotiations were the Tehran Agreement of February 14, 1971, and the Tripoli Agreement of April 2, 1971, which were fated for a remarkably short life. As summarized by Subcommittee counsel, ". . . the companies offered slightly over a $3 billion increase for the Persian Gulf states over the next 5 years and the Persian Gulf states put on the table roughly a $20 billion package, whereupon the second counter-offer the companies went from $3 billion to $6 billion. The Persian Gulf states came down to $15 billion and roughly the agreement was $10 billion."[33] In terms of price, the increase amounted to some 20 cents a barrel. Predictably, a greater increase was secured two months later by Libya in the Tripoli Agreement. Indeed, on February 14 Libya's Deputy Prime Minister Jallud had informed the press that "Libya would get a better deal than the Persian Gulf states received."[34] Affirming its opposition to joint negotiations, the Libyan government on February 25 "reiterated its position that it would negotiate with each company individually and not with one representative acting for all companies."[35] As if to emphasize their opposition to joint bargaining, the Tripoli Agreement was actually a series of separate (though essentially identical) agreements negotiated one by one between the Libyan government and each individual company.

The real impact of this unsuccessful effort at corporate solidarity was not economic but psychological. Faced with a determined show of opposition, the companies had for the first time capitulated not once but twice. In the past they had always managed in any serious confrontation to come out on top: e.g., against Iran during the early 1950's and against Mattei during the 1960's. That on this occasion the companies had given way—and succumbed so easily—was a lesson whose significance was not lost upon the colonels of Libya or the kings and sheiks of the Middle East. The Senate Subcommittee went to considerable lengths in trying to ascertain the reasons for the reversal. In Senator Church's words:

> Well, now, we have a picture then of our Government first having through waiver of the Antitrust Act permitted the companies to join together for a common negotiation. Then a subsequent reversal, apparently, which led to the dissolution of that effort to maintain a united front.

> What accounts . . . for this reversal that took place? I mean after all, the waiver had been granted to let them all join together in one common negotiation and then subsequently the American Ambassador in Iran indicates that the American government would support breaking up the negotiations. Why? Why did the position of the American government change?[36]

Yet there seems little reason to doubt that the explanations given for the rejection were in fact the real reasons. It is not difficult to understand why the Shah of Iran was reluctant to sit on the same side of a bargaining table with representatives of extremist governments who would probably denounce his expected more moderate stand. Nor is it difficult to understand why the Libyan government should oppose placing itself in the same boat with other oil-producing states that lacked its unique advantages. The real question is why the companies and their governments were so ill-prepared to counter an almost certain rejection. The only explanation emerging from the hearings is a vague hope that the U.S. government would back up the companies with some ill-defined types of "pressure." But the nature of this expected pressure is never specified. With their sparse populations, limited industrial bases, and rapidly rising oil revenues, most of the oil-producing states were not likely to be affected by any curtailment of U.S. economic or military aid. The only conclusion to be drawn is that the abortive effort toward a "joint approach" was either an incomprehensible blunder or an elaborate charade, deliberately designed to divert attention away from policy decisions that had already been made at higher levels.

THE LIBYAN TAKEOVERS

Although both the Tehran and the Tripoli agreements were five-year contracts, they endured for less than a year. Only six months after the Tripoli agreements had been signed, Libya's oil minister announced that "Libya would begin negotiations with the companies on participation. OPEC members had decided at the Beirut meeting, which ended on September 22, 1971, that each state would seek participation with the companies operating in their states."[37] This was merely a reaffirmation, though in more explicit form, of OPEC's resolution ten months earlier at its Caracas meeting; what distinguished the Libyan revolutionaries from the other principal oil-producing governments was the rapidity with which they set about to implement it.

The record of nationalizations and participations imposed by the Libyan government on its principal producers is summarized in Table 9-3.[38] By the end of 1973, companies holding concessions to 33 per-

TABLE 9-3

Leading Producers in Libya: Estimated Reserves, Production, and Participation Rate

(000 b/d)

	Est. Reserves Jan. 1970	Avg. Daily Production 1970*	Avg. Daily Production 1973	Participation Rate (State Share)	Tax Rate
Nationalizations					
BP-Hunt	7,887	402	**	100%	
Amoseas (SoCal-Texaco)	1,000			100	
Shell†	658	368	**	100	
Participations					
Majors					
Mobil-Gelsenberg	4,974	277	73	51	55%
Exxon	3,570	752	121	51	55
Independents					
Oasis††	3,951	1,002	393	51	55
Occidental	2,285	717	180	51	60
Total Others	4,975	30	2,176		
Total	29,200				

* First six months.
** 1973 production by state-owned company in former BP-Hunt and Amoseas concessions was 236,000 b/d and 192,000 b/d, respectively.
† 16⅔% share of Oasis nationalized.
†† Continental (33½); Marathon (33½), Amerada (16⅔); Shell (16⅔).
Sources: Estimated Reserves—*International Petroleum Encyclopedia* (see *Chronology,* p. 19).
  Production, 1970—*Chronology,* p. 17; 1973: *The Petroleum Economist,* April 1974, p. 127.
  Participation Rate—*The Petroleum Economist,* April 1974, p. 127.
  Tax Rate—*Chronology,* p. 16.

cent of Libya's 1970 reserves had been taken over completely; in addition, the government had assumed majority participation in companies with an additional 50 percent of its reserves.

Among the independents, Bunker Hunt was nationalized, while Occidental and Oasis (Continental, Marathon, and Amerada) were forced to make the Libyan government a majority partner in their ventures and in addition suffered production cutbacks of 60 and 75 percent, respectively. Of most importance to the majors, Occidental's burgeoning expansion was brought to an end. As compared to an actual 1971 output of 585,000 b/d and a 1975 projection (by Exxon) of 1,100,000 b/d,[39] Occidental's Libyan production was reduced to 423,000 b/d in 1972, to 354,000 b/d in 1973, and to only 332,000 b/d in 1974.[40] Recognizing the handwriting on the wall, Armand Hammer, president of Occidental, announced after the initial curtailment that Occidental "would reduce its Libyan operation considerably."[41] By way of contrast the most conspicuously "crude-short" major, Mobil, was not nationalized, nor for that matter was Exxon, which is generally regarded in the trade as having a good "balance" between its crude production and its marketing requirements. With concessions amounting to over a quarter of the Middle East's proved reserves, BP had for many years been the most outstanding "crude-long" major, supplying such important independent refiners and marketers as the Italian enterprise ENI and the Belgium firm Petrofina. On December 7, 1971, the Libyan government nationalized the holdings of BP, which, with Bunker Hunt, held the concession to the Saris field. With estimated reserves of nearly 8 billion barrels, it was Libya's largest field. The ostensible reason for expropriation was guilt by association, thrice-removed. It seems that the Libyans were angered by Iran's seizure of three islands in the Strait of Ormuz, the sea passage between the Persian Gulf and the Indian Ocean; the British government was assumed to be in conspiracy with Iran; and the British government held a large but minority ownership (48%) in BP. When Bunker Hunt refused to market what had been BP's oil, it too was nationalized, thereby eliminating another important source of supply for independent refiners and marketers.

SoCal and Texaco, both crude-long majors and important suppliers to independent refiners, resisted the demand of the Libyan government for 51 percent participation in their joint company (Amoseas), which was then nationalized. Also taken over was the 16⅔ interest in Oasis held by Shell, which had likewise resisted the Libyan demands. Libya had not only moved a long way toward achieving Colonel Qadaffi's objective of gaining "full control over the sources of oil wealth"; it had taken over or severely curtailed the operations of those companies whose shipments of Libyan oil had most seriously de-moralized world markets.

THE PLIGHT OF THE SMALLER REFINERS: A CASE EXAMPLE

The experience of the New England Petroleum Co. illustrates the problems encountered by independent refiners everywhere when their supply of Libyan crude was cut off. New England had been perform-ing an important service in supplying pollution-plagued U.S. utilities with Libyan residual oil, which was very low in sulphur content. Al-though residual oil was exempt from the quota, the majors had not imported the Libyan product into the United States. On this point the following exchange took place in the hearings of the Senate Sub-committee on Antitrust and Monopoly; the witness was M. A. Wright, vice-president of Exxon:[42]

DR. BLAIR: I would just like to make a brief inquiry concerning residual oil. I am sure Mr. Wright is cognizant of the desire on the part of officials of eastern cities to lower the sulfur content of the residual oil that is burned in their power plants. Standard Oil of New Jersey is one of the major producers of low-sulfur Libyan oil. I believe, Mr. Wright, you have an output in Libya amounting to approximately 750,000 barrels a day; is that correct?

MR. WRIGHT: True.

DR. BLAIR: In the very process of refining that crude into its various products, a certain amount of residual is yielded. Why are you not selling that low-sulfur residual oil to buyers in the United States?

MR. WRIGHT: I believe Libyan crude moves into Europe.

DR. BLAIR: Why?

MR. WRIGHT: Libyan crude moves into Europe.

From a large 500,000 b/d refinery in the Bahamas, owned jointly with Standard Oil of California (SoCal), New England supplied very low sulphur residual to the Public Service of New Jersey, Edison Co. in New York, the New England Gas & Electric System, the Philadel-phia Electric Co., Niagara Mohawk System, the Orange and Rockland counties, and other utilities in the Eastern United States and Canada. According to Edward M. Carey, president of New England Petroleum, the proposal for the joint venture originated with SoCal: "They first went to all of our customers and tried to sell them the oil, but they found we had them under long-term contracts and they were unable to budge them. So after trying to sell our customers they then came around and said, 'If we can't beat you we will try to join you,' and they said they would like to come into business with us and supply us with crude oil and join us in the refinery."[43]

From SoCal's point of view, the arrangement was advantageous in several respects. Already burdened with an excess supply from the Middle East, SoCal needed to find markets for its newer supply from Libya. In the words of Richard de Y. Manning, New England's counsel: "They had huge quantities of oil in Saudi Arabia which they had been unable to move because they had not located markets and this opened up not only that sale but any time a major oil company makes a large sale like that they hope to continue to do so. . . ."[44] Moreover, the establishment of a market near the United States made it possible for SoCal to operate a very profitable tanker run. As described by Carey, "These [SoCal's] ships would work on a triangulated basis. They would load in the Middle East, discharge at Rotterdam, drop down to Libya, reload, go to the Bahamas and discharge, and then back to the Middle East as a very profitable run, which means that the ship is loaded on two-thirds of its voyage."[45]

On September 10, 1973, New England received a cable notifying it "that the government had seized 51% interest of the Standard Oil Co. producing company in Libya [SoCal], that Standard Oil was resisting this takeover and that all deliveries of Libyan crude from Standard's supplying company would be suspended as of September 1."[46] Not only was New England caught between this cutoff in supply and the long-range contractual commitments; it was unable to find alternative sources. In Carey's words, ". . . as far as we were aware there was no other source of this low-sulfur oil because all of the other producing countries had sold their low-sulfur oil and it was placed in other markets and so if New England lost its Libyan source of low-sulfur oil it would be forever lost. . . ."[47] Believing that the reason for SoCal's resistance was to avoid creating a precedent that might be followed by Saudi Arabia, New England offered to take over the Amoseas concession. Manning proposed to Navis of SoCal, "If we . . . had to give in 51 percent to the Libyan government, this would not create any precedent which would be unfavorable to SoCal's interest and the Texas company's interest in Saudi Arabia . . . the Libyan reserves, while insignificant in the Standard Oil of California picture, were highly significant in the New England picture, and I got nowhere with Mr. Navis. He said he feared the Saudi Arabians would see this as a subterfuge, and that it would not accomplish the desired results."[48]

New England then sought to purchase its requirements directly from Libya's own government-owned enterprise. This possibility had been anticipated, however, for on September 13 Texaco (SoCal's partner in Libya and elsewhere) notified New England "that this oil belonged to the Texas Co., and that if New England lifted this oil, that the Texas Co. would pursue all legal remedies to prevent the use of this oil by New England." Shortly thereafter, "within a matter of, it seemed like, minutes, perhaps a half hour," a similar call was received from SoCal. As Manning recounted it, "the conversations were so nearly the same as if . . . these two speakers, the Texas Co. representative and the SoCal representative, were reading from the same script."[49] Shortly thereafter the U.S. State Department also made known its interest: "Within another approximate 30 minutes, another telephone call came in . . . from a Mr. Mau of the State Department. Mr. Mau's conversation was essentially the same as the previous two . . . we were told the State Department felt this was the wrong thing for New England to do, that this would have repercussions in the Middle East, and that the State Department opposed this action. . . ."[50] On the same day, a State Department attorney described to Manning the nature of that opposition: "Mr. Schwebel told me in the event a lawsuit was brought by any of the major oil companies whose interests had been nationalized in Libya and had resisted nationalization, if any lawsuit was brought against us in the United States, the State Department, if requested, would intervene and take a position that this oil had been illegally seized and that the courts should, under the Act of State doctrine, decide the issue of the legality of the nationalization."[51] Under the "Act of State" doctrine, where title to a product produced in a foreign country is at issue in a case brought in a U.S. court, the courts will assume that the foreign government acted in a legal manner, unless the State Department intervenes and asks that the U.S. court decide the question of the legality of the takeover.

In a letter of September 15, 1973, to Secretary Kissinger, Manning argued that unless New England could purchase oil from the Libyan National Oil Co., some 20 million U.S. citizens would be threatened with electricity blackouts; that New England would pay any increase in cost resulting from the Libyan participation; that SoCal could continue supplying New England out of Amoseas's remaining 49 percent share of the concession; that there did not seem to be any just cause for apprehension about compensation since other American companies, including Occidental and three members of the Oasis group, had already accepted the Libyan government's offer; and to the extent that SoCal's resistance was based on a desire to protect its interests, "elsewhere than in Libya," it had no grounds for invoking "force majeure" to cancel the contract. No reply to the letter was ever received.[52]

Despite the warnings, New England purchased crude from the

Libyan National Oil Co. and arranged for it to be refined by an Italian refinery in Sardinia. "Pursuing" what it claimed as its own, SoCal filed a lawsuit in Sardinia, which was still pending at the time of the Senate hearings. But even if SoCal were to win in Sardinia, it would probably gain only a Pyrrhic victory. As Carey pointed out, "Supposing that SoCal was successful in Sardinia in winning this suit and gaining possession of that oil, what do you think we would do? We would immediately file suit to get possession of that oil again under our other contracts because they owe us that oil under the other contract. It is kind of like chasing their own tail."[53]

*   *   *

In addition to the usual symbiotic relationship between the companies and the countries (a higher price inuring to the benefit of both), the relationship in Libya was symbiotic in still other respects. The majors' acute distress over the independents' rapid rise was coupled with a desire on the part of the revolutionary government to increase its unit revenues while conserving its resources. As Henry Schuler of the Bunker Hunt Oil Co. put it: "Well, they began to focus on the question of increasing the unit income that they got per barrel of oil as opposed to depending upon expansion of production. Libya had become one of the fastest growing oil producers, had come from nowhere to rank, I believe, as I recall it, third in the world at one point in a very short time, because the Libyan Government was volume-oriented. With the new revolutionary government this changed; they were more interested in increasing their unit per barrel income in order to be able to cut back on their production."[54] Obviously, this objective was imperiled by the independents, whose success in the world markets depended on their ability to sell more oil at lower prices, and by crude-long majors who, in order to find markets, might well continue to sell to independent refiners, thereby also depressing the price.

To the Libyan government, the curtailments on the independents and crude-long majors meant the attainment of greater revenues with lower output. To the major oil companies, they meant the end of the Libyan danger to the world price structure and to this threat to their prized Middle East concessions. As Carey of New England put it: "Now their [the majors'] financial stake in Saudi Arabia was vastly larger than their financial stake in Libya, and it appeared that they were prepared to sacrifice their Libyan reserves and the concessions there rather than risk the breakdown of their previously negotiated transaction for participation in Saudi Arabia."[55]

To the majors and the government alike, the reduction in Libyan output was the necessary prerequisite to the staggering price increases of late 1973 and early 1974. Had Libyan production by the independents and crude-long majors been running at the rate anticipated five years earlier by Exxon, the supply in 1973 would have been increased by some 1,500,000 b/d. Had it been necessary to find a market for such a quantity, the chances of making the 1973–74 price increases stick would have been exceedingly remote. Whether anticipated or merely the product of fortuitous circumstances, the price increases of 1973–74 had as their necessary prelude the unnoted evisceration of a few independent oil companies operating in one of the world's most sparsely populated and little-known countries.

Confronted with his economist's prediction that the continued rise in Libyan output would require reductions in Mideast production that would not be "politically palatable," C. L. Parkhurst, vice-president of Standard Oil of California, stated: ". . . we were going to have an awful time meeting the demands of the Iranians and the Saudis . . . my only reaction was to tell the people who were trying to move Saudi Arabia and Iranian crude oil, 'Get to work even harder than you have been working because we just can't let this thing happen.' "* And it didn't.

* *Hearings on Multinational Corporations,* Pt. 7, p. 366. In a subsequent memorandum to the subcommittee, Mr. Parkhurst discounted the value of his economist's forecast on the grounds that the predictions for 1973 had been in error. Ignored is the fact that the reason for error—the assumption of a continued Libyan expansion—disappeared after 1970.

THE CRIPPLING OF THE PRIVATE BRANDERS

10

THE MAJOR OIL COMPANIES are engaged in four successive stages of operation: (1) the possession of reserves, (2) the production of crude oil, (3) the refining of crude into finished products (gasoline, fuel oil, etc.), and (4) the sale at retail to the final customer. In addition, they have brought under their control many of the means of transportation used by the industry—gathering lines, pipelines, tankers, tank cars, tank trucks. Thus, for three-quarters of a century they have supplied most of the world's oil requirements from fields which they own (or to which they have producing rights), extracting it by their own wells, transporting it by their own gathering lines, pipelines, and tankers (or those under charter), transforming it into gasoline, distillate fuel oil, jet fuel, petrochemical feedstock, residual oil, and other products in their own refineries, and dispensing it via their own filling stations and other outlets. In the absence of vertical integration, each of these successive stages would be conducted by separate, independent enterprises, producing or marketing at the lowest possible cost and selling at the highest price obtainable. This structure is not just the competitive model of academic economics; it is an accurate description of the way in which business in most industries is actually carried on.

Based on the analogy of the flow of a river, the expansion toward sources of supply is generally referred to as a movement "upstream" (or "backward"), while movement toward the final product is referred to as "downstream" (or "forward") expansion. In the world petroleum industry, companies that have not had enough low-cost crude to supply their own refining and marketing needs have emphasized "upstream" expansion to enlarge their holdings of reserves. Companies that have held crude reserves and production capacity greater than could be accommodated through their own refining and distribution organizations have stressed "downstream" expansion. As a result of the movement in both directions, the oil industry has developed a pattern of vertical integration, both at home and abroad, that is un-approached by any other industry.

The extent to which domestic oil companies have in fact become integrated between production and refining can be measured by deter-mining the proportion of their refinery input derived from their own crude production. Such "self-sufficiency" ratios, and their share of domestic output, are shown in Table 10-1 for the top eight. Only one (Mobil) does not supply more than half of its refinery needs from its own crude production. In the case of three of the companies—Exxon, Texaco, and Gulf—the ratio is more than 80 percent. For these companies integration between production and refining has thus largely been achieved. For the top eight the average, weighted by their 1969 production, is 71.7 percent.

Compared to industry as a whole, the extreme degree of vertical integration in petroleum is something of an anomaly. A study of the ratio of corporate sales to gross corporate product by Arthur B. Laffer disclosed no increase in vertical integration among corporations gen-erally between the late 1920's and the mid-1960's: "The conclusion reached on the basis of this empirical evidence is that there has not been any discernible increase in the degree of vertical integration in the corporate sector. If anything, there might have been a slight decline."[1]

TABLE 10-1

Domestic Self-Sufficiency of the Top Eight, 1969
(millions of barrels)

Company	Share of U.S. Crude Production	Self-Sufficiency Ratio
Exxon	9.8%	87.4%
Texaco	8.5	81.0
Gulf	6.8	87.6
SoCal	5.3	68.8
Standard (Ind.)	5.0	50.5
ARCO	5.1	64.9
Shell	6.0	62.1
Mobil	3.9	42.2
Top eight (weighted average)		71.7

Source: *1973 FTC Staff Report,* pp. 13, 20. (Self-sufficiency ratios based on esti-mates of Kerr, Rice and Company, engineers.)

The explanation for the atypical structure of petroleum lies in a complex of advantages enjoyed by integrated firms in this particular industry, of which the most important have been the benefits accorded petroleum producers under the U.S. tax laws. Percentage depletion and the right to deduct "intangible" drilling costs as business expenses made it advantageous for oil companies to make as much of their total profit as possible at the stage to which these benefits apply—crude production. The greater the proportion of their total revenues made in crude production, the greater the advantage of the integrated firm over their nonintegrated competitors engaged only in refining or marketing. Indeed, as Kahn and de Chazeau have shown, the integrated firms were able to enhance their profits through an increase in the price of crude, even though prices of refined products remained unchanged.[2] Whether a major's operations in the later or "downstream" stages proved to be profitable was secondary to their essentiality as a means of disposing of the product on which the after-tax profit was made. Selling crude to refineries owned by other companies is at best uncertain, while the sale of gasoline to independent marketers depends upon success in what has been a highly competitive market. The key to assured profitability was thus an interrupted flow of crude through refining to the final buyer. To the extent that control over any of the downstream stages rested in the hands of others, the flow might be interrupted, thus curtailing the production of crude and the consequent all-important after-tax profits.

Even without the tax incentives, companies would be motivated toward "backward" or "upstream" expansion by the simple quest for an assured source of supply. It is a natural business motivation to avoid dependence on companies which in the sale of final products are one's competitors. The strength of that motivation is of course enhanced if the supplies involved, as in the Middle East, are spectacularly low in cost.

THE GROWTH OF THE PRIVATE BRANDERS

As contrasted to the major brand gasoline retailer, the private brand marketer represents the epitome of free competitive enterprise. The major brand retailer normally does not own his service station or equipment but leases a completely equipped, supplier-owned or controlled service station; the private brand marketer owns or controls the station or stations which he operates, including land, buildings, and equipment. The major brand dealer agrees in his franchise contract to sell only the gasoline and other products provided by his supplier and only under the major's nationally advertised brand; the private brander is free to seek the best available source and provides his own advertising. The major brand operator benefits from his supplier's advertising program, credit card program, equipment maintenance, travel aid program, business counseling, etc.; the private brander does without all of these services. And perhaps most important, the major brand dealer is protected by an assured gross profit margin; the private brander has no such protection, enjoying only the right to go bankrupt.

The spectacular growth of the private branders dates back to the early postwar years when a massive population exodus began to get under way from the inner city to the suburbs and later to the exurbs. By installing large, multi-pump stations on traffic arteries to the suburbs and undercutting the majors by as much as 5–6 cents a gallon, the private branders soon captured an important share of this rapidly expanding market. Meanwhile, the majors, though also expanding toward the suburbs, were burdened by an excessive number of stations at formerly choice locations in the inner city whose volume was steadily declining. It was the size of the margin needed to cover the costs of these numerous low-volume stations that served as an umbrella under which the high-volume private branders moved in. Their strategy was to emphasize locations where traffic was heavy in the large trading areas, rather than numerous conveniently located stations. And their success was spectacular. In the words of Fred Allvine and James Patterson, "They grew from an estimated 5–10% of the national market to approximately 20% in the late 1950's or early 1960's. They accomplished this by becoming specialists in the local distribution and retailing of gasoline."[3]

Originally located next to railroad sidings in order to eliminate the cost of motor truck transportation, the private branders were quick to introduce self-service stations as well as other innovations in the distribution of gasoline. According to Allvine and Patterson:

> They innovated by erecting large, multi-pump stations along major arteries leading to the suburbs. In addition, they innovated by putting in large, underground storage capacity that could accept full transport trailer loads of gasoline. The large multi-pump stations, with sizeable storage capacity, and strategic location on major traffic arteries gave the private branders the elements that were necessary to do profitable high volume business efficiently at a considerably lower price to the consumer. By following this strategy, the private brand marketers were able to show the strong growth rate that they experienced during the post World War II period.[4]

In effect, the private branders brought to gasoline retailing the economics of modern mass merchandising, with resultant benefits to consumers and to the economy generally. To quote Allvine and Patterson again:

> By running a low unit cost, high volume operation, and by eliminating many of the marketing costs associated with brand name advertising, credit cards, trading stamps, and games of chance, these operators are still able to make money even after substantial price cuts. In the process, they serve an extremely useful function for the gasoline consumer—even those consumers who never patronize the private brander. Specifically, they keep a downward pressure on the retail price of gasoline. Without the continuous pressure of actual or potential price cuts by the private branders, there is considerable likelihood that distribution margins would begin to creep upward, given that generally benign character of the horizontal checks between the major brands.
>
> In addition, they serve those customers who prefer discounts to frills and who are interested in economy. In short, they provide desirable variety in gasoline retailing and represent a viable alternative to the homogenized offer of the majors. Their competitive significance, therefore, extends much beyond their quantitative importance in terms of market share and profitability.[5]

Although private branders had been making inroads on the majors throughout the 1960's, statistical data on retail market shares are available only since 1968 (and for most states only since 1969). Despite the predatory practices used against them, the private branders were continuing to make important gains up to 1972. The following table shows the change between 1969 and 1972 in the share of retail gasoline sales made by the top four and top eight companies, distributed by gallonage of state:[6]

TABLE 10-2

Change in Share of Retail Gasoline Sales, 1969–72

Gallonage (bils.)	Top Four Cos.	Top Eight Cos.
5 or more	−3.76 % pts.	−4.89 % pts.
3–4.99	−5.86	−6.49
2–2.99	−2.82	−5.39
1–1.99	−3.98	−5.28
Under 1	−3.45	−5.01

Regardless of a state's gallonage, the top four and top eight companies accounted for a significantly smaller share of its retail gasoline sales in 1972 than only three years earlier. In the heavy-volume states with a gallonage of over 5 billion barrels, the top four lost 3¾% points and the top eight nearly 5% points. At the opposite extreme, the top four in the smallest-volume states lost nearly 3½% points and the top eight slightly over 5% points. The largest losses took place in states with the next-to-largest gallonage—nearly 6% points for the top four and 6½% points for the top eight. Moreover, the losses were not the result of some episodic occurrence involving a particular year; rather, the trend was steadily downward from each year to the next. Both the top four and the top eight suffered decreases in their market shares in each gallonage category, from 1969 to 1970, from 1970 to 1971, and again from 1971 to 1972.[7]

As a consequence, the number of concentrated gasoline markets sharply declined. As can be seen from Table 10-3, the number of states where the top four sellers accounted for more than 50 percent of the retail gasoline sales fell from sixteen in 1969 to only four in 1972. Included among the dozen markets which shifted to a less concentrated category were one state in the largest-volume category and two in the next-to-largest class; by 1972, the only markets with concentration ratios of over 50 percent were small-volume states. At the same time, the number of states with ratios of 40 percent or less rose from ten to eighteen. Not only were the majors suffering losses in market shares with dismaying rapidity; a relatively large proportion of the losses was centered in the most important states.

TABLE 10-3

**Changes in Distribution of States by Four-Company Concentration
Ratios, 1969 and 1972**

| Gallonage (bils.) | No. of States | No. of States in Concentration Category | | | | | |
| | | 40% and Under | | 41–50% | | Over 50% | |
		'69	'72	'69	'72	'69	'72
5 or more	4	0	0	3	4	1	0
3–4.99	5	1	2	2	3	2	0
2–2.99	9	3	5	6	3	0	0
1–1.99	15	6	7	4	8	5	0
Under 1	17	0	4	9	10	8	4
Total	50	10	18	24	28	16	4

THE DECLINE IN THE MAJORS' DOMESTIC EARNINGS

Despite the impressive advantages of integration the majors, with one notable exception, began during the mid-1960's to suffer a steady deterioration in their *domestic* earnings. The exception was Exxon, which for most of this period was enjoying the fruits of a highly successful advertising campaign, incessantly importuning motorists to "Put a tiger in your tank." The general erosion in profits could not be attributed to any weakness in consumption, since demand was steadily rising by nearly 5 percent a year, and, except for 1970, the economy was singularly free of recessions. Nor could the profit erosion be traced to any general breakdown in the price structure, since the price series for both crude and refined products remained relatively stable. The only explanation was the loss in market shares to private branders offering discount prices.

The profit trends during 1961–73 are shown in Chart 10-1 for the seven largest companies in the United States. The figures, it should be noted, relate to net income in the United States alone and were thus not affected by the vicissitudes suffered in the competitive world market. After showing a moderate but steady improvement during the first half of the decade, net earnings, for all but Exxon, tended to move downward between the mid-sixties and 1972–73. The decline began in 1966 for Standard (Ind.) and SoCal; in 1968 for Texaco, Gulf, and Shell; and in 1969 for Mobil. Particularly pronounced were the decreases registered by Texaco between 1968 and 1969, by Shell between 1968 and 1970, and by Gulf throughout the entire period.

VERTICAL INTEGRATION AND PREDATORY PRACTICES

The gains registered by the private branders were made in the face of a variety of forms of competitive warfare waged against them by the top eight. As vertically integrated firms, the largest companies could, themselves, deny supplies to their nonintegrated competitors, impose on them a "price squeeze," and preempt access to markets. In addition, like all firms with substantial monopoly power in some markets, they could engage in price discrimination.

Evidence of the denial of supplies is to be found in the *1973 Staff Report* of the Federal Trade Commission. Through information collected for 1971 by questionnaire and interviews with the largest independent crude producers, refiners, and marketers, the FTC Staff

CHART 10-1
Seven Companies Comparison United States Net Income

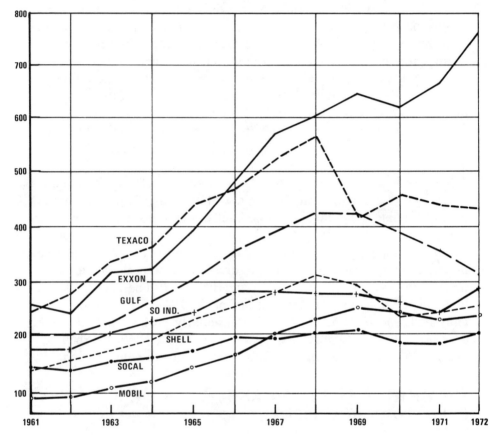

Source: 94th Congress, Senate Subcommittee on Antitrust and Monopoly, *Hearings in the Industrial Reorganization Act,* Testimony of W. T. Slick, Jr., Exxon Corp., January 21, 1975, Exhibit 15.

determined the sources from which the independents obtained their supplies. In 1971, independent marketers in the South and East (Districts 1 and 3) were able to secure from the eight largest integrated oil companies only 4 million out of the 233 million barrels used. During the five-year period ending in 1971, the proportion of their requirements obtained from the top eight ranged from 1.6 (1971) down to 0.5

percent (1968). "The data clearly indicate that the eight largest firms have dealt only nominally with independent marketers; several have testified in investigative hearings that *they will not sell to independents, regardless of price.*"[8]

Even if the nonintegrated independent is able to obtain supplies, he may suffer from a "price squeeze" or narrowing of the margin between the price he pays for his materials and the price he receives for his finished product. The price squeeze may take the form of an increase in the price of materials while the price of the finished goods is held relatively constant or even reduced, or it may take the form of a reduction in the price of the finished goods while the price of materials is held comparatively stable or even increased. Independent petroleum refineries have on occasion experienced the worst possible form of squeeze—an increase in the price of crude and a decrease in the price of refined products.

According to data presented by Alfred E. Kahn before the Senate Antitrust Subcommittee, the margin between the price of crude oil (Gulf Coast) and the average price of refined products (principally gasoline) had remained relatively stable at around $1.00 per barrel throughout 1952 and 1953.[9] Late in 1953 the price of crude was raised, but since a similar advance was made in the price of refined products, no immediate change occurred in the margin. As the 1954 recession got under way, however, the price of refined products began to decline, though the price of crude remained unchanged at its new, higher level. By late 1954, the refiners' margin had been narrowed to less than $.50, and a subsequent recovery early in 1955 only brought it up to around $.75. The same sequence of events, with an even more extreme effect on the margin, was repeated in the 1958 recession. Again the squeeze was preceded by an increase, early in 1957, in the price of crude. Since refined product prices were also advanced, there was again no immediate effect on the margin. But as the recession progressed, the price of refined products fell steadily, though the price of crude again held firm (owing in this, as in the preceding recession, to sharp curtailments in crude output ordered by state proration authorities). By the middle of 1958 the margin had fallen to $.25, and by the end of the year to less than $.10. The recovery did not take place for several years, the margin remaining around $.25 until the middle of 1961.

The transportation problem faced by independent crude producers is a good example of how access to markets can be preempted. About three-quarters of domestic crude output is moved by pipelines: first through gathering lines from the well head to a main trunkline station, and then through a larger-diameter pipeline to the refinery. Al-

most all pipelines are owned by the major oil companies—either
individually or as joint ventures. An independent crude producer so
located that the only nearby gathering line is owned by a major and
flows to the major's refinery virtually has his market determined for
him.[10] The FTC Staff described the nature of the problem as follows:

> Through the pipeline system, crude oil is transported more or less
> on a constant-flow basis. Trunkline stations can pump in a batch
> of crude only when there is a slot in the flow for it and then
> pressure must be increased or decreased to adjust for the desired
> flow speed. The scheduling of pipeline input is very complex and
> must be worked out in advance of the shipment. Because of this
> process, an independent crude producer may have great difficulty
> in securing a place in the flow, especially if he does not have
> storage tanks at the trunkline station and/or ships a relatively
> small amount of crude. The result of this pipeline system is to
> place the major firms who own the pipelines in an excellent posi-
> tion to discriminate against the independent producer. The oppor-
> tunity to require the independent to enter into an agreement to
> sell his product at the well head in order to obtain regular sale
> and transportation of crude clearly exists for the majors.[11]

In addition to using the competitive weapons inherent in vertical
integration, the majors have sought to protect their entrenched position through the use of price discrimination. Referred to variously as
"voluntary price allowances," "temporary dealer allowances," or "competitive price allowances," discounts off the tank wagon price were
granted to the majors' dealers which, after the addition of the dealer's
guaranteed margin, brought his retail price near to or in some cases
even below the private brander's price. Confronted with this tactic,
the private brander then sought an allowance from *his* supplier; but
the independent refiners limited more narrowly the extent to which
allowances were granted off the tank wagon price.[12] The majors seldom if ever granted allowances to all of their dealers in a given market
area, but only to those in a designated zone, usually based on a market
survey designed to delineate the specific area affected by the price
rivalry. The allowances were of course subsidized by higher prices
outside the zone where competition was quiescent, and were terminated when the price rivalry abated.

The most extreme form of conflict between the majors and the private branders was the price war. According to the FTC, price wars
"were especially widespread during the years immediately prior to
mid-1965. One price war brought to the Commission's consideration
lasted for a period of almost four years, and participants in this
struggle claim that gasoline sold below cost for 572 days of the period."

One small refiner testified that in 1959 there were only eight price changes in its marketing area, whereas in 1964: ". . . we were forced to respond to at least 159 major changes in gasoline tank-wagon prices."[13]

The casualties of price wars were not necessarily the least efficient enterprises. An official of one of the lesser majors deplored "the destructive, anticompetitive and even predatory pricing practices that have become symptomatic of gasoline marketing." He went on to state that executives of his company (Tidewater) "do not believe that a man driven out of business because his competition can absorb below-cost sales for extended periods is necessarily inefficient. We believe he is often the helpless victim of competitive cannibalism."[14]

Although its most extreme form, the price war is not the only way in which price discrimination has been practiced in this industry. There has long been consensus that, in order to survive, the private brander's retail price must be at least 2 cents below the major's price, and some independent marketers strove for a spread of 4–5 cents.[15]

As the FTC put it, "The independent claims . . . that if he does not compensate for his inability to engage in massive product differentiation and customer conveniences, he will be in a 'predictably ruinous market position.' "[16] Again subsidizing their dealers with allowances, the majors attacked the private branders by instituting what in the trade are referred to as "one-cent plans." After such a plan is put into effect, the subsequent moves and countermoves take a predictable course, described by the FTC as follows:

> In the great majority of cases, the independent refiners meet such reductions by offering pricing assistance to their customers. Frequently, the proponent of the plan makes a further reduction in tank-wagon price which is almost invariably followed by his fellow majors. Further reductions ensue to the point where retailers are operating under guaranteed margins and the suppliers are bearing the entire burden of the price reductions. Price competition then becomes a matter of staying-power. The independent is determined to sell at a differential in excess of that which the major would impose because as one refiner put it, "surrender to the one-cent plan is encouraged because we know the cost of price wars and there is the hope that perhaps the situation may change . . . [but to] surrender to the one-cent plan means only one thing—slow ultimate death to the independent. I can assure you categorically that this is the inevitable result."[17]

Price discrimination has been supplemented by a variety of other tactics. One has been the introduction of a "sub-regular" brand, designed to be sold at or near the private brander's prices for the regular grade. Another has been the establishment of whole chains of purportedly independent stations, with new and catchy brand names, ostentatiously displaying all the outward appearance of a true private brand marketer. To the majors, they represent merely a legitimate effort to participate in the expanding high-volume, low-price market; to the independents, they represent an invasion under false pretenses into *their* market, subsidized by profits earned elsewhere, and designed to take away their customers and police their prices.

Not infrequently the result of such predatory practices has been the acquisition of the independent marketer by a major oil company. Not only are retail customers thereby deprived of a competitive source of supply, but the effects extend "upstream" to the independent refiner. Between 1958 and 1964, major oil companies acquired forty-eight marketers,[18] most of whom had operated chains of discount filling stations. Commenting on this trend, Allvine and Patterson observed:

> The net effect of these mergers has been a systematic reduction in the number of private brands and a lessening of the important intertype competition that they represent. Nor can we expect the independents to reappear in many of these markets, since such mergers often result in the drying up of supply sources. Typically the majors that purchase outlets in a new market cease to supply the remaining independents in that area since they now have a retail stake in the market which makes "dumping" unattractive. If they do consent to continue to supply an independent, the prices are normally high and the supply terms restrictive. In addition, the rebirth of independents in urban markets is hindered by difficulty in finding suitable new locations with proper zoning.[19]

DENIAL OF SUPPLIES IN THE EARLY SEVENTIES

The gains of the private branders came to an end in 1973; the cause was a sharp intensification of the practices described above—the denial of supplies and the price squeeze. Gasoline available to the private branders began to run into short supply in the spring of 1972. Although a slowdown in refinery construction during the 1960's had left the industry with only a small margin of spare capacity, this was not the cause of the shortage. As Allvine and Patterson point out, "When discussing the refinery shortage question, one should remember that the petroleum product shortage of late 1972 and 1973 was not related to inadequacy of refining capacity. At that time, *there was sufficient refining capacity had it only been scheduled and used properly.*"[20] It is against this background that the action by the integrated companies in sharply lowering the rate of production during the first half of 1972 assumes particular interest.

THE FLOW CHANNELS. The sequence of events that would logically be expected to follow from a reduction in the supply of gasoline
can perhaps be best envisaged by a depiction of the flow channels
through which crude moves to refineries and gasoline from refineries
to marketers. As has been brought out earlier, the domestic industry
is a trichotomy, consisting of the eight largest majors, lesser major
integrated companies, and the independent nonintegrated refiners and
marketers. A flow chart for 1971 was constructed by the FTC Staff,
showing for each of these three types of companies the quantities of
crude produced and sold (or transferred) and the quantities of gasoline refined and sold (or transferred). This information is presented
in summary form in Chart 10-2.[21]

The first and only stage at which most of the output produced and
refined by the largest integrated firms encounters competition is at the
point of sale to the final customer. Hence, it may be more instructive
to read the chart from the bottom up, starting with retail sales. For
the filling stations owned by the top eight, there was in 1971 virtually
only one source: 97 percent of their requirements were supplied by
their companies' refineries. Such shipments constituted 77 percent of
these refineries' output, with 17 percent going to other majors and
only 5 percent to independent marketers. Likewise, the independent
retail outlets obtained over half (51%) of their requirements from
independent refiners. These shipments made up 70 percent of the
independent refiners' output.

Up to this point a certain degree of parallelism can be seen to exist
between the two flows. But unlike the top eight, the independent marketers relied on the "other majors" for a substantial proportion of their
receipts (43%). And these lesser majors were in turn dependent upon
the top eight for much of the supply for *their* filling stations. Although
receiving nearly half (49%) of their refined products from their own
refineries, the retail outlets of the other majors obtained an almost
equally large share (46%) from the top eight. What thus made the
independent marketers particularly vulnerable was the extent of their
dependence on the other majors, whose service stations were in turn
heavily dependent for *their* requirements on the top eight.

Moving upward on the chart, the refineries of the top eight received
the major share of their receipts (61%) from their own wells. But
over a quarter (26%) of their crude intake came from the independent producers. In fact, the top eight were the biggest customers of the
independents, accounting for 44 percent of their output. In addition,
32 percent of their production went to the refineries of the lesser majors. Only 11 percent of the independent producers' output flowed to
independent refiners. The channel from independent to independent,
so evident in the movement of refined products, was constricted and

CHART 10-2
Flow of Domestic Oil and Petroleum Products
Districts 1 and 3, 1971 (millions of barrels)

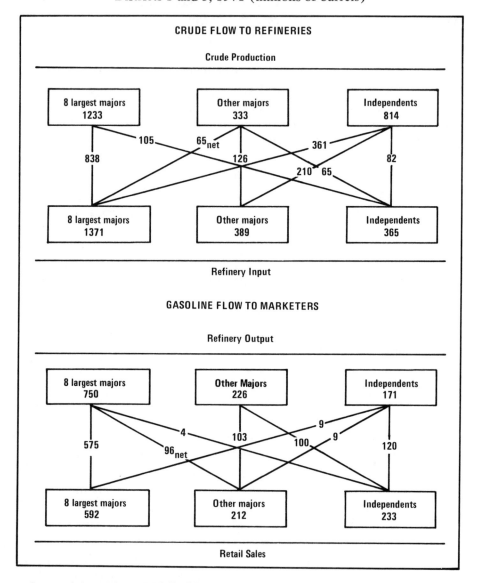

Source: Adapted from FTC Staff Report, 1973.

relatively unimportant in crude production. Whatever the cause, the independent refiners were not an important outlet for the independent crude producers. And this in turn made the independent refiners heavily dependent on their larger rivals, receiving 47 percent of their crude requirements from the majors and only 22 percent from independent producers (the remaining 31% coming in 1971 from imports allocated under the import quota system).

Given the pattern of vertical integration depicted on the chart, the probable consequences of a shortage are readily apparent. Again starting at the bottom of the chart and reading up, the top eight would logically be expected to divert to their own filling stations a good part of the 96 million barrels that had formally gone to the retail outlets of the lesser majors. Since this represents 46 percent of the latter's supply, they would in turn be compelled to divert to *their* stations a good part of the 100 million barrels they have been supplying the independent marketers. As deliveries from the lesser majors have made up 44 percent of their total receipts, the loss of any substantial portion of this supply would place the independent marketers in an almost impossible situation.

Similarly, if either the top eight or the lesser majors—who supplied the independent refiners with 30 and 22 percent, respectively, of their total receipts—were to divert to their own use any substantial proportion of these deliveries, the independents would be hard put to find a replacement. And this in turn would tend to dry up the supply of gasoline available to the independent marketers, who obtain more than half their requirements from the independent refiners.

The private branders were very well aware of the dangers to which they were exposed by these flow patterns. Testifying in 1969 before the Senate Antitrust Subcommittee, Frederick Lichtman of the Society of Independent Gasoline Marketers stated: "An essential element to successful operation is a ready and reliable source of supply of a competitive nature. In recent years, with the decline of independent refiners to less than 10 percent of refining capacity, private brand marketers have been increasingly forced to look to the major oil companies as a supply source. The inequity in bargaining power present in this confrontation leaves private brand marketers largely at the mercy of the major oil companies."[22] Their vulnerability during shortages was well understood by the independents. In Lichtman's words, "In times of plenty many major oil companies are more than willing to sell gasoline to private brand marketers, but little imagination is needed to envision what the situation will be should gasoline come into short supply." By 1972 what they had feared was beginning to become a reality.

THE REDUCTION IN THE REFINERY RATE. During the first four months of 1972, the refiners' rate of capacity utilization (east of the Rockies) fell to 84.2 percent; for the first six months, it averaged 85.4 percent, or 4.5 percent below the first-half average for 1970, 1971, and 1973. Fred C. Allvine notes, "Had this capacity been operated in the first half of 1972, an additional 500,000 barrels of oil per day would have been processed and the condition giving rise to the later recognized petroleum product shortages would not have existed."[23]

The industry's largest firm, Exxon, operated its refining capacity during the first four months in 1972 at an average rate of 86.6 percent, as compared to 95.5 percent in 1971.[24] If the comparison were with capacity, not previous production, the additional amount processed by the industry would have risen during the first half of 1972 to 850,000 b/d, or more than enough to have averted any possibility of shortage. This represents the difference between the 85 percent of capacity actually utilized and an operating rate of 92 percent, considered by staff members of Interior's Office of Oil and Gas to reflect an adequate allowance for normal down-time.[25]

Inasmuch as demand was rising at some 4.5–5 percent a year, the lowering of refinery operations led inexorably to a serious depletion of inventories, first in home-heating oil, and then in gasoline. The refinery cutbacks in the first half of 1972 began to have their effect on fuel oil inventories as early as June. And by October the usual seasonal buildup had fallen far short of normal, leaving fuel oil inventories some twenty-eight days below the corresponding levels for 1970 and 1971. The industry responded by increasing its production of fuel oil, but at the expense of other products, thereby seriously aggravating the gasoline shortage which was already developing. The monthly trends of gasoline stock fell by the middle of 1972 about four days below the corresponding levels for 1970 and 1971; by February 1973, they were eight days below, and by March ten days below: "What followed was a shortage of gasoline, since inventories during the summer months were extremely low and production was not adequate to keep up with the demand for gasoline during the peak driving season."[26]

Here again, Exxon's behavior accorded with that of the industry as a whole. Although assuring officials of the Office of Emergency Preparedness on July 18, 1972, that: "We plan to increase end of summer distillate inventories to maximum and to carry a higher normal inventory position into the first quarter of 1973,"[27] Exxon's distillate inventories at the beginning of the first quarter of 1973 were 18.5 percent below the corresponding average for the three preceding years.[28]

This drop in inventory position was attributed by Exxon to the "abnormally early cold weather in the fall of 1972." Yet during the fall months of September–December, Exxon's average distillate yield (20.2%) was below the average for the first six months (21.1%): "What Exxon was doing was producing the gasoline in the last six months of the year that it had failed to manufacture early in the year when its refinery runs were so noticeably low."[29] But Exxon's gasoline production was not sufficient to meet the needs of its own trade customers. Compared to the first nine months of 1972, sales of gasoline to its large-volume customers were reduced during the period October 1972–June 1973 by 50 percent:[30] "Exxon's second largest wholesale account had been Triangle, one of the larger wholesalers of gasoline to the discount gasoline marketers. Concurrent with a 75 percent reduction in Exxon's sales to Triangle in the final quarter of 1972, Triangle announced its withdrawal from wholesale supply to the independents in mid-Continent area of the United States. Many private brand, discount marketers were left without an alternate source of gasoline."

CASUALTIES AMONG THE INDEPENDENT MARKETERS. The devastating effects of the shortage on independent marketers can be illustrated by a number of examples developed by Allvine and Patterson.[31] Exxon was the supplier of crude to Crown Central, which in turn was the supplier of gasoline to a number of the country's most rapidly growing independent marketers, including the Olé and U-Filler-Up chains. Between the first five months of 1972 and 1973, Exxon's deliveries to Crown Central were reduced by 64.7 percent.[32]

(000's of gallons)

	1973	1972
January	9,602	15,128
February	7,756	13,895
March	9,490	19,737
April	5,155	21,548
May	5,647	33,544
	37,650	103,852

Confronted with a drying up of crude, Crown Central notified these two chains that after April 1973 it could no longer supply them. According to the *National Petroleum News*, these self-service enterprises were started by a lawyer, Lawrence Egerton, who had no prior experience in the gasoline business; they had been "growing like wildfire," and had expanded their number of stations from four in 1968 to 124 by 1972. According to Allvine and Patterson:

> Egerton had financed much of his expansion through short-term bank loans. As supply was cut back, and the cost of remaining material greatly increased, Egerton's ability to keep up with bank payments was seriously jeopardized. This was also true of many other independents for whom quick termination of supply meant being forced to the brink of—or into—financial bankruptcy. . . .
>
> Some of the majors were primary suppliers to lesser oil companies and brokers furnishing the independents. All they had to do was to withdraw the supply from the buffer operations and they could whip the carpet from under many of the new, rapidly growing and financially weak self-service operators. If this action did not bankrupt the independents, it would certainly neutralize them so they could no longer threaten the majors in the marketplace.[33]

The fate of the Egerton chains in the Carolinas was duplicated in Alabama by that of another Crown Central customer, the Romaco self-service chain. Between the fourth quarters of 1972 and 1973, Romaco's supply was reduced by 70 percent, thereby putting an end to its rapid expansion which in three years had brought it to 150 stations. As with the Egerton chains, the curtailment of supply was drastic and abrupt, deliveries dropping by 53 percent between the fourth quarter of 1972 and the second quarter of 1973.

In the case of the Egerton and Romaco chains, the initiator of the chain reaction was Exxon; in the case of Autotronics—the nation's volume leader among the new self-service companies—the initiators were Gulf and ARCO, who supplied the company's brokers, Armour Oil and Foremost Oil, respectively. Featuring newly constructed, attractive outlets, Autotronics had expanded its stations from 66 in 1969 to 550 in 1972: "With an organization built and structured for growth, large insurance and bank financing connections, Autotronics had its sights set on a billion gallons per year of gasoline by 1977, at which time it anticipated being the sixteenth largest gasoline marketer in the United States."[34] After reaching a peak sales volume in March 1973, its supply by May was cut to half that of three months earlier, and by June its sales volume had fallen 49 percent below its peak: "Hundreds of stations were closed and volume was concentrated in the more profitable units. In addition, executives of the company were terminated and major reductions were made in its organizational staff. The wind was definitely taken out of Autotronic's sales and the company was literally a shadow of the organization it had been."[35]

The Petrol Stop chain—supplied partly by Armour and, like Auto-tronics, the ultimate recipient of a cutback initiated by Gulf—had grown from 109 stations in 1969 to 324 in 1972. Made up largely of unprofitable outlets discarded by the majors, these stations under their new management featured exceptionally low prices: "Petrol's method of expansion was just as real a threat to the major brand method of marketing as Autotronic's more capital-intensive approach. If the independents were permitted to pick up the major's 'dogs' and reopen them as low price 'mini' service stations and self-service stations, they would accelerate the decay of the remaining major brand system."[36] After receiving sharp cutbacks in its supply, Petrol's sales volume by May of 1973 had fallen 81 percent below its peak of only five months earlier. As of the following year Petrol's operations no longer existed.

THE EXCLUSION OF IMPORTS. For the independent refiners as well as the marketers dependent upon them, hope of relief came to center on a relaxation of the import quota. At the beginning of 1972, the quota remained at the historical level of 12.2 percent of domestic production, plus a minimal additional allowance of 100,000 b/d for 1970, 1971, and 1972, or a total of some 1,500,000 b/d—approximately 15 percent of the total oil processed. Early in 1972 the larger nonintegrated refiners, e.g., Ashland, Clark Oil, and Standard Oil of Ohio, requested that oil imports be raised by 300,000–350,000 b/d. Through their trade group (the American Petroleum Refiners Association), the smaller independent refiners requested an increase of 350,000 b/d. On May 23, 1972, President Nixon announced an increase of 230,000 b/d. But since the operating rate had been lowered below the first half of 1970–71 by 500,000 b/d, this moderate adjustment did not begin to meet the demand, which itself had been rapidly rising.

Two months later the same companies were again back in Washington, urging a further increase in the quota of some 200,000 b/d. On September 18, 1972, President Nixon took an action which, in effect, transferred the decision-making authority to the companies fortunate enough to have quotas, principally the top eight. Refiners were given the right to increase their previously authorized import quotas by 10 percent, up to an aggregate total of 150,000 b/d, subject however to the condition that any such increase would be counted as an advance against the company's 1973 quota. To the independent refiners, this action represented a Pyrrhic victory, Ashland protesting that it would further squeeze the independent refiner. As Allvine has pointed out, "There was no compulsion for those large petroleum companies controlling more crude oil than they need (produced and purchased from independent producers) to increase their imports. They could simply cut back on sales to independent refiners and increase their own refinery runs, thus further aggravating the growing shortage of petroleum products in the United States."[37] Inasmuch as a number of the majors used their 10 percent "drawing rights" only partly or not at all, the shortage continued.

The position of Exxon on the quota issue remained consistent: opposition to any increase, followed by failure to exercise its rights when the quota was relaxed. In March 1972, at a meeting between the chairman of the Oil Policy Committee and one of Exxon's Washington representatives, the latter (according to a government memorandum) expressed the view that "there was no need for additional crude oil imports in 1972 . . . the crude market seems to be easing."[38] In April, by which time some increase seemed inevitable, an Exxon representative communicated to a Commerce official the need for an increase of only "100,000" b/d, indicating opposition to any increase of 250,000–300,000 b/d then being considered.[39] When in September President Nixon authorized importers to draw against their quota for the following year, Exxon was among the companies that failed to use *any* of their drawing rights. Asked by a Congressional committee to explain its policy, the company answered: ". . . Exxon was able to acquire sufficient quotas to import required crude supplies until the fall of 1972 when world crude supplies became tight and there was simply no additional crude available. Therefore, although Exxon had originally planned to use some of the 'draw' against 1973 quotas, *the worldwide shortage prevented achievement of that intention.*"[40] Yet, while tying the hands of the world's largest oil company, the "worldwide shortage" did not prevent nonintegrated refiners wholly lacking in foreign reserves from being able to use all or most of their drawing rights.[41] Equally uninformative was Exxon's explanation of the reduction in its crude sales to other refining companies: "Through 1972 as crude supplies tightened and our needs increased, spot sales were no longer feasible."[42]

PRICE SQUEEZE IN THE EARLY SEVENTIES

A price squeeze on independent marketers and refiners was the inevitable consequence of the artificial limitation of supply. Trying to find an alternate source of supply, independent marketers, who had been cut off by the major companies, drove up the price of the limited supply of spot market gasoline. Independent refiners, unable to obtain their requirements from customary sources, were forced to do likewise for crude. In both cases, of course, the ultimate effect was an increase in the independents' retail selling price. For the differential between the majors' and the independents' retail prices to be narrowed, it was necessary only for the majors to abstain from price increases. In this particular period, what was obviously to their best interests became a requirement of law with the imposition in August 1971 of government price controls.

What happened to the structure of gasoline prices as this process ran its natural course is strikingly illustrated on Chart 10-3. Compiled by Allvine and Patterson from the Lundberg Survey, weekly retail price series for majors and independents are available from the Lundberg Survey for five Western cities. Clearly, a sharp change in price behavior took place in the middle of 1972. Up to that time, the price had followed a ritualized pattern: established at a relatively high level at the beginning of the month, followed by generally steep declines as the month progressed, only to be reestablished with the beginning of the next month. Both the majors and the independents appear to have followed the same pattern, with the differential between the two remaining relatively stable regardless of the steepness of the decline. But after the abnormal reduction in refinery operations during the early part of 1972, the intra-monthly price declines came to an end. No longer were the majors acting to maintain the established differential by promptly matching every reduction of the independents.

The majors' new stability stemmed from their common discontinuance in mid-1972 of price allowances granted their dealers "to meet competition." And behind this action, according to Allvine and Patterson, was their recognition of the independents' rapidly diminishing strength:

> It is curious how the giant competitors could reach such market stability so quickly in many markets that had been ripped by price wars for years. To many independent discount marketers, it seemed unreal for the majors to ignore their much lower prices. Over several years the majors had engaged the independents in price wars with differentials of two to three cents per gallon on regular gasoline. However, by September and October the independent prices were frequently five to seven cents lower than the majors. The reason why the majors did not respond to the discounters' greater differentials became clear over the next four to eight months, as one price marketer after another experienced sharp cuts in the supply of gasoline available to him. Eventually the price marketers realized that the giants of the petroleum industry had not forgotten them, but, on the contrary, were developing the new tool of supply control to throttle the price marketers.[43]

For those independents wholly unable to secure supplies, the application of this "new tool of supply control" meant a virtually immediate demise. For those more fortunate, it meant the payment of

CHART 10-3

Average Weekly Price of Regular Gasoline: Major and Independent Retailers

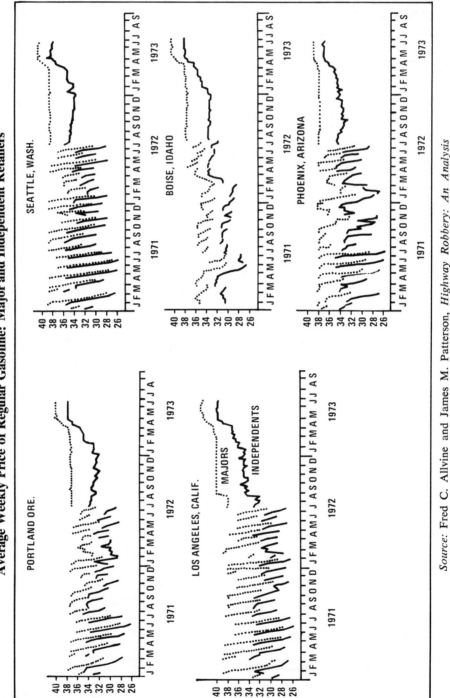

Source: Fred C. Allvine and James M. Patterson, *Highway Robbery: An Analysis of the Gasoline Crisis,* Indiana University Press, Bloomington, 1974 (compiled from Lundberg Survey, Inc.)

premium prices and thus the loss of their most important competitive weapon. By the fall of 1973, the differential between the majors' and the independents' prices had been narrowed to 2 cents or less. And by the end of the year, some independents found themselves the victims of the ultimate price squeeze: to cover their costs they were forced to charge retail prices actually higher than those of the majors.

THE ENDING OF MARKET EROSION

If the objective was to arrest the downward trend in concentration, the slowing down of refinery operations—accompanied by the continued exclusion of imports—more than achieved its purpose. In 1972, the shares of retail gasoline sales made by the leading sellers not only stopped declining; in most states they turned upward. This is illustrated in Chart 10-4, which shows, by regions, the trend of retail gasoline shares accounted for by the eight largest sellers in each of the region's two largest-gallonage states.[44]

The most common pattern is vividly exemplified by the case of North Carolina—a site of conspicuously vigorous expansion by the private branders. Their success is reflected in the sharp decline of the eight-company concentration ratio, from 67.3 percent in 1969, to 55.7 percent in 1972. But as the denial of supplies and the price squeeze took hold, this downward trend was reversed, the share of the eight leaders rising to 63.0 percent in 1973. In a somewhat less extreme form, the same general pattern was exhibited by New York and New Jersey in the Northeast, by California and Texas in the West, and by Illinois in the Midwest. Among a larger group consisting of thirty-three states with 1974 consumption of over 1 billion gallons,[45] the eight leaders were able to improve their market position over the entire period in only one state—Minnesota. But, as can be inferred from Table 10-4, their aggregate losses would have been considerably greater had it not been for the turnaround in 1973. Thus, in nineteen of the thirty-eight states the decline between 1969 and 1972 was followed by a subsequent increase. Of particular interest were the trends within those states in which the leaders had suffered the greatest losses. Of the twenty-one states in which the share of the eight leaders had fallen by 1972 by more than 5 percentage points, no fewer than fourteen, or two-thirds, registered a subsequent increase. Had it not been for the allocation programs imposed by law, requiring the majors to share their crude supplies with independent refiners, these recent increases would undoubtedly have been even greater.

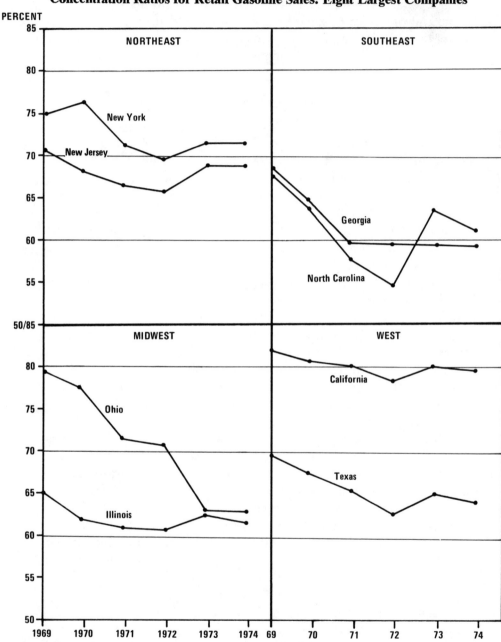

CHART 10-4
Concentration Ratios for Retail Gasoline Sales: Eight Largest Companies

Source: Compiled from Lundberg Survey, Inc., Factbook Issue, *National Petroleum News.*

TABLE 10-4

Retail Gasoline Market Shares, Distribution of Changes in Eight-Company Ratios in Thirty-two States*
(percentage points)

1968–72	1972–1974								
	No. with Increases of:				No. with Decreases of:				
No. of states with decreases of:	Over 5.00	1.01 to 5.00	1.01 & Under	Total	−1.01 & Under	−1.01 to −5.00	Over −5.00	Total	TOTAL
−1.00 or Under			1	1	1			1	2
−1.01 to −5.00	1	1	2	4	3	2		5	9
Over −5.1	2	5	7	14	3	3	2	7	21
Total	3	6	10	19	6	5	2	13	32

* States with 1974 gallonage of over 1 billion gallons.
Source: Compiled from the Lundberg Survey, Inc., Factbook Issue, *National Petroleum News.*

*   *   *

As they entered the 1970's, the largest oil companies were besieged with problems. On the international scene, the Libyan independents had driven the armslength price down to $1.30, while well-known economists had predicted "dollar oil" within the decade. Moreover, the Mideast governments might refuse to accept further curtailments in order to "make room" for the rapidly expanding Libyans, thereby endangering the majors' most valuable concessions. At home, rapid inroads in the retail gasoline market were being registered by the private branders who, because of their superior efficiency, could no longer be held in check by the usual tactics and whose continued expansion was threatening the assured outlets for the flow of the profitable after-tax crude oil.

But in a few short years all this was to change. Abroad, the Libyan independents were either nationalized or forced to accept the government as a majority partner; their production was either preempted or severely limited. At home, independent refiners were rendered desperate for supplies, while the private brand marketers were either forced out of business or were grimly struggling to survive with a greatly reduced margin. Whether the product of a carefully engineered, precisely executed plan or the coincidental result of a series of adroit improvisations, problems that only three years earlier had appeared insoluble were now resolved. Their resolution set the stage for a virtual explosion of prices.

11

THE PRICE
EXPLOSION

BY THE FALL OF 1973, the Libyan independents had either been removed from the scene entirely or rendered incapable of taking advantage of (and thereby hindering) an escalation in world prices. Through an artificial limitation of supplies, the American private branders had been rendered incapable of retarding any upward adjustment of domestic prices made "to meet the competition" of foreign prices. And because the United States had been using up its own oil during the fourteen years of the import quota, this country was no longer able to resolve a world crisis by rapidly expanding its own production. In short, the principal restraints on the exercise of monopoly power were no longer present.

THE PRICE EXPLOSION OF 1973–74

On October 6, 1973, Egypt and Syria invaded Israel, setting off the "Yom Kippur" war. Two days later, a previously scheduled meeting was convened in Vienna between officials of the major oil companies and representatives of the Organization of Petroleum Exporting Countries. The subject for discussion was a revision in the price of oil.

Founded in 1960, OPEC's previous chief claim to fame had been its success in immunizing the oil-producing host countries from the downward trend in world market prices. This was accomplished through an agreement with the majors that tax payments to the countries would be based not on the declining actual or "armslength" prices but on the higher and stable "posted" prices, which accordingly came to be referred to as "tax reference prices." Since the principal effect on the majors was simply to increase their foreign tax credits (and thereby decrease their tax payments to the U.S. Treasury), this accomplishment involved something less than an all-out struggle with the imperialist West. Reviewing OPEC's first ten years of existence,

Edith Penrose was singularly unimpressed. After examining a series of "structural changes" that had taken place in the world industry, she concluded that except for a general strengthening of the producing countries' bargaining power, "OPEC has had either no role at all or a negligible one. OPEC, in spite of its studies, its public relations, its conferences and international ubiquity in the oil world has not, with one exception, been an important factor with respect to the underlying changes that have shaped the industry in the last ten years and are likely to continue to shape it in the future."[1]

In view of OPEC's reputation as a vociferous, pretentious, but largely innocuous organization, the world was ill-prepared for what happened at its meeting of October 6 with representatives of the companies. The OPEC representatives quickly made known their repudiation of the price-determining formulas evolved during the Tripoli, Tehran, and Geneva conferences. They also lost little time in rejecting the industry's offers, initially of an 8 percent, and then of a 15 percent price rise. Instead they proposed, quite simply, that the price be doubled. Although authorized to raise the offer to 25 percent, the industry team decided instead to seek further instructions from the major petroleum-consuming countries; specifically, the governments were asked: "Should the industry voluntarily offer to sweeten the deal to the point where it had a reasonable chance of being accepted by the producing countries?"[2] By their "virtually unanimous" answer in the negative, the consuming governments effectively put an end to the negotiations, thereby opening the door for the unilateral establishment by OPEC of a new price. Promptly taking advantage of the opportunity, OPEC on October 16 announced an immediate increase of approximately 70 percent—from $3.00 to $5.11.

Hardly had oil users adjusted to the October raise before they were hit with a second, even greater increase. At a meeting in Tehran, OPEC announced a further raise, effective January 1, 1974, to $11.65. As can be seen from Chart 11-1, the price of the "marker grade," Saudi Arabia light, had thus risen from its long-established level of $1.80 in late 1970 to $2.59 in early 1972, to $3.01 a year later, to $5.11 in October 1973, and then to $11.65—a sixfold increase in four years. Commensurate increases, variously described in trade accounts as "unprecedented," "staggering," "explosive," "massive," "huge," were instituted for all of the OPEC crudes. In general, the lighter the grade, the lower the sulphur content, and the less the freight required to equalize with other crudes at North European ports, the higher the price.[3] As the chart also shows, the marker grade remained at $11.65 for nearly a year, dropping slightly to $11.25 in November 1974. But in October 1975, the OPEC members took their third

CHART 11-1
Changes in Posted Price of Saudi Arabia Crude Oil*

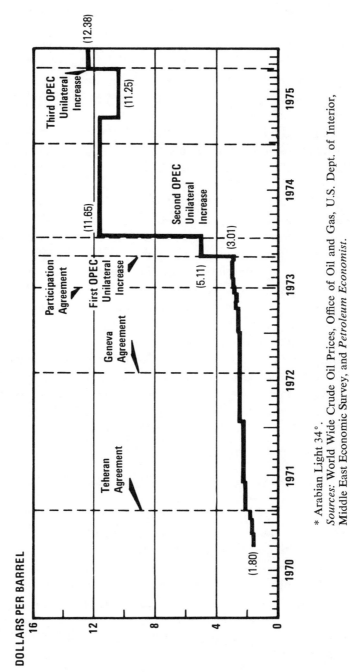

DOLLARS PER BARREL

Third OPEC Unilateral Increase (12.38)

(11.25)

(11.65)

Participation Agreement

First OPEC Unilateral Increase

Geneva Agreement

Second OPEC Unilateral Increase

(5.11)

(3.01)

Teheran Agreement

(1.80)

1970   1971   1972   1973   1974   1975

16   12   8   4   0

* Arabian Light 34°.
Sources: World Wide Crude Oil Prices, Office of Oil and Gas, U.S. Dept. of Interior, Middle East Economic Survey, and *Petroleum Economist.*

unilateral action, raising prices by 10 percent, as a result of which the marker grade rose to $12.38.

The leading proponent of the 1974 increase was, unexpectedly, the Shah of Iran, who had earlier been restored to power with the active aid of the C.I.A., had engineered the highest growth rate of any Mideast country, and as recently as June 1973 had "expressed his opposition to increasing prices on the grounds that it would force Western exporters to raise their prices for the heavy industrial equipment which Iran needed to import."[4]

To support the higher prices, OPEC's Arab members (Saudi Arabia, Iraq, Kuwait, Abu Dhabi, Qatar, Libya, and Algeria) announced on October 17, 1973, that they would cut production below the September level by a minimum of 5 percent in October and by a further 5 percent in each subsequent month "until Israeli withdrawal is completed from the whole Arab territories occupied in June 1967 and the legal rights of the Palestinian people are restored." Because of their conspicuous friendship with the Israelis, the United States and The Netherlands were to be cut off completely. Lending substance to this declaration, crude oil production was reduced between the third and fourth quarters of 1973 in all of the Arab states, the cuts ranging from 20 and 16 percent for Saudi Arabia and Kuwait to 13 and 11 percent for Algeria and Libya, respectively.

In the United States, already suffering from a domestic shortage artificially created earlier in the year, the reaction approached pure panic. Government agencies proferred a succession of rapidly escalating estimates of the "energy shortfall." In a colloquy with John Sawhill, Deputy Administrator of the newly created Federal Energy Administration, Senator Jackson recounted their history:

SENATOR JACKSON: The first estimate we had on Oct. 12 from Mr. DiBona, was 1.2 million barrels per day. On Oct. 24, the Treasury estimate was 1.6 million barrels per day. On October 20 it went up to 2 million; that was a Treasury estimate. The Office of Oil and Gas on October 30 estimated a shortfall of from 2 million barrels to as high as 2.5 million barrels. In early November the Department of Defense estimated 2 million barrels per day.

The President announced on the 25th, in his talk to the nation, a 3.5 million barrel shortfall. Then on December 11, the Emergency Petroleum Supply Committee had the estimate of 2.5 to 2.8. This is what was published.

Then, of course, the figures you and Mr. Simon have given are roughly between 3.26 and 3.27 million barrels.

Do you feel now that you have a more accurate means of making these estimates than we had earlier? Do you now have the ability to collect the data and to marshal the facts and come up with some sensible and accurate estimates?

MR. SAWHILL: I think our estimates on the supply side have improved significantly . . .[5]

The shortfall of 3,270 m b/d cited by Mr. Sawhill was arrived at by subtracting from "unconstrained demand" (plus military demand) the sum total of domestic production plus imports and inventory reduction. This shortfall, however, was to be reduced to 537 m b/d by a series of measures—a 25 percent reduction in airline schedules, reduction in residential and commercial heating, the conversion of power plants from oil to coal, and an allocation program for gasoline.[6] A month later Mr. William Simon, Administrator of the agency, presented a lower estimate of the shortfall, testifying that "the effect of the Arab embargo is to reduce supplies of both crude and product by 2.7 million barrels a day below anticipated demand." This assumed a "realistic, worst case," i.e., a normal growth in demand, a fully effective embargo, and inventory drawdowns to minimum operating levels. The reduction stemmed from a "tremendous response by the American people to our conservation initiatives, from warmer than normal weather, and from leakages in the embargo. The result has been a buildup in our inventory position, and some confusion in discussion of the shortage estimates."[7] Nonetheless, he hastened to reassure the Senators of the gravity of the problem: "Many people still do not believe there is a shortage, but let me assure you that the energy shortage is not contrived."[8]

With motorists forced to wait in long lines, householders forced to live in cold dwellings, and everyone forced to pay much higher prices, the question of whether the shortage was "real" became a matter of intense public interest. On the one hand, the reduction in fourth-quarter production by the Arab countries was an undisputed fact, though production had not been lowered by such important non-Arab countries as Iran and Nigeria. On the other hand, between 1972 and 1973 year-end inventories of petroleum products held by the largest companies rose 5.5 percent.[9] Moreover, there were widespread rumors (usually denied by the industry, the government, or both) that foreign oil was continuing to reach Atlantic ports in quantities greater than reported—a rumor which was given some credence by the fact that the government had relied on the industry's trade association for its import figures; that excess fuel was being stored in tankers whose movement had been slowed to a crawl or in empty tanks of closed-down filling stations; that domestic wells were being capped; that in their offshore operations the companies were restricting production below optimal levels; etc.

THE SHORT-LIVED SHORTFALL

But interest in these and other intriguing subjects of speculation soon began to wane as it became increasingly evident that the shortage, if real, was of remarkably brief duration. During the first quarter of 1974, oil had become generally available throughout the world, but of course at the new price levels. Despite the complete embargo imposed on The Netherlands, supplies reaching Rotterdam had by the end of January attained 80 percent of the pre-crisis level in the case of crude oil and 96 percent in the case of refined products: "The net import figures for three weeks in January show that the Netherlands is now receiving enough crude oil to cover its own needs and that the Rotterdam products market is back in business."[10] In Japan, almost wholly dependent on OPEC oil, crude arrivals during March were "substantially more than forecast earlier"; the government deciding "to ease the restraints on the use of fuel oil and electricity by industry as from 1st March."[11] For Western Europe as a whole, imports for the entire year, 1973, rose by 7 percent, only fractionally below the growth of 7.2 percent recorded for the first six months.[12] In the United States, the total import level was estimated for February to be "about 1 million b/d more than had previously been expected."[13] By April, Mr. Sawhill was acknowledging that previous estimates of the shortfall had been excessive because they "did not take into consideration price elasticity or embargo leakages."[14] As compared to October 1973, the reduction of imports during the next five months reduced total U.S. supply by only 123,580 barrels or 5.5 percent. To this could be added a further reduction of domestic production below the October rate amounting to 29,801 barrels, or 1.3 percent of total supply.[15]

That consuming countries reported, at worst, only minor and temporary interruptions in supplies was due, initially, to the fact that production by OPEC countries for the year 1973 turned out to have been almost identical to the level that would have been expected on the basis of OPEC's historical 9.55 percent growth rate.* In view of the widely publicized embargo and production cutbacks, how was this possible? Part of the explanation lies in the fact that fourth-quarter

---

* The straight-line extrapolation of the regression line and the application of the 9.55% historical growth rate to actual 1972 production (9.8 billion) yield an estimated production figure of 10.7 billion barrels. The application to 1972 production of the slightly higher growth rate of just the last five years (10.4%) yields an estimated output of 10.8 billion barrels. Actual OPEC production for 1973 was 11.0 billion barrels.

output continued to rise over third-quarter levels in a number of non-Arab countries, notably Iran and Nigeria.[16] Of greater importance, however, was the fact that in the Arab countries output had been sharply increased earlier in the year. This is evident from the following table, which contrasts the production decline between the third and fourth quarters of 1973 with the change in output between the first nine months of 1973 and the corresponding period of the previous year.

Change in Crude Oil Output of Arab Producing Countries,
Selected Intervals, 1972 and 1973

	III Q 1973 to IV Q 1973	1st 9 Mos. 1972 to 1st 9 Mos. 1973
S. Arabia	−19.5%	36.4%
Kuwait	−16.1	−5.9
Abu Dhabi	−12.9	30.4
Qatar	−19.2	31.1
Libya	−11.0	1.3
Algeria	−13.4	5.8

Source: Compiled from *The Petroleum Economist,* various issues.

Between the third and fourth quarters of 1973 output declined in all of the Arab countries, the decreases ranging from 11 percent in Libya to nearly 20 percent in Saudi Arabia. The behavior pattern for the first nine months was mixed. As compared to the previous year, a decrease was registered by Kuwait (whose high-sulphur oil was encountering environmental resistance) and only limited increases by Libya and Algeria (whose ambitious nationalization programs had disrupted the movement of their oil to consuming markets). But as compared to a historical annual growth rate of 11 percent, Saudi Arabia's production during the first nine months of 1973 was running 36 percent above the corresponding period of 1972. Increases of nearly a third were also registered by Abu Dhabi and Qatar. A continuation of those high rates of output through the fourth quarter (plus the increases in Iran and Nigeria) would surely have confronted the international oil industry with a distressing glut of "distressed oil."

What is particularly revealing about the 1973 experience is the matter of extent. If OPEC's predetermined growth rate was to be met (but not significantly exceeded), the company-directed accelerations were only slightly in excess of the amounts needed to offset the later country-directed curtailments; or, to put it the other way, the curtailments were nearly sufficient to offset the earlier accelerations. Either the companies in the earlier part of the year correctly anticipated the outbreak of hostilities in October and the resultant curtailments in production; or the countries, after October, correctly tailored their output limitations, so that the increase in actual supply for the year would not significantly exceed (or fall below) the predetermined growth rate.

In fact, both appear to have taken place. Correctly anticipating the outbreak of hostilities, the companies in the first half of 1973 increased the rate of production, particularly in Saudi Arabia. The countries (probably with the aid of the companies) reduced output in October and November by an amount sufficient to offset the earlier increase. But what had impelled the companies to build up the supply? According to Anthony Sampson, Frank Jungers, president of Aramco, paid a courtesy call May 3, 1973, on Saudi Arabia's King Feisel, who "warned Jungers that Zionists and Communists 'were on the verge of having American interests thrown out of the area.'" The King went on to urge "'a simple disavowal of Israeli policies and actions by the U.S. Government.'" The message was made more pointed by the King's chamberlain and close advisor, Kamal Adham, who told Jungers that the Egyptian premier, Sadat, "would have to 'embark on some sort of hostilities' in order to marshal American opinion to press for a Middle East settlement. 'I knew he meant war,' said Jungers later, 'the king liked to give signals, first subtly and then explicitly. It was quite different from his earlier warnings.' Jungers quickly passed on the warning to Exxon and Co. in New York and California."* Whether it was because of this warning or some other information, production was promptly raised in May, and remained at a relatively high rate until the "embargo." For the six-month period May to October, Saudi Arabian monthly production averaged 18 percent higher than in the first quarter.

CHANGES IN "GOVERNMENT TAKE" AND COMPANY MARGINS

How much of the increase in revenues resulting from these drastic price increases went to the host governments? What is generally referred to as the "government take" can be estimated with reasonable accuracy. The method customarily used for this purpose is apparent

---

* Anthony Sampson, *The Seven Sisters,* Viking Press, New York, 1975, pp. 244–245. As his source, Sampson cites Jungers, whom he interviewed in February 1975.

from data obtained in London from Shell and BP and introduced into hearings of the Senate Subcommittee on Antitrust and Monopoly.[17] The figures presented in the first column of Table 11-1 show the results obtained by applying the method in September 1970 to the industry's "marker" crude—Saudi Arabian light.[18] Essentially it consists of (a) subtracting the sum of operating costs and royalties from the posted price, (b) deriving the tax by multiplying the resultant subtotal by the government's share, and (c) adding the royalty to the tax. Compared to $.96 a barrel in 1965, the government take rose to $1.88 in July 1973 and then to $7.00 in January 1974. While due partly to a rise in the government's share (from 50% to 55%), by far the greater part reflects the advance in the posted price from $1.80 a barrel to $3.01 and then to $11.65.

TABLE 11-1

Changes in Government "Take": Light Arabian Crude
(dollars per barrel)

	Nov. 1965	July 1973	Jan. 1974
1. Operating Cost	$ .10	$ .10	$ .10
2. Royalty[a]	.22	.38	1.45
3. Subtotal	.32	.48	1.55
4. Posted Price	1.80	3.01	11.65
5. Less Cost and Royalty (3)	−.32	−.48	−1.55
6. Subtotal	1.48	2.53	10.10
7. Tax Paid	.74[b]	1.40[c]	5.55[c]
8. Govt. "Take" (7 + 2)	.96	1.88	7.00

[a] at 12.5%.
[b] at 50%.
[c] at 55%.

The effect of the OPEC crude oil increases on the majors was ultimately determined by what happened to the prices of refined products. Of the oil obtained in the OPEC countries, the international majors sell relatively little in the form of crude. The great bulk is transferred to their own refineries, entering into petroleum markets only after having been processed into refined products. Any increase in the cost of crude would adversely affect the companies' profit position only if it were *not* passed along in the form of higher prices for refined products. In point of fact, the price explosion in crude was accompanied by sharp increases in refined product prices, as can be seen below for representative grades in world markets:

	Percentage Increase July 1973–Jan. 1974[19]
Aviation Gasoline, Aruba, 100/130	116.7%
Motor Gasoline, Ras Tanura	
95R	120.3
90R	134.6
83R	149.1
Fuel Oil, No. 2, Aruba	200.9
Residual, Bunker C, Aruba	280.8

During the price explosion gasoline more than doubled, light fuel oil tripled, and residual oil nearly quadrupled. Whether these advances exceeded the cost increases incurred by the companies is difficult to determine owing to a series of changes in the relationships between the countries and the companies, all of which affected the latter's costs and margins.

Up to the time of the price explosion, the companies had operated as concessionaires, sharing the total "take" with the host governments (usually on a 50-50 basis) and making most of their payments to the host governments in the form of taxes usable as dollar-for-dollar credits against taxes on other foreign income. Where such was the case, the tax paid was not a cost to be deducted from the price in arriving at the company's margin. This was brought out during Senate hearings in a colloquy with Professor Edith Penrose:

DR. BLAIR: It is not a deduction as a business expense but a dollar-for-dollar credit. This in turn raises the interesting question of whether it is really a cost, does it not?

DR. PENROSE: Tax paid is not a cost. . . . Assuming the company had a U.S. tax liability on its foreign income sufficient to permit an offset, if it did not pay this sum to Kuwait, it would pay it to the U.S. Treasury.[20]

But in the early 1970's the oil obtained by the companies came to be divided between "equity" oil—i.e., what they received in their traditional role of concessionaire—and "participation" oil—i.e., oil accruing directly to the account of the host governments, in their new role as part owners of the operating companies. Since the majors purchase this oil at "buy-back" prices, payment cannot be regarded as taxes and is therefore only a business expense, worth 50 cents on the tax dollar. With the passage of time the OPEC countries increased their ownership interest, resulting in a declining proportion of "equity" oil and an increasing proportion of "participation" oil, until most of the OPEC countries have secured (or will shortly obtain) full ownership. While this will ultimately eliminate the "equity" oil complexity, it introduces other problems, notably discounts off the "buy-back" prices granted to the former concessionaires and fees paid for operating the properties. Therefore, determining the companies' costs and margins would require knowledge of the extent to which tax payments to the host governments have in fact been offset by other tax liabilities, of the changing ratio of participation to equity crude, of not only the published "buy-back" prices but discounts therefrom, and of operating fees and other forms of compensation. As if this were not sufficient to confound the outside analyst, changes have also been made in the royalty rate, the tax rate, gravity differentials, sulphur premiums, and other terms of trade. Indeed, such an informed source as *The Petroleum Economist* has commented: ". . . the multiplicity of instruments employed adds greatly to the confusion surrounding the whole question of oil pricing. Is this perhaps part of the general strategy?"[21]

To the majors it was clear that the critical question was not the cost of crude but whether, regardless of their nature, the new arrangements permitted them to continue as the sole recipients of OPEC's crude. Mr. W. Jones McQuinn, vice-president of Standard Oil of California, and George Keller, vice-chairman of its board, agreed that from the companies' point of view the key objective was to "tie up the crude," preferably in such a way as to "fuzz up the deal."

MR. BLUM: In October 1973, it became apparent that the participation agreement was collapsing and you needed a restructuring of Aramco. Was it your objective in that restructuring to retain the Aramco framework and *retain exclusive rights* to crude through Aramco?

MR. MCQUINN: Yes, very definitely.

MR. BLUM: Were you hoping that you could get the Saudis to give you a more favorable price for crude than other governments perhaps in the Persian Gulf and in a way conceal that or protect it against leapfrogging in the complexity of the Aramco price and corporate structure?

MR. MCQUINN: Yes, sir.

MR. BLUM: . . . I would like to quote in pertinent part from . . . a cable from Mr. Johnston [president of Aramco] of October 25th that says:

". . . Current Aramco management control will remain. (in fact believe we could improve control under some relaxed deal . . .). Revised deal need not contain any lost financial position for current four owners. Saudis quite aware they can control this through postings and tax. (Incidentally got long playback of why unilateral action was taken on posted prices.) Am convinced could *tie up crude* if deal was right. Saudis not really interested in big increased crude volume, especially if we could *fuzz up deal* somehow."

In other words, here what you are dealing with is not encouraging them to increase price, you are centrally interested in *retaining control of the crude*. Am I correct?

MR. MCQUINN: Yes, sir.

MR. KELLER: At as low a cost as possible.

MR. BLUM: And you are counting on the complexity of the financial arrangements, the complexity of the corporate structure to prevent that from leapfrogging up somewhere else?

MR. KELLER: Yes.[22]

THE EFFECTS ON EXCHANGE BALANCES

That the new prices would have a staggering impact on the world's economies was soon made clear through estimates of the resulting transfers of income and exchange balances. According to *The Petroleum Economist,* "the producing countries stand to increase their revenues to well over $100 billion in 1974 if production goes ahead as planned before the cutbacks, compared with the $30 billion they would have received on the basis of the posted price level on 1st October 1973 and $51 billion after the 16th of October increase." Substantial increases in balance of payments deficits were foreseen: "Britain alone faces an extra $4 billion a year for her normal requirements while the U.S.A. and Japan will each have to pay a further $9 billion."[23] The forecasts reached some sort of a nadir with an estimate in July 1974 by the World Bank that the OPEC countries would accumulate an exchange surplus of $643 billion by 1980 and of $1.2 trillion by 1985.[24] These totals can be compared with net foreign assets held by the OPEC countries of $20 billion in 1973 and $5 billion in 1970.

Thereafter a reaction against these high estimates set in. New studies by financial institutions began to make their appearance, indicating a considerably smaller exchange surplus and implying a problem of readily manageable proportions through recycling to be performed, appropriately enough, by financial institutions. Morgan Guarantee estimated the OPEC cumulative surplus by 1980 at $179 billion;[25] the First National City Bank placed it at $189 billion;[26] and Irving Trust proffered two widely differing figures—$248 billion and $22 billion.[27] The World Bank revised its forecast for 1980 downward from $643 billion to $202–403 billion.[28] The hopeful portent of these predictions was illustrated by the accompanying comment by the First National City Bank: "What began in 1973–74 as a ferocious tiger was first declawed and is now becoming a Cheshire cat." One of the bases for these lower estimates was the assumption that the OPEC countries would expand *their* imports of manufactured goods more rapidly than had been expected. Much of these imports consisted, however, of various types of military hardware. In the fiscal year ending June 30, 1974, U.S. arms sales abroad doubled, most of the $8.5 billion going to Mideast countries. Iran alone took $4 billion and Saudi Arabia $700 million.[29] Such expenditures are not likely to continue into the future at anything like the same rate, since the original equipping of a military force obviously calls for greater outlays than its maintenance.

The optimistic view implied by these forecasts has in turn been questioned by the well-known petroleum economist Walter J. Levy, who estimated the 1980 surplus at $449 billion.[30] As compared to the financial institutions, he anticipated a slower increase in OPEC imports and a higher level of oil prices. Levy expected the price to rise from $10.00 in 1975 to $14.65 per barrel in 1980, whereas the First National City Bank anticipated a decline to $9.10 and the Irving Trust Co. postulated a drop to $7.00. The fact that in 1975 the OPEC price was not only maintained but actually increased in the face of sharply falling demand lends strong support to Levy's position. He also pointed out that in borrowing to pay for oil, many consuming countries are incurring substantial interest charges. And unlike borrowing to finance productive investment, loans for current consumption have no potential for generating income out of which future interest charges can be paid. In 1975 OPEC's *investment* income, according to Levy, amounted to $7 billion, or more than its *total* oil revenue as recently as 1970: "By the end of the decade earnings on the reinvestment of OPEC surpluses are likely to reach $30 billion." In the absence of either a dramatic rise in OPEC's imports or a substantial decline in oil prices, the world will be confronted in five years with the unpleasant reality that a dozen countries will have accumulated some $400–500 billion in exchange balances; this happens to be about equal to the sum total of the world's monetary reserves.

On one point there has been virtually no disagreement. It has been apparent from the outset that the price explosion would be particularly injurious to those oil-consuming countries variously referred to as "developing," "under-developed," "poor," and "Fourth World" (the OPEC countries becoming the "Third World"). For example, *The Petroleum Economist* pointed out as early as mid-1974 that against foreign exchange reserves of $629 million in 1973, India's oil bill for 1974 would be $1,241 million. Assuming that India were able to maintain its 1973 favorable balance of trade, the combined total of the balance plus its reserves would still fall more than a third short of meeting its estimated 1974 oil bill. In an even more unfavorable position was the Sudan, whose combined balance and reserves would pay for less than half of its estimated oil bill. Unless their oil consumption were drastically lowered, their balance of trade greatly improved, or financial assistance received from some outside source, India and the Sudan, along with such other important developing nations as Pakistan, the Philippines, and Thailand, would be unable to meet their oil costs in less than two years.

In 1974 the increase in the oil bill of the developing countries, $11 billion, just about canceled out the industrialized world's $11.3 billion in official development assistance.[31] The increase in their oil payments was the single most important factor contributing to the developing countries' trade deficit in 1974 of $35 billion, four times as large as in 1973. In releasing this estimate, the International Monetary Fund raised the question of "the actual ability or willingness" of the rest of the world to finance the deficit.[32] The diversion of resources required to make the oil payments also had the effect of arresting improvements in income and living standards. Referring to a statistical appendix to a World Bank document, Hobart Rowen notes that "the average per capita income of the four OPEC countries with large balance of payments surpluses (Saudi Arabia, Kuwait, Qatar and the United Arab Emirates) soared 115 percent to $7,600 in 1974 from $3,528 in 1973 and others in the OPEC group showed a 36 percent gain to $540 in 1974 from $396 in 1973. But . . . 40 developing countries had zero gain in per capita income, which averaged only $425 and . . . the industrial countries had a 1 percent drop from $5,279 to $5,203."[33]

Spokesmen for the OPEC countries have been quick to point out that they have come to the aid of the poor oil-consuming countries by providing loans, grants, and other forms of assistance. And, indeed, OPEC aid commitments rose from $3 billion in 1973 to $16 billion in 1974. But actual disbursements were far lower, amounting to only $1 billion in 1973 and $5 billion in 1974. Moreover, of the latter only $2 billion represented loans made at less than the current market rates—usually about 8 percent. Furthermore, a substantial portion of

OPEC aid appears to have consisted of war relief or similar war-related grants to the Arab countries (Egypt, Syria, and Jordan) involved in the 1973 war against Israel. According to Rowen, "A [World Bank] document (Sec. M 74-850) prepared . . . on December 20, 1974 shows that 78.6 percent of OPEC subsidized aid disbursed in 1974 went to those three countries for war reconstruction or relief purposes."[34]

In buying oil on credit, the consuming countries may have postponed the ultimate day of reckoning, but they will have done so by incurring interest charges that in the future will have to be met regardless of whether they obtain oil or not. It is thus not difficult to understand the reasons for the International Monetary Fund's conclusion that many of the developing countries will find themselves "in financial difficulty" in 1975 and beyond, with "severe problems" faced by those nations classified by the U.N. as "the most seriously affected."[35]

*   *   *

By now, the commonly accepted explanation for the oil price explosion of October 1973 to January 1974 has become firmly embedded in folklore. Through incessant repetition in every medium of communication responsibility has been effectively transferred to rulers of distant and undeveloped lands whose attitude toward the United States ranges from casual indifference to belligerent hostility. Today's high prices are invariably traced back to the "Arab embargo" and the resultant "shortage." In reality, the embargo occasioned only limited and temporary dislocations. If attaining the historical growth rate of 9.5 percent is regarded as adequate to meet the demand, there was no shortage of OPEC production in 1973. Indeed, in the period of the "embargo"—the fourth quarter of 1973—OPEC output turned out to be virtually the same as in the corresponding quarter of the following year, by which time the concern of OPEC (and the majors) had shifted to a potential surplus.

THE CURTAILMENT OF OUTPUT

12

SINCE WORLD WAR II the price behavior of petroleum has been unlike that of any other industry, resembling neither the cyclical rise and fall of competitive products, the annual or semi-annual ratchet-like "stairstep" increases of oligopolistic industries, nor the steady, secular rise of a material in diminishing supply. Rather, it has featured two enormous jumps—one in the latter forties and the other in the early seventies. Upon the end of wartime price controls, the base price of domestic oil more than doubled, and through the "netback" basing point system, most of this increase also came to be reflected in the Mideast base price. In the recent episode the sequence was reversed, as the initial advance took place in the Middle East, with the domestic prices then being revised upward in accordance with the increase in the world "market" price. Through the planned and systematic restriction of output at home and abroad, the oil companies directed their energies after the first jump toward maintaining domestic and world prices at or above the then unprecedented levels. And until the mid-1960's, these efforts met with a remarkable degree of success. Today, the critical question is whether the sharp increases of the early seventies can be made to endure through similar curtailments in output, or whether they will be eroded away through price shading, secret deals, and downward individual "adjustments."

For the United States, the problem of avoiding price-weakening surpluses has been greatly simplified by the depletion of domestic reserves. In past recessions, an over-supply was avoided only by severe curtailments in output imposed by state prorationing authorities. Since then the need for government intervention has withered away, as production has been moving steadily downward, dropping in the first six months of 1975 13 percent below the 1970 average.[1] This, incidentally, is about the decline to be anticipated on the basis of Hubbert's bell-shaped curve. But for the OPEC countries, particularly

276

those with a high ratio of reserves to output, tailoring production to a declining demand presents a formidable problem. In the case of any cartel the moment of truth arrives when demand begins to undergo a serious contraction. Confronted with the need to subordinate his own self-interest to the industry's common good, each participant has no difficulty in coming up with reasons as to why his allotted share is unfair, unjust, and discriminatory, justifying a departure from the united price front.

For the Organization of Petroleum Exporting Countries, the time of testing began in mid-1974. It had become evident that the developing worldwide recession would lead to a general breakdown of the price structure unless substantial curtailments were made in production. In the United States high government officials and distinguished economists confidently predicted the collapse of the cartel. Anthony Sampson describes the state of anticipation:

> At the Treasury the ebullient William Simon, who had previously been energy "czar," had always been convinced that the free market would make itself felt in oil, as in everything else; a fall in consumption would bring prices down. He had very publicly pinned his hopes on the auction of oil planned in Saudi Arabia in September 1974 and was bitterly disappointed when it was cancelled. But he was still confident of lower prices, and Henry Kissinger was working energetically to break the solid front of OPEC. . . .
>
> Simon and Kissinger waited for OPEC's collapse, and watched the growing indications. To many economists, it seemed a matter of time before the cartel was broken. Milton Friedman, the high priest of the free market, was confidently forecasting that OPEC would collapse. The *Economist* magazine, which had predicted the glut at the height of the shortage, was now saying "I-told-you-so" pointing to the nonsense of high oil prices.[2]

But the expected collapse failed to occur. With a powerful assist from the major companies, OPEC successfully met the challenge. This is shown by Chart 12-1, which contrasts for the eleven OPEC countries and its five leading Mideast members production in 1973, 1974 and 1975 (indicated by *) with their historical growth rate based on output during 1950–72 (indicated by •).

As brought out earlier, the "shortage" of 1973 proved to be more an anticipation than a reality. Output for the eleven OPEC countries slightly exceeded the level indicated by the historical growth rate, the reduced deliveries in the fourth quarter having been more than offset by above-normal shipments earlier in the year. In the following year, for the first time in nearly a quarter of a century, production fell noticeably below the level called for by the 1950–72 growth rate. In

CHART 12-1
OPEC Oil Production: Output in 1973-1975 Compared with Historical Growth Rate

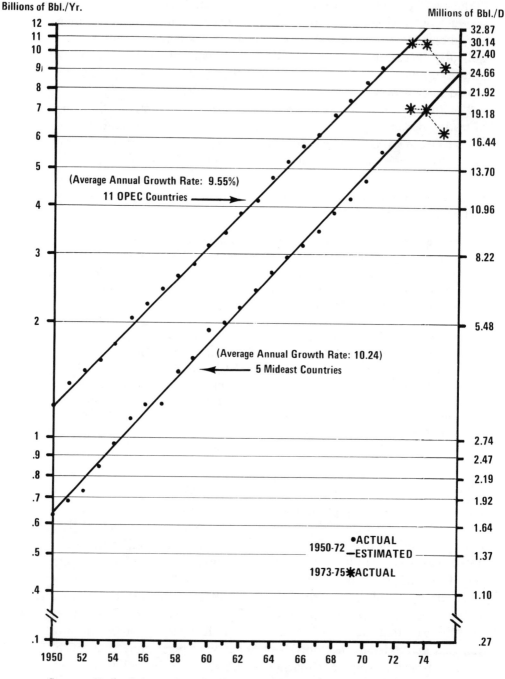

Billions of Bbl./Yr.

Millions of Bbl./D

(Average Annual Growth Rate: 9.55%)
11 OPEC Countries ⟶

(Average Annual Growth Rate: 10.24)
⟵ 5 Mideast Countries

1950-72 •ACTUAL
—ESTIMATED
1973-75 ✳ACTUAL

Sources: Derived from Organization of Petroleum Exporting Countries, Statistical Bulletins and *The Petroleum Economist.*

contrast to an indicated level of 12,000 million barrels, production was held to 10,950 million barrels, or almost exactly the level of the previous year (10,981 bbls.). This could be interpreted as a strategically sound move by a group of sellers uncertain of the severity of the developing recession or the effect of their drastic price increase on demand. The loss of markets was, in effect, assumed to be equal to the historical growth rate. Production could readily have been lowered below this benchmark level had demand continued to decline, or quickly increased had the reverse proved to be true. In 1975, the departure from the historical growth rate was even greater, production (on the basis of the first six months) falling to a yearly rate of 9,500 million barrels. This was 1,450 million barrels (or 13%) under the 1973 figure and 3,500 million barrels (or 27%) below the level called for by the growth rate; the 3,500 million shortfall equaled *total* U.S. production for the year.

In contrast to total OPEC production, output in 1974 for its five principal Mideast members slightly exceeded the area's more rapid growth rate. Much to the displeasure of other OPEC members, production in Saudi Arabia and Iran was not reduced until the following year, thereby imposing on the African and South American countries the entire burden of making the curtailments needed to maintain the price. In 1975, however, the five Mideast countries reduced their output by 800 million barrels below the 1974 figure, or 1,000 million barrels below the historical growth rate. These curtailments of production appear to have accomplished their objective. It is true that Mediterranean crudes were then adjusted downward to equalize with lower delivered prices from the Persian Gulf resulting from lower tanker rates; that certain premiums for quality were eliminated or reduced; that terms of trade (e.g., time for payment) were also eased; and that in a few scattered instances independent refiners were able to negotiate supply contracts directly with OPEC countries, but apparently *not* at prices below those at which comparable grades were available from the majors. In general, overall output appears to have been reduced sufficiently to maintain the price. Looking back on market development during 1975, the *Oil and Gas Journal* in its Annual Refining Report of March 29, 1976, noted that a number of downward adjustments had been made in OPEC prices, such as a reduction of 9.5 cents a barrel in the price of heavy Iranian crude. But these adjustments, it went on to add, were simply designed to bring the price of particular grades into line with existing OPEC prices for comparable grades. Warning against the "danger that policy makers of the world's oil-consuming countries, particularly Americans, will make too optimistic a reading of the move," the *Journal* went on to say:

Much has been written of the possibility that OPEC members, each with differing internal financial needs and oil-production capabilities, eventually would engage in competitive struggle for oil markets that would blow their united pricing policy apart. The big hope of this scenario is that world prices would plunge.

The current price adjustments don't fit any such pattern heralding a general market change. They only reflect realities of the market.

Iranian heavy crude was priced above similar crudes in Saudi Arabia—and still is even after the reduction. In other words, it was out of line with other OPEC crudes, and Iran responded to competition within OPEC. Iran might have gotten by with overpricing in a tight world market but not in a market that is soft. . . . There's no indication any OPEC nation is hurting seriously enough to precipitate price cutting to recover lost sales.

In predicting the imminent collapse of OPEC, the learned authorities and high policy-makers had failed to recognize that, partly for the same and partly for different reasons, the countries and the companies had the same interests. Insofar as the countries are concerned, an ironic paradox is presented: those OPEC countries with the largest oil reserves have the least need for additional funds to carry out ambitious industrialization programs, while those with the greatest need to industrialize have only limited oil reserves. The former are unlikely to seek greater revenues by price shading because they are already hard put to find uses for their existing revenues; the latter are unlikely to cut prices because a greater volume of sales would only accelerate the depletion of their limited reserves.

THE "BANKER" COUNTRIES

An outstanding example of the former group is Saudi Arabia, which occupies the largest land area of any country in the Middle East but whose population numbers only some 8 million persons, making it one of the most sparsely populated countries on earth. In 1974, the government received oil revenues of $27.5 billion, or more than $3,500 per person. Two years earlier, its oil revenues had totaled only $3.1 billion, or less than $400 per person.[3] In a land with virtually no industry or modern infrastructure, the government's problem has been how to make effective use of its enormous existing revenues rather than how to enlarge them further at the expense of its neighbors. In a recorded interview Saudi Arabia's oil minister, Sheik Yamani, stated: "Not only do we lack industry; agriculture; worse still, we lack manpower. I mean educated and trained manpower. We make our young people study and we send them to foreign universities, but it takes time to obtain a degree or a technical diploma. Meanwhile, we have to import engineers, technicians, specialized workers. . . ."[4] Under these circumstances, Saudi Arabia's policy of maintaining a high level of production throughout 1974 became a source of intense irritation to other OPEC countries. Referring to the resentment felt by other states, *The Petroleum Economist* observed: "Threats have been made to reduce production if Saudi Arabia increases its own as a means of implementing its price-cutting policy, and there is reason to believe that the 'hawks,' notably Iran, Kuwait, and Algeria, have actually agreed to a level of production cutbacks in such an eventuality."[5] By early 1975, however, the worsening worldwide recession made it impossible for Saudi Arabia to continue to produce at its existing rate without giving rise to "distressed oil"; the additional curtailments that would have been required by other countries were not within the realm of probability. Confronted with the alternatives of expanding its output at a lower price or reducing its production to maintain the price, Saudi Arabia opted for the latter. Although its production had been declining for several months, Saudi Arabia in March 1975 specifically authorized Aramco to lower its rate of production from 8.5 to 6.5 million b/d. According to Sheik Yamani, the reduction had been requested by Aramco because there were "no markets."[6] But this was not the full extent of the reduction. According to the interview conducted in mid-1975, Sheik Yamani was quoted as saying:

> We can produce as much as 11 million barrels a day. . . . This makes us a power to be reckoned with both by producing and consuming countries. To ruin the other countries of the OPEC, all we have to do is produce to our full capacity; to ruin the consumer countries, we only have to reduce our production. In the first case, the price would fall noticeably; in the second, the price would rise not by 35, but by 40, 50, or even 80 percent. We can dictate our conditions to all, even within the OPEC.[7]

On this occasion, however, Sheik Yamani indicated that Saudi Arabia was in opposition to a "drastic increase" in price. When asked who did favor such an increase, he replied:

> The ones who want that are first and foremost, the oil companies. Obviously, when the price rises, their profits increase. And unless the system changes, unless, for instance, Saudi Arabia takes over 100 percent control of Aramco, as I hope will happen in the future, the companies will keep on demanding increases. Side by side with the companies, in any case, I'd mention Venezuela, Ecuador, Algeria, Iraq, Gabon, Libya.[8]

Occupying an area of 6,000 square miles, with a population of only 830,000 (of whom less than half have citizenship), and without any natural resources other than petroleum, Kuwait epitomizes the "banker" producing country. After providing its citizens with the world's highest per capita income as well as lavish social services (including free medical treatment and higher education anywhere in the world), Kuwait's remaining oil revenues are far beyond any conceivable internal use. Attempts at "downstream" integration have not been particularly successful; the Kuwait Petrochemicals Industries Co. has consistently run at a loss, while BP and Gulf sold their 20 percent interests in the Kuwait Chemical Fertilizer Co. not finding it an economic operation. Unlike widely publicized industrialization "programs," the line of activity in which Kuwait has been most successful, banking and overseas investment, places no particular pressure on the government to secure additional funds, but rather represents a logical way to use existing surplus revenues—which in 1974 exceeded $8 billion, compared to $1.7 billion in 1972.[9] It is therefore not surprising that Kuwait has been a leader in urging (and practicing) the curtailment of production: ". . . in 1972, following Libya's example, Kuwait became the first exporting country of the Gulf to limit production, ostensibly on the grounds of conservation although the country's estimated reserves of at least 66 billion barrels would have been sufficient to last for nearly 60 years at the existing level of output." While an increase to 4.0 million b/d had been planned, production had been reduced by 1974 to 2.2 million, with the downward trend continuing in 1975.

THE "INDUSTRIALIZING" COUNTRIES

In contrast to the philosophic attitude of the sparsely populated countries, the approach of OPEC's more populous members has been aggressive in the extreme. It is the Shah of Iran who has been generally credited with engineering the second unilateral price increase—from $5.11 to $11.65 in January 1974. And on the occasion of the third unilateral increase in October 1975, the figure finally agreed upon (10%) was widely reported to be a compromise between the restrained position of Saudi Arabia and the more aggressive demands of Iran, Venezuela, and other "industrializing" countries. As means of enhancing revenues, however, a distinction must be drawn between price increases and price shading. The former will be strongly supported by the "industrializing" countries, since it means greater revenues without a necessary increase in output. But their pursuit of the latter will be more tempered since, if successful, it will result in an increase in production, thereby hastening the depletion of reserves.

The importance of this restraint on individual behavior has long been recognized by Venezuela, which in the fall of 1974 announced that it would lower 1975 output to 2.6 m b/d, or 23 percent below the 1973 level, aiming toward a reduction to around 2 m b/d by 1980. The reasons given for the planned cutback included the "need to conserve crude oil reserves, now estimated at between 13 and 14 billion barrels compared with an estimated 20 billion at the end of 1967."[10] In addition, the government explicitly recognized the need for output restrictions to stabilize the market, a government official noting "the need to shield crude oil prices by 'drying up' an oversupply of crude on the world market caused by increasing production and a simultaneous drop in demand as consuming nations have become more cautious in the use of oil."[11] Moreover, the Venezuelan government has for some time made known its desire to lessen the importance of oil in the Venezuelan economy and to expand those industries that offer greater employment and are less subject to foreign control. As P. R. Odell noted in 1968:

> The Government has, however, quite deliberately adopted a policy of maximizing its "take" from existing levels of petroleum production (this "take" per barrel is now, on average, about $1) in the full knowledge that this would cause the international Companies to switch their interest in increasing production and production capacity to other parts of the world. The rationale for this policy stems from the belief that the oil sector of its economy is too dominant—accounting for over 90 percent of exports and about 20 percent of the GNP; but, at the same time, giving employment to only two percent of the labour force in a situation in which a population growing at a rate of about 3.5 percent per annum demands a large number of new job opportunities. The oil industry, moreover, the Government argues, is in foreign hands with no degree of Venezuelan control over decisions taken in New York or London but which vitally affect the Venezuelan economy.[12]

As the prime mover in the original formation of OPEC, and a vigorous advocate of restrictionism, Venezeula would find it somewhat awkward to abandon the cause for which it has been the leading proponent. In Odell's words:

> . . . The Government has to face up to the immediate practical difficulty that its policy, to be effective, has to secure universal acceptance amongst oil producing and exporting nations—for restrictions on production by any one nation to maintain prices may be offset by any willingness elsewhere to expand without control. It was to overcome this fundamental difficulty that Venezuela sought informal contacts with the Middle Eastern producers "to understand mutual problems, to directly exchange points of

view on the world oil situation and to achieve coordinated action in the future." These contacts later provided the initial basis for the formation of OPEC in 1960. Since then Venezuela has taken every opportunity to convince its fellow exporting countries of the validity of its arguments. Within the Organization itself the 1965 agreement on the following year's production levels represented a success for Venezuela.[13]

Like Venezuela, Algeria has announced ambitious plans for industrialization; but also like Venezuela, its aims appear to be well beyond its reach. In June 1974, the government launched a $30 billion four-year economic plan to be financed by revenue from oil production, which was expected to increase 30 percent by 1977 and 50 percent by 1980. Instead, as compared to 1973, crude oil exports declined 7 percent in 1974 and a further drop of 22 percent was expected in 1975. Had Algeria embarked on a truly competitive policy, there is a real question how long its limited resources (amounting to only 10 billion bbls. of proved reserves) could have sustained the resultant rise in production. Thus, *The Petroleum Economist* attributed the 1974 decrease in its output to "difficulties in the grudgingly yielding Saharan oilfields as much as sluggish export sales. It is suggested that even now Algerians are trying to squeeze too much production from existing fields for the sake of revenues."[14] According to *The New York Times*, "Algeria's oil fields are expected to be depleted by 1995—the main one at Hassi Messaoud is already showing signs of depletion. . . ."[15]

With over 30 million persons (as compared to only 8 million in Saudi Arabia, and but 800,000 in Kuwait), Iran has a larger population than all of the other Mideast oil-producing countries combined. The Shah has repeatedly made known his determination to greatly expand his country's industrial base, which even before the price explosion of 1973–74 employed more than 700,000 persons in manufacturing—far more than any other OPEC country.[16] Commentators have frequently speculated that if any country were to depart from OPEC's united front on prices, it would be Iran, citing as reasons its urgent need for industrialization and its long-time close association with the United States. As the only non-Arab state in the Middle East, Iran has not been involved in the Arab-Israeli differences and has not always had the friendliest relationships with its Arab neighbors. Thus, when Iranian oil was being boycotted following the nationalization of BP, the Arab countries lost no time in taking over Iran's market position, a move that was promptly reciprocated by Iran during the 1956–57 Suez conflict. Perhaps because of these factors, Iran's production remained relatively stable throughout 1974. But production in 1975 turned noticeably downward; by the second quarter of 1975, output was 14.8 percent below the level of a year earlier. Despite the pressure for industrialization and its "friendship" toward the United States, Iran, like its neighbors, had elected to cut production rather than price. In addition to the natural desire to avoid touching off a price war with lower-cost rivals (notably Saudi Arabia and Kuwait), the policy would find justification in the fact that Iran's reserves, though hardly negligible, cannot be considered large by Mideast standards. Indeed, one of the reasons advanced to explain the Shah's unexpectedly "hawkish" position on price has been his desire to finance industrialization with oil revenues before Iran's reserves are used up.

Among the more important producing states, only Iraq and Libya fall between this dichotomy of "banker" countries that have the reserves but not a compelling need and "industrializing" countries that have the need but not the reserves. On the basis of the hypothesis suggested here, they would be the most likely sources of price cutting.

With over 10 million persons, Iraq ranks second to Iran in population among the Mideast countries. And, like Iran, it has an ambitious development program, oriented principally toward the improvement of agriculture. But unlike Iran, Iraq's oil reserves are immense, though even their approximate dimensions are unknown. Not only did the long-continued restriction of the country's output by the owners of the Iraq Petroleum Company (Exxon, Mobil, BP, Shell, and CFP) work against exploratory activities; new fields were shut in and news of their discovery deliberately suppressed. As a consequence, in the words of *The Petroleum Economist*: ". . . Unlike most other Middle Eastern countries, whose oil potential is known with reasonable accuracy, Iraq still has areas which have not yet been thoroughly explored and the possibility, according to Iraqi officials, of at least doubling its reserves, to place them perhaps second only to Saudi Arabia."[17] Although with the takeover in 1972 of the Iraq Petroleum Co., the country lost the marketing outlets of the major companies (except for BP's subsidiary, the Basrah Petroleum Co.), Iraq has been able to expand its output through the use of a well-trained work force left behind by IPC and through technical assistance provided by the Soviet Union and East European countries. In sharp contradistinction to the other leading OPEC countries, the trend of Iraq's output in 1974–75 was steadily upward, rising 31 percent between the second quarters of 1974 and 1975. At least some of this gain appears to have been the result of price concessions: ". . . in spite of denials to the contrary, there is more than a suspicion that INOC [the state-owned Iraq National Oil Company] has been trimming its prices to increase sales. This is especially evident in the East Mediterranean where exports of crude from Kirkuk and the northern fields have been approaching near record levels of 1 million b/d, whereas Tapline, the other major East Mediterranean pipeline, has closed down entirely because of the high cost differential on its deliveries of Saudi Arabian crude compared with the cost of Saudi crude at the Persian Gulf."[18]

Although Libya, like Saudi Arabia and Kuwait, is a land of few resources other than oil and sparse population (some 2 million persons), it has embarked on an ambitious industrialization program, primarily for the ideological purpose of gaining "full control over the sources of oil wealth." Libya's ability to finance its industrialization program, however, has been imperiled by the drastic decline in its production—from 3.3 m b/d in 1970 to only 1.1 m b/d in the first half of 1975, or little more than half the 2 million figure regarded by its officials as the desirable balance between revenue needs and conservation requirements. Among the causes of the unusually sharp cutback was Libya's nationalization of BP, SoCal, and Texaco, which ended the flow of its oil through their marketing facilities. Moreover, Nelson Bunker Hunt, the owner with BP of the concession to Libya's biggest field, Saris, which was nationalized by the Libyan government, filed suit against buyers of oil taken from that field. Another factor has been the worldwide easing of anti-pollution controls and the consequent lessening of demand for Libya's premium-price, low-sulphur oil. Finally, the fall in supertanker rates from the Persian Gulf caused oil from Libya to be "out of line" with delivered prices from the Middle East. To reverse the fall in output, Libya reduced its contract prices from $16.00 a barrel in January 1974 to $11.86 in January 1975 and to $11.10 in June 1975. The reduction appears to have had the intended effect, since by the middle of 1975 output had begun to rise. In one of the few open displays of acrimony among OPEC members, Algeria refused to meet Libya's lower prices, contending that the reductions were greater than necessary to meet the lower delivered prices from the Persian Gulf: "The announcement that no change was to be made in Algeria's third quarter price was accompanied by a bitterly-worded statement by the official Algérie Presse Service news agency declaring that Algeria refused to take part in a price-cutting spiral and that as a result of 'unjustified' cuts, Iraqi, Nigerian and Libyan crudes were underpriced in relation to Algerian oil, which was priced exactly in line with Gulf crudes."[19]

CRUDE PRODUCTION AND REFINED PRODUCT PRICES

Whether because of the differing motivations against price cutting governing the "banker" and "industrializing" countries or some other factors, it seems evident that during the 1974–75 recession any temptation toward individual self-aggrandizement was subordinated to group interest. The reductions in crude output were sufficiently large not only to maintain the crude price structure; they even made possible a 10 percent advance in November 1975 and in addition enabled the companies to make a number of advances in refined product prices. This can be seen from Chart 12-2, which compares the monthly trend of aggregate crude production of eleven OPEC countries with the price movements in international markets of three representative refined products—motor gasoline (90 R Ras Tanura), fuel oil (No. 2 Aruba), and diesel fuel (marine, Ras Tanura).*

From the middle of 1973 to the end of 1974, total monthly production of these OPEC countries remained, with only three exceptions, within a range of 850 to 950 million barrels. But in January 1975 output fell to below 800 million barrels, remaining until the middle of the year at around 750 million barrels. Presumably "to beat" the OPEC price rise scheduled for late in the year, production then moved up in July, August, and September to the 800–850 million range, only to fall sharply in the last quarter. But, as can be seen from the lower half of the chart, the downward trend in supply was accompanied— *after* the October 1973–January 1974 price explosion—by three increases in the price of motor gasoline, by two increases in the price of diesel fuel (following the recision of a slight decrease) and, apart from seasonal variations, by a general pattern of price stability for fuel oil. Of particular interest are the price increases registered by each of the products during the last quarter of 1975, when production had fallen to the 700-million-barrel range.

By way of comparison, the OPEC price for crude remained unchanged from January to November 1974. Yet during this period the price of gasoline was raised, effective October 10, 1974, from 32.6 cents to 34.3 cents a gallon. Then, effective November 1, the OPEC prices were reduced, the "marker" grade of Saudi Arabian light falling from $11.65 to $11.25 a barrel. A little more than three weeks later, the price of gasoline was raised, on November 26, 1974, from 34.3 cents to 35.3 cents a gallon. It should not be thought, however, that refined product prices are completely insensitive to the trend of crude since, when OPEC instituted a 10 percent increase in October 1975, the prices of all of the refined products were promptly increased—gasoline from 35.3 to 37.7 cents, diesel fuel from 28.8 to 30.6 cents, and fuel oil from 33.7 to 35.7 cents.

* The eleven are those for which monthly production figures were available— Venezuela, Saudi Arabia, Kuwait, Iran, Oman, Libya, Nigeria, Iraq, Qatar, Abu Dhabi, and Algeria. In 1972 their production amounted to 25,381,000 b/d, or 96.8% of OPEC's total output of 26,218,000 b/d.

CHART 12-2
Crude Production and Refined Product Prices, July 1973–December 1975

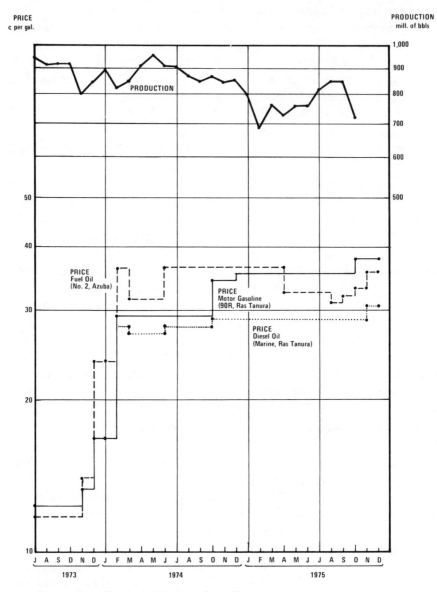

Source: Compiled from *The Petroleum Economist.*

THE LOCUS OF RESPONSIBILITY

Exactly how the responsibility for the price explosion of late 1973–early 1974 should be apportioned between the international majors and the OPEC countries remains a matter of speculation. Of equal importance is the locus of responsibility for the validation of those stratospheric price increases through subsequent and substantial curtailments in output. If output was to be effectively controlled by the OPEC countries, they would have to develop some mechanism of control similar to that perfected over a long period of years by the companies. Without it, they would have to develop, *de novo,* knowledge (and means of implementation) on such difficult matters as: (a) the growth rate of overall supply that prevents the appearance of "distressed oil"; (b) the effect on overall supply of alternative growth rates of the various producing countries; (c) the extent to which other countries would have to limit their output to offset excessive production by one or more suppliers; (d) the amount by which production in each of the countries can be permitted to grow without significantly disturbing their agreed-upon or at least implicitly accepted market shares; and (e) the ways and means of maintaining output in established countries at levels which they would regard as "just and equitable" while at the same time accommodating the "national aspirations" of newcomers with a potential for rapid expansion. Just to list the problems—and there are others—is to reveal the difficulty of achieving in any short period of time what it has taken the best brains of the world's largest companies half a century to perfect.

Early in 1975, *The Petroleum Economist* predicted (somewhat prematurely) the imminent breakdown of OPEC and the restoration of "the normal forces of the market." In answer to its own question, "What will hold this dozen of exporting countries together in the days to come?" it observed:

> They are left with one common purpose—that of enforcing a price-level fifty to one hundred times the level of costs. In all other respects they are competitors, as will become more and more evident from now on. As world oil consumption flags and alternative energy sources are progressively developed, the oil exporting countries will be able to achieve their last objective only by rigorously enforced controls on production. The idea of controlling or "programming" production has, of course, been in the governments' minds for years past. *But its effective implementation necessitates fixing basic quotas for individual producing countries*

*and devising machinery to enforce production decisions and im-
pose sanctions for non-compliance. At present, this loose-knit
organization simply does not have the staff or the expertise to
operate an effective cartel in the conditions envisaged.* All past
experience suggests that, as the present excess capacity within the
industry gradually swells, some of the exporters of crude oil will
start to trim their prices in order to boost their sales. When this
occurs, the cartel will crumble and the normal forces of the market
will determine the supply price of oil.[20]

The failure of the OPEC countries to remedy this deficiency has
not been for want of awareness. On several occasions the OPEC
Secretariat has importuned the governments to set up the necessary
machinery. Speaking of one such effort, Dr. Marwin Inlander, general
manager of Middle East Economic Consultants, stated, "The heads
of state were called upon to adopt a production program for oil to
keep supplies from exceeding demand. No such program was
adopted."[21] Because of its large population, its obvious need for
economic development, and the magnitude of its reserves, Iraq has
regarded any production-control program as beneficial to its interests;
but its support has not been sufficient. According to *The Petroleum
Economist*:

> . . . it is not surprising that Iraq has been one of those OPEC
> members pressing for a coordinated system of production pro-
> gramming, since on the basis of such criteria as oil reserves, his-
> torical position and financial needs for development, Iraq would
> have a higher share of total OPEC production than at present.
> Some economists and OPEC's own Secretariat consider that only
> by regulating production according to world market demand can
> OPEC maintain high crude oil prices, preventing attempts by
> individual countries to trim prices in order to increase their exports
> and thus their revenues. *But so far, it has not been possible for all
> the OPEC members to reach agreement on such a policy, nor any
> formula on which it could be carried out.*[22]

In a study of "The OPEC Process" published in late 1975, Zuhayr
Mikdashi points out that an objective of one of OPEC's "fathers,"
Venezuela's Perez Alfonso, was "to permit the governments to operate
as a cartel. The instrument for this cartel function was to be the joint
prorationing of oil production in the member countries." But in
Mikdashi's view, this objective has not been realized:

> An export cartel not only must include rigid agreements on price,
> but also related agreements in such key areas as production con-
> trol and market sharing. The export cartel must also be respon-

sible for monitoring the activities of its constituent members with a view to policing violations and penalizing violators. The OPEC member governments do not perform any of these cartel functions. Their agreement on oil export prices is strictly voluntary, and does not carry with it sanctions or rewards. Moreover, the agreements leave to the discretion of each member government the setting and changing of prices within ranges considered reasonable by OPEC members. A close scrutiny of OPEC's statutes and resolutions shows that the Organization does not have supernational powers. Member countries do not delegate to any central body their policy—or decision-making power. Indeed, they jealously guard their sovereignty, and consider their freedom of action to be paramount.[23]

Implementing programs of production curtailment (which are bound to give rise to aggrieved feelings on the part of some of the members) will probably remain beyond OPEC's ability, as long as decisions continue to require a unanimous vote and the Secretariat's staff members have only limited freedom of action on their own. As Mikdashi points out, "The staffing of the Secretariat is restricted to OPEC nationals, and these are almost always on loan from government civil service, or, more recently, from the management of the national oil companies. It is difficult to see how, in the absence of a tenure system, the OPEC staff can have a large measure of freedom of action to work for the 'common interest'; it is not even clear that a tenure system could offset national loyalties."[24]

If the OPEC Secretariat has in fact lacked the necessary competence and authority, the function of precisely tailoring supply to a diminishing demand must have been the work of the companies which, by limiting their "offtakes," have simply continued their historical role of stabilizing the market at the existing level of price. That such is the case has, in effect, been conceded by Clifton C. Garvin, Jr., chairman of the board of Exxon Corporation. In a televised interview on *Face the Nation*, November 16, 1975, the following exchange took place between Garvin and one of the questioners, Morton Mintz of the *Washington Post*:

MINTZ: Mr. Garvin, you said that if the President signs the bill, we'll have to become more dependent upon imports, and I want to ask a question that I think grows out of that. Last month, the Arabian-American Oil Company, of which Exxon, SoCal and Texaco each owns thirty percent, made a staggering cutback in production in Saudi Arabia. As you know, the cutback was 2.47 million barrels a day. . . . Now doesn't this prove that ARAMCO, and not Saudi Arabia, is calling the shots, and doesn't this prove that without the support of Exxon and the other major oil companies, the cartel would collapse and the prices of oil would drop?

MR. GARVIN: No, it does not. . . . Europe is having a big recession; Europe is having a mild fall so far. *There just hasn't been the demand. As a result, we've had to cut our production of oil. It's just that simple.*[25]

Later in the program, Mintz pursued the matter further:

MINTZ: How could the cartel survive without you? You people decided that there would be a 2.47 million barrel a day cutback in Saudi Arabia. . . . Who's calling the shots? You haven't answered. . . . The *Petroleum Intelligence Weekly*, which is it for this industry, called that cutback, and I quote again, stunning. Now that—you were trying to say it's just ordinary, but these people are expert and they say—

MR. GARVIN: Well, I'm not going to try to say what the PIW, or whatever you called it, does. These are the facts. It's true that the program is trying to move oil, to get maximum inventories, consistent with the way that demand is seen for the winter by November 1. The truth of the matter is that you've seen what a pleasant fall they've had in Europe. *Believe me, the recessionary effects in Europe are still deeper than we like to talk about, and our estimates of what the oil demand was going to be just didn't materialize, so we had to cut back.*[26]

If the companies elect not to send tankers to a producing country or process the crude in their refineries, what options are available to the country? It has only two ultimate weapons: nationalization or direct sales to independent buyers. In the absence of adequate compensation and other arrangements satisfactory to the companies, nationalization will mean the loss of assured outlets provided by the companies' refining and marketing facilities. Discount sales to independent buyers represent, if anything, an even more dangerous undertaking. Every OPEC country is fully aware of the utmost seriousness with which the majors view this course of conduct. Indeed, in 1974 Saudi Arabia used precisely this threat to bring Aramco to heel: "It was the threat by Saudi Arabia—following its recent agreement with Abu Dhabi and Qatar—to offer over 3 million barrels daily for direct sale on the world market to third parties, specifically excluding the major companies, at prices lower than Aramco was paying, that compelled the Aramco companies to accept complete take-over."[27] Thereafter, an accommodation appears to have been reached, for in November 1975 Saudi Arabia was reported to have abandoned the threat. According to an industry trade journal, "Saudi Arabia, as a matter of policy, currently plans to limit any new direct crude oil sales to state-to-state deals for the foreseeable future, PIW learns. This new policy hasn't been publicly announced but has been made known lately to potential third-party buyers inquiring about supplies following the December expiration of Petromin's [the state-owned company] 1973 contracts. It's more explicit than earlier unofficial hints that contracts might not be forthcoming for smaller independent private companies anyway."[28]

Although available to Saudi Arabia and perhaps one or two other countries with huge reserves, the threat to sell to independents may be of little value to less essential OPEC countries. Were they to embark on such a policy, they might well find themselves cut off by the majors entirely—a risk which none of the OPEC countries seems anxious to take. In short, while both the companies and the countries have the power to set effective ceilings on production, only the companies can set effective floors.

*   *   *

Exxon's chairman and Saudi Arabia's oil minister were in agreement: the initiative for the 1975 production cutbacks came from the oil companies. Had it not been for the cutbacks, the market would have been flooded with "distressed" oil, OPEC would indeed have broken down, and oil prices would have fallen sharply. That none of this occurred stems from the nature of the relationship between the companies and the countries. Among economists, the term "bilateral monopoly" refers to situations where a monopsonist (one buyer) or oligopsonist (a few large buyers) buys from a monopolist or oligopolist. In such situations, the relationship of the two parties is that of adversaries, each seeking to profit at the expense of the other. But where, as in oil, one party holds a concession from another, with each receiving its compensation as a fixed percentage of total revenues, or where their common interest in the maintenance or enhancement of price transcends their interests as individual buyers or sellers, the relationship is not adversary but symbiotic, defined in Webster's *New World Dictionary* as the "intimate living together of two kinds of organisms, especially where such association is of mutual advantage." The structure created in the Middle East more than half a century ago and continued to this day can properly be described as a form of bilateral symbiotic oligopoly.

PROFIT CENTERS AND TARGET RETURNS

13

AS IT HAS BECOME increasingly evident that the new price levels for petroleum will be continuing into the foreseeable future, explanations of the price explosion have begun to make their appearance. Put forward by some members of the academic community, a "free market" theory would explain the price explosion as merely the normal response of a competitive industry to rising demand and limited supply. While it is recognized that most Mideast crude enters into integrated corporate structures, the course of free market prices, it is contended, is indicated by bids offered at auction sales held by national, state-owned companies. Fearful that they would be cut off by the widely publicized embargo, independent refiners and a few consuming countries did, in fact, bid up the price to "fantastic" levels at auctions held by Iran, Nigeria, Venezuela, Libya, Algeria, and Indonesia. This upward spiral culminated in a record-breaking bid offered in December 1973 to the National Iranian Oil Co. of $17.34 per barrel—a bid cited by the Shah as evidence of oil's true market value. Such sales, however, constituted an extremely thin market, equivalent to only 2.5 percent of Middle East production.[1] Moreover, once the momentary panic had subsided, the auction prices began to decline. As early as March 1974, *The Petroleum Economist* reported: "Auction sales of state crude are revealing the sharp downturn in going prices. Most recently, bids for 85 million barrels failed to reach the levels hoped for—most were reported around $9 a barrel—although a limited quantity was later sold at the posted price of $11.54. Earlier, Iranian crude bought at $17 in December was reported reselling at $13 . . . some buyers of Libyan state oil at over $16 have since withdrawn and in Nigeria buyers have failed to sign firm deals for 150,000 b/d of the crude which drew as high as $22.60 late last year."[2] Reporting in September 1974 that "panic buyers are no longer in the market," the journal commented on "the disappearance of the fantastic prices that were quoted for marginal sales earlier this year. In

294

this sense it is true that the free market has been showing a downward trend."[3] If, as a proxy for the "free market" price, the rise in these auction bids provided an explanation for the price explosion, their subsequent decline should logically have been accompanied by reductions made by OPEC in the price of crude and by the companies in the prices of refined products. No such decreases have taken place.

A quite different explanation, widely accepted in European intellectual circles, attributes the upward movement in OPEC prices during the early 1970's to strategic maneuvering by the U.S. government, designed to improve the competitive position of U.S. industry in world markets. In the words of the French economist Jean-Marie Chevalier, "By encouraging the rise in the prices of non-American crude she [the U.S.] strengthened her competitive position with regard to Europe and Japan, since she produced far more than they imported, at a lower cost. Furthermore, the price rise benefitted the development of the replacement sources of energy that the United States possessed: coal and oil shales."[4] The fact that the leading Mideast proponent of higher prices has been a long-time ally of the United States is seen as especially significant: "It was no mere quirk of fate that the Shah of Iran decided to become the spokesman for the producing countries, thus succeeding in channelling their demands in the direction desired by the United States, causing a rise in non-American crude prices. . . ."[5] This line of argument has of course been severely undermined not only by the rise in the U.S. crude price but by the greater increase in the particular petroleum product used by industry as raw material— petrochemical feedstock.[6] As a result of these domestic price increases, the opportunity for U.S. industry to register the gains envisioned by Chevalier has been irretrievably lost.

To comprehend not merely the fact of the price increases but their specific nature requires a grasp of complex, little-understood motivations governing both the countries and the companies. Thus, the OPEC countries were motivated not merely by a general desire to increase revenues but to do so in a highly specific way, i.e., to attain a predetermined target objective described in an OPEC communiqué as a "government take of $7 a barrel." The derivation of this figure was described by *The Petroleum Economist* as follows: "The calculation of government take proceeds through the solemn fiction that, for example, Arabian light crude now posted at $11.65 a barrel, yields a production profit of some $10.10 after deducting the production cost and the 12½ percent royalty; this fictional 'profit' is subject to tax at a rate of 55 percent. The total government take on Arabian light crude (royalty plus profits tax) is now $7 a barrel, compared with $1.52 a year ago."[7] This target objective was specifically referred to by the leading proponent of the price advances: ". . . the Shah of

Iran, in a press conference in Teheran, insisted that a seven-dollar-a-barrel government take represented the minimum cost of developing alternative energy, notably the extraction of oil from shale or the liquification or gasification of coal."[8]

For the companies, the specific objectives were to reduce their reliance on crude production as the source of profits, and to improve their ability to generate and attract capital. The former was achieved by widening the refining profit margin; the latter by raising and meeting new and higher target returns on investment.

WIDENING THE REFINING MARGIN

In March 1974 Otto Miller, former chairman of the board of Standard of California, was asked in a congressional hearing whether his company had sought "to move profits downstream," to which he delivered the unenlightening response that his company had always endeavored to make refining and marketing "economical."[9] The head of one of the nation's largest independent refining companies was somewhat more candid. Orin Aikins, chairman of Ashland Oil, referred to the industry's practice of deriving the "great bulk of its profits from its raw material sources and on more occasions than not has 'given away' its finished product at little or no profit in order to market that basic material." But, he emphasized, "This day is over, and in the future all segments of the oil industry must be made profitable." He went on to add, "The profit from refining, marketing and transportation could be substantial and frankly would be a new experience for many in the oil industry."[10]

That the domestic refinery margin has in fact undergone enlargement is implied by a comparison of the price movements of crude oil with those of refined products. Between 1972 and the end of 1974, all of the refined products, with the exception of gasoline, had registered a greater price increase than had crude oil:

	Percentage Price Increase 1972 to Dec. 1974
Crude Oil	96.0%
Gasoline	95.4
Light Distillate	141.7
Middle Distillate	169.6
Residual Oil	224.2

Source: Bureau of Labor Statistics.

The price movements of these product classes are also shown over a longer period of time, by month at the end of quarter, in Chart 13-1. Except for a falling off during the first quarter of 1975, the price trend of gasoline closely paralleled that of crude oil in both timing and extent. But over the entire period, the other products outpaced the rise in crude, with the heavier products generally registering the greatest increases.

These differences in price increases suggest an interesting hypothesis: The easier it is for buyers to pass along a higher price to their customers, the greater the increase. Thus, the largest increase was for residual oil, used principally in the generation of electric power by private utilities—a type of enterprise singularly able to shift to its users the increased cost of any material or supply. The next largest increase was in the middle distillates (principally diesel fuel and petrochemical feedstock). Like the utilities, the regulated trucking firms are permitted to incorporate higher fuel costs in their rates, while the manufacture of petrochemicals is sufficiently concentrated to allow the large chemical companies to incorporate higher costs in their prices. In contrast, the users of light distillates (principally home-heating oil) are unable to pass along higher fuel costs to anyone; moreover, too high a price might cause them to switch permanently to other fuels. Finally, the smallest increase was for gasoline, whose buyers also cannot pass along the increase and who, though unable to switch to other fuels, can nonetheless make further reductions in consumption.

Another possible explanation for the differential increases is suggested by the remarkable uniformity achieved by 1974 in actual prices. Historically, the lighter the product, the higher the price. At the top (and the first to be taken off in the cracking process) was gasoline, followed by the slightly heavier kerosene, and so on down until the lowest-price product was reached—residual oil (literally what remains after the other products have been taken off). But by the end of 1974, these historical product differentials had been virtually erased. If the objective was to eliminate differences among the prices of refined petroleum products, regardless of form or use, that goal had been largely accomplished. The prices as of mid-1969 and the end of 1974 for the four major types of refined products are shown in the table on page 299.

That the refining margin widened is obvious from a comparison of changes in crude versus refined product prices; the question of how much it widened could be answered definitively only by the use of cost data, which of course are unavailable. Unable to secure access to cost data, economists have frequently made use of "engineering estimates." Such an approach, combined with price information, can be

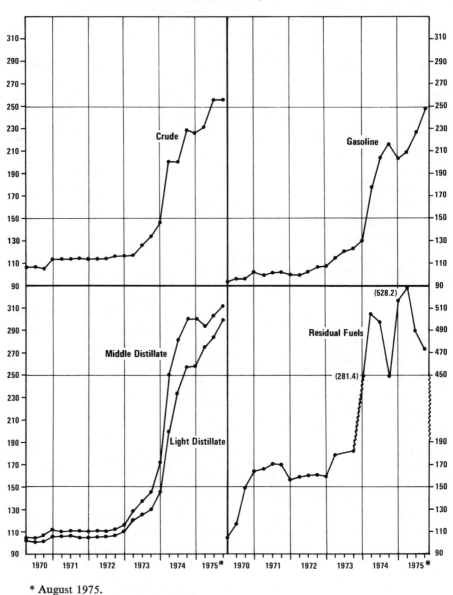

CHART 13-1
Price Movements of Domestic Crude and Refined Products
Month at End of Quarter (1967 = 100)

Crude

Gasoline

(528.2)

Middle Distillate

Residual Fuels

(281.4)

Light Distillate

1970 1971 1972 1973 1974 1975*   1970 1971 1972 1973 1974 1975*

* August 1975.
Source: Bureau of Labor Statistics.

Prices of Refined Petroleum Products
(cents per gallon)

Product	Mid-1969	End 1974	Increase
Gasoline	12.8¢	28.9¢	125.8%
Kerosene	11.1	28.8	159.5
Other Heating and Diesel Oils	10.5	27.4	160.9
Residual	4.7	26.4	461.7

Source: Platt's Oilgram: July 22, 1969, and Dec. 30, 1974. Prices at N.Y. Harbor.

used to shed light on the change in the refining margin. On the basis of an engineering estimate, the output of a typical modern refinery can be distributed among its various refined products; the value of each product can be determined by multiplying its quantity by its price; from the aggregate value of the refined products the cost of crude can be subtracted; this leaves an aggregate refining margin which, when divided by the refinery's output, represents the margin per barrel.

Specifically, in Table 13-1, the output of a typical modern 150,000 b/d refinery located on the East Coast is distributed on the basis of information obtained from industry sources among its various refined products—58 percent gasoline, 7 percent kerosene and other light distillates, 23 percent for other heating and diesel oils, 7 percent for residual, and 5 percent for other by-products. The values for each product were determined by multiplying its quantity, so derived, by its price, as obtained from *Platt's Oilgram*, for July 1968 and December 1974. For these two months, the price of crude plus the costs of getting it to the refinery were taken as $3.75 and $8.45 per barrel, respectively. The subtraction of the cost of crude from the aggregate value of the refined products left aggregate refinery margins of $143,-226 for the former period and $635,192 for the latter, or refinery margins per barrel of, respectively, $.95 and $4.23.

While adequately portraying the trend of the refining margin, Table 13-1 tends to understate for the majors the actual level of costs. This is because of the implicit assumption that the refinery input consists entirely of "purchased" crude, acquired at costs of $3.75 in 1969 and $8.45 in 1974. But as Table 10-1 shows, purchased crude makes up only 30 percent of the top eight's refinery input, the rest consisting of their own "captive" crude. For the latter, the only costs incurred are the expenses of operating existing facilities, or "operating costs." Except for marginal, high-cost wells accounting for only a very small share of U.S. output, operating costs are known to average well below

TABLE 13-1

Change in Refining Margin, Typical (150,000 b/d) East Coast Refinery, July 1969 and December 1974

Product	Product Yield	Output (000's) bbls.	Output (000's) gals.	At Crude Input Prices of: $3.75 (7/69) Price	$3.75 (7/69) Value	$8.45 (12/74) Price	$8.45 (12/74) Value
Gasoline	58%	87.0	3,654	12.8¢	$467,712	28.9¢	$1,056,008
Kerosene	7	10.5	441	11.1	48,951	28.8	127,008
Other Heating & Diesel Oils	23	34.5	1,449	10.5	152,145	27.4	397,026
Residual	7	10.5	441	4.8	21,168	26.4	116,424
Other Refined Products	5	7.5	315	5.0	15,750	20.0	63,000
Total: Refined Products	100%	150.0	6,300		705,726		1,759,466
Cost of Crude Oil				3.75	562,500	8.45	1,267,500
Refining Margin Total					143,226		635,192
Per Barrel					.95		4.23

Sources: Product yields: Engineering Estimate (*Hearings on Governmental Intervention*, Pt. 3, p. 1,276).
Refined product prices: *Platt's Oilgram*, July 22, 1969 and Dec. 30, 1974.
Crude oil prices: 1969—Wellhead price of $3.10 plus $.50 for transportation and $.15 for gathering, loading and terminal charges.
1974—Weighted average of $5.25 for "old" oil (60%) and $10.75 for "new" oil (16%), "released" oil (11%) and "stripper" oil (13%); plus $.80 for transportation and $.20 for gathering, loading, and terminal charges.

price. In 1965, for example, Professor Henry Steele found that operating or "lifting" costs averaged approximately $.50 a barrel for the United States as a whole (and undoubtedly somewhat less for the majors, who tend to operate lower-cost wells). To operating costs Steele suggested additions of $.20 for severance taxes and approximately $.10 for royalties, or a total of "short-run" costs of $.80 a barrel (see Chart 15-1).

If in July 1969 a major oil company operating the typical 150,000 b/d East Coast refinery depicted in Table 13-1 had bought crude for 30 percent of its requirements at $3.75 and produced crude for 70 percent of its needs at an operating cost (including severance taxes and royalties) of $.80, its total crude input costs would have been $1.68. The subtraction of this input figure from the weighted average price of its refined products (as shown in Table 13-1 adjusted to a "per barrel" basis) would have yielded a refining margin of $3.02 per barrel.

How does such a figure compare with the same refinery's margin, operating with the same proportions of "purchased" and "captive" crude, in December 1974? By this time the weighted average price of its refined products would have risen to $11.73 per barrel, while its costs of purchased crude (30% times $8.45) would have mounted to $2.53. What is missing is the cost of "captive" crude. For some inexplicable reason, the Federal Energy Administration, armed with several thousand employees and ample reporting powers, has failed to duplicate for a recent year the cost study made before the price explosion by a lone professor working with published Bureau of Mines data. Because of the lack of operating cost data, no upper limit is shown on the accompanying Chart 13-2 for captive crude in 1974.

If between 1969 and 1974, operating expenses had risen by half again (to $.84), the crude input cost would have been $3.37, leaving an operating margin of $8.36; if they had doubled (to $1.12), the crude input cost would have been $3.65, leaving a margin of $8.08. Thus, even under conservative assumptions the operating margins of this typical refinery would have risen from about $3.00 a barrel in July 1969 to around $8.00 a barrel in December 1974. It thus seems clear that the majors used the price explosion as an opportune occasion to widen appreciably their domestic refining margin, thereby achieving a substantial measure of financial independence from the price of crude and immunizing themselves against the loss of its tax benefits.

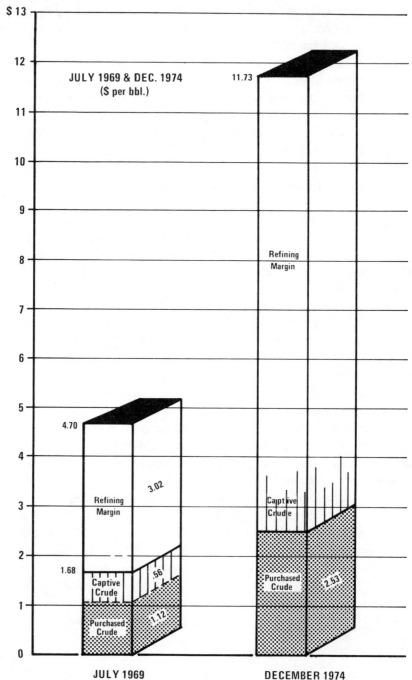

CHART 13-2
Costs and Refining Margins, Typical (150,000 b/d)
East Coast Refinery, July 1969 and December 1974
(dollars per barrel)

Avg. Refined Product
Price & Cost ($ per bbl.)

$ 13

12   JULY 1969 & DEC. 1974   11.73
          ($ per bbl.)

11

10

9

8   Refining
                                     Margin
7

6

5
   4.70

4   3.02

3   Refining   Captive
         Margin   Crude
2
   1.68   .56
         Captive   Purchased   2.53
         Crude   Crude
1   Purchased   1.12
         Crude

0
         JULY 1969   DECEMBER 1974

RAISING THE TARGET RATE OF RETURN

At about the time of the 1973–74 price explosion, the international majors made another far-reaching change, which also contributed powerfully to the price increases of refined products. Briefly stated, they raised the profit rate, or "target rate of return," which they regard as appropriate and necessary for their line of business.

As control over the market has been strengthened by both private and public means, the role of profit for the largest companies in American industry generally has undergone a progressive transformation from "what is left over" to, in effect, a predetermined "cost." Under competitive conditions, "profit" is of course the surplus (if any) remaining after deducting the costs of putting on the market the quantity called for by the existing level of demand. But with increasing control over the market, the leading companies in oil, as in other industries, have gained a substantial discretionary authority over price —the lower limit of which is a price so low that it covers only the inescapable costs of production, and the upper limit one so high that the resultant reduction in demand decreases revenues more than they are increased by the higher price. Where both the inescapable costs and the price elasticity of demand are low, as in petroleum, the range of discretionary authority is exceptionally wide. Target return pricing is a method of establishing, within this range, a price that reconciles aspiration with reality in such a way that performance can be empirically measured. It may be defined as the establishment of price in relation to costs (both direct and indirect) at such a level that the profit margin on sales at a "normal" or "standard" volume of production will yield a predetermined profit rate on investment.[11] A variant of "full-cost" pricing, target return pricing is, in Heflebower's words, ". . . a direct challenge to two tenets of generally accepted economic theory; i.e., (1) that demand as well as supply conditions, or costs, enter into price determination (for which Marshall used the 'two blades of the scissors analogy'); and (2) that the rational solution of all price problems requires the equating of *marginal* revenue and *marginal* costs."[12]

First outlined in 1924 in a series of articles by Donaldson Brown, vice-president of General Motors,[13] target return pricing has come to be employed by such important price leaders as General Motors, U.S. Steel, Aluminum Corp. of America, E. I. du Pont de Nemours— and Exxon. A company endeavoring to meet a *given* target return will tend to raise its price under two circumstances: (1) when increases in costs resulting from a new labor contract, higher prices for materials and supplies, etc., lower its actual profit rate below the target, even though production remains at or above the standard volume; or (2) when, as a result of a decline in demand, production falls below the standard volume, resulting in increases in unit labor and unit fixed costs. The price will also be increased if the company elects to raise the target return itself. An example was provided by the efforts of U.S. Steel during the middle and later fifties to raise its target return by 4 percentage points—from 9 percent to 13 percent at an operating rate of 80 percent.[14]

Throughout most of the post-World War II era, none of these circumstances served as the occasion for any material increase in oil prices. The principal objective of the companies appeared to be simply to maintain an established, apparently satisfactory return on investment—a goal which in the face of growing competition from independent suppliers was proving increasingly difficult of realization. On the basis of interviews with corporate officials, this author estimated that during 1953–68 the target return of Exxon, the industry's "reference seller," was 12 percent of net worth. Demonstrating a remarkable ability to meet that objective, Exxon's actual profit rate during the period averaged 12.6 percent:

> Changes in petroleum-refining activity are kept within narrow limits through a combination of market demand proration and import quotas limiting supply to demand. And so also have changes in Standard Oil's [Exxon's] profit rates been kept within narrow limits. The only conspicuous deviations were above-target performance in 1956, which is traceable to a 5.6 percent price increase during the first Suez crisis, and a below-target performance in 1958, which was the product of an 8.8 percent price decline resulting from the breakdown of the "voluntary" import program. With the subsequent imposition of the mandatory quota the profit rate moved upward during the next two years. In the ensuing 8 years the profit rate displayed a remarkable degree of stability, moving between 1.1 percentage points below and 1.2 percentage points above the target return.[15]

THE DECISION TO RAISE THE TARGET RETURN. Coincident with the price explosion of late 1973–74, Exxon, as well as the other leading companies, made known their intention to raise the target return. In hearings during January 1974 before the Senate Permanent Subcommittee on Investigation, Senator Percy propounded the following question to officials of the seven leading companies assembled, *en masse*, before the Subcommittee:

> . . . I would like to ask a question of the industry as to what the rate of return on net worth or capital should be to provide a level

of profits that would create necessary incentives for development, exploration and further investment. Is the proper figure 10, 11, 12, 15 percent? What does the industry feel to be adequate incentive? What would be considered reasonable profits—against which we could measure; what might be excessive or windfall profits?[16]

Although spokesmen for some of the companies demurred from offering at the hearings quantitative expressions as to what would be an "adequate incentive" or "reasonable profits,"* all but Texaco later submitted written, and presumably well-considered responses. Perhaps reflecting a desire to mollify irritated Senators, the figures originally proffered "off the cuff" at the hearings usually turned out to be lower than those contained in the prepared statements. Among the officials refraining from answering at the hearings was Roy A. Baze, senior vice-president of Exxon, who stated: "I don't think I would want to answer that question today, sir. My company operates worldwide, not just in the United States. Some areas are much more risky than others."[17] But in its written response, Exxon called attention to the constancy of its past profit performance, pointing out that its "return on average shareholder's equity had not varied more than one percentage point above or below a 12.5% return for 10 years. . . ."[18] Such a rate, the company maintained, "did not compensate for the accelerating rate of capital expenditures necessary to satisfy demand for petroleum." If the company was to secure the capital needed for future expansion, a higher profit rate was held to be essential:

> In the case of Exxon, in order to sustain the level of investment we foresee, in order to maintain a balance in our capital structure between equity and debt (including capitalized leases) which will sustain the corporation's financial ability to approach the capital markets, in order to finance working capital requirements, and in order to attract new (as well as compensate existing) investors we have concluded that a return on equity *at least* in the 14%–16% range is required and therefore adequate. Worldwide inflationary pressures, rapidly increasing working capital requirements in refining/marketing functions due to the increased costs of carrying higher priced inventories and receivables, and most particularly, acceleration in the anticipated rate of capital expenditures could require that an adequate return be *above* the 14%–16% range.[19]

In the past, the company stated, funds had come principally from internal savings (i.e., from the consumer). But in recent years there

---

* References to the target return concept are frequently to be found in reports by industry groups and accounts in its trade journals: e.g., referring to a report on Ocean Petroleum Resources issued in March 1975 by the National Petroleum Council, *The Oil and Gas Journal* stated, "A 20% return on total invested capital will be necessary to attract industry, the study indicated by using this figure in its calculations." (March 24, 1975.)

had been a growing need to supplement this source with recourse to the capital market. And to attract outside capital in the future, the company's existing rate of return was held to be inadequate:

> Until the mid-1960's Exxon, and the oil industry as a whole, relied principally on internally generated funds to finance investments. However, from the end of 1964 to the end of 1972, Exxon's long-term debt tripled in size ($851 million to 2.6 billion) while the rate of dividend payout decreased from 67% to 56% (39% in 1973), meaning that even with an increased rate of retained earnings and a rights offering to shareholders in 1970 which brought $376 million in new equity capital to the corporation, massive amounts of new debt had to be taken on.[20]

With a few minor variations, Exxon's theme was echoed by the other companies. At the hearings, Allen E. Murray, vice-president of Mobil, responded to Senator Percy's question by stating: "I can't give you a precise answer but obviously we have to compete in money markets in the United States and once again I am talking about just the United States, not international. We would have to have a return, I would say, comparable to general manufacturing in order to compete in the money markets." To Senator Percy's query, "Which would be around 12 percent?" Murray responded, "That would be my guess; yes."[21] In Mobil's written response, the 12 percent figure became the lower limit of a range: "to finance our business and attract the necessary capital," the rate of return "would probably be in the range of 12–15%. . . . In addition, we would expect, and require, a higher rate of return on investment in foreign companies generally than we would require in the United States of America because of the higher risk involved in these foreign investments."[22]

Citing "the capital intensive nature of our business . . . the high risk of petroleum exploration," and the "size of the capital investment program," Standard of California felt that "a rate of return on total capital employed of *at least* 16% is appropriate and proper for our company."[23]

R. H. Leet, vice-president of Standard Oil of Indiana, stated at the hearings: ". . . it might well take rates of return on total capital employed in the neighborhood of 18 percent in order to meet the estimated demands for capital in the future. That, however, is nearly twice the rate of return that has been accomplished by the industry. I would think a target of 14 to 15 percent would be something well within reason to look toward in order to generate and attract enough capital for the future levels."[24] In the company's prepared statement, the figure of 14 percent disappeared, while 15 percent became the lower limit of a range whose upper limit was 19 percent. "Based on our assessment of the requirements of the domestic petroleum industry, an after-tax rate of return on stockholders' equity of 15 to 19 percent will be required to make the necessary contribution to a national self-sufficiency in energy within the next 10 years."[25]

Shell's response represented another case of upward revision. During the hearings, its president, Harry Bridges, had said, "I would suggest that the industry needs to earn between 14 and 15 percent on shareholders' investment, to do the kind of job it needs to do."[26] But in its prepared statement, Shell offered a rationale for a considerably higher rate. Thus, because of their "high-risk" nature, the oil companies would have a "difficult time in attracting capital" unless they could earn "a premium of 1½ to 2 points above that of a public utility." Since the median return for utilities "has averaged 11.5%" (the equivalent of 12.5 to 13% under comparable accounting procedures for oil companies), the addition of the risk premium means that a "typical (median) domestic integrated oil company must average 14 to 15% return." But this, the company went on to say, was for the "long pull"; to make up for past "difficult" years (1969–73), it would take five very successful years with returns on equity of "around 18 to 20%."[27]

In direct response to Senator Percy, Z. P. Bonner, president of Gulf, stated: "I think between 12 and 15 percent would be a reasonable number that would allow us to reinvest the money. I would urge that when we think of this percent, and I am talking about net employed capital, I would urge that we think of the whole business."

TARGET RETURNS AND PROFIT PERFORMANCE. The new profit target objectives, together with the actual rates of return in 1974, are shown in Table 13-2. In bringing the target returns together, a number of steps were taken to achieve comparability. Thus the goals of SoCal and Gulf, originally presented to the Senate Committee in terms, respectively, of "total capital employed" and "net employed capital," were adjusted upward by 1 percentage point to place them on the basis of net worth.* Only the upper limits of Exxon's 14–16 percent range and Mobil's 12–15 percent range are shown, since in both cases even the upper limits were presented as minimal objectives. For Standard (Ind.), Shell, and Gulf, the objective ranges were 15–19 percent, 14–15 percent, and 13–16 percent. What emerges is a remarkable consensus: large firms in the oil industry should, in

---

* For the period 1964–72, SoCal's return on net worth averaged 0.97% point above its return on total capital employed, while Gulf's averaged 0.77% point above its return on net employed capital.

TABLE 13-2

Comparison of Target Objectives with Rates of Return

	Target Objective	Rate of Return	
		1963–72	*1974*
Exxon	16.0%	12.8%	21.3%
Mobil	15.0	10.3	17.2
SoCal	17.0	11.2	18.1
Standard (Ind.)	15–19	9.3	21.0
Shell	14–15	11.9	18.6
Gulf	13–16	11.3	17.9
Average	15.9*	11.1	19.0

* Based on midpoint of range.
Source: 1963–72—FTC; 1974—Compiled from Moody's Industrials.

their view, be able to secure a return on their net worth (after taxes) of 15–17 percent.

This uniformity assumes heightened significance in the light of the petroleum industry's structure, which is that of a "symmetrical" or "barometric" oligopoly. Such a structure differs from an "asymmetrical" oligopoly in that no single firm is clearly dominant, the various oligopolists being of about the same size and holding roughly similar market shares. In an asymmetrical oligopoly, it is the leader who effectively sets the price, which is customarily met by the other firms. Where, as in automobiles, the leader is superior in profitability (and presumably in efficiency), his price must be observed, since in a price war the lesser oligopolists would be driven out of business. Where, as in steel, the leader is less profitable (and presumably less efficient), his prices are generally observed out of custom and a healthy respect for the leader's powers of retaliation through predatory practices. In a symmetrical oligopoly, however, each of the leading producers enjoys a far greater degree of freedom. Such is the case in petroleum, where two companies (Exxon and Royal Dutch Shell) are, worldwide, about the same size, while within the United States shares of the top four are separated from each other by less than 1 percentage point in reserves, refining capacity, and retail gasoline sales.[28] Under these circumstances, there would be no way by which one oligopolist could prevent any of the others from embarking on an independent pricing policy designed, say, to improve its long-range position by sacrificing short-term profits. If, however, all of the oligopolists are seeking the same short-run target return, the price behavior will approach that of an asymmetrical oligopoly. Assuming no marked differences in costs, the pursuit of identical profit rates will tend to result in identical prices.

In comparing their new target objectives with subsequent profit performance, it must be borne in mind that recent profit rates indicated by published financial reports often understate profitability. This stems from a number of changes in accounting procedures, among which was a change in evaluating inventories from the FIFO ("First-in-First-Out") to the LIFO ("Last-in-First-Out") method. In periods of rising prices, the use of FIFO maximizes inventory profits because of the widening spread between the cost at which materials had been acquired (and are carried on the books) and the mounting prices at which products are sold. To provide a closer correspondence between inventory costs and product prices, certain of the oil companies switched to full or partial LIFO in 1974 and 1975. From the 1974 annual reports, it would appear that the effect on profitability was so great that the reported figures should not be used for SoCal. Had it treated inventory on the same basis in 1974 as in prior years, its rate of return on net worth would have been 18.1 percent, as compared to its reported return of 15.8 percent.

Despite such understatements, the price increases instituted by the major oil companies enabled them in 1974 to surpass their new profit goals, which at the hearings they had described as "adequate," "appropriate," and "proper." At their average profit rate of the previous decade, it would have taken the six companies nine years to pay off their stockholders' investment; at the rate called for by their new target objectives, the average pay-out period would be shortened to slightly more than six years; and at the rate of their actual 1974 performance, it would be reduced to about five years.

During 1975, the worst recession year since World War II, only Exxon and Shell achieved their target objectives, the group falling about 2 percentage points below their new goals. Aside from the downward bias arising from accounting changes, the decrease is the product of several causes, of which the most important was the decline in demand. In the second quarter of 1975, U.S. supply was 7.8 percent below the corresponding period of the previous year, itself a depressed period. Domestic crude production was down by 4.8 percent, crude imports by 2.0 percent, and refined product imports by no less than 30.0 percent.[29] In other consuming centers the deterioration was even more severe. Between the first halves of 1974 and 1975, combined net imports of crude and major refined products by the five leading countries of Western Europe dropped from 250 million to 200 million tons, a decline of 20 percent.[30] But with the economic recovery in the first quarter of 1976 the rate of return for the largest international majors rose slightly above its announced target objective, while that of the largest domestic major came well within its desired range. According to *Business Week,* Exxon registered a return on common equity of 16.1 percent while Standard of Indiana recorded 16 percent (May 24, 1976).

In an industry of high fixed costs, such as petroleum, a decline in demand takes its toll on profit rates in two ways: revenues tend to fall more rapidly than investment, and unit costs tend to rise. The latter is the product of increases in both unit fixed costs (as overhead costs are spread over a smaller number of units) and unit labor costs (as firms reduce their output more rapidly than their employment).[31] As production falls below the level (or "standard volume") prevailing when the price had been set, these increases in costs will tend to narrow the profit margin. If the target return is to be achieved, this will in turn require an increase in price. In 1975 precisely this sequence of events appears to have taken place in the petroleum industry. The decline in demand proved to be more serious than had been anticipated; the resulting increase in unit costs so narrowed the profit margin as to make it impossible to attain the target objectives; and as a consequence, in mid-1975 the domestic price of gasoline was raised. This action, it should be noted, was in no way precipitated by OPEC, whose prices remained unchanged until near the end of the year.

A necessary preliminary to the price increase was a reduction in gasoline inventories. Contrary to the usual seasonal pattern, gasoline production was cut back during the first half of 1975, dropping from 6,515,000 b/d in January to 6,075,000 b/d for the months March through May. As a result, gasoline inventories fell from 245 million barrels in March to only 198 million barrels in June, or just slightly above the so-called peril point of 195 million barrels. During this same period, inventories of middle distillates and residual fuel followed their usual seasonal trends, and in June 1975 stood at approximately the same levels as a year earlier. While crude oil stocks were 10 million barrels higher than in June 1974, stocks of gasoline were 20 million barrels lower. Having created a tight supply situation, the oil companies then raised gasoline prices just before the heavy driving days of July 4th holidays. Further increases brought the price by August to 21.5 percent above the January level. Lesser increases were imposed on crude (14.8%), light distillates (17.9%), and middle distillates (4.6%).[32]

INTERNATIONAL VERSUS DOMESTIC COMPANIES. One other effect of the price adjustments made during and shortly after the price explosion was the elimination of the long-standing divergence in profitability between the international majors and the predominantly domestic companies. For years the former had enjoyed a more rapid increase in earnings and a higher rate of return. Whether so intended or merely another in a series of remarkable coincidences, the upward adjustments in domestic prices of crude, and particularly refined products, had the effect of bringing about substantial uniformity in profit rates between the two groups of companies. As can be seen from Chart 13-3, this was the product of greater increases in earnings shown by the "domestic" companies than by the "international" firms. The upper half of Chart 13-3 compares the average profit trend (before and after taxes) of five "international" majors (Exxon, Mobil, SoCal, Conoco, and Marathon) with that of six "domestic" majors (Standard of Ind., Shell, Phillips, Cities Service, Union, and Standard of Ohio). The basis for differentiation was the average percentage of foreign income taxes to the company's net income before taxes during 1970–73. For the international majors, it was more than 50 percent; for the domestic majors, less than 15 percent. The lower half of the chart contrasts the profit showings of pairs of companies, one member of which is an international major, the other a domestic major—SoCal[33] versus Standard (Ind.), Conoco versus Phillips, and Marathon versus Cities Service.

Except for a slight decline in 1969, the profit trend of the five international majors between 1965 and 1972 was steadily but moderately upward, their aggregate net income (before taxes) rising from $2,882 million to $6,591 million. In contrast, the earnings of the six domestic majors remained almost unchanged during 1965–69, declined during the 1970 recession, and moved slightly upward in the next two years. In 1965, their aggregate net income totaled $1,043 million; in 1969, $1,334 million; and in 1972, $1,368 million. During the period 1967–71, when the "international" group was enjoying a pronounced rise in earnings, the domestic majors were suffering a slight decline. For the international companies the rise in income just about kept pace with the corporations' expansion, while in the case of the domestic majors it lagged behind. As a consequence, the average rate of return for the former remained virtually unchanged at around 12 percent, while for the latter it moved downward from about 11 to 8–9 percent.[34]

These differences in trends to 1972 are confirmed by the showings for the individual "pairs of companies." Thus, the moderate upward trend of SoCal contrasts with the stability of earnings displayed by Standard of Indiana. In the other comparisons the difference was even more marked: Conoco displayed the steady upward trend character-

CHART 13-3
Trends of Net Income, International Versus Domestic Majors

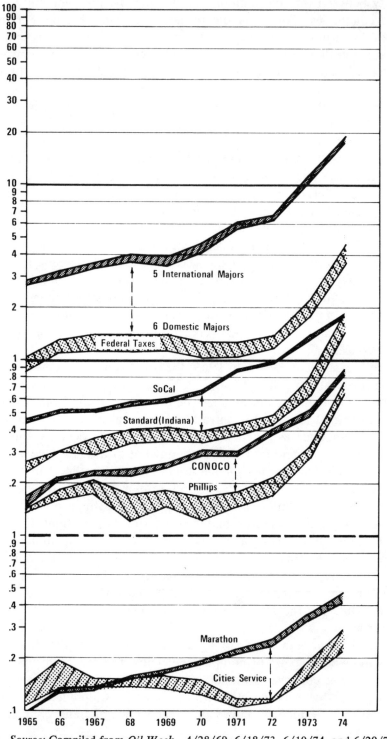

$ BILLIONS

Source: Compiled from *Oil Week*—4/28/69, 6/18/73, 6/10/74, and 6/20/75.

istic of the international majors, while Phillips showed little change in either direction. Marathon moved steadily upward, while Cities Service registered an actual decline.

In 1973–74 the pattern was reversed. The opportunities were presented (or created) to make breathtaking profits, and both the international and the domestic majors (but particularly the latter) were quick to realize them. Apparently, what was gained domestically from the application to captive "new oil" of the higher prices being paid for purchased "new oil," plus the widening of the domestic refining margin, proved to be greater than what was gained from production abroad where "equity" crude was in the process of being replaced by the less profitable participation crude. The change in earnings trends between 1965–72 and 1972–74 is summarized below for the two types of companies.

Percentage Increase in Net Income (before federal taxes)

	1965–72	1972–74
Five international majors	128.7%	167.9%
Six domestic majors	31.1	221.7
SoCal	106.1	87.1
Standard (Ind.)	78.7	261.7
Conoco	190.1	116.0
Phillips	28.9	247.7
Marathon	164.0	13.0
Cities Service	90.1	146.2

That the profit gains of 1972–74 were greater at home than abroad explains what would otherwise have remained an enigma. In response to Senator Percy's question, officials of the domestic majors, it will be recalled, proclaimed for their companies target returns more or less on a par with those of the international majors. On the basis of their earlier profit showings, the attainment of such a parity would have been so much wishful thinking.

HISTORICAL COMPARISONS. A broader perspective on these new target returns and recent profit rates can be gained by comparing them with profit performance over a larger period. There are two series of long-term profit rates in the oil industry. The First National City Bank issues annual rates of returns (after taxes) on the book value of net assets for "integrated operations" and for "oil and gas operations." The former is made up of major oil companies; the latter of nonintegrated oil and gas producers. The Federal Trade Commission publishes annual rates of return (after taxes) on net worth (i.e., stock-holders' investment) for the "four largest" and for eight other large companies engaged in petroleum refining. The First National City Bank series are shown in the lower grid of Chart 13-4; the FTC series on the upper grid. Taken in juxtaposition, these various series provide an indication of profitability in the industry's principal sectors—the very largest companies, other majors, the majors as a group, and independent oil and gas producers.

As will be seen, the average rate of return for the four largest companies reached 17.0 percent by 1973 and 20.7 percent by 1974; for the next eight, the profit rates averaged 12.5 percent in 1973 but 17.4 percent in 1974. These gains reversed a downward trend beginning toward the end of the sixties, which was undoubtedly the result of the inroads made by the Libyan independents in world markets and by the private branders in the domestic market. That decline, in turn, ended a period of relative stability in profit rates which had set in with the effective implementation of the mandatory import quota. Although introduced on March 11, 1959, the quota's mechanics of operation and enforcement had to be set up, while imports from Canada were not integrated into the quota until 1963. By that year, profit rates had recovered to a plateau where they remained until nearly the end of the decade. The quota thus arrested and reversed the sharp decline in profits affecting *all* sectors of the industry during 1957–59. Culminating in the collapse of the voluntary import control program, these were the years when low-cost foreign oil was making its way through Eastern seaboard ports as far as Western Pennsylvania. Profit rates in each of the industry's sectors dropped by about a third. The bringing in of foreign oil had in turn ended the industry's halcyon days when an earlier plateau had been achieved, lasting from the late 1940's to the latter 1950's. This was a period when prorationing was effectively limiting domestic production to predicted demand, thereby enabling the industry to enjoy the fruits of the doubling of the domestic price between 1946 and 1948. Through the international basing point system, this increase had also been transmitted to the majors' expanding low-cost operations in the Middle East. The history of the industry's profits during the past twenty-five years has thus been a composite of two plateaus of relative stability, two short-lived periods of declining profitability (following the outbreak of competition), and most recently a precipitous advance.

THE RATIONALIZATION OF PROFITS

How can these new target returns and higher profit rates be rationalized? Over the years, the oil industry's profits have been justified by a

CHART 13-4
Long-Term Trend of Profit Rates

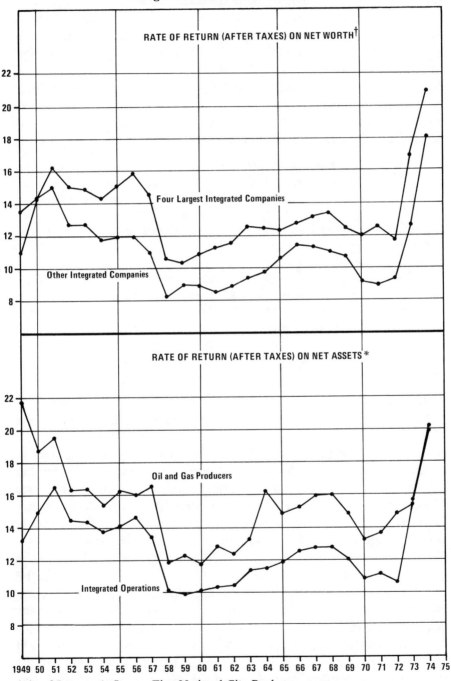

RATE OF RETURN (AFTER TAXES) ON NET WORTH†

Four Largest Integrated Companies

Other Integrated Companies

RATE OF RETURN (AFTER TAXES) ON NET ASSETS *

Oil and Gas Producers

Integrated Operations

1949 50 51 52 53 54 55 56 57 58 59 60 61 62 63 64 65 66 67 68 69 70 71 72 73 74 75

* As of January 1. *Source:* First National City Bank.
† Net Worth Average beginning and end of year / Federal Trade Commission, *Rates of Return of Selected Manufacturing Industries.*

variety of rationalizations, ranging from proper refutations of naïve criticisms to sophisticated distortions of fundamental economic concepts. The industry's defenders are constantly faced with the need to stress the impropriety of criticisms based simply on the magnitude of the industry's profits or the rapidity of their increase. Immediately after the price explosion of 1973–74, the favorite line of attack, both in and out of Congress, took the form of showings of *percentage increases* in the industry's *dollar profits*. It has been repeatedly pointed out that profits cannot be legitimately criticized by ignoring the investment required to generate them; Edward Symonds of the First National City Bank made a statement to this effect in 1969:

> People outside the petroleum industry are apt to suffer from an optical delusion—that oil is "the most profitable American industry." By a kind of optical foreshortening, they see clearly that industry earnings add up to a huge total. According to our tabulations, the U.S. industry declared net earnings after taxes totalling more than $6 billion, and they have been rising . . . by some 8 percent annually.
>
> But many observers perceive dimly, if at all, that, to generate these earnings, the companies had to sell goods and services which last year were valued at more than $60 billion. To maintain their pace of activity, these petroleum companies—most of which have been in business 50 years or more—have had to build up net assets totalling some $47 billion and yet receive a rate of return of 13 percent. . . .[35]

A corollary argument is that the industry's earnings, when related to investment, have not been particularly high. Thus, Symonds went on to point out that the industry's 13 percent rate of return "is below that of other U.S. industries." Or, in the words of Kenneth E. Hill of Eastman, Dillon Union Securities: "Historically, the oil industry has not enjoyed exceptionally high profits. In fact, its return on net worth has consistently averaged slightly less than the rates for all manufacturing."[36] Even before the price explosion, however, this argument was of doubtful validity. In a comparison of the 1971 rates of return of the eight largest oil companies with those of the eight leaders in eighteen other major industries, the oil firms ranked fifth.[37] The oil industry was certainly not the most profitable of these nineteen important fields of production, that honor—as had been true for many years—being reserved for the drug industry. The profit performance of the top eight oil companies was also surpassed in 1971 by the eight leading firms in cigarettes, malt liquors, and motor vehicles. At the same time, the average rate of return for the eight leaders in oil was more than *twice* that of the leading firms in machine tools, steel, broadwoven fabrics and yarn, aircraft, radio and television, nonferrous metals, and pulp and paper. It is true that the oil industry's profitability was exceeded by "other" industries, but not by many. After the price explosion, the argument became even more difficult to sustain— and hence has been heard with rapidly diminishing frequency.

In recent years the most frequently invoked and seemingly plausible rationale is the need for a profit rate "adequate" to ensure the industry's future growth. To the extent that the necessary funds are to be supplied out of internal savings (i.e., by the consumer), this argument implies the absence of an adequate capital market through which outside investors, both individual and institutional, could provide the needed capital formation by purchasing new equity offerings. To the extent that new capital is to be provided by outside sources, it implies the need for a relatively high profit rate to attract the needed funds. Both assumptions are considerably less than self-evident. It has yet to be demonstrated that this country's highly developed capital market is incapable of meeting the capital needs of petroleum or any other industry. In its statements to the Senate Investigation Subcommittee, Exxon made no effort to come to grips with the issue of whether the taking on of "massive amounts of new debt" could have been avoided by raising additional venture capital. The reluctance to make greater use of new stock offerings has stemmed more from a desire to avoid the "dilution" of outstanding securities than from any concern over the market's possible inadequacy.

As to the need for a higher profit rate to attract outside capital, the argument represents a confusion in tenses. A higher profit rate is claimed to be needed *now* to attract capital at some time in the future. What inducements will be required years hence to interest investors is of course a matter of sheerest speculation, which involves assumptions on the state of the country and the economy, the condition and prospects not only of the oil industry but of all alternative investment opportunities as well, the rate of inflation, the state of the law and government policy, propensities to save and consume, etc. To ignore these and numerous other variables, and to assume a direct cause-and-effect relationship between current profitability and future outlays by investors, is to indulge in the most extreme form of oversimplification. Even if the oil companies were not among the most profitable of all enterprises, investors might still be attracted to the world's largest industrial companies, occupying commanding positions in a huge, dynamic, and essential industry that enjoys highly favorable growth prospects.

Quite apart from the validity of this rationale, other limits must be drawn around its applicability to the oil companies. Usually, it is presented in the form of a justification for funds required to discover and produce additional supplies of oil, often in inhospitable and costly

locales. Obviously, such a justification has little to do with the takeover by Mobil Oil Corporation of Montgomery Ward; nor should
it properly be invoked to justify the funds required by the oil companies in their attempt to monopolize through merger and acquisition
competing forms of energy—coal, uranium, etc. Again, it is not clear
why their profits should be sufficient to enable the oil companies to
invade the chemical industry. Not only is the U.S. chemical industry
by far the world's largest; it has shown no inability to raise sufficient
capital to meet its domestic needs and, despite the effects of the import quota on its materials costs, become the largest earner of dollar
exchange of any U.S. manufacturing industry. In 1973, 7.1 percent
of the oil companies' net investment in fixed assets both within the
United States and worldwide was in chemical plants.[38]

Of even greater quantitative importance are the capital requirements for retail distribution, principally the outlays needed for gasoline service stations. In no other industry are the capital requirements
for *retail* distribution generally assumed to be a burden to be borne
by the manufacturer. Within the retail sector, capital costs are normally borne by the retailer himself, out of savings, borrowings, security
offerings, or retained earnings. An expansion by the supplying company may require a correlative expansion on the retailer's part, but
the cost is rarely included in the supplier's projected capital requirements. Yet in 1973, no less than 15.5 percent in the United States and
13.6 percent worldwide of the oil companies' net investment in fixed
assets was in marketing.[39] To use similar proportions in projecting the
industry's future capital requirements implies an inability of existing
outlets to handle the expected increase in demand, which in turn rests
upon the absurd assumption of full utilization of existing service stations. Moreover, there is the purely physical problem of finding
enough street corners to accommodate any vast expansion in the number of filling stations.

All these forms of capital investment—in competing energy industries, in chemicals, in gasoline filling stations, in mail-order houses,
and a variety of miscellaneous activities—are included in the majors'
consolidated financial reports and often in projections. Since profit
rates in these other fields are usually below those of oil, the companies'
reported overall profitability understates the attractiveness of investment in their traditional field. By the same token, projections of their
future financial requirements frequently overstate the capital needs for
the exploration, discovery, production, and refining of petroleum.

Transcending these considerations is the argument against internal
savings *per se*. In the words of Paul Frankel, "It is a negation of the
general principle on which the capital market in a free-enterprise sys-
stem is based, according to which money for investments is provided

from *all* the savings of the community, the priorities being established
—with some guidance from the center being provided by the Finance
Minister and/or the National Bank—by the actual and the potential
profitability of the individual project or enterprise."[40] Frankel went on
to point out the consequences of the ability to "plough back" earnings: "This term with its agricultural flavor of fresh air and virtuous
thrift, does more to confuse than to enlighten the public. These profits,
before they can be ploughed back, have first to be made, and the
industry which makes them subjects all others to a kind of compulsory
saving."[41] At the heart of the matter, he argued, was the very principle
of a "free-flowing capital market":

> If there was not so much of the profit reinvested, profits of this
> magnitude would never be made since they could not be dis-
> tributed without attracting unfavorable attention. . . . Some indus-
> tries, of which oil is only one, are so organized as to be able to
> be judges in their own case. If they take to self-financing, by
> setting their profit target sufficiently high, the very principle of a
> free-flowing capital market will be affected. This capital market is
> normally fed by savings of many individuals and by profits of *all*
> enterprises. If it becomes a general habit of "strong" industries to
> preempt a large slice of what is available, we are getting into a
> vicious circle; because the capital market is insufficient, some
> industries intercept the money before it gets there; thus, the capital
> market gets weaker still and so on *ad infinitum*.[42]

*   *   *

In a competitive market sellers are "price-takers," forced to accept
the price determined by the free play of the forces of supply and demand. In a controlled market sellers are "price-makers," enjoying a
substantial measure of discretionary authority over price that enables
them to choose among a variety of alternative pricing policies. During
some intervals—e.g., the early 1930's, the mid-1950's, and the late
1960's—the major oil companies have been forced to be "price-
takers." During most of the remaining time they have been "price-
makers," largely as a consequence of their tight control over Mideast
supply and the helpful market-stabilizing interventions by U.S. governmental bodies. For sellers with discretionary power over price the
critical question is what standards will be used to govern its use. For
the OPEC countries the objective of the price explosion was to achieve
a fourfold increase in the government "take." In the case of the "industrializing" countries this huge increase in revenues could, at least
conceptually, be put to good use. In the case of the "banker" countries the rationale for draining away far more revenues than they can
use is much less clear.

The role played by the major companies in the price explosion and earlier in the evisceration of the Libyan independents remains obscure. But the majors must clearly bear the responsibility for curtailing supplies to the American private branders, for raising prices more than any increase in costs occasioned by the OPEC actions (as is indicated by the rise in their profit rates), and for bringing about a curtailment in supply during the subsequent recession sufficient to maintain the price at its new and sharply higher level. Behind these actions, it appears, were the twin objectives of shifting the locus of profit-making downstream and achieving a higher target rate of return, plus the corollary goal of raising the profit rates of the domestic majors up to the level of the international majors.

It also seems clear that little consideration was given by either the OPEC countries or the major companies to the broad economic and social consequences of their actions, e.g., retarding the development of the world's poorer countries by draining away their limited foreign exchange balances, aggravating a serious worldwide recession, and imperiling the monetary basis of conducting world trade. At some time in the not too distant future the consuming countries will be forced to abandon their reliance on fashionable, simplistic solutions and come to grips with these and related problems. But until then, the prospect is for steady deterioration. Only a breakdown in the symbiotic relationship between the majors and one or more of the largest producing countries would halt the trend. And here the chances seem remote. Thus, except on one issue, the owning companies and Saudi Arabia appear to have arrived at an amicable solution to the takeover of Aramco. Reporting on a conference held at Panama City, Florida, the *Wall Street Journal* of March 15, 1976, stated:

> The companies which depend on Aramco for a significant part of their worldwide crude oil requirements could continue to have access to volumes of Saudi oil roughly equivalent to what they are currently taking, or between six million and seven million barrels a day. The lower figure is understood to be approximately what Saudi Arabia wants the companies to commit themselves to take at "competitive market prices" . . . the companies . . . are pressing for some sort of "mechanism" (requiring a major concession on Saudi Arabia's part) that would permit them to sharply reduce their volumes of Saudi oil if market or other conditions dictated.
>
> One concept which has been accepted is that "Yamani will set the price, but it has to be a competitive market price, and the companies have to be able to count on a mechanism that will permit them to pull out if conditions warrant," another source said.[43]

Part
FOUR

PUBLIC POLICY

In theory, the easiest way to resolve any shortage of supply is simply to rely on the operation of price in a free market. By attracting investment, a higher price will bring about an increase in supply; by curtailing consumption, it will lower demand to the available supply. Belief in the effectiveness of the free market has of course been the ostensible reason for opposition to price controls, for the drive to permit the price of "old" oil to rise to the level of "new" oil, and for the condoning of domestic price increases (such as those of mid-1975) not occasioned by any OPEC action. Quite apart from the fact that the oil industry bears only a passing resemblance to a free market, this approach to the energy crisis suffers from a fatal deficiency: both supply and demand are comparatively unresponsive to changes in price.

The assumption that supply is responsive to price has two components: a higher price is presumed to increase supply by increasing the amount of new oil discovered and by expanding output from existing wells. With respect to the former, history provides little support for the proposition that discovery is a function of price. Indeed, an argument can be made that if a relationship exists, it is inverse. Thus, the price of oil reached its all-time low during the early thirties, which was also a period of great expansion in supply arising from the discovery of the East Texas and other important fields. During the years of the import quota (1959–72), when the domestic price was artificially enhanced by $1.25 a barrel, the discovery of new oil fell below the rate of the preceding decade. And the price increases of the 1970's have been accompanied by a steady decline in new discoveries. If not inversely related, the rate of discovery has certainly been independent of price.

As to expanding output from existing wells, the high ratio of fixed or non-operating costs (most of which are in the nature of "sunk" costs) means that, after they have been incurred, production is likely to be much the same, as long as price covers the operating or direct costs of production. As Henry Steele has put it:

It is important to keep in mind . . . that costs of exploration are "sunk" costs and must logically be disregarded once oil is found and the decision becomes one of whether or not to develop it. For example, it may cost a million dollars to find half a million dollars worth of oil, but it will still make sense to exploit the field if the costs of developing and producing the oil are less than half a million dollars . . . *once a flowing field is discovered, the low ratio of out-of-pocket costs to price means that the risk of production being curtailed by price declines is relatively small.*[1]

Much the same is true of demand. The available evidence indicates that an increase in price would not result in a significant decrease in demand. Studies suggest that a 100 percent increase in price would be accompanied by only a 5–15 percent decrease in gasoline demand. Short-run price elasticities for gasoline range from —.16 (Houthakker and Taylor[2] and Data Resources, Inc.[3]) to —.11 (Phlips)[4] and even down to —.06 (Chamberlain).[5]

Because of the lack of responsiveness of both supply and demand, little progress can be made in resolving the energy crisis by relying on the "free play of market forces." Instead, the need is for direct and affirmative measures, carefully designed to achieve highly specific objectives.

These objectives lie in the worlds of both technology and law. Technological change holds forth the promise of increasing the supply of energy and reducing demand (without seriously sacrificing the utilities provided by petroleum). The specific technologies that appear to offer the greatest promise are examined in Chapter 14. How to achieve a more equitable distribution of what is available—how, in short, to keep a bad situation from becoming worse—lies within the province of law. The specific legal approaches that could be followed for this purpose are the subject of Chapters 15 and 16.

THE TECHNOLOGICAL POTENTIAL

14

IF IN THE LONG TERM the United States and the world are to have adequate sources of energy at all, and if in the near and mid-term the United States is to have any measure of energy independence, direct and affirmative measures must be adopted to increase supply and lessen demand. This requires making better use of existing methods and processes, as well as developing new technologies. If we were to adopt the general principle of giving the highest priority to those measures that offer the most gains in the shortest time, with the least resource expenditure, this would mean emphasizing available over undiscovered sources and existing over potential new technologies. In fact exactly the reverse seems to be taking place.

The glamorous new technologies which are receiving the greatest attention today are only potentialities for the future, and in most cases the distant future. Yet the more strongly attention is riveted on what the future may promise, the more difficult it is to arouse interest in what the present already offers. The principal victims of the resultant neglect are unexploited energy sources whose existence has long been known and those technologies which, though relatively new, are commonly used for other purposes. Though relegated to the limbo of the mundane and commonplace, it is the available sources and the existing technologies that offer the best hope of resolving the energy crisis.

Just as there has been this tendency to favor future potentialities over what is presently available, so also has greater emphasis been given to technologies replacing less important as opposed to more important petroleum products. Thus, nuclear fission (both conventional and the new breeder reactors), nuclear fusion, coal gasification, wave and tidal energy, magno- and electrogasdynamics are replacements for residual oil, which accounts for only 15 percent of the total U.S. petroleum demand. More than four-fifths of the residual used in the United States is imported (principally from refineries in the Caribbean), while the remainder is produced as a necessary by-product of petroleum refining. Thus, even a complete and immediate replacement of residual oil would lessen only slightly the demand for domestic crude oil. The failure to distinguish more important from less important products has arisen logically from the widespread—but erroneous—assumption that the different petroleum products, and indeed, all of the various fuels, are interchangeable, since all are sources of energy. This assumption underlies such forms of analysis as measurements of concentration[1] for the "energy market" or the "energy industry," generally, in which the various fuels (petroleum, natural gas, coal, nuclear power) are converted to a common denominator (usually BTU's). But this approach ignores the fact that petroleum acquires utility only after it has been refined into its various products; there is no use, and thus no demand, for crude oil itself. And once refined, the different petroleum products are for the most part not substitutable for each other, but serve different and discrete markets. No lower fraction can physically be substituted for a higher fraction; residual oil cannot be used in a residential furnace; home-heating oil cannot be used to power an automobile. Although some substitution can be made in the opposite direction (e.g., light fuel oil for residual), it seldom makes economic sense to do so because of the difference in price. True, some inter-fuel competition is to be found in electric power generation and in heating. But in petroleum's most important use, direct competition among fuels waits on the replacement of the gasoline-powered automotive engine by such unlikely creations as a lightweight coal-burning mechanism or a small, portable, and safe nuclear converter that can be conveniently fitted under the hood.

When the different petroleum products are examined individually, it immediately becomes apparent that any real easing of the energy crisis depends primarily on improving the supply-demand relationship for motor fuel. The transport sector uses the equivalent of 53 percent of all the crude oil consumed in the United States; for Europe, the figure is 28 percent.[2] Yet most programs advanced to resolve the energy crisis, including the "National Plan for Energy Research, Development and Demonstration," submitted on June 28, 1975, by the Energy Research and Development Administration,* are tangential to this central problem—the transportation uses of petroleum. For the near term (to 1985), the Administration accords the "highest priorities" to coal, nuclear power, gas, and oil from new sources and enhanced recovery techniques, as well as energy extraction from waste

---

* Section 6 of the Federal Nonnuclear Energy Research and Development Act of 1974 requires the Energy Research and Development Administration to develop a comprehensive plan for energy research, development, and demonstration.

materials. For the mid-term (1985–2000), priority would be given to "the development of new processes for the production of synthetic fuels from coal and for extraction of oil from shale," as well as to geothermal and solar energy. And for the long term (past 2000), they would go to nuclear breeders, fusion, wind power, thermal, and photovoltaic approaches. The only reference to any new technology that would increase the supply of fuel for transportation is to *new processes* that need to be developed for the production of synthetic fuels. Exactly what is wrong with the existing process for shale oil, considered adequate in 1969 by the Bureau of Mines, is not made clear. And this "development" is put off to the "mid-term," which does not begin for a decade.

An even graver deficiency is the omission, except for the "long-term," of any technology that would reduce the demand for petroleum's transportation products. At some time after the year 2000 the plan would accord priority to "technologies to use the new sources of energy. . . . As an example, long term efforts are needed to develop a full range of electric vehicle capabilities." No reference is made to the fact that at the time of the plan's submission electric vehicles capable of meeting the needs of a family's second car were already commercially available.

TERTIARY RECOVERY

The logical first step in increasing the supply of petroleum is to raise the rate of recovery from known reservoirs. Oil is extracted from the ground by three methods: primary, secondary, and tertiary. In the first, oil is brought to the surface by natural gas pressures ("free-flowing") or by pumping. In the second, additional oil is "squeezed" by pressure out of the reservoir, usually through the injection of water. In tertiary recovery, detergents, supplemented by other chemical agents, are injected to facilitate the release from the surrounding sandstone of oil droplets which may then be brought to the surface. Conceptually, the three processes are often regarded as constituting a logical sequence that will somehow inevitably take place, but in practice tertiary recovery may prove to be impossible of attainment on a commercial basis. As with solar energy, the potential of tertiary recovery is enormous, but so also are the practical problems of transforming it into a reality. In solar energy, the problem is the diffusion of sunlight; in tertiary recovery, it is the quantity and cost of the detergents, the comparative lack of basic scientific knowledge on important aspects of the process, and the heritage of prorationing.

Some idea of what awaits the development of a successful process of tertiary recovery can be gained from the fact that after the use of *both* primary and secondary methods, there still remains in the ground about two-thirds of the reservoir's original supply. On the average, about 20 percent is removed by primary recovery and about 13 percent by secondary processes. In older fields, which suffered the most severe losses of natural gas pressures from overexploitation, as much as 80 percent of the supply may remain in the ground, though in newer fields the percentage has been reduced to 55–60 percent. An increase of only 1 percent in the average recovery rate would add approximately 4 billion barrels to recoverable domestic reserves—or more than a year's total production. The hopes of the Federal Energy Administration for an expansion of domestic production (outside of Alaska) appear to be largely centered on tertiary recovery. According to a table introduced in the *Congressional Record* by Senator Adlai Stevenson, the FEA estimated that in 1985 tertiary recovery would supply 93 percent of the increased production which it expected would result from the lifting of price controls and a rise in the price of crude from the then-existing level of $5.25 a barrel to $12.50 a barrel.[3] In the FEA's view the higher price would call forth from old fields employing primary methods an increase of 49,000 b/d and from those using secondary recovery a gain of 68,000 b/d, or only 2.7 percent and 3.7 percent respectively, of the total expected increase.

The objective of tertiary recovery is to reduce the "interfacial tension" of oil droplets, i.e., their tendency to adhere to the surrounding

TABLE 14-1

Crude Oil Production in 1985, With and Without Price Controls

Expected lower 48 crude oil production (000 b/d)

	At $5.25/bbl.	At $12.50/bbl.	Increase
New fields:			
New primary	3,345	3,345	0
New secondary	312	312	0
New tertiary	85	85	0
Old fields:			
Primary	2,210	2,259	49
New secondary	2,192	2,260	68
New tertiary	0	1,714	1,714
Exempt oil	400	0	−400
Totals	8,544	9,975	

Source: Federal Energy Administration, *Congressional Record,* October 7, 1975, p. S17671.

sandstone, thereby permitting the droplets to assume shapes that enable them to escape through narrow necks of pores in the rock and coalesce into a continuous oil bank, which in turn coalesces with others, causing further displacement of oil. Fortified with other chemicals to lower viscosity, the chemical agents utilized are detergents, much like those employed for household use. Approximately 500,000 pounds of detergent would be required per acre, which, at the current price of around $1.00 a pound, would make tertiary recovery an extremely costly method of expanding the supply of energy. Moreover, there are purely physical limitations. The amount of detergent required for just one 20-acre experimental field (10 million pounds) represents more than half the annual output of a good-sized detergent plant. Moreover, although the gain in oil output would be greater than the amount used, the detergents are themselves produced from petrochemical feedstock. A further problem is the lack of basic scientific knowledge on what actually takes place within the reservoirs in the presence of these chemical agents. Despite the current widespread interest in the subject, tertiary recovery is still very much in the research and experimental stage. For a process contributing nothing to commercial production at the present time, the FEA is expecting a great deal when it assumes that tertiary recovery could in ten years provide nearly all of the expected increase in total domestic production.

In the event that some scientific breakthrough were to resolve the technical difficulties, there would still remain the problem of cost. Granting a higher price to *all* producers in order to help the minority who could or would employ tertiary recovery would not be a particularly effective means of enlarging the recoverable supply. Far less costly and more effective would be a federal government program to provide the necessary chemicals at no charge to those producers who wished to use them.

A further possible obstacle, already alluded to, is the absence in the nation's largest producing states of a compulsory unitization law, which has been described as the "irreducible *sine qua non*" for the adoption of advanced recovery methods. Here again, the federal government should directly assume the responsibility. To the question whether it has the necessary jurisdictional authority, an obvious precedent is provided by the Connally "Hot Oil" Act. If the federal government during a period of over-supply can prohibit the movement in interstate commerce of oil produced in excess of state law, it should be able during a period of inadequate supply to prohibit the movement in interstate commerce of oil produced under conditions resulting in a needless and irretrievable loss of an irreplaceable resource essential to the national interest and general welfare. By forging an instrument which utilized the powers of the federal government to stabilize and enhance the price, the framers of the Connally Act unwittingly provided a precedent for the use of those same powers to enlarge the country's recoverable supply.

SHALE OIL

In addition to petroleum, the United States contains two other sources of energy embodied in fossil fuels—coal and oil shale. Although both can be transformed into a liquid and thus made suitable for automotive use, the process of liquefaction is far more complex for coal than for oil shale. While the latter, or "kerogen," is made up of 80 percent carbon and 10 percent hydrogen, coal contains in addition up to thirty-six other elements, including sulphur and chlorine, which makes it difficult to handle and manipulate chemically. When used in the complex processes required by liquefaction, it clogs equipment, corrodes valves, and fouls controls. And a process which works with one of the many types of coal may not work with others. Although research into coal liquefaction has been going on for over half a century,[4] and although new processes continue to be proposed,[5] the only coal-to-oil plant operating in the United States is one developed by the FMC Corporation, which has encountered a series of technical problems.[6]

Coupling coal with shale under the heading "synthetic fuels" conveys the impression that the formidable technical difficulties of extracting liquid fuel from the former are also applicable to the latter. But, in point of fact, the processing of oil shale is the essence of simplicity. In the conventional method, the rock is simply mined and crushed, and then heated to a temperature of 480°C, at which raw shale oil (a close equivalent of petroleum) is released. Involving no special mineral preparation, high pressures, or difficult catalytic procedures, the process is far less complex than is currently required for many other minerals. In fact, a sophisticated and efficient extracting device, the Pumpherston Retort, was developed in Scotland as far back as 1894.[7] In a sense, oil shale's principal attributes and liabilities are the reverse of those of petroleum. Whereas the major problem presented by petroleum is its discovery, the location of vast bodies of oil shale is well known; whereas the natural state of petroleum is liquid, shale oil achieves this state only after processing.

RESERVES AND COSTS. The deposits of oil shale are enormous in extent but highly centralized in location. According to the National Academy of Sciences, the "identified" shale oil resources of the Green River Basins of Colorado, Utah, and Wyoming total 1,818 billion barrels. In addition, the area holds 625 billion barrels in the form of "hypothetical" resources, or a total of over 2,400 billion barrels. Of the 1,818 billion barrels of identified resources, 418 billion are in the form of rich deposits containing 25 to 100 gallons per ton. The remaining 1,400 billion are in leaner deposits, containing 10 to 25 gallons per ton.* But the former, alone, is ten times our proved petroleum reserves and would last about a century at current rates of consumption. The origins of this immense repository of captured sunlight have been described by Welles:

> The staggering dimensions of this resource were created by a huge inland sea which covered much of the western United States well over 60 million years ago. As the sea slowly evaporated, two large, rather shallow, fresh water lakes covering about 34,000 square miles remained. What geologists call Lake Gosiute covered southern Wyoming and was separated from Lake Uinta, which covered Utah and Colorado, by a wide plateau. The lakes were surrounded by high hills and frequent rains washed huge amounts of plant and animal life into the water. Meanwhile, the deep earth forces which were thrusting up the Rocky Mountains raised the lakes, eventually as high as 9,400 feet above sea level. This 'crustal upwarp' cut off outlets and sources and the lakes became stagnant. Broad swamps and mud flats developed along the shore lines, which were later to become coal deposits. The accumulating organic matter in the water acted as a kind of natural pollutant, not unlike the manmade variety of Lake Erie today in that it stimulated the growth of immense quantities of algae. Bacteria, fungi, protozoa and other microorganisms also flourished. Vast accumulations of plant spores, pollen and other grains added to the debris. Over perhaps 10 million years of remarkably constant climatic conditions, this material sank to the bottom to form thick layers of ooze, along with sedimentary clay and sand with which it chemically combined. As the lakes continued to shrink, the ooze was covered with layers of volcanic ash and other rock torn loose from the convulsive forming of the nearby mountains. Though in some sections pools of conventional oil and gas were to form, the upwarp did not allow most of the organic material to progress beyond the kerogen stage.[8]

It has been estimated that 84 percent of the oil reserves of the Green River formation (occupying 64% of the surface) lies in the public domain; that 10 percent of the reserves (occupying 21.8%

---

* National Academy of Sciences, *Mineral Resources and the Environment,* 1975, p. 95. According to the Academy, the Midcontinent holds 200 billion barrels of "identified" and 800 billion of "hypothetical" resources, both with 10 to 25 gallons per ton. Although their deposits are considerably smaller than those of the U.S., other countries with shale oil resources include Brazil, Scotland, Estonia, Russia, Yugoslavia, China, Zaire, South Africa, and Australia (*ibid.,* p. 95).

of the surface) are patented (privately owned) lands; and that 4.9 percent of the reserves (with 13.5% of the surface) are on unpatented and presently contested lands.[9] Hence the policy of the federal government has been a critical determinant in the development of oil shale, or rather its lack of development.

On the face of it, the costs of simply lifting a liquid out of the ground should be less than the combined costs of mining a mineral, crushing the rock, removing its oil content, and disposing of the residue. But the difference tends to narrow if there is added the prior cost of discovery. Over time, the difference between production *plus* exploration costs for crude oil and production costs *alone* for oil shale may completely disappear. Exploration costs will tend to rise as the nation's fixed stock of discoverable crude reserves decreases and new reserves become more expensive to locate, while the production costs of shale should tend to fall as new techniques are introduced, "bugs" are eliminated, and better use made of men and machinery all along the line.

Over a period of four decades beginning in 1916, the Bureau of Mines intermittently conducted research on extracting oil from shale, on the basis of which a vast body of information relating to production techniques and costs was developed. Spurred by fears during World War I that the nation was "running out of oil," the Bureau set up two experimental retorts near Rifle, Colorado, and a research center on refining techniques near Boulder. The former were closed in 1929 and the latter in 1930. Again impelled by fear of domestic insufficiency, research and development was resumed shortly after World War II under the Synthetic Liquid Fuels Act of 1944. Sponsored by Senator Joseph C. O'Mahoney and Representative Jennings Randolph, its purpose was to obtain "cost of engineering data for the development of a synthetic liquid-fuel industry." At a total capital and operating cost to the taxpayers of $24 million, pilot plants were constructed at Anvil Points near Rifle, Colorado. During the next ten years important technological gains were recorded in both mining and retorting. On January 14, 1953, Under Secretary of the Interior Vernon D. Northrop was able to write Senator John Sparkman, "it now appears that costs have been reduced to a point approaching a level with petroleum products." Similarly, a Bureau of Mines pamphlet published in March 1954 stated, "Recent cost estimates . . . show that the commercial cost of making shale gasoline and other liquid fuels on a large scale would closely approach the cost for the corresponding petroleum products."

Based on an extensive study of costs in 1962, updated to 1965, Professor Henry Steele stated in 1967: "It is my view that in all likelihood shale oil costs are at present low enough to allow crude shale oil to be produced profitably at current crude petroleum price levels. There may be many obstacles to entry of firms into shale oil production on a commercial scale, but the present level of production costs to prices does not appear to be among them."[10] Adding to the production cost of $1.25 an estimate of $.71 for transportation costs to Los Angeles would have yielded a delivered cost of around $1.96 a barrel, or $.89 below the price of crude oil then prevailing in that market, which would have yielded a return of about 15 percent after taxes on average invested capital.[11] Officials of Union Oil Co., which in the 1950's operated a pilot plant, repeatedly expressed satisfaction with its plant's cost performance. On July 8, 1958, Albert C. Rubel wrote that we "can with complete assurance proceed with the building of a shale plant which we know will work . . . and at a price closely comparable to current crude prices." And on February 27, 1959, Fred L. Hartley wrote, "As a result of our very large-scale shale demonstration plant and mining program, we have been able to establish firm costs . . . we believe that today's cost of producing shale oil is of the same order of magnitude as today's cost of *finding and producing* new sources of domestic crude oil."[12]

For a large company, producing oil from shale now offers another important economic advantage. The Tax Reduction Act of 1974 eliminated the right of companies producing more than 10 million barrels a year to take percentage depletion on petroleum, but left the percentage depletion provision on oil shale unchanged. In 1970, the value of oil shale's depletion allowance (15%) was greatly enhanced by a provision changing the point of its application from mined rock to the much higher-valued oil after extraction. Keeping the percentage allowance and the point of application unchanged in 1974 was not the result of a legislative oversight but reflected a deliberate Congressional intent to spur the development of oil shale. The economic value of the shale deposits has also been increased by the recent discovery of valuable minerals, nahcolite and dawsonite, tightly embedded in the rock. Thus, its mining and processing would yield valuable quantities of by-products used in making such important products as soda ash and alumina.

OBSTACLES TO DEVELOPMENT. Currently, the most frequently cited objections to oil shale development concern its effect on the ecology, particularly the effect on the water supply. A large-scale shale industry, it is argued, would increase the salinity of the Colorado River through depletion of the area's fresh water supply. Writing in *Science,* William O. Metz states, "shortages of water will probably limit shale oil production to a few percent of the U.S. petroleum consumption, no matter what the crude oil price."[13] Yet, even for a large-scale (1 m b/d) facility that would produce "semi-refined shale oil," the supply of water was considered "ample" by the Bureau of Mines. It is in refining, not mining or retorting, that large quantities of water are required.[14] In the petroleum industry, refineries have long been located near the centers of consumption. If crude petroleum can be transported thousands of miles from the deserts of Arabia to the refineries of Rotterdam, the task of moving crude shale oil a much lesser distance to U.S. refinery locations should not be beyond the capability of American industry. Another frequently cited drawback is the disposal of spent shale. Because it has a low energy value per ton of raw material (one barrel of oil requiring about 1.5 tons of shale), large volumes of slag would be left by the conventional process of mining and retorting. And because the application of heat causes the shale to expand, the slag takes up more space than the untreated rock, which of course means that it cannot all be put back in the mine. The area abounds with canyons and gulches, however, into which the residue could be dumped. It has been estimated that the spent shale from a 50,000 b/d plant would fill a gulch to a depth of 250 feet in seven years, leaving on top about 700 acres of bare shale,[15] which is about the area occupied by one typical Western wheat farm. Protection against sliding could be secured by planting top-soil or native grasses (three of which have been found to grow in the slag).

This is not to imply an absence of any ecological problems, but even apart from the probable economic necessity of its development, the ecological damages would to some extent be offset by ecological advantages. For one thing, oil from shale has a low sulphur content; its use would thus tend to reduce the sulphur emitted by automobiles and central power plants, making America's cities less obnoxious areas in which to live and breathe. Also to be considered is freedom from the peril of oil spills, a danger that will inevitably increase as the United States obtains more and more of its petroleum supplies from imports and offshore drilling. Whatever ecological damage is done by an oil shale industry would be largely centered in those sparsely populated parts of three states which have been described by a resident as the country's "most arid, desolate and unscenic" area, where the destruction already wrought by nature "would be hard for man to match."[16]

The development of oil shale has also been held back by a heritage of America's past, the "Teapot Dome" syndrome, defined by H. Byron Mock (former administrator for the Bureau of Land Measurement) as "the recurrent omnipresent fear of the charge of scandal felt by

each federal employee who issues a permit or license or other permission that allows private developers to make a profit from public
land." To strongly dedicated government employees, something more
than fear of criticism is involved. The prevention of "giveaways" of
the public's resources for private gain becomes a sacred obligation.
While noble in motive, the syndrome "has made it more difficult than
ever for Interior to produce a single development program, to do anything but let the shale remain under the ground."[17] It has also weighed
heavily in the minds of members of advisory committees appointed to
study the shale oil problem. Thus, a committee appointed by Secretary
Udall recommended a "two-stage" program under which commercial
development would have been delayed until after the completion of
still more research and study. One reason for this cautious approach
was cited by the Secretary: "We had a 'Teapot Dome' controversy—
scandal, in my judgment—because the Secretary dared to make policy
in the dark of night and that is the last thing we would propose to do
on this subject."[18] Another reason was the Committee's inexplicable
optimism concerning the adequacy of our petroleum reserves. In
Udall's words, "Our known and potential reserves, according to present
technology, are adequate to carry us into the next century at or about
present costs."[19] But the principal obstacle to the development of oil
shale has been the opposition of the oil companies. To firms whose
chief concern over the years has been in preventing price-weakening
surpluses, oil shale has been more of a threat than a promise. From
its inception the elaborate mechanism used to control domestic oil
production could at any time have been thrown badly out of gear
by the appearance of a new source of supply. Moreover, the attempt
to integrate Colorado shale oil into the mechanism would have presented special difficulties. If total oil supply was to be kept within
the Bureau of Mines' forecasts of demand, quotas for the new product
would have had to be granted to the shale states (at the expense of
course of the crude-producing states). Prorationing systems (for
which there existed no base periods) would have had to be set up
within the shale states, covering each producing facility. Inasmuch as
most of the deposits are owned by the federal government, leases
would probably have had to be open to all comers, making it exceedingly difficult to keep outsiders out. Furthermore, the federal government (or members of Congress) might not be sympathetic to output
restrictions by a new industry in which it had a sizable investment.

As early as World War I Union Oil, a lesser major primarily engaged on the West Coast, began acquiring oil shale properties and
studying methods of extraction. In 1948, it established a small pilot
plant; and in 1957, it began operating a "demonstration" plant of

"semi-commercial" size, four-stories high and designed to process 360 tons of shale per day. Despite many expressions of satisfaction by corporate officials with its performance,[20] the plant was shut down on June 30, 1958. The president of Union attributed its abandonment to the fact that "the 1958 oil imports were coming into the country with no regulations whatsoever"[21] and to oil shale's lower depletion allowance. But, as Welles observes, "Neither of these explanations seems wholly adequate." Voluntary import controls were in effect and indeed were in the process of being replaced by the mandatory program, while Union had certainly been aware of the difference in the depletion allowance before spending $12 million on the project. Interestingly enough, at the time merger negotiations were under way with Gulf, which was as conspicuously "crude-long" as Union was "crude-short." In April 1956, Union sold to Gulf $120,000,000 of 3½ percent twenty-five-year subordinate debentures which, if converted into common shares, would have given Gulf a 23 percent interest in Union, enough for working control. Union also entered into a long-term contract under which Gulf committed itself to supplying Union enough crude to meet its demands. Although the merger was abandoned at the insistence of the Department of Justice, the long-term supply contract remained in effect, thereby greatly relieving Union's need for another source of supply.

Not only did the majors show little interest in oil shale themselves; they were keenly interested in preventing its development by the federal government. As has been noted, after both World War I and II the federal government launched research and development programs on oil shale. In each case the programs were carried on by the Bureau of Mines for about a decade, only to be abruptly ended by higher authorities.

On April 15, 1930, President Hoover issued Executive Order No. 5327, "Withdrawal of Public Oil Shale Deposits and Land Containing Same for Classification," which remained in effect for more than three decades:

> Under authority and pursuant to the provisions of the Act of Congress approved June 25, 1910 (36 Stat. 847), as amended by the Act of August 24, 1912 (37 Stat. 497), it is hereby ordered that subject to valid existing rights the deposits of oil shale, and land containing such deposits owned by the United States be, and the same are hereby temporarily withdrawn from lease or other disposal and reserved for the purposes of investigation, examination and classification.
>
> This order shall continue in full force and effect unless and until revoked by the President or by Act of Congress.

It will be recalled that a committee of the American Petroleum Institute, concerned over the "too rapid development" of oil fields, had recommended on March 15, 1929, that "1928 production of crude oil in the United States should be considered as peak requirements for 1929 and subsequent years. . . ."[22] This recommendation, it will also be noted, was almost identical to the first principle of the Achnacarry "As Is" Agreement adopted September 17, 1928.[23] Not only would the development of an entirely new, and potentially very large, source of supply have contravened such a recommendation; it would have enormously complicated the task of setting up the domestic control mechanism, then in its formative stages. And accordingly, the development of an oil shale industry was stopped in its tracks by the Executive Order and by the closing of the Bureau of Mines pilot plants at Rulison in 1929 and at Boulder in 1930.

Again, the government's large facility at Anvil Points, established under the authority of the O'Mahoney-Randolph Act, was closed in 1956. According to Welles, ". . . it is undeniable that a group of high-ranking oil industry executives desired that the plant be closed, and that both the Interior Department and the Congress acceded to this desire." In 1950 Secretary of the Interior Oscar Chapman asked the National Petroleum Council, an advisory group of oil officials, to make an appraisal of the facility's cost data. Not unexpectedly, the Council found that "all methods of manufacturing synthetic liquid fuels . . . are definitely uneconomical under present conditions."[24] Another industry committee to study the Bureau of Mines' operations was then appointed by Felix E. Wormser, the new Assistant Secretary for Mineral Resources. In its recommendations of May 1954, this committee was even more explicit:

> The experimental work done solely by the Bureau on the production of oil shale and oil from shale at Rifle, Colorado *shall cease* and . . . *no further work be done* with the new retort [heating mechanism] unless there is a substantial contribution by industry under a cooperative agreement. If industry feels that no further experimental work is necessary, then the facilities will have served the purpose for which they were developed and constructed, and disposition should be made in accordance with established procedures.[25]

The retorts were shut down at the end of June 1955, and the entire facility closed a year later. In a speech on the Senate floor, Senator Estes Kefauver on March 1, 1957, said: "It is difficult to conceive of a more clear-cut case of oil-company domination of the policy of the United States Government." He went on to quote an editorial from the Denver *Post*: "If a jury of railroad presidents was asked to decide whether the trucking industry should be allowed to use public highways, there would not be much doubt what the verdict would be. We do not leave decisions on whether the government should subsidize the airlines to committees composed of bus-company executives. . . . The oil industry is just about as anxious to have competition from shale oil as the Republicans are to have Democrats win the November election."

REVIVAL OF INTEREST. Shortly after the energy crisis burst upon the world, the federal government shelved President Hoover's withholding order of 1930, opening up a number of oil shale tracts for competitive bidding. In January 1974, Standard Oil (Ind.) and Gulf jointly won the right to develop a 5,089-acre tract, containing an estimated 1.3 billion barrels of recoverable high-grade shale oil. A year and a half later they were still gathering environmental and geological data. At Anvil Points a consortium of seventeen oil companies was engaged in a modest ($7.5 million) project, apparently directed toward making further improvements in retorting. Union Oil had renewed its interest, while Superior Oil, a large independent, was undertaking experimental work.

The project that has elicited the greatest interest is *in situ* processing, being pioneered by the industry's long-time maverick, Occidental Petroleum. Because it dispenses with mining, conveying the shale to the surface, and conventional retorting, *in situ* processing holds the promise of important economic and ecological gains, causing no air pollution, using little water, and presenting only limited disposal problems. Conceptually, the process is the essence of simplicity. About a fifth of an underground cavity is mined out. The remaining four-fifths is then blasted with explosives, creating a rubble-filled cavern of broken oil shale.[26] Shale at the top of the cavern is ignited, with the fire controlled by the amount of air pumped into the chamber through holes drilled in the fracture lines. After several smaller experimental "burns," Occidental in the fall of 1975 ignited shale in an underground chamber 120 ft. square by 310 ft. high. By early 1976 the project was reported to be achieving its target of 450–500 barrels a day. Quoting an official of a Denver engineering firm, *Business Week* reports: " 'There is every indication that the Oxy people are tickled to death about their current project. They're the only oil shale people who aren't crying and they're spending more than anyone else' " (March 29, 1976).

Aside from Occidental, the oil companies have continued their long-standing posture of skeptical indifference. In early 1973 ARCO, the operator for a group that had assured control from a pioneering independent (Tosco),[27] shut down its 1,000 ton/day experimental retort, and a year later announced that a 50,000 b/d facility, expected to be in commercial production by 1978, was being postponed indefinitely. According to *Business Week,* the industry's restraint stemmed from a desire for "protection not only against inflation but against a catastrophic decline in world prices."[28] Another factor was the rejection by the House of Representatives on December 11, 1975, of a $6 billion loan guarantee amendment to the federal energy program under which private shale oil developers would have received up to $1 billion on federal guaranteed loans. Thereupon two of the partners in a consortium that bid $117.8 million in 1974 for a 5,000-acre federal oil shale tract in western Colorado withdrew from the project.

A TVA FOR OIL SHALE. The resistance of the major oil companies to oil shale has lasted so long and proved so effective as to constitute a reasonable basis for the assumption that only the federal government can be relied upon to transform this invaluable resource into an actual supply of energy. Fortunately, a detailed blueprint for such an undertaking already exists in the form of a little-known report, issued in 1969 by the Bureau of Mines. Prepared by L. W. Schram of its Division of Mineral Studies, the report, "Estimated Cost and Producing Capacity of a Government Assisted Shale Oil Industry, 1970–1980," contemplates that in ten years "shale oil production capacity could be expected to grow to about 1.0 to 1.5 million barrels daily and thus to fill one-fourth to one-sixth of the estimated 6 million a day gap in scarce oil supply that has been projected in connection with removal of oil import controls."[29] Thereafter, production could readily be pushed to higher levels: "Eventually shale oil in quantities of the order of 6 million barrels a day could be supplied by the oil shales of the Green River Formation in Colorado, Utah and Wyoming." Three years after the program was launched, three 35,000 b/d plants would be in operation. Production would gradually be raised by 200,000 b/d a year, with the goal of 1,000,000 reached seven years after the first plant began operations. The report assumed the use of the conventional mining and crushing process. To the extent of course that it could be replaced by *in situ* processing, the entire operation would be greatly simplified, problems of waste disposal would be virtually eliminated, and costs would be reduced. What would be required by the conventional process was described as follows:

> Production of 1,000,000 barrels of semi-refined shale oil a day, primarily in Garfield County, Colorado . . . would involve the opening of at least 20 large oil shale mines in the southern Piceance

Creek Basin area. The total output of the mines would be approximately 1,730,000 tons of shale per day. Crushing and screening facilities would prepare the shale for retorting. The retorting plants would require at least 150 commercial size retorts and would include oil recovery equipment and spent shale transportation and disposal systems. The refineries would include not only the oil processing units but also hydrogen generating plants and sulphur and ammonia recovery plants. Some of the auxiliary facilities would be steam and electric power generating plants, a water supply and distribution system, roads, shops, warehouses and office buildings. . . .

An area of 100 square miles of oil shale reserves in the southern part of the Piceance Creek Basin would be required, assuming that each mine should have a 20-year shale supply. The reserves would be ample.

To construct and operate the facilities would require 35,000 workers, involving a total population increase of some 250,000 people. No overcrowding problems were anticipated since there are now in the area "only a few small towns." The capital expenditures required for the industrial development *and* the new housing and community facilities would total $6 billion. For both an initial "first-generation" plant (35,000 b/d) and an improved plant (62,000 b/d) the report compares production costs with the price for a "high quality semi-refined shale oil" required to yield a 12 percent rate of return on investment. The price required to achieve the 12 percent return for the initial first-generation plant ($3.59 a barrel) would have slightly exceeded the average Texas field price of early 1969 ($3.27), but operations would still have been profitable since costs ($2.10) amounted to less than two-thirds of the prevailing price. The price required for the "improved" plant ($2.72) would have been $.50 below the prevailing petroleum price, and its costs ($1.07) would of course have been even lower. The showings of the shale oil plants would have appeared even more favorable had they been credited with byproduct minerals assumed to be valued at $.61 a barrel. It is realized, of course, that because of higher wages and prices costs in 1976 would have been considerably higher than the figures shown for 1969, but it seems unlikely that the cost increases would have matched the rise in petroleum prices. Hence, production of shale oil, even by plants using the conventional technology, should have yielded profits well in excess of a 12 percent return. That despite the prospect of such returns (plus percentage depletion) the oil companies continue to be apathetic suggests that if oil shale is to be developed, it will be only through the direct and affirmative involvement by the federal government, preferably through an agency for comprehensive industrial and environmental development modeled along the lines of the Tennessee Valley Authority.

SOLAR ENERGY

It has become customary in discussions of solar energy to begin with references to its abundance: if just one-half of 1 percent of the sun's energy annually reaching the continental United States could be collected and converted, we would be provided with three and a half times our total 1974 national energy consumption from all sources. In addition, solar energy is non-polluting, inexhaustible, and available nearly everywhere. The problem is that sunlight is a highly dilute source of energy, difficult to concentrate in quantities sufficient to replace conventional fuels for most purposes. Moreover, energy from the sun is subject to interruption by clouds, rain, snow, haze, and dust. If not used when collected, it must be stored, increasing the cost and decreasing the usable supply.

On the basis of present and foreseeable technologies, the principal potential market for solar energy would appear to be the heating and cooling of buildings which, it will be recalled, accounts for nearly a fifth of total petroleum demand. The use of sunlight for this purpose is of ancient origin. Adobe dwellings were designed by American Indians in the Southwest to insulate against the midday sun and release the stored heat during the cool evening hours. Some solar hot water heaters used on rooftops by homeowners in Arizona, California, and Florida in the early 1900's are still in use today, as is Solar House Number 1 of the Massachusetts Institute of Technology, which began operation in 1920.

The essentials of the process are little changed today. The sun heats a "collector," a flat plate insulated on its underside and painted black to absorb the sun's heat, usually containing passages through which air, water, or some other working fluid can pass and be heated. The air or fluid then moves to a storage container or directly to a heat exchanger, which delivers heat for hot water and space heat. For heating only, the collector must raise the temperature of the working fluid to 80–85°; for cooling, the temperature needed ranges from 190° to 200°.[30] With existing technology both are attainable, but cooling is considerably more costly.[31] According to the Energy Research and Development Administration, "The application of this technology to user needs must be demonstrated convincingly, production increased and prices reduced appreciably before a sufficient market can be developed."[32] At present, the additional cost of equipping a new house with solar heating is generally estimated at around

$10,000. Even though savings in fuel costs would permit recapture in eight to ten years, such an increase in the cost of a home greatly circumscribes the development of a mass market.

To promote the use of solar energy, the Energy Research and Development Administration has made research grants to improve hardware and has also developed "demonstration" projects to broaden public awareness. Limiting its role to providing an "appropriate stimulus to industry" and assisting "industry with development and demonstration,"[33] the Administration anticipates a rather leisurely rate of adoption: "Based on this possible progression in 1980, solar heating will supply the energy equivalent of 10,000 barrels of oil per day, and in 1985 the energy equivalent of 100,000 barrels of oil per day."[34] Needless to say, a program that envisions the replacement in ten years of only about 2 percent of the petroleum used for heating and cooling has come under sharp criticism. According to Dr. Jerry D. Plunkett, head of a small research and development firm, the research program "was based upon a misjudgment of the state-of-the-technology, and thus proceeded to re-invent the wheel six or seven times; ignored the potential contributions of small firms and individual inventors; and was overly oriented to big firms, large-scale projects, and abstract academic research":

> The federal government has what I believe is an almost incurable habit of undertaking large-scale projects. Given two equally valid technical responses to a national program, it is my opinion that the technology that is larger in scale will invariably be preferred to the smaller more decentralized technology. . . . Technologists have not yet learned from the scientists that the best, most elegant solutions are simple in both concept and execution. . . . Much federally supported research ends up as a report. Paper is the product . . . a research contract is almost certain to appear successful. Work will be performed, experiments conducted, data recorded and a report drafted. But innovation and directed development are a very different matter; specific targets must be set and the work measured against goals. Failure is visible and likely. Given these basic but perhaps only slightly overstated differences, it is clear that the average federal contract or grant monitor will opt for the safer research operation.[35]

Criticism to the same effect has been offered by Dr. O. G. Lof, a pioneer in solar energy research and director of the solar lab at Colorado State University: "There is a misplaced emphasis in a program that gives millions of dollars in grants to large, name companies or universities with no experience in solar energy to develop giant systems that are of no use to anybody."[36]

While technical improvements can be expected in the conventional process of collecting, storing, and using heat from the sun, the most promising opportunity for a radical technological breakthrough is offered by the solar or "photovoltaic" cell, which, like chlorophyll, converts sunlight directly into energy. Although the principle that light protons striking certain materials can cause electrons to move was discovered in the last century, it remained a laboratory curiosity until 1954, when scientists at Bell Laboratories created a silicon-based semiconductor solar cell. The first practical application was in providing electric power for NASA's Skylab space station, providing the power needed for nine astronauts. In the solar cell thin wafers of silicon (the second most abundant material on earth) are infused with minuscule amounts of impurities, such as boron and phosphorus, creating two sections that behave like the opposing poles of a battery. Protons of light striking the cell create a positive charge in one and a negative charge in the other, causing current to flow. When the cells are combined into modules and into still larger solar panels, significant wattages can be achieved.

Like other promising technologies, the solar cell is still caught in the low-output and high-cost cycle. Prospects for automating the manufacturing process, currently performed by hand, appear promising, as the cell lends itself to mass production techniques and indeed is a simpler device to make than an integrated circuit. Another source of economies is in the cost of materials, as the growth in demand should make possible large-scale purchases of silicon, specifically designed for solar-cell use.

LIGHTWEIGHT MATERIALS

The simplest and best way of reducing demand for gasoline would be to lighten the weight of motor vehicles. In a perceptive appraisal of the various methods of meeting the energy crisis, Great Britain's Central Policy Review Staff considered the reduction of vehicle weight to be far more effective than severe speed limits, car pooling, or switching from the private car to mass transit. The latter were rejected not on the grounds of undesirability, but because the savings would not foreseeably outweigh the social strains. By the year 2000, savings of only about 2 percent of transport sector energy requirements would result from either the imposition of a 50 mph speed limit or a switch of one-third of urban car travel at peak periods to mass transit. The Staff stated:

> Broadly speaking, the energy provided by the engine of a car is used in four different ways: to power the car's accessories such as the fan, the generator and the heater; to overcome the rolling

resistance caused principally by the tire; to overcome aerodynamic drag; and for acceleration and for climbing hills. Acceleration and hill-climbing are the most important power-consuming activities and they depend directly on the weight of the car. The weight of the vehicle is, therefore, the single most important parameter affecting fuel economy and the use of lighter cars would be expected to bring the largest savings within the limits of existing technology.[37]

In its evaluation, the Staff had in mind only a shift to smaller, conventional steel-body cars, having rejected the use of thinner gauge steel because of the "loss of mechanical strength," the use of aluminum as "prohibitively expensive," and the use of plastic materials (including fiberglass) for no stated reason whatsoever. But even within the severe limitations of the assumption, the report concluded: ". . . a switch to the use of smaller vehicles appears by far the greatest potential for significant energy savings in the passenger transport sector."[38]

In the United States, over a quarter of a million of General Motors' Corvettes plus several thousand Avantis have been made with fiberglass bodies. In Great Britain, the Reliant Motor Works at Tamesworth makes three- and four-wheel automobiles with fiberglass bodies (the former qualifying for a lower tax). Reliant not only assembles but manufactures in its own plant all the parts and components except the engine and the gasoline tank. In a measured test in the United States, one of Reliant's three-wheel models achieved 52 miles per gallon.[39]

Compared to steel, the advantages of fiberglass (often referred to as FRP or "Fiberglass Reinforced Plastic") are a higher strength-to-weight ratio, greater resistance to damage without permanent deformation, one-fifth the specific gravity of steel, freedom from rust corrosion, excellent heat and electrical insulation properties, the capability of being molded in larger, complex shapes impossible to draw in one piece of metal, and tooling costs about one-eighth those for similar metal parts.[40] Concerning weight savings, its strength-to-weight ratio ranges up to three and a half times that of steel. In one test, steel sheets used in a typical automobile body collapsed when a weight of 8.57 lbs. was dropped from a height of 13 ins., but the type of fiberglass used for the same purpose did not buckle until the weight reached 16.5 lbs.[41]

For use in automobiles, the principal disadvantage of fiberglass has been its higher costs—*on models with large production runs*. But where volume is limited, its extremely low tooling and set-up costs give fiberglass an advantage, which gradually narrows with increasing output until a "crossover point" is reached. The economies of using fiberglass rather than steel were discussed with Robert S. Morrison, whose company made the Corvette body for General Motors:

DR. BLAIR: Mr. Blauvelt [of Owens-Corning] gave his opinion that if the car bodies were designed from their inception to utilize fiberglass the crossover point for fiberglass would be in the vicinity of 70,000 to 100,000 vehicles. Is that in accordance with your impression?

MR. MORRISON: I think so. That would assume you design it from the tires up because you would not need as heavy tires. For example, you could take a thousand pounds out of a station wagon which would include taking considerable weight out of the chassis and chassis components as well as the body. Passenger cars might be 600 pounds lighter. . . .

DR. BLAIR: In that connection . . . taking up the matter of station wagons, Dodge has two of approximately the same length, Coronet at 208 inches and the Plymouth Belvedere at 207 inches, of which combined sales totalled only 45,000 in 1966. Would you think that for such a limited production the use of fiberglass would be more economical?

MR. MORRISON: It would be if they started back about 2 or 3 years before.[42]

When asked why fiberglass was not used more extensively by the automobile manufacturers, particularly on models with limited production runs, Morrison stated:

> . . . there are individuals within companies who wield considerable influence—we call them steel benders—who do not want any part of fiberglass and we have run into that problem which is one of the reasons . . . maybe why much higher quality products are not developed. A man does not want to go through the problems of getting a new assembly up, and a new type of assembly operation going.[43]

In 1962, Owens-Corning embarked on an ambitious effort to persuade the automobile makers to shift production of car bodies from steel to fiberglass. In a brochure, the company stated: "A square foot of an FRP panel one-tenth of an inch thick weighs about half as much as the same size piece of standard .036″ steel. This makes it possible to reduce the weight of an automobile body made from FRP to slightly more than half the weight of a comparable steel body." Moreover, the reduction in body weight makes possible other weight savings, less power is required of the engine, less weight must be borne by the suspension system, and less strain is placed on the transmission and brakes: "Reduction in weight of an automobile makes possible corollary weight savings in other components such as the engine chassis, drive line, transmission, brakes, suspension, and tires."[44] The corollary weight reduction was estimated at 1.25 of the savings in body weight.[45]

TABLE 14-2

Comparisons of Vehicle Weight in Steel and Fiberglass (lbs.),
Five Representative Models

	Luxury Car	4-Door Sedan	Convert- ible	Station Wagon	Trav- eler
Total Car Weight (Steel)	5,600	4,200	4,500	4,700	3,100
Steel Body Weight	1,260	1,059	884	1,120	1,115
FRP Body Weight	780	659	571	703	695
Difference	480	400	313	417	420
Corollary weight reduction	600	500	391	520	525
Total weight reduction	1,080	900	704	937	945
Total Car Weight (FRP)	4,520	3,300	3,796	3,763	2,155
Total Weight Savings	19.3%	21.4%	15.6%	20.0%	30.5%

Source: Compiled from data furnished by Owens-Corning Fiberglas Corp.

Comparisons presented by the company for representative models of several types of passenger cars are summarized in Table 14-2.

Despite the 20 percent saving in overall weight, plus the advantages of fiberglass in tooling costs, design flexibility, dimensional stability, and suitability for large moldings, the auto makers have continued to be firmly wedded to steel for their car bodies. Accordingly, Owens-Corning has been forced to lower its sights, emphasizing the desirability of the new material for specific parts and components. In this effort the company has met with a fair measure of success. Thus, it was able to report that in 1975, twenty-seven different models, nine more than in 1974, had fiberglass front end panels. The savings in weight have frequently been extraordinary.[46]

An argument frequently made against fiberglass (or any plastics-based material) is that the savings in petroleum achieved by weight reduction would be offset by the greater use of petroleum in the production of the plastic resins. But only about 30 percent of fiberglass consists of petroleum-based resins, the remainder consisting of the glass fibers (30%) and inert materials (40%). Moreover, a rather considerable amount of energy is required to produce the alternative material, steel. In a comparison of the energy needed to make an automotive hood, Eldon Trueman, an engineer for Owens-Corning, estimated the energy requirements (including the "potential fuel value of resin raw materials") at 40,000 Btus per lb. for fiberglass and 28,000 for steel. Although steel was thus shown to have somewhat lower energy requirements in production, this advantage was readily over-borne by the savings in use. Taking both production and use together, he concluded that: "A one-piece fiberglass/plastic hood would represent an energy savings of well over five million Btu [slightly more than a barrel of oil] when compared to its steel counterpart. . . ." He went on to point out that further savings are likely in the future "as work continues toward the recycling of reinforced thermoplastics and toward the use of all discarded fiberglass/plastics as a source of fuel."[47]

While superior to steel in terms of strength, fiberglass has no advantage in terms of the other principal determinant of a material's value—its ratio of stiffness-to-weight. But new "high-performance" composites are appearing which are superior in terms of both strength and stiffness. The greater its strength, the greater the ultimate load that a structural member can carry; the greater its stiffness, the less its deformation or deflection. Of the emerging new composites, the most promising appear to be those made of graphite (also referred to as carbon) and boron, i.e., plastics reinforced with fibers of graphite or boron. In contrast to steel or aluminum, whose structural properties are invariant, fixed by nature itself, graphite and boron composites can be constructed with a wide range of properties. Being synthetics, their stiffness and strength-to-weight ratios can be made to vary, depending on the specific type of fiber used, the plastic material with which it is combined, the general construction of the composite, and so on. The upper limits of the graphite composites far exceed the traditional materials in terms of both strength and stiffness. It is possible to get with the graphite composites the same strength as steel with as little as one-quarter the weight; the same stiffness with as little as one-fifth the weight.

The result of original research at the Hartwell facility of Britain's Royal Aircraft Establishment, graphite fibers have been described as threads of ". . . pure carbon having enormous strength and looking like fine strands of shiny dark grey hair." How low their price would have to fall to make them serious candidates for use in automobiles is a matter of conjecture, depending partly on the prices of competitive materials. But their suitability for this use has been emphasized by Dr. Stephen Tsai, formerly director of the Materials Research Laboratory at Washington University: "For the same performance, we can use smaller engines and less fuel, both of which will reduce air pollution. . . . Safety can increase because cars made of composite materials can be made more maneuverable, and more energy absorbing. There are indirect effects as the weight of the vehicle reduces; examples include the possible elimination of power steering and power brakes, which further reduces the size of the power plant required."[48]

ELECTRIC CARS

Until the latter part of the eighteenth century, power had been drawn from the wind, from the movement of water, from animals, and from men themselves. The age of fossil fuels dates back some two hundred years, when James Watt was able to put to practical use the "Carnot" or heat cycle on which the functioning of modern industrial economies still depends. Watt's steam engine converted chemical energy embodied in coal into heat (and thus steam), which was then transformed by pressure on a piston into mechanical energy. When, a century later, the German engineer Nikolaus August Otto invented the internal combustion engine, the only changes were the use of a liquid (and portable) fuel and the generation of mechanical energy by the explosion of a mixture of the fuel with air rather than through the expansion of steam. Obviously, converting chemical energy into heat and thence into mechanical energy by such a complicated process is wasteful in the extreme. Energy is lost in the overly rich mixture of gasoline and air in the carburetor, in the movement of the piston and connecting rods, in the opening and closing of the valves, and in the turning of the crankshaft. Up to three-fourths of the energy content of petroleum is lost in its conversion to motor power for transportation.

That the United States has run through its petroleum reserves so rapidly is due in large part to its single-minded dependence on power generation through the Carnot cycle. Almost wholly neglected have been alternatives which, while currently offering less in the way of performance, also consume far less of our irreplaceable resources. One means of improving the efficiency of energy generation has been available for many years—the battery. Another has been brought through research and experiment to a high level of development—the fuel cell. By converting chemical energy directly into electrical and thence into mechanical energy, they eliminate the heat stage with its enormous energy losses. Moreover, among the alternative energy sources, they are portable and thus practical substitutes for the critically important transportation uses of petroleum.

By the reaction of chemically different materials through a surrounding electrolyte, batteries produce an electric current in a circuit connecting its plates; by reversing the process, the battery can be recharged. Although interest in batteries dates back to the Middle Ages, experimentation was first documented in the work of Alessandro Volta in 1800, while the lead-acid battery was invented by Gaston Planté in 1860. Shortly after the turn of this century, vehicles powered by lead-acid batteries became a commercial reality. By 1915, some one hundred manufacturers had put on the market electric cars with a range of about 20 miles and a speed of around 25 mph. In that year production reached a high of 6,000 passenger cars and 4,000 commercial vehicles. The first taxis produced for use in New York City were electric. But like automobiles generally, they soon gave way to gasoline-powered vehicles. In 1910 gasoline was selling for 12–15 cents a gallon, and operating costs were only about half a cent a mile. With higher operating costs, plus the inconveniences of limited range and recharging, the electric vehicles were unable to meet the competition. Their demise was dramatized in 1915 by the reluctant decision of Henry Ford and Thomas Edison to abandon a joint undertaking to develop and produce an electric car.

For nearly half a century research on batteries for vehicular use lay in a state of torpor, resulting from three widely held but erroneous impressions. First was the assumption that the power plant weight, including batteries, would be about the same as in a gasoline-powered car, i.e., 25 percent of the gross vehicle weight.[49] Yet, through the use of plastics, fiberglass, and aluminum alloys, ratios in excess of 50 percent have easily been achieved. In the second place the maximum energy density of the lead-acid battery was assumed to be 8–12 watt-hours per pound.[50] But, as Raymond Jasinski, author of *High Voltage Batteries,* has pointed out, this represents merely what is required to turn over and start an internal combustion engine, not the battery's full potential capability: "Now, some preliminary experiments indicate that you are actually using maybe 30 percent of the active material and that . . . you can double or triple this. . . ."[51]

Finally, there has been the view that an electric car, to be considered a success, would have to duplicate the performance of Detroit's traditional high-horsepower "big" car. But this assumption overlooks the fact that a substantial portion of total automobile mileage is made up of short trips—to and from a nearby office, shopping center, school, etc. According to 1967 data compiled by Professor Lloyd Orr,[52] trips of less than 10 miles accounted for more than three-quarters of the number of trips and made up nearly 30 percent of the miles traveled; trips of less than 20 miles accounted for more than 90 percent of the number of trips and nearly half (48%) of the mileage. Making four trips daily of less than 10 miles, or two of less than 20 miles, an electric car with a 40-mile range could take over about half of the total passenger car usage. According to a more recent study, the average automobile made 1,315 local trips a year and only 3.6 long-distance trips (over 100 miles), with an average trip length of 7.3 miles. Aside from the long-distance trips, the average vehicle made 3.7 trips per day, with an average length of 5.7 miles, traveling 21 miles per day,[53] or only *half* the range of commercially available battery-powered cars. An unknown but obviously very large proportion of these short trips was made by the family's second (or third) car—clearly the logical market for the battery-driven car.

By 1975 battery-powered cars were commercially available at retail prices of less than $3,000. With a range of some 50 miles, a top speed of about 40 mph, and an ability to accelerate to 25 mph in 6 seconds, their operating costs are said to average about 1 cent a mile.[54]

This performance was attained by the use of the lead-acid battery, which has been materially improved in recent years. In Jasinski's words, "It works well, it is durable, and it is cheap."[55] Or, as Schrade F. Radtke, vice-president of the International Lead Zinc Research Organization, has described it:

> The lead-acid battery is still King of the hill because it is still far and away the best that modern science can offer. The lead-acid battery is a completely reliable system. This has been conclusively demonstrated over the past decades. Next, it is economic, as everyone knows. It is simple in operation, simple in principle, and simple to produce. It is non-polluting of the air, it is quiet. Noncritical materials, which are readily available, are used in its construction, and the lead is salvaged for re-use again and again. And finally it offers high performance—good power and long service life.
>
> It is true that today's lead-acid battery will not provide sufficient power to compete in performance with the standard American automobile, but we know it is capable right now of powering various limited mission vehicles including the typical family second car.[56]

In various stages of testing and development are higher performance batteries: e.g., zinc-air, zinc-nickel, lithium-chlorine, and sodium-sulphur, of which the last may have the greatest potential. With a projected power density of 100 watt-hours per pound, it would give a compact car a range about three times that of the lead-acid battery. Now under investigation by fifteen research groups throughout the world, including the Ford Motor Co. and Dow Chemical, the sodium and sulphur electrodes are kept in a liquid state separated by a solid, ceramic membrane (electrolyte). Electrons moving from the sodium to the sulphur electrodes through the external circuit serve to extract energy produced by the chemical reaction and convert it to useful power. Among its important advantages is its light weight, a sodium-sulphur battery weighing one-tenth to one-sixth as much as the standard lead-acid battery. It is constructed of abundant and inexpensive materials (sodium, sulphur, and aluminum oxide) and should therefore be low in cost. Because the reactants are liquid and the ceramic membrane is inert, the battery suffers little deterioration, even after continuous recycling. Tests by Ford suggest that a sodium-sulphur battery weighing 350 lbs. should enable a 1,350 lb.-commuter car to cruise at 40 mph for 200–300 miles, or at 60 mph for 125–200 miles, and to attain a top speed of 70 mph. The chief disadvantage of the sodium-sulphur battery is the high temperature of operation (300°C). Since a cold start is impossible, auxiliary heating must be provided, or the battery must be kept hot continuously; the latter would present no problem for an urban-suburban vehicle garaged for overnight recharging. The high temperature would also present a safety problem, since the escape of hot sulphur and sodium in the event of an accident must be prevented. Here the solution would be the development of adequate containers.

The fuel cell resembles the battery in that it converts chemical energy directly into electrical energy, but also resembles the internal combustion engine in that it uses an externally stored and replenishable fuel. Its potential advantages are overwhelming. According to Donald J. Looft, chief of the Electrotechnology Laboratory of the U.S. Army Mobility Equipment Command:

> . . . the fuel cell is the only device that directly converts chemical energy in a fuel to electrical energy, consequently it is a highly efficient device not limited by the heat cycle barrier. Further, there is no combustion process, there is no combustion exhaust, only reaction products which are in almost all systems an inert gas and water. Still further, the conversion process in fuel cells is a chemical reaction not accompanied by controlled explosions such as those in a combustion chamber so that except for pumps and blowers to bring the fuel and oxidant to the reaction site, remove reaction products and provide cooling and conditioning as required, the process is silent and static. All these characteristics make fuel cells potentially an ideal power source.[57]

First developed by Grove in 1836, hydrogen-oxygen fuel cells were neglected for more than a century until in 1965 they were used to provide the power for space capsules. Their success in the space program established the reliability of hydrogen fuel cells, which, however, present handling and distribution problems that make them impractical for use in a motor vehicle. Of the available alternatives, the U.S. Army has indicated its preference for the chemical hydrazine, a colorless liquid with an odor like ammonia. The Army arrived at its choice by testing all available "power systems" at its Mobility Equipment Research and Development Center located at Fort Belvoir, Virginia. Testifying in 1967, the Army representatives stated: "The most advanced of the special fuel approaches is the hydrazine-air system. Though hydrazine has roughly half the energy per unit weight of hydrocarbons, hydrazine in a water solution is a highly reactive compound and can be oxidized directly on a fuel cell anode. . . . Hydrazine fuel cells are clearly superior to any other available silent power source."[58]

Although first prepared by Lobry de Bruyn in 1894, hydrazine remained a laboratory curiosity until late in World War II. Recalling its high specific impulse, German scientists took hydrazine off the shelf and put it to use as a rocket fuel. In the immediate postwar years it also became the preferred rocket fuel of this country; but when the decision was made to shift to solid-state propellants, the market for hydrazine all but disappeared, since its other uses are relatively minor —as raw material for pharmaceuticals, as plant growth regulators, and for miscellaneous chemical purposes.

To test actual performance, the Army replaced the original 94-horsepower internal combustion engine in a standard ¾-ton military truck with a 20-kilowatt hydrazine-air fuel cell. It should be noted that the truck had a cargo capacity of 2,300 lbs., far greater than would be required in a passenger vehicle. The vehicle was subjected to 500 miles of testing under military requirements which, as Looft pointed out, are more "severe" than those faced by commercial vehicles in terms of cross-country, towed load, extreme environment, and standby power capabilities. Terming the results "quite encouraging," the Army representative stated: "Test data accumulated during 500 miles of testing shows that performance equivalent to that provided by the original 94-horsepower reciprocating engine and mechanical drive can be expected with a 40-kilowatt (approximately 53-horsepower) fuel cell electric drive system." He concluded by saying: "feasibility . . . has been demonstrated; cost is a major barrier at this time to their use."[59]

Hope for reducing the cost of hydrazine lies in the adoption of new and more efficient processes for the manufacture of hydrazine, one of which has been developed by a noted chemical engineer, Dr. Ju Chin Chu.[60] In this new process[61] the raw materials, ammonia and chlorine, would be fed into a fuel cell instead of a conventional reactor, thereby greatly reducing the amount of power required which, in Chu's words, "is the main reason why hydrazine still commands a high price today." Compared to the existing Rasching process, the saving in power was estimated by Dr. Chu as "at least 70 percent."[62] The fuel-cell reactor would serve the dual function of producing hydrazine solution and furnishing power for the concentration of hydrazine in the latter stages of production. In other words, a large stationary fuel cell would be used to produce the fuel to be used by smaller fuel cells propelling vehicles. Although he recognized the difficulty of calculating cost savings, Chu estimated that with his process, ". . . up to 40 to 45 percent of the reduction in the production cost can be made possible."

*   *   *

The difficulty of arousing interest in this process represents a classic case of the need for direct government action to break the endless cycle of restricted production resulting in high costs and prices which in turn limits production. Dr. Chu reported that his efforts to interest chemical companies had met with little success: "Because of the change of the requirement in . . . the missile systems, we even have some standby plant facilities not in operation. In other words, we still have excess capacity of plant for producing hydrazine. For this reason very few industrial firms will be interested to explore any new process." His attempts to interest the Air Force had proved equally unproductive: "It was brought to my attention that existing plant capacity is actually more than enough. Most people are not really interested in any new manufacturing technique at all."[63]

THE REMEDIES AT LAW:
The Regulatory Approach

15

Resolving a physical shortage depends primarily upon advances in science and technology. Bringing about a more equitable distribution of what is available lies within the province of law. Conceptually, there are only three public-policy approaches to the problem of substantial monopoly power: to control it through government regulation, to eliminate it through the antitrust laws, or to preempt it through public ownership.

The last refuge of an outraged citizenry, the ownership approach does not appear to be a realistic prospect for the United States, at least for the foreseeable future. The government is a majority owner of the leading oil companies of both Great Britain (BP) and France (CFP). Neither provides evidence that government ownership affords protection against either monopolistic prices or egregious inefficiency. Indeed, their behavior has been at least as rapacious as that of privately owned companies.* No member of Congress in the long and at times heated debate on energy policy during 1975 advocated the nationalization of the oil companies. But a very real debate developed over the other two alternatives, with the Congress opting for the regulatory approach, at least for the time being. In the process the arguments in Congress brought out in dramatic form the attributes and weaknesses of both the competitive and regulatory approaches not only for petroleum but for industry generally.

With the signature by President Ford on December 22, the Energy Policy and Conservation Act of 1975 (Public Law 94-163) became

---

* According to Sampson, "In London the Foreign Office was more sceptical of BP after the Iranian disaster [touched off by the refusal of BP to grant concessions similar to those already made to Venezuela by the American majors], but the Treasury still regarded oil companies as geese laying golden payments: by 1956 BP and Shell were reckoned to supply £323 million a year—more than half of Britain's receipts from all overseas investments." (Anthony Sampson, *The Seven Sisters,* Viking Press, New York, 1975, p. 137; cf. also pp. 114, 199–201, 263.)

the law of the land. It has been described as marking "an assertion of the right of public regulation and surveillance of petroleum prices and responsibility for maintaining authority to correct inequities which is unprecedented in peacetime in the United States in a period not clearly identified as an emergency."[1] It has also been termed a "99-page filibuster." Industry spokesmen have referred to it as a less undesirable alternative to proposals to break up the oil companies. In the words of *Business Week*, "many oilmen are concerned that continued resistance to Congressional pricing will heighten threats on Capitol Hill to break up the big oil companies. So some are willing to go back with almost any pricing scheme, so long as they can be sure it will stick. 'Better the devil you know,' says one resigned oil-man, 'than the devil you don't know.' "[2]

THE ENERGY POLICY AND CONSERVATION ACT

Repeatedly criticized in the congressional debate as "needlessly complex and difficult to administer,"[3] the ninety-nine pages of the law make up a *potpourri* of mandatory provisions, optional and discretionary authorizations, invocations to planning, and reporting requirements, ranging far and wide over the entire range of energy issues. But what has been gained in breadth has been lost in clarity. Indeed, if obfuscation had been the intention, the manner in which the statute is drafted could not have more successfully accomplished the purpose.

Apart from the pricing provisions, perhaps the most important mandatory provisions are the fuel economy requirements set for automobiles. The "product mix" of each car maker must average at least 17 miles per gallon in the 1977 model year, 18.0 in 1978, 19.0 in 1979, 20.0 in 1980, and 27.5 by 1985. It remains to be seen whether these new standards, which promise dramatic savings of up to 2,000,000 b/d, will actually go into effect or be relaxed once again in the face of expected industry opposition. The new statute also requires the establishment of a Strategic Petroleum Reserve of up to 1 billion barrels, of which 150 million barrels must be set aside in three years. And it extends the authority of the Federal Energy Administration to direct power plants and other major fuel-burning installations to convert to coal.

In addition to the mandatory requirements, the statute authorizes the President to take a variety of actions, if he so elects. Thus he is authorized to restrict the exports of coal and petroleum—a power that he is not likely to exercise. Restricting the exports of coal would not alleviate the developing shortage of gasoline and other lighter products, while exports of petroleum are minuscule. The President is also authorized to require that wells produce at their rate of "maximum efficient recovery." Behind that power is the doubtful assumption that a significant volume of output is being withheld by wells producing below their MER rates. The act abounds in references to planning, particularly for conservation. "Energy contingency plans," including a "gasoline-rationing contingency plan," are to be submitted by the President; a federal grant-in-aid program of $150 million is authorized to assist states in developing and administering state energy conservation programs; "energy-efficient targets" are to be set for the ten most energy-intensive industries; and all federal agencies are required to develop ten-year plans for energy conservation. In keeping with the philosophy of a statute that seeks an accommodation with monopoly power, international agreements to allocate petroleum products are exempted from the antitrust laws, but joint bidding by the majors for leases on the Outer Continental Shelf is prohibited. If nothing else, the act will provide employment for a small army of statisticians and clerks needed to collect, process, and prepare the numerous schedules and reports called for by its various provisions.

The most important, and controversial, provisions are of course those relating to price. In a return to the medieval concept of a "just price," Congress decreed that for forty months the maximum price for domestic crude should be $7.66 per barrel. This is to be the weighted average of the prices for "old" and "new" oil. "Old" oil is what is produced and sold from "a property" at or below its average monthly volume of September–November 1975; "new" oil can thus be not only oil produced in newly discovered fields but the output of existing wells above their base period volumes. Increases in the weighted average price of up to 10 percent a year may be made by the President as a "production incentive" or "to take into account the impact of inflation," with the former not to exceed 3 percent. Subject to exemption are up to 2 million barrels a day "transported through the Trans-Alaskan pipeline" (regardless of destination). Also subject to exemption are secondary and tertiary production. Although the prices for "old" and "new" oil can vary (as long as the weighted average does not exceed $7.66), the price of the former is expected to continue near its existing level of $5.25—the ceiling price for such oil set by the Cost of Living Council in August 1973.[4] For "new" oil the price used in deriving the $7.66 average was the figure submitted by the Federal Energy Administration as the "free market" price in January 1975—$11.28 a barrel. Allowable increases in the cost of crude can be "passed through" to later stages, but, to prevent pyramiding, only on "a dollar-for-dollar basis." Another provision limits the right of refiners to load a disproportionate share of higher crude costs onto specified products; i.e., they are not permitted to pass through crude oil increases on a "greater than direct proportionate by volume basis" to number 2 oils, heating oil, diesel fuel, propane, and aviation fuel. And in an effort to prevent the ceiling from becoming the floor, the act specifies that the President "shall have no authority . . . to prescribe minimum prices for crude oil . . . or any refined petroleum product."

While the establishment of a price ceiling in terms of a specific dollars-and-cents figure may appear to be a new high in congressional economic illiteracy, it represents merely a further step toward the subordination of what is economically and legally logical to what is administratively enforceable. Stemming from efforts by governmental bodies to restrain the behavior of "natural monopolies," the underlying rationale of regulation, to use Justice Holmes's famous words, has been to strike a "bargain" between protecting consumers on the one hand and permitting a monopoly to enjoy "the most profitable return that could be got" on the other. Over the years there has evolved the regulatory principle that prices must be low enough to be "just and reasonable" but high enough to cover operating expenses, depreciation, and taxes, and also provide a "fair return" on the "fair value" of the capital invested in the business. Although beset with difficulties, particularly in choosing between "original cost" versus "reproduction cost," regulation has been at least administratively workable in areas with relatively simple industry structures, e.g., electric and gas utilities, telephone service, and transit companies. But in fields with more complex structures, regulatory agencies have tended to replace the traditional regulatory standards with simplistic formulae and rules of thumb. Thus, during "Phase II" of 1972 the Price Commission virtually abandoned the traditional standards, coming to place principal reliance on what it called "term-limit pricing."[5] Such agreements were entered into with 185 firms representing about $124 billion in sales. Under this type of agreement each firm was simply required to limit the weighted average price increase for all its products to a specific percentage of its sales volume (originally 2 percent and later 1.8 percent), with the maximum increase for any individual product limited, originally, to 8 percent and later 6 percent. The justification was administrative workability: "it was necessary to minimize the administrative load that multiproduct companies would impose if individual decisions were required on each and every product."[6] The standard of price control set forth in the Energy Act differs only in that it specifies, not a weighted price increase, but the weighted price itself.

THE LEGISLATIVE DEBATE

The defense of the bill largely revolved around what was perceived as the only likely alternative—the complete decontrol of oil prices which had been under one form or another of price control since August 1971. Reflecting a widely expressed point of view, Representative Gude announced his intention, "albeit reluctantly," to vote for the bill on the grounds that the only alternative "may well be no bill at all, meaning immediate price decontrol and a rapid resurgence of inflation. That this path is less desirable is the best argument for the bill."[7] To Senator Cannon the consequences of decontrol would be calamitous: "Uncontrolled prices would destroy the present economic recovery and throw the country back into renewed recession. Business costs would increase at rates that would force many businesses and factories to close, increasing the unemployment rate beyond any acceptable level. Increased consumer costs would jeopardize economic recovery, worsen inflation, and produce general, social and economic hardship and dislocation."[8] The consequences of decontrol on prices were described by Representative Brown: "Under immediate decontrol $5.25 oil—most of it in the hands of the major oil companies—will immediately go to the domestic market price, $13.70 with the $2 tariff or $11.70 without it." After adding in the high-priced foreign crude, this means that "gasoline prices will go up from 3.5 to 6 cents per gallon."[9] In Representative Rogers's view the only restraint on oil prices in the event of decontrol would be the decline in demand resulting from a collapsing economy: "Why not $25 per barrel oil? Because there are limits to what you can do to the economy in this way. And everyone has discovered this." Castigating the administration for its "bankrupt, single-minded devotion to higher prices," he stated: "It has never made sense to me that in January 1975, when the uncontrolled price of oil had been raised to about $11.28 by OPEC, that this country should say, 'We don't think that's high enough' and raise the price another $2 by imposing an import fee . . . intended only as a brake on consumption."[10] To Senator Glenn, the measure incorporated the last possible concession that could be made to the administration's constant importunities for ever-higher prices: "This final position represents the acceptance of a substantial move upward in pricing for many members of Congress, and there was a general feeling that 'enough is enough,' no more give on this or other points."[11]

To its opponents, the bill represented an intolerable interference with "free markets." Invoked in opposition was Milton Friedman, who, in Senator Fannin's words, "eloquently articulated" the relationship between supply and price: "Do you want to produce a shortage of any product? Simply have Government fix and enforce a legal maximum price on the product which is less than the price that would otherwise prevail. Do you want to produce a surplus of any product? Simply have Government fix and enforce a legal minimum price above the price that would otherwise prevail."[12] Intellectual support from an unexpected source was helpfully provided by a staff report of the Federal Trade Commission's Bureaus of Competition and Economics. Economic behavior under price controls was compared with the performance expected in a theoretical "free market" in which supply and demand are brought into equilibrium by a "market-clearing" price.[13] Not surprisingly, the necessary evil of controls suffered by comparison with the theoretical ideal: "When the price of a commodity such as gasoline or crude oil is held by government controls below the level which would prevail in a freely operating market, a situation of excess demand is created. . . . We conclude, therefore, that the microeconomic benefits of decontrol are likely substantially to outweigh any costs associated with injury to the vigor of competition."[14] The rejoinder to this line of argument was a repeated insistence that the real world of petroleum is a far cry from what the FTC staff referred to variously as a "free market," "a freely operating market," and an "unfettered market." As Senator Hartke put it, "a free market in oil does not exist because the Arab cartel effectively sets not only its own price but the market price of domestic oil; therefore the so-called free market price is nothing more than the OPEC-dictated price."[15]

Another argument against the measure was the contention that, over time, the price of "new" oil under the "weighted average" formula would inevitably decline, thereby reducing the incentive for exploration and discovery. As Representative Long explained, "Any student of oil production and all knowledgeable oil men know that there is a downward graph of production predictable in any downstream field. . . . As the 'old oil' production goes down in total volume, the 'new oil' will become a greater percentage of the composite and will have to be reduced in price to maintain the weighted average now set at $7.66.[16] Senator Bentsen quantified the decline: "Old oil approximates 60 percent of production today; new oil 40 percent. Should this ratio change to 59 percent–41 percent, new oil prices must drop an average of 16 cents per barrel—and so on, as the ratio shifts to new oil. What this means is that the Congress is discouraging the production of new oil."[17] In rebuttal, it was argued that the rates of new oil production were not a function of price. As Senator Abourezk pointed out, "With the threefold increase in oil prices—

from $4 a barrel to $13.50—production of new oil has not increased. Total domestic production declined from 9.2 million barrels a day in 1973 to 8.3 million barrels a day in 1975."[18]

Other reasons for opposition included the argument that a 1 to 3 percent gasoline price decline, expected to occur shortly after the bill's passage, would stimulate consumption, thereby aggravating the shortage. In Representative Frenzel's words, "The counter-productive nature of the bill is enhanced by the fact that it not only reduces domestic supplies, but also its artificial rollback encourages demand."[19] What he termed this "weird policy" would result from the use of the earlier and somewhat lower price of January 1975 as the base figure for "new" oil. But Representative MacDonald objected on the grounds that "Projections by prominent economists and even FEA officials show that the elasticity of demand on all oil products is very low. . . . Does a reduction from 60 cents per gallon to 58 cents per gallon mean that people will start a surge of demand for gasoline?"[20] Even the cause of higher education was invoked in opposition. Introduced into the record was a letter "fervently" opposing the measure from Edward Clark, a member of the Texas University System's Board of Regents, which happens to be endowed with 2,100,000 acres of oil-bearing lands: "Such bills, if signed into law, will have far-reaching adverse effects on the Permanent University Fund Endowment of the University of Texas, and the . . . countless thousands of Texans who are directly or indirectly dependent upon the health of the oil and gas and related industries. . . ."[21] But the objections were to no avail. On December 16 the bill was passed in the House of Representatives by a vote of 236 to 160, and two days later in the Senate by 58 to 40.

EVALUATION

In evaluating the Energy Act of 1975, it is important to bear in mind that overhanging every stage of the bill's gestation was the constant threat of a presidential veto which, as the final vote indicated, could not have been overridden. Hence, the measure's legislative history was one of constant compromise with the Ford administration in general and the Federal Energy Agency in particular. In view of what they regarded as a commitment, supporters of the bill professed "amazement" at reports that "the President's decision to sign or not is on a knife's edge—a 50–50 chance." In Representative MacDonald's words, "the conferees were in continuous contact with the administration. All of the provisions of the bill, especially the oil pricing section, were worked out with the full knowledge and in many cases the demand of the administration . . . we would never have agreed to many of the compromising amendments if we had not had the assurance of a Presidential signature."[22] Supporters were moved to accept the administration's demands partly because they had succeeded in incorporating several desirable features: the fuel economy requirements, the authority to order power-plant conversion, the establishment of a reserve stockpile, and authorization for the Government Accounting Office to audit oil company books.

As an example of legislative draftsmanship, the act is singularly devoid of merit. In the words of Senator Mathias, "The program which is to be offered to the American people is not creative, is not decisive, is not comprehensive—in short, it is not adequate. S.622 is rife with vague, voluntary programs which encourage or promote conservation, but which do little to ensure that conservation will become a potent force."[23]

Evaluating the price provisions involves a weighing of opposing considerations. On the one hand, failure of Congress to enact controls would certainly have meant an almost immediate doubling of prices for some three-fifths of domestic production, imposing a heavier burden on petroleum-using industries and the consuming public. Without some protective mechanism, it would have ensured the demise of the remaining independent refiners, who, forced to pay some $11 for *all* of their domestic crude, could not have long competed with crude-long majors with far lower operating costs for their captive crude oil. Two-tier pricing can also be justified on the grounds that it represents at least an effort to cope with a fundamental, intransigent problem in an industry of declining resources: the sharp dichotomy between high (and rising) costs of finding and developing new supplies and the much lower operating costs of producing from known and established sources. As the search for oil is carried on in increasingly difficult locales and as wells are drilled to greater and greater depths, the divergence between the costs of discovery and the costs of operation may be expected to widen. To rely on "free markets" as the sole form of public policy is to assume that the economy can withstand the shock of prices for *all* oil high enough to call forth the needed *additional* supply. This is an assumption that the majority in Congress was not prepared to make. In the words of Representative Gude, "faced with an inevitably declining resource, it makes little sense to sacrifice everything for that last barrel of oil or that last cubic foot of gas."[24] These considerations, however, must be weighed against serious shortcomings of the prices used for both "new" and "old" oil.

THE PRICE OF "NEW" OIL. Since "new" oil is, by definition, oil "produced and sold from a property" in excess of the property's monthly average of September–November 1975, production by an existing well above its base period volume qualifies as "new" oil. Except by enhancing the owner's income, such production not only contributes nothing toward new discovery but accelerates the depletion of known reserves. Even more unfortunate is the incentive imparted toward drilling unnecessary duplicate wells in established producing fields, thereby reducing the reservoir's ultimate recoverable supply by causing further waste of irrecoverable natural gas pressures.

If the purpose is to stimulate exploration, the reward of the "new" oil price should logically be limited to oil produced from fields that are in fact newly discovered. Determining what would qualify should not be beyond the technical competence of industry and government. In fact, data have been collected and published in the *Oil and Gas Journal* distributing "exploratory successes" according to whether they represent "new fields," "new pays," or "extensions." "New fields" are true discoveries where oil and gas have not previously been found; "new pays" represent the location of additional subsoil producing horizons above or below the levels currently being produced in an existing field; and "extensions" are the extension of the geographical limits of an existing field through "step-out" drilling. In other words, the latter two types of "successes" take place where oil and gas are already known to exist. To the extent that production in a "new pay" brought an existing well's output above its base period volume, it would qualify for the "new" oil premium. So would most of the production in "extensions" which require the drilling of new wells whose output would necessarily be above any base period.

If the premiums for "new" oil were limited to oil extracted for a specified number of years from reservoirs not previously known and exploited, the principal recipients would be the independents who make most of the "new field" discoveries. As Table 15-1 shows, in 1972, 602, or 80 percent, of the 754 new oil and gas fields were discovered by independents, compared with only 92, or 12 percent, by the majors, with the remaining 60 (or 8 percent) being discovered by drilling funds. In the case of oil alone, the independents recorded an equally impressive showing—81 percent as compared with 10 percent by the majors and 9 percent by the drilling funds. The vast majority of oil and gas successes registered by the majors, 470, or 84 percent, were "new pays" or "extensions"; only 16 percent were "new field" discoveries. In contrast, 41 percent of the much greater number of successes by the independents were in "new fields." Not only did the majors put much less effort than the independents into domestic exploration, but the effort they did make was largely confined to areas where success was virtually guaranteed.

To provide a stimulus and compensation for discovery, there is no gainsaying the need for a premium of some kind above the "old" oil

TABLE 15-1

Exploratory Successes in United States Oil and Gas Fields, 1972

	New Fields Oil	New Fields Gas	New Pays Oil	New Pays Gas	Extensions Oil	Extensions Gas	All Exploratory Successes	% of Total
TOTAL U.S.								
Majors	38	54	127	228	68	47	562	25.5
Independents	317	285	215	295	208	165	1,485	67.5
Funds	35	25	24	28	18	24	154	7.0
Total	390	364	366	551	294	236	2,201	

Source: The Oil and Gas Journal, July 2, 1973.

price; the question is the desirability and appropriateness of the particular premium provided in the Energy Act. The $11.28 figure is (with minor adjustments for transportation charges) the OPEC price and, as such, bears no necessary relationship to the outlays actually required to cover the costs and provide the incentives necessary to bring in new fields of production. It is certainly conceivable that what is required in the United States for this limited and specific purpose is less than what rulers of underdeveloped countries regard as necessary to transform their entire economies almost overnight into modern industrial states. Moreover, the linkage to the OPEC price will impart a strong inflationary thrust to the U.S. economy, not only because of continuing upward price revisions by OPEC itself, but also because of the increasing importance of "new" oil in the composition of U.S. output. To Senator Hollings it seemed illogical to denounce OPEC for its price-raising actions and at the same time adopt the OPEC figure as the price for "new" oil: "If we accept the pricing actions of OPEC as being arbitrary and capricious, then, by implication, the legislated price of $11.28 is arbitrary and capricious, because it is no different than that established by OPEC."[25] The relationship between the movements of the "new" oil and OPEC prices is apparent from Table 15-2. Based on new reports to FEA, the table shows "wellhead prices" (for both "old" and "new" oil) and refiner acquisition cost (for both domestic and imported oil). According to the Federal Energy Administration, "the price series for uncontrolled domestic production from February 1975 forward is a 'moving target' that is clearly going in the same direction as imported crude prices but with lags in timing that cannot be measured precisely nor estimated with any precision."[26] Rather, as can be seen, it is the import price that is the "moving target."

TABLE 15-2

Prices of Domestic and Imported Crude Oil, 1974–75
(dollars per barrel)

	Wellhead Prices		Refiner Acquisition Cost			Imports and "New" Dom.
	"Old" Dom.	"New" Dom.	Total Dom.	Im- ported	Com- posite	
1974						
Jan.	$5.25	$ 9.82	$6.72	$ 9.59	$ 8.46	− .23
Feb.	5.25	9.87	7.08	12.45	8.57	+2.58
Mar.	5.25	9.88	7.05	12.73	8.68	+2.85
April	5.25	9.88	7.21	12.72	9.13	+2.84
May	5.25	9.88	7.26	13.02	9.44	+3.14
June	5.25	9.95	7.20	13.06	9.45	+3.11
July	5.25	9.95	7.19	12.75	9.30	+2.80
Aug.	5.25	9.98	7.20	12.68	9.17	+2.70
Sept.	5.25	10.10	7.18	12.53	9.13	+2.43
Oct.	5.25	10.74	7.26	12.44	9.22	+1.70
Nov.	5.25	10.90	7.46	12.53	9.41	+1.63
Dec.	5.25	11.08	7.39	12.62	9.28	+1.54
1975						
Jan.	5.25	11.28	7.78	12.77	9.48	+1.49
Feb.	5.25	11.39	8.29	13.05	10.09	+1.66
Mar.	5.25	11.47	8.38	13.28	9.91	+1.81
April	5.25	11.64	8.23	13.26	9.83	+1.62
May	5.25	11.69	8.33	13.27	9.79	+1.58
June	5.25	11.73	8.33	14.15	10.33	+2.42
July	5.25	12.30	8.37	14.03	10.57	+1.73
Aug.	5.25	12.38	8.48	14.25	10.81	+1.87
Sept.	5.25	12.46	8.49	14.04	10.79	+1.58

Source: Federal Energy Administration, reproduced in *Congressional Record,* December 16, 1975, p. S22,404.

The OPEC price explosion of October 1973–January 1974 promptly raised the landed cost of imported crude from $.23 below to some $3.00 above the price of "new" domestic oil. By the latter part of 1974, however, a steady rise in the "new" oil price had brought it within about $1.50 of the import cost. During 1975 President Ford imposed tariff fees of $1.00 a barrel on February 1 and again on June 1. Because of what the FEA referred to as "weakness" in world markets, only about half of these charges came to be reflected in the landed cost. The increases, however, were promptly matched by roughly corresponding advances in the domestic series. Thus, a $.49 increase in the landed cost between January and April was accompanied by a $.36 rise in the "new" oil price; a $.76 increase between May and July in the former was paralleled by a $.61 rise in the latter. By September the differential had once again been narrowed to approximately $1.50.

The parallelism in movement (after short time-lags), as well as the size of the "normal" differential, suggests a continued use of the industry's international basing point pricing system, with one important change. Instead of determining the Mideast price by adding to the Texas base price freight to New York and then subtracting freight back to the Middle East, the sequence appears to have simply been reversed: the OPEC price is the "base" price and the U.S. price is the "netback" price. Support for this hypothesis is provided by the fact that in 1975 tanker freight from Texas to New York harbor averaged about $.80 a barrel, the deduction of which would reduce the $1.50 differential by about half. And even the remaining difference might well disappear if allowance were made for the probable greater weight of higher-priced grades and qualities in the composition of imports. As compared with domestic production, imports probably contain a lower proportion of heavy, "sour" crudes and a higher percentage of low-sulphur and lighter grades.[27]

THE PRICE OF "OLD" OIL. Although its purpose is simply to provide a reasonable profit for producing oil with existing "properties," the "old" oil price was not based on cost data but is simply the product of historical happenstance and arbitrary adjustments. In August 1973 the Cost of Living Council froze petroleum prices for the different grades and qualities at the levels prevailing on May 15, 1973. To this the Council added the arbitrary figure of $.35, yielding an estimated average of $4.25. The result of freezing prices as of that date was to include the $1.25 premium of domestic over foreign oil resulting from the import quota. After OPEC's first unilateral increase to $5.11 in October, the Cost of Living Council on December 18, 1973, raised "old oil" to $5.25, where it has since remained. Citing cost data of the Federal Power Commission, Senator Abourezk stated that this price level is "too high because it simply does not cost the oil companies that much to produce their oil. . . . The oil companies are not making 10 cents a barrel, or 50 cents a barrel. They are making much more on their old oil."[28]

The image of the United States as a high-cost producing area is of fairly recent vintage, since for the first half of the century the United States was by far the world's leading petroleum producer and exporter. The image is traceable to the existence of a multitude of low-volume, high-cost wells which in the aggregate account for only a small proportion of total U.S. output. According to Paul T. Homan, "Of the approximately 550,000 wells currently producing oil in this country, just under 10 percent are producing by natural flow, while the other 90 percent use artificial lift. But although the flowing wells number only one in 10, they produce about 75 percent of all oil."[29] Between the exempted stripper wells, i.e., those producing less than ten barrels a day, and the flowing wells were about 100,000 non-exempt smaller wells. If these latter wells could produce profitably under the "old" oil price of $5.25, the flowing wells, accounting for three-fourths of the nation's output, should be able to enjoy a generous profit margin.

AN ALTERNATIVE: TRADITIONAL REGULATION

There is nothing inherent in the oil industry that makes it necessary to dispense with the traditional regulatory standards designed to strike a proper "bargain" between the conflicting interests of consumers and investors. The products of the oil industry are not differentiated but, with accepted quality differentials, homogeneous and substitutable. The companies' profits, for the most part, are made in petroleum, which facilitates comparison of product prices with corporate earnings. Among different producers, there is a greater uniformity of profit showings than in most other industries. The fact that demand is inelastic will enable a regulatory body to subordinate the effect on demand in considering alternative prices. Finally, the most important empirical basis for regulation, i.e., cost studies, can be made.

In a brilliant application of statistical methodology to economic concepts, Henry Steele constructed a short-run supply schedule based on operating costs for domestic crude oil production. His study shows how much crude oil was produced in 1965, as well as how much could have been produced in the absence of prorationing, by wells with successively higher operating costs. The basic source of data was a comprehensive statistical compilation by the Bureau of Mines distributing daily oil production in fourteen states by rate of production and well depth.[30] As Steele observes, "Purely physical considerations of reservoir engineering suggest that—other things being equal—the lower the daily rate of production, the higher the average cost per barrel produced, and the deeper the well, the greater the average cost per barrel produced."[31] He then applied to this body of data the findings of statistical studies relating operating costs to production rate and to producing depths. Increments of production in terms of sixty cost categories were ranked in order of increasing costs, starting with the lowest-cost category, which, as expected, consisted of wells with the highest production rate and the shallowest depth. At the opposite extreme were low-output stripper wells operating at great depths. As between production rate and well depth, the former appeared to be more important, with deep wells producing at high rates tending to have lower costs than shallow wells producing at low rates. To determine what the supply curve would have been in the absence of prorationing, actual production was adjusted upward by the extent to which it was below capacity; in 1965 there were six states for which this adjustment was required.[32] The results of the analysis are shown in Chart 15-1: "A" is the actual distribution of crude oil production by wells with successively higher operating costs; "B" is what it would have been in the absence of prorationing. Because prorationing resulted in a greater restriction of low-cost than high-cost wells, curve "B" is well below curve "A." These figures, it should be emphasized, do *not* include the costs of exploration and development; i.e., the costs of finding a field, drilling wells and installing gathering, processing and shipping facilities. It is, of course, proper that exploration and development costs not be included in cost schedules for "old" oil. Nor do they include severance taxes or royalties. They are, in short, the operating or "lifting" costs incurred by existing facilities.

What is most arresting is the highly skewed slope of the curves. With or without prorationing, operating costs exhibited only a very slight rise through almost the entire range of production. Only at the very last increments, accounting for only a minute proportion of total supply, did the cost curves turn upward, and then they rose precipitously. The flatness of the cost curves through nearly all the range of output was commented on during hearings of the Senate Subcommittee on Antitrust and Monopoly:

DR. BLAIR: Your curve B has only a very slight upward slope until it reaches the extreme right hand part of the chart. Thus it crosses the 30-cent line at approximately 2.4 billion barrels.

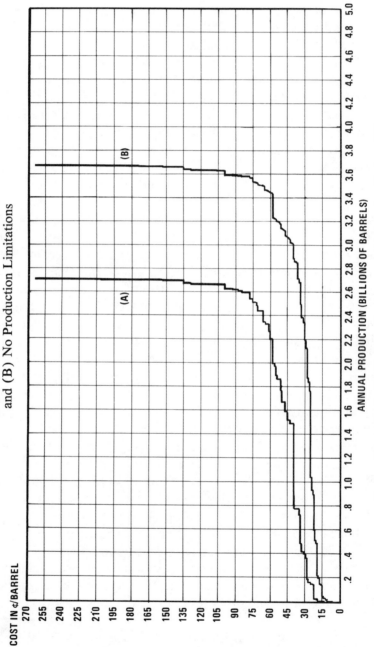

CHART 15-1

Short-Run "Supply" Schedules for Crude Oil Produced at the Wellhead, United States, 1965

Assuming (A) Production Limitation Controls as Operative in 1965,

and (B) No Production Limitations

Source: Henry Steele, *Hearings on Governmental Intervention,* Pt. 1, p. 219.

DR. STEELE: Yes.

DR. BLAIR: This is only 300 million barrels less than actual production in 1965.

DR. STEELE: That is right.

DR. BLAIR: Am I correct in my understanding that at an operating cost of only 30 cents, all but some 300 million barrels of our actual output in 1965 would have been covered by wells whose cost would have been 30 cents a barrel or less, in the absence of limitations on production?

DR. STEELE: Yes. That is what the schedule indicates. The short-run supply costs or lifting costs would be only that much for that rate.[33]

In 1965 the average price was $2.86 a barrel; the highest-cost wells had operating costs of $2.65 a barrel; actual production totaled 2.7 billion barrels. In the absence of prorationing, this total would have been met by wells with operating costs of less than $.35 a barrel. The 1974 level of output (3.2 billion barrels) could have been produced in 1965 at an operating cost in that year of less than $.60 a barrel, and 3.0 billion barrels, or 94 percent, at less than $.40 a barrel.

Similar cost schedules for more recent years could readily be developed, particularly by a regulatory agency with subpoena powers. On the basis of such data it would be possible to determine both average and marginal costs. Because of the industry's highly skewed cost distribution, it would be particularly important to determine what might be thought of as the "near-marginal" cost, i.e., costs covering, say, all but that last 5–7 percent of extremely high cost output.* (In 1965 a "near-marginal" cost would have been about $.40 a barrel.) The addition of appropriate increments for royalties and severance taxes would yield a total approaching the economist's concept of "short-run marginal costs." (For 1965 Steele suggested increments of $.20 for severance taxes and $.10 for royalties, or a total of $.70 a barrel.†) Such a cost schedule (and appropriate increments) would provide the basis for determining the relationship of alternative ceiling prices to gross profits and thus to return on investment. This in turn would permit the use of a traditional regulatory standard (e.g., the competitive cost of capital) on which to base the permitted profit rate and thus the ceiling price.

---

* If their output were considered essential, the high-cost producers could be paid a subsidy representing the difference between their cost and the "near-marginal" cost; as compared with basing the price on *their* costs, the savings would be enormous.

† ". . . the true short-run supply schedule should be increased by perhaps 20 cents per barrel to recognize average per barrel production costs and by another 17 percent to reflect the impact of the average royalty rate on production costs. Thus an indicated 50 cents per barrel might be increased to 78.5 cents on an operating interest basis" (*Hearings on Governmental Intervention*, Pt. 1, p. 216).

There would still remain the problem of the premium needed to cover the additional costs of exploration and development. Here again, the fundamental basis should be cost data, specifically the total costs incurred in bringing in "new fields" (as distinct from "new pays" and "extensions"), to which an appropriate and generous profit allowance could be added. The premium could be paid through a higher price for "new field" oil or possibly as a direct subsidy.

*   *   *

The pricing provisions of the Energy Policy and Conservation Act reflect only one concession to the consuming interest: the requirement of a lower price for "old" than for "new" oil. It is, however, impossible to say whether the profits earned under the weighted average price of $7.66 represent a "fair return" on a "fair" value. Under the act the standard of price determination floats in a conceptual limbo. There is no technical, administrative, or substantive reason why it should not be replaced by the standards traditionally used by utility commissions in determining a "just and reasonable" return.

THE REMEDIES AT LAW:
The Competitive Approach
16

THE COMPETITIVE APPROACH offers four fundamental theoretical advantages: prices are set at an economically desirable level, the level needed to bring forth the supply required to meet the existing level of demand; there is a constant downward pressure on costs, as less efficient producers must either modernize to meet the competition of their lower-cost rivals or go out of business; a constant stimulus is provided for the discovery and development of new products and processes; and resources automatically move out of industries where they have become redundant and into those where they are needed. For the regulatory and ownership approaches, attaining a "fair and equitable" price is within the area of possibility; the other three are difficult or impossible of attainment.

As its extraordinary efforts to control the market attest, petroleum is very definitely not one of those industries from which competition has been precluded by the requirements of technology or any other inherent barrier to entry. Despite the diminishing domestic supply, the operations of OPEC, and the majors' control over refined products, the potential for competition has been heightened by a number of recent developments. For one thing, the nationalization of concessions and the growth of "participation" arrangements has placed the international majors in what for them is the novel role of buyers. OPEC, by its successful drive for participation and nationalization, has created a fissure in the mutuality of interests inherent in the old "equity" arrangements, opening up a Pandora's box of possible conflict with oligopsonistic buyers. As long as refined product prices continue to be controlled by the majors, the prospects for such competition seem remote, even though a lower price for crude would widen profit margins, giving rise to at least some pressure for lower input prices. But the principal source of competitive pressures is the extraordinary margin between price and costs—a margin that is probably exceeded by no other major industry, except possibly drugs. Although the margin is at its peak in foreign crude, the domestic majors have raised the umbrella of re-fined product prices to such heights as to yield generous profits at considerably lower prices. The temptation to undercut will be particu-larly strong for those lesser majors who are well supplied with their own captive crude as well as for independent refiners able to obtain domestic oil. The objective of public policy, therefore, should be to take advantage of the industry's potential for competition, such as it is, by a sophisticated use of the three thrusts of antitrust: against collusion, against monopolistic acts and practices, and against existing concentration.

While the objectives of antitrust are, admittedly, long-range in char-acter, arising from the maintenance of a free, open, and competitive economy, near-term benefits can sometimes be realized by directing action against an industry's Achilles heel, which in petroleum is the control of crude. Specifically, the thrust of the law against collusion should be directed toward ending the concerted restriction of crude production; the thrust against monopolistic practices, toward forcing the majors to share more of their crude with independent refiners; and the thrust against existing concentration, toward breaking up the majors' vertically integrated structures. Only the last would necessitate new legislation. The first could probably be attained under existing law, and so also might the second, though new legislation would be preferable.

THE CONCERTED RESTRICTION OF PRODUCTION

If during 1950–72 the international majors had not been able to closely gear foreign production to a predetermined industry growth rate, sur-pluses of "distressed oil" would inevitably have developed, resulting in lower prices to buyers everywhere, including the United States. The remarkable success of the international majors in so precisely limiting output over so long a period raises the question, certainly of more than routine interest to the Justice Department and the Federal Trade Commission, of whether it was achieved through at least an implied "agreement, arrangement, or understanding" in violation of Section 1 of the Sherman Act, or a "planned common course of action" in violation of Section 5 of the Federal Trade Commis-sion Act.

The illegality of collusive restrictions of production has been well established. As early as 1902, the Circuit Court of Appeals in *Gibbs vs. McNeeley* held illegal a program designed to fix prices for red cedar shingles by shutting down mills and otherwise curtailing output whenever supply exceeded demand. The court stated:

> The combination in the case before the court is more than a combination to regulate prices. It is a combination to control the production of a manufactured article more than four-fifths of which is made for interstate trade, and to diminish competition in its production, as well as to advance its price. These features, we think, determine its object, and bring it under the condemnation of the law.[1]

Apart from lumbermen's associations, which have frequently been prosecuted for their attempts to maintain prices by limiting production,[2] the Department of Justice has proceeded against a cartel of magnesium producers which operated not only through agreements to limit output but also through the use of patent pools to exclude newcomers.[3] Similarly, American Can and Continental Can, which reportedly produced about 85 percent of the metal cans manufactured in this country, pleaded *nolo contendere* to a charge of limiting the production of certain types of cans.[4] On its part, the Federal Trade Commission has ordered producers in a number of industries, e.g., vitrified pipe,[5] veneer packaging,[6] and paper containers,[7] to "cease and desist" from limiting production.

While there can be little doubt of the illegality of such restrictions, there is the further question of evidentiary requirements; i.e., what is needed in the way of evidence to establish a violation of law? Where the restriction is the result of explicit agreement (as is usual with unsophisticated, small-business industries), direct evidence of collusion in the form of letters, agreements, minutes, memoranda, etc., is not too hard to come by. But in the case of large and very sophisticated companies, proof of illegality must usually (though not always) be established by circumstantial or indirect evidence of the agreement's operations and effects. The ability of the antitrust laws to reach restriction through such evidence is well established[8]—a fact that apparently is little understood by officials of the oil companies, who seem to labor under the impression that the laws proscribe recorded meetings and signed agreements but countenance everything else.[9]

Thus, Piercy of Exxon testified, "We are not a cartel in any way. We are not a monopoly."[10] Commenting on what he "sensed" as a "feeling" that Congressional inquiries had "monopoly overtones, oligopoly and so forth," he objected that "this antitrust thing permeates a lot of our problems."[11] Piercy's protestations of innocence ignore a substantial body of antitrust law directed against "implied conspiracies" or "conscious parallelism" developed by the antitrust agencies and the courts over a long period of time. Although woefully neglected in recent years, these doctrines have never been overturned and must still be regarded as the law of the land.

It has long been recognized that express proof of agreement is not required to establish a violation of Section 1 of the Sherman Act, to say nothing of Section 5 of the Federal Trade Commission Act. In the well-known *Interstate Circuit* case the Supreme Court held: "Acceptance by competitors, without previous agreement, of an invitation to participate in a plan, the necessary consequences of which, if carried out, is restraint of interstate commerce, is sufficient to establish an unlawful conspiracy under the Sherman Act."[12] The doctrine was reiterated in *American Tobacco Co. vs. United States,* in which, without direct evidence of meetings or agreements, the Court found a conspiracy from the parallel business behavior of three major cigarette manufacturers: "No formal agreement is necessary to constitute an unlawful conspiracy. . . . Where the circumstances are such as to warrant a jury in finding that the conspirators had a unity of purpose or a common design and understanding, or a meeting of the minds in an unlawful arrangement, the conclusion that a conspiracy is established is justified."[13]

The high-water mark in the development of the law against parallel behavior was a decision by the Supreme Court that upheld a Federal Trade Commission order charging manufacturers of rigid-steel conduit with engaging in unfair methods of competition in violation of Section 5 of the Federal Trade Commission Act. In one count, the Commission's complaint charged that the respondents had *conspired* to use a delivered price system of pricing, and in another, that the respondents had *independently* followed a *common course of conduct,* each with the knowledge that the others were doing likewise. Under the latter the Commission held it to be illegal for any seller individually to quote prices under a basing-point system with the knowledge that his rivals were doing the same and with the result that competition among them was eliminated. Splitting four to four, the Supreme Court sustained the decision of the Seventh Circuit Court of Appeals on May 12, 1948, upholding the Commission.*

With respect to the international industry the question is whether the evidentiary requirements could be met by showing: (a) that the seven international majors tailored their yearly output of crude (outside the United States and the Communist countries) to achieve (and not exceed) the same predetermined industry growth rate; (b) that to offset expansion in some countries, which otherwise would have caused the growth rate to be exceeded, compensating reductions were made

---

* 168 Fed. 2 at 175. Justice Minton, who as a member of the Circuit Court had joined in its decision, abstained when the case reached the Supreme Court to which he had been appointed in the interim. His vote, presumably, would have resulted in a 5 to 4 decision in favor of the Commission.

elsewhere; and (c) that during the 1974–75 recession output was reduced by the companies sufficiently to maintain the sharply increased OPEC prices.

On the first count, it has already been established that the companies did in fact set for themselves an overall growth rate (outside North America and the Communist countries) of 9.5 percent; that during 1950–72 they were able to achieve this goal so closely that an assumption that production would increase at such a rate would explain all but one-tenth of 1 percent of the actual change; and that this objective was achieved in the face of differing and sometimes widely disparate production trends among the producing countries. There is also the evidence relating to the common use by all of the seven international companies of a formula (and a most curious one at that) to determine the level of Iranian output; the use of Aramco's owners (Exxon, Mobil, SoCal, and Texaco) of the Iranian production level to determine the production rate for Saudi Arabia; the use of Kuwait's output (controlled by BP and Gulf) as an "evener" to secure conformance with the overall growth rate; and the long-continued (and deliberately disguised) repression of Iraq's production by four of the seven companies.

Concerning the second count, the most telling body of evidence would of course be that relating to the majors' reaction to the Libyan independents' rapid expansion, including internal memoranda demonstrating their apprehension and specifying the curtailments in Mideast output needed to prevent the production of "distressed oil." Also included would be data showing not only how the objective was accomplished but how Mideast output was accelerated following the ending of the Libyan danger. Similarly in point would be evidence relating to the rapid increases in output by Kuwait and Saudi Arabia following the Iranian nationalization and the subsequent leveling off after Iranian production was resumed. In these and other instances the point to be stressed is not merely that compensating adjustments were made, but that their extent was such as to make the actual increase in overall supply accord almost exactly with the predetermined growth rate.

The final count, and the one with the greatest current significance, concerns the means by which supply from the OPEC countries was reduced during 1974–75. Without this reduction the amount of "distressed oil" produced would undoubtedly have been sufficient to bring about widespread price concessions and probably the disintegration of the OPEC cartel. If, as is suggested in Chapter 12, the OPEC members have neither agreed on standards of allocation nor set up the necessary allocating machinery, the responsibility for the curtailments necessarily rests with the companies.

With respect to the domestic industry, the question is whether the failure of the majors to expand refining capacity in the face of rapidly rising demand during 1959–66 (as shown in Chapter 6) and their failure since the price explosion to construct a single new domestic refinery can be regarded as evidence of collusive restriction of production. Between late 1973 and early 1976 a shortage of refining capacity has been avoided partly by the falling off of demand associated with the 1974–75 recession, and partly by the industry's expansion of *existing* facilities. But the relaxation of pressure on supply resulting from both factors may prove to be temporary. And on the supply side that portion of the industry's capacity which is unsuited to the production of unleaded gasoline will become increasingly obsolete. There is a real question whether the addition to capacity to manufacture unleaded gasoline (of acceptable octane ratings) will prove adequate to meet the expected rise in demand, particularly if recessions are avoided. Under such circumstances the failure of the industry to construct new "grassroots" refineries designed for the production of unleaded gasoline could become a serious source of shortage.

In enacting the antitrust laws Congress sought to frame a body of law, expressed in general principles, that would remain *au courant* with changing circumstances and business practices, recognizing that when it came to devising new and more ingenious ways of suppressing competition, "the inventiveness of the mind of man knows no bounds." So far as the first thrust is concerned, this congressional objective has been substantially realized through the historical development of the "implied conspiracy" and "conscious parallelism" doctrines. Their availability makes the application of the antitrust laws against systematic, concerted restrictionism a viable possibility in terms of the law and a potentially important source of relief in terms of economic effect.

THE DENIAL OF SUPPLIES

It is a demonstrated empirical fact that competition can act as an effective restraint on petroleum prices, *if a stream of oil can be opened up that flows around the major companies.* During the 1960's the oil produced by the Libyan independents flowed largely to relatively small, independent European refiners who sold gasoline and other refined products to independent marketers, who in turn quickly gained from 10 to 25 percent of Western Europe's gasoline markets. During the same period the growth of the American private branders was made possible by their ability to acquire gasoline from the lesser majors and independent refiners. Thus, in both Western Europe and the United

States the powerful restraint on the majors' product prices exercised by the independent marketers derived from flows of oil circumventing the largest companies.

Within the United States, reestablishing such an "outside" flow will become more and more difficult as U.S. reserves continue to dwindle. If in the long run independent refiners are to remain an effective source of competition, their source of supply will increasingly have to be the OPEC countries. In the interest of maintaining a stable price structure, the latter may wish to sell only to the majors, while the majors may wish to use their imported crude exclusively in their own refineries. For the independents, the result would be a classic case of denial of supplies. This monopolistic practice is difficult enough to deal with when the seller is a U.S. firm; it would seem to be impossible of solution where the seller is a foreign entity.

Relief under existing law might be obtained by a judicial finding that the withholding of foreign crude from independent refiners was the consequence of collusion among the majors. Given such a finding, the courts would enjoy wide latitude in devising ways and means of assuring an adequate flow of imported oil to independent refiners.

Alternatively, new legislation might be enacted, equipping an appropriate U.S. procurement agency with "set-aside" powers analogous to those enjoyed by the Small Business Administration. In its effort "to mobilize" the facilities of small business during World War II, the Smaller War Plants Corporation designated individual firms as capable of supplying specific procurement contracts. After the war the successor agency (the Small Business Administration) was granted mandatory powers to require such set-asides. Hence, for over two decades a government agency has had the power to require that specific defense contracts (or portions thereof) be reserved exclusively to small firms. In the same way, a federal procurement agency can be given the power to require that shares of crude oil imports be set aside for the exclusive use of independent refiners. Such "set-aside" oil would be used to make up the difference between crude obtained by independent refiners from all other sources and some base period percentage representing their "normal" share of total crude input.

To be of any value, the "set-aside" crude would have to be made available at a price low enough to enable the independent to compete with the majors. Such a price might consist of the sum of (a) the amount paid by the majors for their purchases of "participation" (including "nationalized") crude, (b) tax payments for their "equity" crude (minus the value of any credits used in the United States as offsets against such foreign tax payments), and (c) transportation costs to the United States, with the total value divided by the quantity of imports of both "participation" and "equity" crude.* The product would be a price equal to the true landed cost to the majors of their imported crude. Thus, no subsidy to aid small business would be involved. No drain on the U.S. taxpayer need arise, since the cost of administering the program could easily be borne through a small fee accruing to the procurement agency. On foreign oil it would merely enable the independent refiners to begin the competitive race from the same starting line as the majors. It is to be differentiated from the proposal made by Professor M. A. Adelman and others that the United States follow the lead of a number of other consuming countries (e.g., Brazil and Uruguay) and centralize in the government the procurement of foreign oil. By confronting the oligopolistic selling power of the OPEC countries with monopsonistic buying power, the U.S. government, it is argued, would be able to play one country off against another, securing better prices through its massed buying power than could be obtained by the companies individually. Apart from the question whether this would be sufficient to break the sellers' cartel, the proposal is based on the optimistic assumption that on oil resold by the government to the majors, the benefits of such lower prices as are obtained from the producing countries will be passed on to the consumer in the form of lower prices for refined products.

MERGERS AND ACQUISITIONS

Channeling a stream of oil around the majors to independent refiners will promote competition only to the extent that independent refiners have not been absorbed by mergers and acquisitions. Restoring independent status to at least the more important of the recently absorbed companies would substantially increase the refining capacity available to independent marketers.

Between 1951 and 1968 the number of refining companies decreased from 218 to 135, 61 disappearing through merger and the remaining 22 through dissolution. During this period the combined refining capacity acquired by the majors amounted to 848,650 barrels per day, or 8.1 percent of total U.S. capacity in 1966. Indeed, during

---

* Assume for illustrative purposes a division between "participation" and "equity" crude of 60–40%; an OPEC price of $10; a "buy-back" price for participation crude of $9; a tax rate of the host government on "equity" crude of 50%; taxes owed the U.S. Treasury on other foreign income of $1.5 mm; and a production of 1 mm bbls. Hence:

Participation crude (1 mm × 60% × $9)	$5.4 mm	
Equity crude (1 mm × 40% × $10 × 50%)		2.0
Less foreign tax credit		1.5
Net	.5	
Total and Cost per bbl.	$5.9 mm and $5.9 per bbl.	

TABLE 16-1

Acquisitions of Large Refining Companies[1] by Major Oil Companies, 1960–70
(millions of dollars)

Acquiring Company	Assets[2]	Acquired Company	Assets	Year
		TOP 8		
Exxon	$9,894.7	Monterey	$ 102.2	1960
SoCal	2,782.3	Standard (Ky.)	141.9	1961
Exxon	2,925.7	Honolulu Oil	99.2	1961
ARCO	2,450.9	Sinclair	1,851.3	1969
		OTHER MAJORS		
Marathon	469.9	Plymouth	80.8	1962
Union	916.5	Pure	766.1	1965
Atlantic	960.4	Richfield	499.6	1966
Sun	1,598.5	Sunray (DX)	749.0	1968
Total			4,290.1	

[1] Assets in excess of $50 million.
[2] At time of acquisition.

the 1960's a veritable wave of mergers resulted in the disappearance of some of the country's most important regional independents. As can be seen in Table 16-1, no fewer than eight refining companies with combined assets of over $4.2 billion disappeared between 1960 and 1970, four being acquired by companies among the nation's largest majors and the remaining four merged with other regional independents to form national or quasi-national majors. In either case, the effect was the removal of an important source of competition in a particular marketing area.

The simplest competitive injury to comprehend (and the one to which the Antitrust Division has largely limited itself) is the impact of mergers of competing firms selling in the same market area. Thus, the combining of Sun with Sunray eliminated a direct competitor in Kentucky, Indiana, and Michigan. Because both Atlantic Refining and Sinclair had been operating in the same states, ARCO was required to sell $400 million of Sinclair's assets and 1,800 of its 10,500 service stations to British Petroleum.

But there are other and in some ways more serious adverse effects on competition than that resulting from the mere elimination of a direct competitor. Among the most important is the constraint on a nearby area exercised by a firm that is currently not operating in that area but whose size and resources are sufficient to permit penetration should it be motivated to do so. In any given area, prices and profit margins are thus constrained by the threat of entry on the part of sizable firms operating in neighboring areas. Once a regional independent joins the ranks of the national majors through merger, the constraint is lost. No longer do the existing firms have to fear the entrance into their region of a sizable firm struggling for a position in a new market. The newcomer has become a national major itself, and would suffer as much as the older majors from the outbreak of competition in any given market. It is in this respect that the mergers of Union with Pure, Atlantic with Richfield, and SoCal with Standard of Kentucky have been destructive of competition.

The change in a firm's identify from a regional independent to a national major also exerts a limiting constraint upon the supply available to independent marketers. Owing to the unpredictability of the weather, unexpected transportation problems, bottlenecks in storage and distribution facilities, and similar unexpected eventualities, what is produced may be more than the refining company can get into consumption through its own outlets. When this happens to a regional concern, the natural market for its excess supply consists of private-brand marketers, particularly those operating in a different market, since whatever happens to price there would have little effect on its own market area. When, through merger, the regional firm becomes a national major, however, what happens to price in any market becomes a matter of real moment to it. The surplus gasoline available to private-branders tends to dry up not only for this reason but because of the ability of the new national major to absorb in one region any surpluses it has produced in another. Even if the distance and transportation problems are such that the surplus cannot be physically moved, the company will probably be able to work out an exchange agreement with another major, under which the latter will absorb the former's surplus, providing the equivalent amount elsewhere. Thus, by increasing the firm's ability to accommodate its own excesses, the transformation of regional oil companies into national majors tends to reduce the supply formerly available to the independent marketers.

A strong case can be made that most or even all of the mergers shown in Table 16-1 could have been challenged under the Celler-Kefauver Amendment to Section 7 of the Clayton Act. It is true that proceedings under that act have been permitted to become so time-consuming as to make it singularly ineffective to deal with a current crisis. But much of the prolonged (and lengthening) duration of proceedings is the product of causes that are not inherent in the law or its enforcement. These include unnecessary legal rules and procedures, the natural desire of defense attorneys "to keep the meter ticking," the desire of the defendant companies to prolong the period in which they can enjoy the fruits of their actions, and the tendency of the antitrust agencies to "overtry" cases by introducing vast quantities of tangential or even irrelevant evidence, most of which then serves as the basis for interminable refutation. Although none of these problems is likely to disappear overnight, the antitrust agencies could greatly foreshorten the proceedings if they would give an overriding priority to the act's basic purpose: to nip monopolies, trusts, and conspiracies in the bud and before consummation.

DIVORCE, DIVESTITURE, AND DISSOLUTION

An antitrust case against the concerted restriction of production would undoubtedly increase the difficulty of nicely gearing world supply to the existing level of demand, thus giving rise to sporadic outbreaks of price competition. Likewise, creating a flow of oil around the majors would assure a source of supply through independent refiners to independent marketers who can prosper only through price competition. Neither, however, would come to grips with the fundamental problem of size and integration represented by the major oil companies. For this purpose the competitive approach requires "divorce, divestiture, and dissolution"—trust-busting in the literal sense. The requirements for transforming petroleum into a structure approaching the model of competitive theory have been well summarized by Walter Adams:

> *First*, we must terminate the symbiotic relationship between a monopolistic industry and a compliant government. *Second*, we must break asunder the horizontal dominance of the petroleum majors, whether it rests on mergers, exchange agreements, joint ventures, or financial interlocks. *Third,* we must halt the invasion of competitive areas of energy supplied by the petroleum giants. *Fourth,* we must put an end to the majors' vertical control over crude, refining, marketing and transportation by divorcement and divestiture action. *Finally,* we must restructure the multinationals which currently perform the conflict-of-interest role as producers in, and marketing agents for, the OPEC nations.[14]

The objective of ending the majors' "vertical control over crude, refining, marketing, and transportation" would be accomplished by a bill, S.2387, introduced in the Senate on September 22, 1975, by Senator Bayh for himself and Senators Hart (Michigan), Abourezk,

Tunney, and Packwood. Offered as an amendment to a pending measure to decontrol natural gas, the bill would require each company engaged in the four stages of the petroleum industry—crude production, transportation, refining, and marketing—to select that stage in which it wanted to continue doing business and then to divest itself of all interests in the other three. Specifically, it provides that "three years after enactment of this act it shall be unlawful (1) for any major petroleum producer to own or control any interest, direct, indirect, or through an affiliate in any refining, marketing, or transportation asset"; similar provisions relate to any "petroleum transporter," "major refiner," and "major marketer." Containing, in addition, only definitions, reporting requirements, and a provision vesting administration in the Federal Trade Commission, this bill, in its brevity and clarity, is a refreshing contrast to the 99-page Energy Policy and Conservation Act. Although it was defeated on a roll-call vote, the margin was so close (45 to 54) as to be a source of pleasant surprise to the amendment's supporters and astonished dismay to the oil industry. If the bill had gone through the regular Senate procedure of hearings before a legislative committee, instead of being introduced as an amendment on the Senate floor, the vote would probably have been even closer.

ARGUMENTS FOR DIVESTITURE. To the amendment's supporters the central issue was the destruction of competition inherent in companies which are not only of "immense" size but vertically integrated from "wellhead to pump." The majors' overwhelming structural dominance was described by Senator Hart of Colorado: ". . . there is still a lack of general comprehension of the size of companies that we are dealing with where we talk about the so-called giant oil companies. The fact of the matter is that 7 of the largest 15 domestic U.S. corporations are oil companies, 9 of the largest 20 are oil companies, and 20 of the largest 100 are oil companies."[15] Senator Nelson pointed out that if Exxon "retained its crude oil and exploration facilities alone, it would still be the largest privately owned company in the world."[16]

But more important than reducing the size or increasing the number of sellers would be changes in motivation. No longer could those majors electing to remain in production afford to calmly accept (if not welcome) OPEC actions raising the cost of crude, secure in the knowledge that they could pass it along in the prices of refined products. And since they could not look for profits at other stages, those majors remaining in refining could be expected to exert a continuous downward pressure on *their* costs. Moreover, since producers would have to *sell* to refiners and refiners to marketers, the task of preventing the appearance of distressed oil would become infinitely more difficult.

What Senator Stevenson referred to as the "supreme irony in this debate" was the fact that the high prices stemming from the majors' control of the market were without redeeming economic value. Beyond a point well below the OPEC price, "you do not get more oil and gas. You get an extremely high-priced energy industry. You get windfall profits. But the country does not get more oil and gas."[17] Similarly, Senator Moss stated: ". . . even if we assume that we got a great expansion of effort in the industry, we still do not have the capacity to raise our reserves and supplies of natural gas suddenly, or oil, for that matter."[18]

Not only does a higher price fail to increase supply, it does not reduce demand. In the words of Senator Stevenson, there is "no basis" for the "expectation of this administration that the increased price decreases consumption . . . the evidence, much of it based on recent experience, indicates the demand for energy in the United States is highly inelastic." The studies, according to the Senator, show that "Even in the case of gasoline [where] theoretically, there is more elasticity than in the case, for example, of fuel oil with which to heat homes and businesses, gasoline consumption has proven highly unresponsive to increases in price." Demand is elastic with respect to income, not price: "The only way that energy consumption is significantly decreased is by causing recession, depression, by bringing down the level of industrial activity, and that has brought down the consumption of oil in the world."[19] Not only do higher energy prices fail to reduce demand; they are extremly regressive in their effects. Senator Biden called attention to a joint study by the Office of Income Security (HEW) and the Office of Consumer Affairs (FEA) which explored the economic impact of rising home-heating costs on low-income families. According to the Senator, "Low-income families spend an average of more than 11 percent of their income on natural gas and electricity as compared to less than 2 percent for households with annual incomes over $16,000. Yet the poor consume 56 percent as much electricity as the nonpoor and 82 percent as much natural gas." For poor families the chances that further price increases would bring about additional voluntary savings in the use of fuel are exceedingly remote: "Because fuel consumption by these close to 5,000,000 low-income households is already narrowed to the most essential uses, they, unlike higher-income families, face utility shutoffs due to nonpayment rather than curtailment of nonessential uses as a result of higher energy costs."[20] The case that the cost of higher prices is out of all proportion to their benefits was summarized by Senator Humphrey: "The administration itself has claimed that immediate oil price decontrol would cut consumption by only 3 percent by 1977 and boost production by 1 percent. This tiny step toward energy independence would cost the American consumers close to $30 billion per year, assuming complete tariff removal."[21]

Since there is thus little in the way of public benefit to offset the huge cost of the recent price rises, it was argued that the time had come to break up the monopolistic power that had made them possible. Until recent years the inherent "suspicion of bigness and power in Middle America" had, in Senator McIntyre's words, been "like a low-grade fever that manifested itself in . . . vague public mutterings about monopoly, the depletion allowance, and the proliferation of oil millionaires." The fever had remained "low grade and vague as long as gasoline sold for 29 cents a gallon. . . . But now the concern has escalated, and with that has come a broadening and a sharpening of public understanding about the real dimensions of the industry's power and influence and its overall effect on America's energy destiny."[22] Senator Metcalf recalled a prediction that power, once obtained, would be abused: "nearly 20 years ago Estes Kefauver warned us that concentration of economic and political power in the oil industry would result in increasing prices and controlled supply all along the line, from the wellhead to the gas pump. . . ." Time, he emphasized, was running out: "the people are going to demand that we stop talking about this issue of oil company power over the consumer, and do something positive to restore free and independent competition to the industry."[23]

The available alternatives for coping with the abuse of power stemming from vertically integrated size were summarized by Senator Abourezk: "By separating the producing phase of the oil and gas business from the transporting and refining and marketing phases, we create a situation where all of the companies will compete against one another on a more equal basis for the best price possible. Without this competition, the market is simply a distribution mechanism run by wealthy men in boardrooms. . . . The only protection against that is either to pass a regulation saying the price will be controlled by the government according to costs or to see that there exists competition. . . ."[24] Senator McGovern's remarks were to the same effect: "We can regulate the industry. This is a clumsy and often ineffective approach, particularly when egregious loopholes like the interstate-intrastate distinction in natural gas make effective regulation nearly impossible." Another possibility is "full or complete nationalization," which, the Senator recognized, "is a frightening word for many

Americans." The remaining alternative is "tough and vigorous anti-trust action aimed at restoring competition to the industry by forcing the vertically integrated corporations to break up."[25]

ARGUMENTS AGAINST DIVESTITURE. In the first of four counterarguments, opponents acknowledged the size of the oil companies but denied its significance. Great size, it was contended, is an inherent characteristic of the industry, and further, the leading companies' share of the market is comparatively modest. In Senator Fannin's words, "concentration figures of the oil industry show that it is much less concentrated than most other industries." The Senator put into the record statistical tables contrasting the four-company concentration ratios for oil (27 percent in production, 33 percent in refining, and 30 percent in gasoline marketing) with those for thirty-nine other industries, in each of which the ratio exceeded 60 percent.[26] In reply, the proponents argued that in this industry the injury to competition stems not so much from horizontal or "market" concentration as from vertical integration. Senator Hart (Colorado) offered an illustration: "Since World War II, the main profit-taking level of this industry has been at the crude level. Little profit was taken at the marketing, storage or refining levels—because of the incentives, such as depletion allowances and such—which make the crude level so attractive. Obviously, for independents facing [competition] from subsidiaries which did not have to make money, things were tough."[27]

A second and related line of defense was based on the industry's long-term profit showings. According to Senator Bartlett, "the long-term profitability record of the oil industry is not one to indicate that the companies have any market power whatsoever." He went on to quote from testimony offered by Professor Edward Erikson of North Carolina State University:

> Profitability is an important indicator of the existence and exercise of monopoly power. The record of long-run profitability in the petroleum industry indicates that the firms in this industry do not enjoy substantial, systematic market power. This index of effective competition yields positive results whether the comparison is to all U.S. manufacturing, Moody's 125 industrials, Moody's 24 public utilities, or a group of industrial firms known to possess market power.[28]

The response was to the effect that the relevant issue was not the industry's "long-term" profit record but its current and probable future performance. In Senator Stevenson's words, "The return on stockholders' equity of the 20 largest oil companies in 1973 was 15 percent, and 19 percent in 1974, higher than the average generally for industry in the United States. The rates of return declined in 1975 with a downturn in business activity generally, but with decontrol and an OPEC price increase of $1.50—we have already experienced $1.35 of that increase—the rate of return would increase by 85 percent in 1976 over the present levels in 1975."[29]

Opponents also cited the practical problems of divestiture—the costs and mechanics of asset redistribution, the drain on capital markets, and the effect on investors. In effect, the very problem which had given rise to the divestiture proposal, i.e., the great size of the oil companies, was said to have made the remedy of divestiture impossible. Senator Eagleton asked, "Is it practical to think such a massive disposal of assets can take place in a period of 5 years? What organizations outside of the major oil companies themselves would have the capital necessary to take over the relinquished operations? What would be the impact on our ability to produce and distribute petroleum in the critical years ahead?"[30] Senator Bartlett warned, "The monumental task, both mechanical and financial, of trying to separate assets, find buyers, finance the acquistions for close to $50 billion of net fixed assets will upset many markets for years." The affected companies, he pointed out, "have a market value of 10 to 15 percent of all securities traded on the New York Stock Exchange. . . . The market will react to this type of action as if it was confiscation and a selloff should take place. Not only will petroleum stocks be affected but the whole market will suffer with the belief that if it can happen to the petroleum industry it can happen to all."[31]

In reply, the proponents pointed out, first, that divestiture had a long and honorable history in the United States, without occasioning any of the predicted dire consequences, and, second, that by "spinning off" the stock to owners of the existing enterprises, the requirements for new capital would be far less than the companies' assets. Senator Hart (Colorado) recounted a number of past episodes:

> In 1935, the Public Utilities Holding Act forced certain companies to divest themselves of either gas or electricity distribution facilities. That act also required that they divest themselves of all non-utility-related assets, such as oil wells, bus companies and coal mines. That was in 1935.
>
> In 1934, the year before, in the McKellar-Black Airmail Act of that year, Congress required a number of firms to divest themselves of either air carriers or aircraft manufacturing facilities. General Motors, for example, was required to sell off its interest in Eastern, Western, United and TWA.
>
> Earlier than that, in the Glass-Stegall Act of 1932, Congress

forced financial institutions to rid themselves of either their commercial or their investment banking activities.

Even dating back to 1906, the beginning of this activity, in the Hepburn Act, the railroads were required by Congress to get out of the business of producing coal and other commodities.[32]

In the view of Senator Hart (Michigan), opponents had "vastly overstated" the "disruption" that would arise from divestiture: "It is highly likely that the mechanism used would be spinoffs whereby the stock of the new entities simply is split up among the stockholders of the existing company. This would eliminate the need for going to the capital market for vast sums of money."[33] To prevent any small group of owners of the original enterprise from holding control over the spun-off companies (as the Rockefeller interests had done with successors to the old Standard Oil Trust), Senator Abourezk proposed a limitation: that "shareholders above a certain size—say 1 percent of the new firm's voting stock—must sell their shares within a limited period of time."[34] In contrast to the $50 billion figure being bruited about, Senator Abourezk offered an estimate that "Total equity requirements for refining and marketing and pipeline divestiture would be some $15 billion, an amount which could be readily handled by the domestic capital market.*

The final, and substantively most important, argument against divestiture concerned the effect on efficiency. The question was raised by Senator Dole: "Would not some of the actions result in lost economies of scale and increased inefficiency which would in the end mean higher prices?"[35] Senator Bartlett was more specific: "How much will divestiture increase consumer costs? The integrated structure of the firm in the petroleum industry developed because of greater efficiency and economies of scale, in order to reduce costs, and to not duplicate human, technical, managerial, and physical efforts."

---

* *Congressional Record,* October 7, 1975, p. S17,681. Assuming that the companies would elect to remain in crude production, Senator Abourezk arrived at the $15 billion figure by estimating the total value of their assets in refining, marketing, and transportation and applying thereto percentages representing the proportions made up of stockholders' equity. The value of refining capacity (excluding depreciation) he estimated at $11.2 billion, derived by multiplying 11.2 million b/d capacity by a value (excluding depreciation) of $1,000 per barrel of daily capacity. Marketing properties were placed at 75–80 percent of the value of refining properties yielding a "total value of refining and marketing properties of $20 billion." If new enterprises in refining and marketing were "set up with, say 60 percent equity, the rough average for the industry, the equity requirement would be no more than $12 billion." For transportation, oil pipelines, according to ICC data, had an asset value in 1973 of $5.6 billion which, after allowing for growth and the value of nonreporting lines, would be $8 billion. Applying the proportion of the value of ICC pipelines made up of equity (38 percent) yields an "equity requirement for divestiture of pipelines" of some $3 billion, which when added to the $12 billion for refining and marketing yields a total equity requirement for divestiture of $15 billion" (*ibid.*).

In addition to operating economies, he raised the question of the effect on industrial creativity: "What will happen to the research efforts of the integrated firms? They are capable of supporting this effort now. Will they be after divestiture? Frequently, the R & D organization of the integrated firms serves more than one functional department. This whole structure would be destroyed."[36] To this line of argument the bill's proponents offered no rebuttal whatever, a failure which is most surprising in view of the preeminence of the efficiency rationale as monopoly's first line of defense. In view of its importance, this defense of bigness, as it relates to the petroleum industry, warrants further examination.

THE EFFICIENCY RATIONALE

The efficiency rationale breaks down into three components: the technological, multiplant, and invention-innovation arguments. Under the first, it is regarded as self-evident that size is inevitable to the extent that it stems from the requirements of technology, i.e., the need for large plant and heavy capital outlays to secure the available economies of scale. Similarly, size must be accepted as inevitable to the extent that it results from economies arising from multiplant operations, i.e., the securing of net gains in efficiency through bringing together and operating separate facilities under common ownership and control. And size is also inevitable to the extent that it stems from the requirements of modern research and development, i.e., the need for large concerns to support the costs of maintaining laboratories, purchasing expensive testing equipment, and employing the teams of scientific specialists needed for modern research. Each of these rationales can be examined as it relates to the petroleum industry.

With respect to the technological rationale, the amount of capital required in exploration and drilling is not a significant barrier to entry. Were this not true, independents could not possibly have been responsible for most of the "new fields." Moreover, such increases as the explosion in exploratory and developmental wells from 24,600 in 1945 to 57,200 in 1956 could not possibly have taken place. In the production of crude oil the pumping capacity of the well is not among the principal determinants of productivity. Far more important are such factors as the rate of flow, the depth of the pool, the amount of pumping required, and whether the field is operated under maximum efficient rate (MER) prorationing.

It is at the refinery stage that capital costs are sufficient to constitute a formidable barrier to entry. In a speech before the Economics Club of Detroit in March 1973, Rawleigh Warner, Jr., chairman of

Mobil Oil, stated that the minimum economic size for a new refinery was about 160,000 barrels a day; such a refinery would cost around $250 million and would account for 1.2 percent of the industry's capacity. In terms of physical volume this engineering estimate is quite similar to one offered more than two decades earlier by Joe S. Bain, who found the minimum size of an efficient refinery to be an output of 120,000 barrels a day, representing 1.75 percent of the industry's capacity.[37] In a recent study Frederick N. Scherer found that a refinery with a capacity of 200,000 barrels a day would "achieve all significant economies of scale at the single-plant level, assuming 1965 technology and economic conditions.[38] Estimates of minimal efficient size ranging from 100,000 to 200,000 b/d have been made by other investigators.[39] And support for these "engineering estimates" is provided by studies employing the "survivor technique."*

That concentration in refining is largely a function of multiplant operations is indicated by the fact that in 1969 the "top eight" companies operated a total of 70 domestic refineries, ranging from a high of 11 for Standard (Indiana) to a low of 4 for Gulf. Both Texaco and Shell operated 10 refineries, Mobil and SoCal operated 9, while 8 were operated by Exxon and 7 by ARCO. Although one giant refinery had a capacity of more than 400,000 b/d (Exxon's facility at Baton Rouge, Louisiana), 51 of the 70 had capacities of only 30,000 b/d or less.[40] Such facilities would appear to be well below the minimal size required to achieve the available economies of scale, but in determining plant size, operating economies are not the only factor to be taken into consideration. In Scherer's words, "Most refineries of the Big Eight have been built at scales considerably smaller than 200,000 bbl/day because of limited market absorption potential and/or because the cost savings from operating larger, less decentralized refineries would be more than offset by increased product transportation costs except where excellent water or product pipeline transportation facilities exist."[41]

Gains in efficiency may result not merely from operating a refinery of optimal size; they may also be achieved by rationalizing output among different refineries, by bulk purchasing, by broadening product lines, by securing easier access to capital and credit, by better financial controls, and by other managerial actions that are possible when

---

* George J. Stigler found that the most rapid growth between 1947 and 1954 was in plants with between 0.5% and 2.5% of the industry's capacity, from which he concluded that this was the most efficient size. Employing the same technique for the period 1958–1961 Leonard Weiss found the minimum efficient size for a multiproduct refinery to be 150,000 barrels a day (George J. Stigler, "The Economies of Scale," *Journal of Law and Economics,* October 1958, p. 69; Leonard W. Weiss, "The Survivor Technique and the Extent of Suboptimal Capacity," *Journal of Political Economy,* June 1964, p. 249).

separate plants are operated under common ownership and control. On the other hand, such potential economies may be offset by diseconomies, such as waste inherent in hierarchical structures, impediments of "proper procedures," inescapable conflicts between line and staff, diseconomies arising from advancement, resistance to change, and others.[42]

In their recent study Scherer and his associates concluded that in petroleum "a firm operating only one efficient-sized refinery experienced anywhere from a very slight [less than 1 percent] to moderate [2 to 5 percent] price/cost handicap relative to a firm enjoying *all* the benefits of multi-plant operation."[43] More specifically, the Scherer study examined for eleven "functional areas" the extent to which "single-plant refiners were handicapped relative to multi-plant firms." For one of these areas (managerial and staff economies), it was found that multiplant operations were "probably disadvantageous." For four others, no advantage was found.[44] And in an additional group of four, the advantage of the multiplant firm was described as "slight" or "slight to moderate."[45] Only in "vertical integration" and "access to capital" did the multiplant firm enjoy as much as a "moderate" advantage. And the last is more a product of an institutional financial gap in the economy than a shortcoming of smaller firms.

With respect to the invention-innovation rationale, few enterprises have failed more conspicuously than the oil companies to provide evidence in support of their creativity. For the first half of this century the significant inventions in petroleum involved the chemical process of cracking—the splitting of large hydrocarbon molecules into smaller ones. The search centered on developing a process that could be operated continuously, without closing down the facility every day or so to be cleaned out. During the 1920's four major continuous terminal cracking processes were introduced. Each was the creation of an individual inventor, although in two cases major oil companies assisted in transforming the invention into a commercial reality.[46]

Important as was the achievement of a continuous operation, it was overshadowed by a revolutionary new concept, catalytic cracking, which, by introducing chemical agents, greatly accelerated the speed and productivity of the process. According to John L. Enos, the individual responsible epitomized many of today's independent inventors—a highly trained scientist who preferred to work by and for himself:

> It was the next invention and innovation in the historical sequence which most savored of the heroic. By devoting himself and his fortune to the study of catalysis, a French inventor, Eugene

Houdry, developed the first practical catalytic cracking process. Commencing after World War I, Houdry carried out research into the nature of catalysis and its effect upon the cracking operation. It was not until 1927, however, that he first successfully produced motor gasoline from a heavy petroleum fraction. Like the inventors of the continuous thermal cracking processes, Eugene Houdry was not originally employed by an oil company. He differed from them in that he alone directed the subsequent development of the invention into a commercial process.[47]

Aided financially by Mobil and Sun, Houdry established the Houdry Process Corporation, which by 1936 had overcome the difficulties in the design of equipment and was in commercial operation. Since the Houdry process was only semicontinuous, the next stage was to transform it into a fully continuous operation. While several processes were developed by Houdry and others, the nation's largest oil company used its scientific resources to avoid the payment of royalties: "Standard Oil (N.J.) . . . deliberately tried to invent around the Houdry patents."[48]

Reviewing the whole history of "inventions and innovations pertaining to the manufacture of motor gasoline from a heavy hydrocarbon material," Enos concluded:

> These inventions and innovations occupied a period of approximately forty-five years from 1913 to the present and permitted the manufacture of products of higher qualities and greater yields at successively lower costs. The processes utilized first heat and pressure and then catalysts to promote the cracking reaction. They were initially noncontinuous and subsequently continuous in operation. *In almost all cases the inventions were made by men close to the oil industry but not attached to the major firms.*[49]

In a recent study Edwin Mansfield examined the question whether the largest petroleum companies spend more on research and development than somewhat smaller firms.[50] Using data for nine major petroleum companies, "the evidence seems to indicate the answer is no." Petroleum is thus no exception to the conclusion for industry generally: "Although there is a certain threshold size, which varies from industry to industry, that must be exceeded if many kinds of development projects can be undertaken effectively, a firm's R & D expenditures generally do not increase in proportion to its size in the range much above this threshold size."[51]

Not only do the largest oil companies fail to put more into research and development relative to their size; they fail to get more out of what they do spend. Based on listings of important inventions and innovations in petroleum and petrochemicals, Mansfield constructed an "index of inventive output," which was then regressed by size of firm. Again the conclusions were similar to what has been found for industry generally: "Thus, there is no evidence, based on this very crude analysis, that the productivity of R & D expenditures is higher in the biggest firms than in somewhat smaller ones. Moreover, there is no evidence of economies of scale in R & D in this range of variation of R & D expenditures."[52]

Mansfield also sought to determine whether the research and development work carried on by the eight largest oil companies differed from that of large, established firms generally, which he described as follows: ". . . the bulk of their R & D seems to be directed at relatively safe, short-term objectives, the radical advances often come from outside their laboratories, and they seem to be better at adapting, developing, and improving the novel inventions of others than coming forth with their own."[53] From his examination of the oil companies he concluded: ". . . the bulk of the R & D projects carried out by these firms is regarded as being relatively safe from a technical point of view, the median probability of technical success being at least 75 percent in most of the firms. . . . only a small percent of the money goes for basic research, and most of the R & D projects are expected to be finished and have an effect on profits in 5 years or less."[54]

Unimpressive as it has been, research by leading oil companies has been in a state of decline. Mansfield notes that "between 1963 and 1966, the petroleum industry's R & D expenditures increased by about one-third, between 1966 and 1969 they increased by about one-quarter, and between 1969 and 1971 they did not increase at all." This change in trend was not accidental; rather, it stemmed from top management's disenchantment with in-house research and development.

Ironically, the retrenchment followed in the wake of an internal survey made only a few years earlier by the same division of the same company. In 1966 Esso Research and Engineering had conducted a retrospective study of over one hundred of their inventions in the previous twenty years. According to Mansfield, "the findings indicated the critical importance of real novelty in obtaining commercial success and the small returns, if any, from developing run-of-the-mill innovations based on well-known science and obvious needs."[55]

It is sometimes argued that a "tradeoff" is inherent between the "cost" of higher prices resulting from monopolistic control of the market and the "benefit" of greater efficiency and creativity resulting from large size, which in turn makes monopolistic control inevitable. Insofar as the petroleum industry is concerned, there is very little evidence that the "cost" is in any significant way offset by the "benefit." Not only does the size of the major oil companies far transcend that required for optimal efficiency, but they have been a remarkably infertile source of new products and processes. Without the achievement of these benefits, the principal objection to divestiture disappears.

Nonetheless, as the Congressional debate over divestiture has intensified, industry spokesmen have been placing increasing emphasis on the presumed economies of size, particularly those held to result from vertical integration. The very term conveys an impression of economies achieved through a series of gears nicely meshing with each other or an assembly line moving smoothly from lower to higher stages of fabrication. A long-cited example drawn from the steel industry, i.e., the elimination of reheating steps by integrating furnaces with rolling-mill operations, has been borrowed by defenders of the oil industry. Where, as in that case, the economies are secured within the same plant, the example has little relevance to divestiture or any other public policy issue, as no one since the Luddites has advocated breaking up physical plants. A relevant argument would be that economies are achieved from a better flow of materials and products by bringing separate, successive plants under the same corporate roof. In the petroleum industry, evidence, or even examples, of such economies are conspicuous by their absence.

Another argument is that vertical integration can be a source of economies, if at a series of successive stages the integrated firm becomes a repository of unique technological and managerial expertise or "information." At many stages of the petroleum industry, however, the principal repositories of such expertise are specialty firms *not* engaged in the production, refining, or marketing of oil. Highly expert at their particular stage, these specialists are not divisions, subsidiaries, or affiliates of oil companies but independent enterprises retained by contract to perform a specific function. Thus, one group of firms (e.g., Seiscom Delta and Western Geophysical) specialize in making geophysical surveys preparatory to offshore drilling, while a different group (Levingston, Avondale Shipyards, Marathon Manufacturing, and Bethlehem Steel Corp.) make nearly all of the nation's offshore drilling rigs. And the large offshore production platforms are made by a third group (e.g., J. Ray McDermott, Brown and Root as well as Avondale). There are literally hundreds of firms engaged in onshore drilling, while most refineries are constructed by companies such as W. M. Kellogg, Bechtel, Fluor, and C. F. Braun. And pipelines and gathering lines are laid by still another group, led by Brown and Root. A variety of highly specialized but critically important types of geophysical and geological work is provided by many firms, notably de

Golyer and McNaughton and Schlumberger. And, of course, the oil companies rely on firms such as Cameron and Hughes Tool for their tools and equipment. At such stages the effect of divestiture should be to heighten the demand for the specialty firms' services by increasing the number of potential contractors.

In addition to the expertise provided by such specialty firms, the efficiency of nonintegrated companies at a number of stages would appear to be comparable, if not superior, to that of the majors. In view of their lack of monopoly power, the private-brand marketers could have made their surprising gains in retail gasoline market shares only by superior efficiency. Similarly, independent fleet owners have increased their share to about half of the world's tanker tonnage. And in operating a refinery a company with "all the benefits of multi-plant operations" enjoyed, according to Scherer, no significant cost advantage over "a firm operating only one significant-sized refinery." At these stages divestiture, by lessening the majors' ability to control supply and foreclose markets, should have the effect of opening up opportunities for expansion by the efficient nonintegrated firms.

*   *   *

It is sometimes said that against this industry, antitrust has been tried and found wanting. Yet the last occasion when a "big" antitrust suit against the oil companies was carried through to final adjudication was the case against the old Standard Oil Trust in 1911. Since then three broad-scale antitrust actions have been launched against the majors, only to be halted in midstream by intercession of higher authority. An antitrust action against this industry, once launched, has invariably generated political opposition sufficient to ensure its demise. The manner in which the *International Oil Cartel* case of the 1950's was eviscerated and eventually, like ancient Carthage, "sown to salt" has already been described. A decade and a half earlier, the Department of Justice had brought an antitrust action against virtually all of the majors and the American Petroleum Institute. Although referred to as the "Mother Hubbard" case, reflecting its broad coverage, the suit actually followed traditional antitrust lines in that the end sought by the companies ("monopolization") was held to have been accomplished by unlawful means. The government had charged twenty-two major oil companies with monopolizing crude oil production, transportation, and marketing by the use of a variety of predatory and discriminatory practices, including tie-in arrangements and exclusive dealing contracts in violation of the Sherman, Clayton, and Elkins acts. In addition to injunctive relief, the Department sought divestiture of the majors' transportaion and marketing operations. But with World War

II looming on the horizon, the argument was put forward that the case interfered with "national defense." Attorney-General Jackson then worked out an innocuous consent decree with the advice of the oil advisory committee of the Council for National Defense; nine of the eleven committee members were connected with either Exxon or Shell, both defendants in the case.[56]

During the early stages of the first Suez conflict, when it was widely and erroneously feared that the blockade of the Suez Canal would lead to widespread shortages, the oil companies raised their prices in the United States at about the same time by the same amounts. The similarity of the increases and the uniformity in their timing aroused suspicion in the Department of Justice, which in early 1957 filed a case accusing twenty-nine U.S. oil companies of using the Suez crisis as a convenient pretext for increasing the price of gasoline. Criminal price-fixing indictments were returned by a federal grand jury empaneled in Alexandria, Virginia (hence the reference to the "Alexandria" case). Included in the evidence were executive diaries showing that telephone meetings had taken place and that the companies knew what price increases their competitors were going to make before their announcements. Inexplicably, the case was transferred to Tulsa, Oklahoma, where Judge Royce A. Savage dismissed all charges against the companies. A year later Judge Savage resigned from the bench to become a vice-president of Gulf, one of the defendants.[57]

The record of nonfeasance on the antitrust front has continued since the energy crisis. While a sweeping antitrust complaint was issued early in 1974 by the Federal Trade Commission, it is so broadly defined and imprecisely focused that two years later it is still in the investigating stage and final disposition, according to Senator Hart, may be as far away as 1988. The conclusion is not that antitrust has failed; for over sixty-five years it has not been tried.

AN ACTION PROGRAM

THE COMBINATION OF declining U.S. production and growing dependence on the world's politically most explosive area should make immediate action imperative. But the types of action required are held back by a number of conceptual barriers. There is the common failure to recognize that, at least insofar as the United States is concerned, the crisis in energy is largely centered in transportation. To meet the requirements for heating and electric-power generation other fuels are available: coal, solar energy, and—if the safety problems are resolved—nuclear energy. A second conceptual problem is the assumption that "the" solution will be provided by some future technological breakthrough, if only scientific research is adequately funded. Quite apart from the doubtful assumption that discovery can be programmed, the danger is that reliance on what the future may hold will divert attention away from what can be done in the here and now. Finally, it is essential that the federal government (notably the Energy Research and Development Agency) dispense with its self-imposed restraint of limiting itself to financing or conducting research in the hope that implementation will be provided by private industry (preferably by one or another of the large corporations). There are many reasons why the large corporations may fail to exploit even the most promising new technologies.[1] Given the gravity of the energy crisis, allowing private corporations to profit from research and development financed by the taxpayer may be offensive, but it is probably tolerable. But permitting promising fruits of such research to remain unutilized is intolerable.

The single most effective step toward increasing the supply of energy would be the development of oil shale, using the *in situ* process, if possible, or the conventional mining-and-crushing process, if necessary. During the many years when their principal preoccupation was the prevention of "excess" production, the oil companies could have been expected to resist the development of any new source of supply. But a country confronted with a real and growing energy crisis should no longer tolerate their continued procrastination, intended to secure both a "satisfactory" guaranteed price and government financing of

396

development. Just as the private utility companies' long-standing reluctance toward developing the electric power potential of Muscle Shoals led to the formation of the Tennessee Valley Authority, so also should the oil companies' long-standing apathy on oil shale lead to the establishment of an Oil Shale Authority. As was the case of TVA itself, this new agency should be designed to integrate economic development with the protection and improvement of the environment. On the basis of the time schedule set forth in the Bureau of Mines' 1969 blueprint, such an agency should be able in a few years to produce 1 million and eventually 6 million barrels of motor fuel a day.

At the same time, direct financial assistance should be provided to home-owners installing solar energy, thereby reducing the demand for another "light" refined product—home-heating oil. Since the introduction of solar heating and cooling is on an application-by-application basis, the logical role of government should be to assume all or a substantial part of the difference in initial cost between the solar and the conventional systems, thereby making the subsequent savings in fuel costs the inducement to purchase.

On the demand side the single most effective step would be to lighten the weight of the automobile, thereby accelerating the replacement of steel with fiberglass and other light, synthetic materials. This could be done by placing a sharply graduated tax on the weight of automobiles or, alternatively, by imposing limits on the number of "heavy" cars that could be produced or on the amount of "heavy" materials, such as steel, that could be used for automobile manufacture.

The preference of consumers for a vehicle capable of both long and short trips over one capable of only short trips should be modified by government assistance to those who purchase electric cars. Although not finally enacted, a provision of the "Energy" bill (H.R. 6860), as passed by the House of Representatives on June 19, 1975, would have granted a tax credit of $750 on the purchase of an electric car.

In addition, "crash" research programs should be instituted on specific transportation-related technologies where the technical obstacle is known, the research and development costs are limited, and the time period between a research breakthrough and widespread commercial acceptance promises to be short—notably high-performance batteries, fuel cells, the solar cell, and boron and graphite composites. Any successes that may be achieved will hasten the arrival of a whole new era of industrial progress.

Two centuries ago the Industrial Revolution burst upon the world as the consequence of a symbiotic relationship between a new source of power and the raw material of industry. The steam engine made possible an unimagined expansion in the use of iron, and later steel, by providing power so that machine tools and other types of machinery could work this hard and resistant material, by pumping air into blast furnaces so that coke from coal could replace charcoal from the disappearing forests, by driving the "puddling" rods for stirring pig iron so that coke could be used for making wrought iron, and by pumping water out of the mines so that coal could be economically extracted. At the same time, iron opened up vast new opportunities for the use of the steam engine. Replacing wood, which, because of its heterogeneity, had not lent itself to mass production, iron and later steel provided a uniform consistent and durable material which could economically be worked by a procession of new metal-working machines powered by steam.

After two centuries of interaction between coal, oil, the steam engine, and the internal combustion engine on the one hand and iron and steel on the other, there now appears to be aborning a new or Second Industrial Revolution, with symbiotic relationships again developing between new sources of power and new materials. In the transportation sector alone, the interaction between plastics, fiberglass, and the high-performance composites on the one hand and batteries and fuel cells on the other has the potential of resolving the energy crisis, abating air pollution, and reducing the cost of transportation. The technological potential is clear; what is not clear is whether the institutional heritages of the past will prevent its realization.

As to the remedies at law, traditional utility-type regulation is feasible for the domestic petroleum industry. It suffers, however, from two serious drawbacks—one inherent in the approach itself and the other of especial importance to this particular industry. Although capable of preventing prices from being "excessive" in relation to costs and profits, regulation does so at the expense of impairing the industry's efficiency. Not merely is competition's constant downward pressure on costs forgone; regulation gives rise to an actual cost inflation. Expenditures that would never be countenanced, or even possible, in a competitive industry are frequently tolerated and even incorporated into a regulated company's rate base, thereby tending to increase its permitted volume of profits.

In addition to this perverse economic consequence, the regulatory approach rests upon the assumption that government would place the public interest over what has been described as "the greatest aggregation of effective economic and political industrial power which the world and nations have ever known."[2] Such a turn of events would fly in the face of all recorded history. Whether by transferring valuable publicly owned reserves to the oil companies (Teapot Dome and more recently Elk Hill), or by implementing the domestic production control mechanism, or by preventing for nearly a decade and a half the importation of low-cost foreign oil, or by transferring to other U.S. taxpayers the burden of making up the revenue losses stemming from the industry's preferential tax advantages, or by eviscerating the *International Petroleum Cartel* case and other antitrust actions, or by countenancing recent price increases of refined products not warranted by changes in either costs or demand, or by channeling the great bulk of federal research and development funds into technologies that will not disturb (and may actually benefit) the oil companies, or by restraining the development of oil shale, or by a myriad of other actions too numerous to mention, the historical role of the federal government has been not to restrain the industry but to make more effective its exploitation of the public interest. To expect government to change the habits of a lifetime and embark on a course of bringing to heel these great "aggregations of effective economic and political industrial power" would be simply to invite a continuation of history's mistakes.

If a regulatory agency were to propose any action strongly opposed by the industry, the probable subsequent sequence of events is not too difficult to predict. On the one side the agency's few overworked lawyers and economists would try to make a case based on the limited amount of publicly available data, supplemented by such fragmentary information as could be pried out of the companies. On the other side, a veritable army of industry lawyers would not only contest the substance of the case but delay interminably any final resolution through an endless series of procedural motions and objections. Based on "accepted" accounting principles, leading accounting firms would testify to the oil companies' financial impoverishment, while outstanding economists would emphasize the need for "adequate" earnings to support the industry's growth. Meanwhile, highly skilled public relations firms would be drumming up "grassroots" campaigns against harassment of the industry and planting propaganda in the form of slanted TV news broadcasts and documentaries, newspaper stories, magazine articles, etc. Washington lobbyists would be pointing out to members of Congress the industry's importance not merely as a supplier of energy but as a contributor to political campaigns and, in some cases, to the legislators' own financial well-being.[3] Subsequent attacks on the agency in the pages of the *Congressional Record* could be expected as a matter of course. Attacks, criticisms, and various forms of sabotage are also to be expected from other government agencies, many of which have long ago been infiltrated by the industry.

Regulation necessarily requires that government be deeply involved in the affairs of an industry. In the very process of applying regulations, government officials become knowledgeable not only of the industry's economic characteristics—its organization, structure, costs, prices, profits and ways of doing business, etc.—but of its problems and difficulties. And from an awareness of its problems come understanding and not infrequently sympathy. This combination of expert knowledge with sympathetic understanding tends to vitiate all attempts at effective regulation, provides an effective shield against attacks by public-interest critics, and makes the staff of the regulatory agency exceedingly attractive to the regulated companies.

In contrast, by merely establishing the rules and conditions for the automatic operation of the market mechanism the competitive approach operates at the margin. Once an antitrust action is instituted, the relationship between the agency staff and the defendant companies is one of adversaries. Instead of mutual understanding, the prevailing attitude is one of antagonism. In such a climate influence and corruption do not thrive. And this is the fundamental reason why in the long run the antitrust approach offers greater protection to the public interest than any conceivable form of regulation. In mutual dislike rather than in mutual understanding there is strength. Moreover, by making an industry's behavior depend on the judgment and actions of many buyers and sellers, the competitive approach minimizes the harm that can be done by any small group of individuals, thereby making influence and corruption more cumbersome, expensive, and of most importance, ineffective.

Notes

Preface

1. 91st Cong., 1st Sess., Senate Subcommittee on Antitrust and Monopoly, *Hearings on Governmental Intervention in the Market Mechanism*, 1969, Pt. 1, p. 10.
2. *Ibid.*, p. 263.
3. Joint Committee on Atomic Energy, 1973. "Understanding the National Energy Dilemma," Staff Report of the Joint Committee on Atomic Energy, August 17, 1974.
4. National Academy of Sciences, *Mineral Resources and the Environment*, 1975, p. 272.

Chapter **1.** THE ENERGY CRISIS

1. 85th Cong., 1st Sess., Report of the Senate Subcommittee on Antitrust and Monopoly, *Petroleum, the Antitrust Laws and Government Policies* (Senate Report No. 1147), 1957, p. 97.
2. *Ibid.*
3. *Ibid.*, p. 98.
4. *The Petroleum Economist*, January 1974, p. 17. In the opinion of this source, the U.S. had the production capability to offset an even larger curtailment: "Although it would have taken several months of field development work to bring into production the U.S.A.'s total surplus capacity of some 2.5 million b/d, America could have made up for most of the deficiency had a similar 25 percent reduction in Arab oil supplies occurred in 1967."
5. M. King Hubbert, "World Energy Resources," paper before the 10th Commonwealth Mining and Metallurgical Congress, 1974, p. 48.
6. 91st Cong., 1st Sess., Senate Subcommittee on Antitrust and Monopoly, *Hearings on Governmental Intervention in the Market Mechanism, The Petroleum Industry,* 1969, Pt. 1, pp. 18–19. (Hereafter referred to as *Hearings on Governmental Intervention.*)
7. *The Tampa Tribune*, "Icebergs May Be Danger," October 15, 1975.
8. *The New York Times*, September 26, 1975.
9. *The New Republic,* May 15, 1976.
10. *Hearings on Governmental Intervention,* Pt. 2, pp. 1021–1028; cf. also pp. 660–667, 857–859.
11. *Ibid.*, p. 1023.
12. Thus, referring to "Dr. Blair's plot of 'new oil found,'" an exhibit submitted by M. A. Wright, vice-president of Exxon, stated: "For the specific area [the Continental U.S. excluding Alaska] the downtrend is probably a

401

reasonable expectation and does not differ significantly from Humble's outlook" (*Hearings on Governmental Intervention*, Pt. 2, p. 1,054).

13. *Ibid.*, p. 731 (emphasis added).
14. *Ibid.*, pp. 697, 699, 700, 761. Forecasts by the Department of the Interior, Standard (N.J.), Standard Research Institute, and the Texas Eastern Transmission Corp. placed 1980 demand for petroleum and natural gas liquids at around 18 million barrels a day (*ibid.*, p. 697).
15. M. King Hubbert, "Energy Resources," in *Resources and Man,* National Academy of Sciences, National Research Council, 1969, p. 43.
16. Hubbert, "Energy Resources," p. 48. Among the estimates made at this time were figures of 145 billion (Pratt), 150 billion (Hubbert), 170 billion (Prague and Hill), 173 billion (Knebel), and 200 billion (DeGolyer and MacNaughton).
17. 99th Cong., House Ways and Means Committee, Statement of M. King Hubbert, March 10, 1975. See also Hubbert, "Energy Resources," p. 49.
18. T. A. Hendricks, "Resources of Oil, Gas and Natural Gas Liquids in the United States and the World," 1969. U.S. Geological Survey, Circular 22.
19. P. K. Theobold, S. P. Schweinfirth, and D. C. Duncan, "Energy Resources of the United States," 1972. U.S. Geological Survey Circular 650.
20. V. E. McKelvey, "Revised U.S. Oil and Gas Resources Estimates," 1974. U.S. Geological Survey, News Release, March 26, 1974.
21. *Hearings on Governmental Intervention*, Pt. 2, p. 769.
22. National Academy of Sciences, *Mineral Resources and the Environment*, 1975, p. 88.
23. *Ibid.*
24. Department of the Interior, U.S. Geological Survey, "Geological Estimates of Undiscovered Recoverable Oil and Gas Resources in the United States," Geological Survey Circular 725, June 1975, pp. 1, 46.
25. The estimate of the National Science Foundation for undiscovered recoverable crude oil was 113 billion barrels for crude oil and natural gas liquids, which would also work out to 82 billion for crude alone. (National Academy of Sciences, *op. cit.*, p. 90.)
26. M. King Hubbert, "World Energy and the Fossil Fuels," *Drilling and Productive Practice*, 1956.
27. *Business Week*, March 10, 1975, p. 77.
28. Hubbert, "Energy Resources," pp. 57–58.
29. The figures on world reserves and production are from various issues of *World Oil*. For figures from *World Oil* for 1944–67, see *Hearings on Governmental Intervention*, Pt. 1, pp. 577–578.
30. *Hearings on Governmental Intervention*, Pt. 1, p. 204.
31. 93rd Cong., 2nd Sess., Senate Committee on Foreign Relations, Subcommittee on Multinational Corporations, *Hearings on Multinational Petroleum Corporations and Foreign Policy*, 1974, Pt. 7, p. 541, Telegram to W. J. McQuinn of SoCal. (Hereafter referred to as *Hearings on Multinational Corporations*.)
32. *Ibid.*, pp. 537–538. Telegram of June 27, 1973.
33. *Ibid.*, p. 539 (emphasis added). Telegram of July 25, 1973.
34. *Ibid.*, Pt. 7, p. 309.
35. *The Petroleum Economist*, February 1975, pp. 44–45. Excluded is the publication's admittedly highly speculative forecast of "possible" exports of 100 million tons (.750 million bbls.) from China. Its projected 1980 annual output for the other principal new areas are as follows: North Sea (1.4 billion barrels), the North Slope of Alaska (1.5), Brazil (.75), and Malaysia (.5). Further increments were also expected from Greece, Zaire, and Mexico.
36. *Ibid.*, p. 45.

37. *Ibid.*, June 1975, p. 203.
38. *Ibid.*, p. 204 (emphasis added).
39. C. R. Bedoun and H. V. Dunnington, *The Petroleum Geology and Resources of the Middle East*, Scientific Press, Ltd., Beaconsfield, Bucks, England, 1975.
40. National Academy of Sciences, *op. cit.*, p. 93.
41. *Ibid.*
42. *Ibid.*, pp. 12, 260, 261.
43. *Ibid.*, p. 312.

Part ONE   THE CONTROL OF FOREIGN OIL

Chapter **2.** THE EVOLUTION OF CONTROL: Supply

1. Department of the Interior, Bureau of Mines, "1974 Figures on Worldwide Crude Oil Production, Imports and Exports," September 4, 1975.
2. 82nd Cong., 2nd Sess., Senate Small Business Committee, *The International Petroleum Cartel*, Staff Report of the Federal Trade Commission, 1952, p. 47. (Hereafter referred to as *International Petroleum Cartel*.)
3. Fritz Fischer, *Krieg der Illusionen,* Droste Verlag, Düsseldorf, 1969, pp. 424–425.
4. *Ibid.*, p. 50.
5. 66th Cong., 2nd Sess., S. Doc. No. 272; 67th Cong., 1st Sess., S. Doc. No. 672.
6. 66th Cong., 2nd Sess., S. 4396.
7. See *International Petroleum Cartel*, pp. 37–45.
8. *Ibid.*, p. 41.
9. *Ibid.*, pp. 109–110.
10. *The Petroleum Times* (London), May 2, 1936, p. 563. (Cited in *International Petroleum Cartel*, p. 115.)
11. *Hearings on Multinational Corporations*, Pt. 7, p. 57.
12. *Ibid.*, p. 58.
13. *International Petroleum Cartel*, pp. 110–111.
14. *Ibid.*, p. 115.
15. *Ibid.*
16. *The Petroleum Times*, July 4, 1936, p. 8.
17. *International Petroleum Cartel*, p. 121.
18. *Ibid.* (emphasis added).
19. *Hearings on Multinational Corporations* (Testimony of Barbara Svedberg), Pt. 7, p. 81.
20. *Ibid.*, p. 82.
21. 93rd Cong., 2nd Sess., Senate Foreign Relations Committee, Subcommittee on Multinational Corporations, *Report on Multinational Corporations and U.S. Foreign Policy*, 1975, p. 48. (Hereafter referred to as *Report on Multinational Corporations and U.S. Foreign Policy.*)
22. *Ibid.*
23. *Ibid.*
24. *Ibid.*, p. 49.
25. *Ibid.*, p. 47.
26. Temporary National Economic Committee, Monograph No. 29, *The Distribution of Ownership in the 200 Largest Nonfinancial Corporations*, 1940.
27. *Ibid.*, pp. 127–128. (See also Chapter 6.)
28. For an account of these maneuvers, see *International Petroleum Cartel*, pp. 99–107.
29. *Hearings on Multinational Corporations* (Testimony of Barbara Svedberg), Pt. 7, p. 82.
30. *International Petroleum Cartel*, pp. 120, 122.

31. *Ibid.*, pp. 135–136.
32. *Ibid.*, p. 83.
33. *Hearings on Multinational Corporations*, Pt. 7, pp. 87, 89.
34. *International Petroleum Cartel*, p. 162.
35. *Ibid.*, pp. 145–162.
36. *Hearings on Multinational Corporations*, Pt. 7, p. 304.
37. Testimony of Richard Funkhouser, *ibid.*, Pt. 7, p. 132.
38. *Hearings on Multinational Corporations* (Memorandum from W. B. Watson Snyder to Messrs. Worth Rowley and William Fugate, "Participation in Iranian Consortium") March 10, 1955 (Justice File: 60-57-140), Pt. 7, pp. 248–249.
39. *Ibid.*
40. *Ibid.*, p. 295.
41. *Ibid.* (Testimony of E. L. Shafer, Vice-President, Continental Oil Co.), Pt. 7, p. 244.
42. *Ibid.*, p. 302.
43. *Ibid.*, p. 303.
44. *Ibid.*, pp. 299, 303.
45. *Ibid.*, p. 304 (emphasis added).
46. *Ibid.*, p. 303 (emphasis added).
47. 80th Cong., 1st Sess., Special Senate Committee investigating the National Defense Program, 1947–48, Hearings, N.S. Rept. No. 440, *Navy Purchases of Middle East Oil*, 1948, Pt. 5.
48. Economic Commission for Europe, Secretariat, *The Price of Oil in Western Europe*, United Nations, Geneva, 1955, pp. 14–15.
49. Wayne A. Leeman, *The Price of Middle East Oil*, 1962, pp. 64–66.
50. Charles Issawi and Mohammed Yeganeh, *The Economics of Middle Eastern Oil*, Frederick A. Praeger, New York, 1962, p. 91.
51. Zuhayr Mikdashi, *A Financial Analysis of Middle East Oil Concessions, 1901–65*, Frederick A. Praeger, New York, 1966, p. 168.
52. *Platt's Oilgram*, News Service, May 26, 1967.
53. Paul G. Bradley, *The Economics of Crude Petroleum Production*, North-Holland, Amsterdam, 1967; see also *Hearings on Governmental Intervention*, Pt. 1, p. 285.
54. *Ibid.*, p. 294.
55. *Hearings on Governmental Intervention*, Pt. 1, p. 8; see also M. A. Adelman, "Oil Production Costs in Four Areas," *Proceedings of the Council on Economics*, American Institute of Mining, Metallurgical and Petroleum Engineers, 1966; summarized in *Petroleum Press Service*, May 1966.
56. Helmut J. Frank, *Crude Oil Prices in the Middle East*, Frederick A. Praeger, New York, 1966, p. 143.
57. Mikdashi, *op. cit.*, p. 42.
58. *Ibid.*, pp. 42, 43.
59. *Ibid.*, p. 244.
60. *Ibid.*, p. 211.
61. *Ibid.*, pp. 182, 195, 212, 221.
62. A. H. Tariki, *Towards Better Cooperation between Oil Producing and Oil Consuming Countries*, Fourth Arab Petroleum Congress, Beirut, November 1963, p. 10.
63. Mikdashi, *op. cit.*, pp. 195, 221, 212–214, 182.
64. *Ibid.*, p. 220.
65. *Ibid.*, p. 210.
66. See *Hearings on Governmental Intervention* (Testimony of Edith Penrose), Pt. 1, p. 431.
67. Computed from Organization of Petroleum Exporting Countries, *Statistical Bulletin*, 1973.

68. Paul H. Frankel, *Mattei: Oil and Power Politics*, Frederick A. Praeger, New York, 1966, p. 87.

Chapter **3.** THE EVOLUTION OF CONTROL: Marketing

1. *International Petroleum Cartel*, p. 198. Much of the material in this chapter is derived from this document.
2. *Oil and Gas Journal*, September 20, 1928, cited in *ibid.*, p. 199.
3. *International Petroleum Cartel*, p. 229.
4. *Ibid.*, p. 231 (emphasis added in IPC report in this and the quotations that follow).
5. *Ibid.*, p. 261.
5a. *Ibid.*, p. 259.
6. *Ibid.*, p. 257.
7. *Ibid.*, p. 282.
8. *Ibid.*, pp. 232–233.
8a. *Ibid.*, p. 261.
9. *Ibid.*, p. 261.
10. The exception was SoCal, which at that time had not yet become an important supplier of Mideast oil nor a significant factor in European markets.
11. *International Petroleum Cartel*, p. 245.
12. *Ibid.*, p. 244.
13. *Ibid.*, p. 263.
14. *Ibid.*, p. 263.
15. *Ibid.*, p. 263.
16. *Ibid.*, p. 265.
17. *Ibid.*, p. 266 (emphasis added).
18. *Ibid.* (emphasis added).
19. *Ibid.*, p. 210.
20. *Hearings on Multinational Corporations*, Pt. 5, p. 114.
21. *Ibid.*, p. 134.
22. *The Economist*, December 21, 1929.
23. *International Petroleum Cartel*, p. 235.
24. *Ibid.*, p. 291.
25. *Ibid.*, p. 288.
26. *Ibid.*, p. 320.
27. *Ibid.*
28. *Ibid.*, p. 246.
29. *Ibid.*, p. 296.
30. *Ibid.*, p. 295.
31. *Ibid.*, pp. 314, 318. Although quota figures for Great Britain are available only for individual products, the share for the "as is" companies ranged in 1936 from a low of 79.8% for gas oil to a high of 93.9% for fuel oil; for gasoline it was 81.1% (*ibid.*, p. 317).
32. The "as is" group consisted of Exxon, Shell and BP, plus Mobil where the last was a significant factor in the market.
33. In the case of Great Britain the quota figures were accountable only on the basis of individual products while the figure on trading results related to all "controlled" products as a group.
34. *International Petroleum Cartel*, p. 323. "Negotiations for a reconstruction of the cartel were going on in late 1936, according to a memorandum written by an official of Exxon."
35. *Ibid.*, p. 266.
36. *Hearings on Multinational Corporations*, Pt. 7, p. 25.
37. *The New York Times*, November 19, 1974.
38. *Ibid.*

39. Some of these documents were secured by the Senate Subcommittee on Multinational Corporations and introduced into the record of its hearings.
40. *International Oil Cartel*, Preface, p. vi.
41. *Hearings on Multinational Corporations* (Testimony of Leonard J. Emmerglick), Pt. 7, p. 99.
42. *Ibid.* (Testimony of David T. Haberman). According to Haberman, one of the attorneys assigned to the case, the FTC report's "carefully researched 378 pages provided a most exquisite blueprint for the Justice Department staff; indeed, it became our bible in the preparation of the oil cartel case" (*ibid.*, p. 15).
43. *Ibid.*, pp. 104–105.
44. *Ibid.*, p. 106.
45. President Truman said that he was conditioning the change on a belief (which he would be powerless to implement) "that the companies involved agreed to the production of the documentary materials" called for in the criminal proceedings (*ibid.*, p. 106).
46. *Ibid.*, p. 107. This testimony was given on February 21, 1974. In response to inquiries by the press, General Bradley stated that he could not recall having made any such recommendation to President Truman.
47. *Ibid.*, p. 109.
48. *Ibid.*, p. 110.
49. *Ibid.*, p. 132.
50. *Ibid.*, p. 130.
51. *Ibid.*, p. 125.
52. *Ibid.*, p. 148.
53. *Ibid.*, p. 32.
54. *Ibid.*, p. 109.
55. *Ibid.*, p. 73.
56. *Report on Multinational Corporations and U.S. Foreign Policy*, p. 74.
57. Memorandum on *Artificial Restraints on Basic Energy Sources*, prepared by Worth Rowley and Associates for the American Public Power Association and the National Rural Electric Cooperative Association, February 25, 1971, pp. 48–49.

Chapter 4. THE EXCLUSION OF OUTSIDERS

1. *Report on Multinational Corporations and U.S. Foreign Policy*, p. 58.
2. *Ibid.*, p. 59. (The source cited in the report is *Present at the Creation*, by Dean Acheson, p. 507.)
3. Mikdashi, *op. cit.*, p. 155.
4. *Hearings on Multinational Corporations* ("Internal State Department Memoranda by Richard Funkhouser"), Pt. 7, pp. 122–134.
5. Mikdashi, *op. cit.*, pp. 155–156.
6. *Ibid.*, pp. 158–159.
7. See Chapter 5, Chart 5-2.
8. Mikdashi, *op. cit.*, p. 157.
9. *Report on Multinational Corporations and U.S. Foreign Policy*, p. 59.
10. *Ibid.*, p. 64.
11. *Hearings on Multinational Corporations*, Pt. 8, pp. 537–541. The case cited was Anglo-Iranian Oil Co. Case [Jurisdiction], Judgment of July 22, 1952, ICJ Report, 1952, p. 93.
12. *Ibid.*, p. 540.
13. Digest of *International Petroleum Cartel* report prepared by Central Intelligence Agency and published in *Hearings on Governmental Intervention*, Pt. 1, pp. 554–577.
14. See Chapter 9.
15. *Hearings on Multinational Corporations*, Pt. 7, p. 309.

16. *Ibid.*, Pt. 7, p. 310 (emphasis added).
17. Memorandum from Anthony M. Solomon to Nicholas D. Katzenbach, October 13, 1967. This and other internal State Department memoranda cited in this section have been declassified and placed in the public record of the Senate Subcommittee on Multinational Corporations, *Hearings,* Pt. 8.
18. State Department, Memorandum for the Under Secretary from Andreas Lowenfeld on "Iraq Petroleum Situation," October 24, 1964 (*Hearings on Multinational Corporations,* Pt. 8, pp. 537–541).
19. *Ibid.* (emphasis added).
20. Department of State, Memorandum of Conversation, Subject: "Sinclair Interest in Iraq Oil Concession," May 6, 1974 (*ibid.*, pp. 532–534).
21. Department of State, Memorandum of Conversation, Subject: "Standard of Indiana's Interest in Iraq," May 19, 1964 (*ibid.*, p. 534).
22. Department of State, Outgoing Telegram from Under Secretary Ball to American Embassies (London, Baghdad, Rome), Subject: "IPC Negotiations," July 8, 1964 (*ibid.*, p. 536).
23. Department of State, Outgoing Telegram from Secretary Rusk, November 19, 1964 (*ibid.*, p. 544).
24. Department of State, Outgoing Telegram from Secretary Rusk to Embassies (London, Paris, The Hague), Subject: "Iraq Oil," August 24, 1967 (*ibid.*, p. 548).
25. *Ibid.*
26. Department of State, Incoming Telegram from Ambassador Bruce (London), May 13, 1967 (*ibid.*, p. 545).
27. *Ibid.* (emphasis added).
28. Department of State, Incoming Telegram from Ambassador Reinhardt (Rome), Subject: "ENI-Iraqi Oil Involvement," May 13, 1967 (*ibid.*, p. 545).
29. *Ibid.*
30. Department of State, Outgoing Telegram from Secretary Rusk, October 17, 1967 (*ibid.*, p. 552).
31. Department of State, Incoming Telegram from Ambassador Bohlen (Paris), Subject: "Iraq Oil," October 23, 1967 (*ibid.*, pp. 553–554).
32. *The Petroleum Economist,* March 1974, p. 105. However, an IPC affiliate, the Basrah Petroleum Co., which holds a concession in N. Rumaila, instituted proceedings against purchasers of oil from that field. Basrah Petroleum was itself nationalized in late 1975.
33. An ambitious expansion program was announced by the Iraq National Oil Co., but its objectives have subsequently been reduced.
34. Frankel, *op. cit.,* p. 90.
35. *Ibid.*
36. *Ibid.*, pp. 98–99.
37. *Ibid.*, p. 124.
38. *Ibid.*, p. 131.
39. *Ibid.*, p. 131.
40. In Frankel's view a further factor contributing to this failure was the fact that in Central Europe Mattei lacked the direct support or participation of any government. But, given the right of the established companies to counter his invasion as they did, it is difficult to see how such support could have done anything more than postpone the failure.
41. Frankel, *op. cit.,* p. 99.
42. 94th Cong., 1st Sess., Hearings Before the Senate Subcommittee on Multinational Corporations, prepared statement by Archie Monroe, July 16, 1975, mimeographed, p. 3.
43. *Hearings on Multinational Corporations,* Pt. 2, pp. 268–313, "Internal

Audit Report of the Special Budget/Special Budget Bank Account of Esso Italiana," August 30, 1972.

44. *Hearings on Multinational Corporations*, Pt. 12, pp. 246–247.

45. *Ibid.*, "Internal Audit Report."

46. *Ibid.*, "Internal Audit Report."

47. *Ibid.*, p. 256.

48. *Ibid.*, "Internal Audit Report."

49. *Ibid.*, p. 316.

50. *Ibid.*, pp. 317–318. Mr. Checkett stressed the fact that the first and third measures were adopted before Mobil began to make political contributions, but they did not antedate Exxon's far larger contributions.

51. *Ibid.*, p. 316.

52. *The Petroleum Economist*, January 1975, p. 22 (emphasis added).

Chapter 5. THE INTERNATIONAL CONTROL MECHANISM

1. *Hearings on Multinational Corporations*, Pt. 7, p. 307 (emphasis added).

2. *Ibid.*, p. 308.

3. *Ibid.*, p. 342.

4. *Ibid.*, p. 328.

5. *Hearings on Multinational Corporations*, Pt. 8, p. 591.

6. *Ibid.*

7. *Ibid.*, pp. 591–606.

8. Exxon, *Forecast of Free World Supplies*, 1967 (emphasis added). (*Hearings on Multinational Corporations*, Pt. 8, p. 601.)

9. The equity ownership of the Iranian Consortium is BP 40%, Shell 14%, CFP 6%, Exxon 7%, Mobil 7%, SoCal 7%, Texaco 7%, Gulf 7% and Iricon 5%. A "consortium within the consortium," Iricon's current membership is American Independent 2/12; Getty Oil 2/12; ARCO 4/12; Sohio 1/12; Charter 2/12; and Conoco 1/12.

10. *Hearings on Multinational Corporations* (Testimony of E. L. Shafer), Pt. 7, pp. 253–254.

11. *Ibid.*, Pt. 7, p. 254. The figures under "Nomination" have been added. They were derived by multiplying the figures for "Total Program" by the participants' equity percentages.

12. *Hearings on Multinational Corporations* (Statement of E. L. Shafer), Pt. 7, p. 261.

13. *Ibid.*, p. 303.

14. *Ibid.*, p. 266.

15. *Ibid.*, p. 267.

16. *Ibid.*, p. 268.

17. *Ibid.*, p. 304.

18. The equity ownership of Aramco is Exxon 30%, SoCal 30%, Texaco 30%, and Mobil 10%.

19. *Hearings on Multinational Corporations*, Pt. 8, p. 491 (emphasis added).

20. *Ibid.*, p. 492. For comparative purposes the schedule showed the 1972 "Liftings from Aramco" which were contrasted to the "Minimum Lifting Obligation or Provision." It also contained a "Statement of Excess Credits" for prior years.

21. The February 15 "estimated" schedule was revised on March 12, with the "growth ratio" changed from 1.364% to 1.270%. For reasons not made clear but probably reflecting adjustments for prior years, a higher ratio, 1.638%, was applied to Texaco (*ibid.*, p. 493).

22. *Ibid.*, p. 309.

23. The same language, "Kuwait estimates are by difference," is used in other annual *Forecasts*, e.g., those of 1960, 1961, 1962.

24. In this connection it should be noted that companies with influence in Kuwait's production include not only the concession holders, Gulf and BP, but through long-term contracts Exxon and Shell.

25. *Hearings on Multinational Corporations,* Pt. 8, p. 605.

26. *Hearings on Multinational Corporations,* Pt. 7, p. 309.

27. *Petroleum Times* (London), "Adjustment in Prices of Bunker Oil Supplies," May 13, 1944, p. 298. (Quoted in *International Petroleum Cartel,* p. 356.)

28. 80th Cong., Hearings before a Special Committee Investigating the National Defense Program, "Petroleum Arrangements with Saudi Arabia," 1947, 1948, and "Navy Purchase of Middle East Oil," S. Rept. 440, 1948.

29. *International Petroleum Cartel,* p. 359.

30. See Chapter 8.

31. *Petroleum Times* (London), January 17, 1948, p. 55. (Cited in *Hearings on Governmental Intervention,* Pt. 1, p. 200.)

32. *Ibid.,* July 24, 1953.

33. *Hearings on Governmental Intervention,* Pt. 1, pp. 343–344.

34. For the analysis of these changes, see *International Petroleum Cartel,* Ch. 10; *Hearings on Governmental Intervention,* Pt. 1 (Testimony of Helmut J. Frank), pp. 339–363; and Frank, *Crude Oil Prices in the Middle East.*

35. *International Petroleum Cartel,* pp. 361–362.

36. *Hearings on Multinational Corporations,* Pt. 5, p. 3.

37. *The New York Times,* January 5, 1975.

38. *Hearings on Multinational Corporations,* Pt. 4, p. 68.

Part TWO THE CONTROL OF DOMESTIC OIL

Chapter 6. CONCENTRATION IN DOMESTIC OIL

1. Temporary National Economic Committee, *Hearings on the Petroleum Industry,* Pt. 14, 1940, pp. 7,593–7,594.

2. *Ibid.,* p. 7,595.

3. *Standard Oil Company of New Jersey, et al.* v. *United States,* 221 U.S. (1911).

4. Federal Trade Commission, *Report on the Petroleum Trade in Wyoming and Montana,* 1922, p. 3.

5. Adolf A. Berle and Gardiner C. Means, *The Modern Corporation and Private Property,* rev. edn., Harcourt, Brace, New York, 1967, pp. 320–321.

6. John W. Wilson, "Market Structure and Interfirm Integration in the Petroleum Industry," *Journal of Economic Issues,* June 1975, p. 324.

7. 93rd Cong., 1st Sess., Senate Committee on Government Operations, "Preliminary Federal Trade Commission Staff Report on Its Investigation of the Petroleum Industry," Committee Print, 1973. (Hereafter referred to as the *1973 FTC Staff Report.*)

8. *Hearings on Governmental Intervention,* Pt. 1, pp. 133–134.

9. *1973 FTC Staff Report,* p. 18, n. 18.

10. Derived from 94th Cong., 1st Sess., Hearings before the Senate Subcommittee on Antitrust and Monopoly on the Industrial Organization Act (Testimony of W. T. Slick, Jr., Exxon Corp.), January 21, 1975, Exhibit 15.

11. *Oil and Gas Journal,* March 30, 1969; April 6, 1974.

12. 93rd Cong., 1st Sess., Senate Interior Committee, *The Gasoline Shortage: A National Perspective,* Background paper prepared by the Legislative Reference Service, Committee Print, p. 35.

13. *Chemical and Engineering News,* June 16, 1969.

14. Fred C. Allvine and James M. Patterson, *Highway Robbery: An Analysis* *of the Gasoline Crisis*, Indiana University Press, Bloomington, Ind., 1974, p. 166.

15. *Oil and Gas Journal*, March 1972.
16. 93rd Cong., 1st Sess., Senate Subcommittee on Antitrust and Monopoly, *Hearings on the Natural Gas Industry*, Pt. 1, *Competition and Concentration in the Nation's Gas Industry*, 1973, p. 499 (emphasis in original). (Hereinafter referred to as *Hearings on the Natural Gas Industry*.)
17. Commissioner of Corporations, *Report on the Petroleum Industry*, Pt. 1, 1907, pp. 48, 51.
18. Thomas G. Moore, "The Petroleum Industry," in *The Structure of American Industry*, ed. Walter Adams, 4th edn., Macmillan, New York, 1971, p. 130. For refined products the proportions are 27% by pipeline, 30% by water carrier, and 43% by truck.
19. *1973 FTC Staff Report*, p. 26.
20. *Ibid.*, p. 26.
21. *International Petroleum Cartel*, p. 28.
22. *Ibid.*, pp. 27–28.
23. *Hearings on Governmental Intervention* (Memorandum from W. T. Pecora, Director, Geological Survey), May 26, 1966, Pt. 4, p. 1,800.
24. Walter J. Mead, "The Competitive Significance of Joint Ventures," *Antitrust Bulletin*, Fall 1967, p. 839.
25. *Hearings on the Natural Gas Industry*, Pt. 1, p. 482.
26. 94th Cong., 1st Sess., Senate Subcommittee on Antitrust and Monopoly, *Hearings on S. 2387 and Related Bills*, Pt. 1, pp. 51–70, Statement of Walter S. Measday, September 23, 1975.
27. Wilson, "Market Structure," *Journal of Economic Issues*.
28. *Ibid.*
29. 63rd Cong., 2nd Sess., H. Rept. 627, Report of the Committee on the Judiciary, House of Representatives, to accompany HR 15657, May 6, 1914, pp. 17–18.
30. *Ibid.*, p. 19.
31. USC, Title 15, Sec. 19.
32. See Federal Trade Commission, *Report on Interlocking Directorates*, 1951, p. 15.
33. *Ibid.*, p. 377.
34. *Ibid.*, p. 377.
35. *Ibid.*, p. 377.
36. *Ibid.*, p. 366.
37. *Ibid.*, pp. 365–366.
38. The 1972 data on the interlocking directorates are compiled from Stanley H. Ruttenberg and Associates, *The American Oil Industry: A Failure of Antitrust Policy*, 1974. In 1972, Gulf had no interlocks with other major oil companies.
39. In 1970 these six firms held 44.3% of the refining capacity in District 2 (*1973 FTC Staff Report*).
40. See John M. Blair, *Economic Concentration*, Harcourt Brace Jovanovich, New York, 1972, p. 78.
41. Ruttenberg and Associates, *op. cit.*, pp. 78–79.
42. Berle and Means, *op. cit.*, pp. 76–77.
43. Temporary National Economic Committee, Monograph 29, *The Distribution of Ownership*, pp. 127–128.
44. R. H. Larner, "Ownership and Control in the 200 Largest Nonfinancial Corporations, 1929 and 1963," *American Economic Review*, September 1966.
45. Jean-Marie Chevalier, "The Problem of Control in Large American Corporations," *Antitrust Bulletin*, Spring 1969.

46. See Lundberg Survey, *National Petroleum News*, 1973, Factbook Issue, pp. 113–120.
47. Wilson, "Market-Structure," *Journal of Economic Issues*, p. 326.

Chapter 7. THE DOMESTIC CONTROL MECHANISM

1. Erich W. Zimmerman, *Conservation in the Production of Petroleum*, Yale University Press, New Haven, Conn., 1957, pp. 138, 139, n. 50.
2. *Hearings on Governmental Intervention*, Pt. 2, p. 714 (emphasis added).
3. *Report of the Federal Oil Conservation Board*, Pt. I (May 28, 1930).
4. *Ibid.*, p. 14.
5. Zimmerman, *op. cit.*, p. 144.
6. *Ibid.*, p. 92.
7. Temporary National Economic Committee, *Hearings on the Petroleum Industry*, Pt. 14, 1940, p. 7,102.
8. Zimmerman, *op. cit.*, p. 121.
9. Federal Oil Conservation Board, *Fourth Report*, May 1930, pp. 17–24.
10. Walter S. Measday in *Hearings on Governmental Intervention*, Pt. 1, pp. 579–582.
11. Zimmerman, *op. cit.*, pp. 123, 127.
12. *International Petroleum Cartel*, p. 212 (emphasis added).
13. *Ibid.*, p. 213.
14. Cited in *ibid.*, p. 213.
15. Federal Oil Conservation Board, *Fifth Report*, October 1932, p. 24 (emphasis added).
16. *Ibid.*, pp. 23–24.
17. See *International Petroleum Cartel*, pp. 236–239, 249–251, 268–272.
18. In this "Paris" agreement, the Rumanians obtained the right to sell anywhere, though the international majors were given the right of first refusal to purchase; the majors also agreed to buy from the Rumanians specified amounts of gasoline and kerosene.
19. *Petroleum Times* (London), May 13, 1933. (Cited in *International Petroleum Cartel*, p. 251, n. 98.)
20. *Ibid.*, p. 251.
21. *Ibid.*, p. 239.
22. *Ibid.*, p. 212.
23. Paul H. Frankel, *The Essentials of Petroleum*, 1946, pp. 116–117.
24. Zimmerman, *op. cit.*, p. 147.
25. *Ibid.*, pp. 145, 153.
26. *Ibid.*, pp. 151, 153.
27. Temporary National Economic Committee, *Hearings on the Petroleum Industry*, Pt. 14, pp. 7,596 and 7,597.
28. *Ibid.*, p. 7,603.
29. *Ibid.*, p. 7,138.
30. *Ibid.*, p. 7,139 (emphasis added).
31. *Ibid.*, p. 7,140.
32. *Ibid.*, p. 7,141.
33. Zimmerman, *op. cit.*, p. 207.
34. *Ibid.*, p. 209.
35. *Ibid.*, p. 194.
36. Temporary National Economic Committee, *Hearings on the Petroleum Industry*, Pt. 14, p. 7,307.
37. 81st Cong., 1st Sess., Senate Small Business Committee, *Final Report*, S. Rept. 25, p. 13.
38. The way in which prorationing was administered also helped to raise costs. With respect to one of the principal determinants of cost (well depth), the regulations incorporated an unusual principle: the higher the cost, the greater the permitted output. As Kahn pointed out:

Production allowables vary with the depth of the producing reservoir; the deeper the reservoir, the larger the allowable. . . .

This sounds quite reasonable to people brought up in the medieval tradition of just price: after all, costs of production are much greater at the greater depths, and producers could not survive, in those deep wells, with 74 barrel-a-day allowables. But this is only another way of saying that the higher the cost, the larger the share of the market a firm should be given. Put that way it does not seem quite so obvious or just; and in economic terms it is utterly irrational. (*Hearings on Governmental Intervention*, Pt. 1, p. 137.)

39. *Hearings on Governmental Intervention*, Pt. 1, p. 134.
40. *Ibid.*
41. Erich W. Zimmerman, *Conservation in the Production of Petroleum*, Yale University Press, New Haven, Conn., 1957, p. 76.
42. *Ibid.*, pp. 347–348.
43. *Oil Daily*, May 10, 1972.
44. *Ibid.*
45. Federal Oil Conservation Board, *Fifth Report*, 1932, pp. 23–24. In this context the "prorationing" referred to would have been international in scope.
46. *Hearings on Governmental Intervention*, Pt. 1, pp. 138–139.
47. See Chapter 13, Chart 13-4.
48. *Report of the President's Task Force on Oil Import Control*, 1970, Pt. 1, Sections 106–113, 117–130, p. 8.
49. *Hearings on Governmental Intervention*, Pt. 1, p. 30. At Adelman's request the sentence was italicized in the *Hearings*.
50. *Ibid.*, pp. 30–31.
51. *Washington Post*, July 16, 1970.
52. *Hearings on Governmental Intervention*, Pt. 1, p. 105.
53. Since they were not licensed, actual Canadian imports, not surprisingly, regularly exceeded the authorized amounts.
54. *Hearings on Governmental Intervention*, Pt. 3, pp. 1,486–1,502.
55. *Hearings on Governmental Intervention*, Pt. 3, p. 1,177.
56. *Hearings on Governmental Intervention*, Pt. 3, p. 1,252. With the exception of purchases of 3,700 barrels by Union Carbide and 163 barrels by a small trading company, these represent all of the purchases of quotas made in 1968.
57. The methodology employed is the same as that set forth in Table 13-1, with the additional step that the lower aggregate values of the refined products (at the $2.00 level) were distributed among the various products on the basis of the same proportions that their values bore to the aggregate total at the $3.75 level.
58. *Hearings on Governmental Intervention*, Pt. 1, p. 274.
59. *Ibid.*, pp. 306–307.
60. *Ibid.*, pp. 306–307.
61. Also affected was the Southeast. See *ibid.*, pp. 1,370ff.
62. *Ibid.*, p. 253. For further expositions concerning the quota's effects on New England, see Testimony of Governor Kenneth Curtis of Maine and A. Thomas Easley, Executive Vice-President of the New England Council. (*Hearings on Governmental Intervention*, Pt. 3, pp. 1,406ff and 1,191ff.)
63. *Ibid.*, Pt. 3, p. 1,305.
64. *Ibid.*, p. 1,407.
65. *Ibid.*, pp. 1,407–1,408.
66. *Ibid.*, p. 1,408.
67. *Hearings on Governmental Intervention*, Pt. 3, pp. 1,202, 1,262, 1,285, 1,400.

68. *Ibid.*, pp. 1,235ff.
69. *Ibid.*, pp. 1,343ff.
70. *Ibid.*, pp. 1,268ff.
71. *Ibid.*, pp. 1,397ff.
72. *Ibid.*, pp. 1,367, 1,375ff.
73. *Ibid.*, pp. 1,352ff., 1,357.
74. *Hearings on Governmental Intervention*, Pt. 4, pp. 1,707–1,708.
75. "Summary Guide to Task Force Report on Oil Import Control," reprinted in *Hearings on Governmental Intervention*, Pt. 4, p. 1,782.
76. *Ibid.*, pp. 1,734–1,735.
77. Robert E. Hardwicke, "Oil Well Spacing Regulations and Protection of Property Rights in Texas," *Texas Law Review*, 1952, p. 111.
78. Zimmerman, *op. cit.*, pp. 338, 340.
79. *Ibid.*, p. 340 (emphasis in original). The case referred to is *Railroad Commission* vs. *Humble Oil and Refining Co.*, 193 S.W. 2nd 824,832 (1946).

Chapter **8.** PREFERENTIAL TAXATION

1. *Oil Week*, June 30, 1975.
2. *Hearings on Multinational Corporations*, Pt. 4, p. 19. (Cited in Testimony of Stanford G. Ross.)
3. *Hearings on Governmental Intervention*, Pt. 2, p. 845. (Computed by the Internal Revenue Service from data taken from the IRS *Source Book Statistics of Income*, July 1965–June 1966.)
4. *Hearings on Governmental Intervention*, Pt. 1, p. 134.
5. 65th Cong., 3rd Sess., S. Rept. No. 617, December 6, 1918 (emphasis added).
6. Joint Committee on Internal Revenue Taxation, Staff Report, *Legislative History of Depletion Allowances*, 1950, p. 2.
7. *Ibid.*, p. 3.
8. 65th Cong., 3rd Sess., 57 *Congressional Record* 801 (Cited in *ibid*).
9. Cited in Staff Report of Joint Committee on Internal Revenue Taxation, *op. cit.*, p. 6.
10. Cited in *ibid.*, p. 6.
11. Ronnie Dugger, "Oil and Politics," *Atlantic Monthly*, September 1969, Vol. 224, No. 3, pp. 66–90, at 70.
12. 69th Cong., 1st Sess. (Confidential committee print), January 1926. (Quoted in Staff Report of Joint Committee on Internal Revenue, *op. cit.*, p. 6.)
13. Quoted in *ibid.*, p. 7.
14. Cited in *ibid.*, p. 7.
15. Quoted in *ibid.*, p. 7.
16. Alfred E. Kahn, "The Depletion Allowance in the Context of Cartelization," *American Economic Review*, June 1964, pp. 286–314.
17. Philip M. Stern, *The Great Treasury Raid*, Random House, New York, 1964, p. 25.
18. *Ibid.*, p. 33 (emphasis in original).
19. Estimate of Federal Tax Expenditure for 1972 prepared by the Staff of the Treasury Department of the Joint Committee on Internal Revenue Taxation (cited by Ross, *loc. cit.*).
20. *Hearings on Multinational Corporations*, Pt. 4, p. 36.
21. *Ibid.*, pp. 118–119.
22. IRS Statistics of Income, 1961, Supplementary Report, *Foreign Tax Credit Claimed on Corporation Income Tax Returns*, GPO, Washington, D.C., 1967, Table 1. For twenty-three integrated petroleum companies, total taxable income amounted to $1,063 million; their foreign source income to $906 million, or 85.2%.

23. The obstacles to relatively free election are minimal. Since all companies were on a per-country basis in 1960, the Act provides simply that after January 1, 1961, taxpayers may elect to move to the overall basis. At first glance this appears to be an irrevocable decision, but it is not. Should a company which has made the first "free" election to shift from the per-country to the overall limitation find that this was a mistake, it may shift back again with the permission of the "Secretary of the Treasury or his delegate" (who has been designated since as the Commissioner of Internal Revenue). At a still later date, it can with permission return again to the overall basis. In short, the only legal barrier to free election, as the law now stands, is the necessity that the taxpayer secure the permission of the Secretary of the Treasury or the Commissioner of Internal Revenue for changes beyond the initial election.

24. After the liberalization in 1960, most of the major oil companies have found it advantageous to use the per-country limitation. In this way they were able to maximize the tax value of losses arising from the rapid write-off privilege for untangible drilling expenses; thereafter the foreign tax credit becomes operable. More recently, however, some of the largest companies have been using the overall basis. (See Joint Committee on Internal Revenue, *Energy Taxation: Possible Modifications in the Tax Treatment of Foreign Oil and Gas Income*, Study No. 3, Committee Print, February 21, 1974, p. 6).

25. *Hearings on Multinational Corporations*, Pt. 4, pp. 84–85.

26. *Ibid.*

27. *Ibid.*, p. 91.

28. *Ibid.*, pp. 88–90.

29. *Ibid.*, pp. 96–97.

30. *Hearings on Multinational Corporations*, Pt. 4, p. 13.

31. 85th Cong., 1st Sess., Senate Antitrust Subcommittee and Senate Interior Committee, *Hearings on the Emergency Oil Lift Program and Related Oil Problems*, Pt. 2 (1957), p. 1,441.

32. Originally a secret document, the Treasury ruling approving the change in the treatment of payments was itself made part of the tax code in 1955—Rev. Ruling 55-296, 1955-1, CB 386. (See Ross statement, *Hearings on Multinational Corporations*, Pt. 4, p. 124.)

33. *Hearings on Multinational Corporations*, Pt. 4, p. 97.

34. *Hearings on Governmental Intervention*, Pt. 1, p. 162.

35. *Ibid.*, pp. 43, 68.

36. *Hearings on Multinational Corporations*, Pt. 4, pp. 14–31.

37. Six thousand cubic feet of gas is treated the same as a barrel of oil.

38. A special limitation provides that oil and gas percentage depletion may not exceed 65% of the taxable income for the year (computed without percentage depletion). In the case of gas selling under a contract fixed before February 1, 1975, the 22% depletion rate continues. It also continues until July 1, 1976, for gas regulated by the FPC (Section 501(a)).

39. For 1975 the limitation is set at 52.8% and for 1976 at 50.4%.

Part THREE EROSION AND RESTORATION

Chapter 9. THE EVISCERATION OF THE LIBYAN INDEPENDENTS

1. See Chapter 5, Chart 5-2.

2. *Allen & Co.* vs. *Occidental Petroleum Co.*, 67 CIV 4011: Southern District of N.Y.

3. *Ibid.*

4. *Ibid.*

5. *Hearings on Multinational Corporations*, Pt. 5, p. 106.

6. *The New York Times Magazine*, February 16, 1975, p. 30.

7. *Hearings on Governmental Intervention*, Pt. 1, pp. 48, 57. Where prices from several suppliers were shown for a given year, the lowest price is cited.

8. *Ibid.*, p. 246.

9. *Ibid.*, p. 76 (Grades 31–38).

10. *Ibid.*, Pt. 2, p. 798.

11. M. A. Adelman, *The World Petroleum Market*, Johns Hopkins University Press, Baltimore, Md., 1972, p. 173.

12. (Emphasis added.) The predicted peak of Libyan output, 3.5 million b/d, was only 6% above the actual peak of 3.3 reached in 1970.

13. *Hearings on Multinational Corporations* (Memorandum from S. E. Watterson, Assistant Manager, Economics Dept., to W. K. Morris, Manager of Foreign Operations Staff, Standard Oil Co. of Calif.), December 6, 1968, Pt. 8, p. 761.

14. The slightly higher totals under "B" and "C" for the Free World supply reflect adjustments for inventory: "We also raised our estimates of inventory build-up for 1969 in the two adjusted cases."

15. The memorandum notes that "These estimates are those reported in the Blue Book."

16. (Emphasis added.) Similar apprehension was expressed over the forecast for Nigeria, which was based on the assumption that "the Civil War would last through 1969 . . ." But recent press reports had suggested the possibility of an earlier settlement: "Hence, our estimate for Nigeria could be too low by at least 200 m b/d, which would suggest that our Middle East production would be too high by a corresponding amount."

17. *Hearings on Multinational Corporations, Chronology of the Libyan Oil Negotiations, 1970–71*, p. 4 (reprinted in Pt. 4 of *Hearings*). (Hereafter referred to as *Chronology*.)

18. *Ibid.*, Pt. 5, p. 3.

19. *Ibid.*, Pt. 5, p. 4.

20. *Ibid.*, pp. 7–8.

21. *Ibid.*, p. 7.

22. See Table 9-1.

23. *Hearings on Multinational Corporations*, Pt. 5, pp. 10–11. For defenses of Occidental's producing practices by its petroleum engineers, see Charles L. DesBrisay and E. Leon Daniel, "Supplementary Recovery Developments of the Inestar 'A' and 'D' Reef Field, Libyan Arab Republic," *Journal of Petroleum Technology*, July 1972, and Charles L. DesBrisay, John W. Gray, and Allen Spivak, "Miracle Flood Performance of the Inestar 'D' Reef Field, Libyan Arab Republic," Society of Petroleum Engineers of AIME, p. SPE 5080, 1974.

24. See *Chronology*, p. 9.

25. *Hearings on Multinational Corporations*, Pt. 5, p. 79.

26. See Chapter 7.

27. *Chronology*, p. 10.

28. *Hearings on Multinational Corporations*, Pt. 5, p. 248. According to George Schuler of Bunker Hunt, ". . . the genesis of this solidarity movement was Shell. Shell had some very forward-thinking people in an office that followed OPEC affairs . . ." (*ibid.*, p. 80).

29. *Ibid.*, p. 113 (emphasis added).

30. *Ibid.*, p. 81.

31. *Ibid.*, p. 251.

32. *Ibid.*, Pt. 6, pp. 11–13.

33. *Ibid.*, Pt. 5, p. 19.

34. *Chronology*, p. 15.
35. *Ibid.*, p. 15.
36. *Hearings on Multinational Corporations*, Pt. 5, pp. 87–88. Schuler's response was: "But oftentimes the representative of the United States becomes the representative of the country to which he is accredited" (*ibid.*, p. 88).
37. *Chronology*, p. 17.
38. Generally similar terms were imposed on smaller companies operating in the country. (See *The Petroleum Economist*, April 1974, pp. 127–128.)
39. See Table 9-1.
40. *The Petroleum Economist*, March 1975, p. 88.
41. *Chronology*, p. 12.
42. *Hearings on Governmental Intervention*, Pt. 2, p. 800.
43. *Hearings on Multinational Corporations*, Pt. 5, p. 32.
44. *Ibid.*, p. 33.
45. *Ibid.*, p. 34.
46. *Ibid.*, p. 39. For the text of the table and subsequent related communications between SoCal and New England Petroleum, see *ibid.*, Pt. 5, pp. 49–54.
47. *Ibid.*, p. 38.
48. *Ibid.*, p. 37.
49. *Ibid.*, pp. 44–45.
50. *Ibid.*, p. 45.
51. *Ibid.*, pp. 46–47.
52. Cf. *ibid.*, pp. 49–51.
53. *Ibid.*, p. 48.
54. *Ibid.*, p. 107.
55. *Ibid.*, p. 37. Production in 1973 by the Libyan National Oil Co. in the former BP-Hunt concession totaled only 236,000 b/d in 1973, as compared to 402,000 b/d in the first half of 1970; and in the former Amoseas concession, it amounted to only 192,000 b/d in 1973, as compared to 368,000 in 1970.

Chapter 10. THE CRIPPLING OF THE PRIVATE BRANDERS

1. Arthur B. Laffer, "Vertical Integration by Corporations, 1929–1965," *Review of Economics and Statistics*, February 1969, pp. 91–93.
2. See Alfred E. Kahn and Melvin de Chazeau, *Integration and Competition in the Petroleum Industry*, Yale University Press, New Haven, Conn., pp. 212–222.
3. *Hearings on Governmental Intervention*, Pt. 3, p. 1,290. (Joint Statement of Fred C. Allvine and James M. Patterson.)
4. *Ibid.*, p. 1,291.
5. *Ibid.*, p. 1,291.
6. The source of Tables 10-2 and 10-3 is *The Independent Retail Gasoline Marketer* by C. David Schultz, Jr., 1974 (Master's thesis, University of South Florida, mimeo). The figures were compiled from the *Lundberg Survey*, published in the annual *National Petroleum News Fact Books*.
7. *Ibid.*, pp. 21–22.
8. *1973 FTC Staff Report*, pp. 8–11 (emphasis added).
9. 89th Cong., 1st Sess., Senate Subcommittee on Antitrust and Monopoly, *Hearings on Economic Concentration*, Pt. 2, "Mergers and Other Factors Affecting Industry Concentration," 1965, pp. 591–608. (Values read by inspection of charts.)
10. *1973 FTC Staff Report*, p. 11.

11. *Ibid.*, p. 24.
12. Federal Trade Commission, *Report on Anticompetitive Practices in the Marketing of Gasoline*, mimeographed, 1969, p. 20.
13. *Ibid.*, p. 13.
14. *Ibid.*, p. 27.
15. *Hearings on Governmental Intervention*, Pt. 3, p. 1,290. (Joint Statement of Allvine and Patterson.)
16. Federal Trade Commission, *Report on Anticompetitive Practices*, pp. 22–23.
17. *Ibid.*, p. 24.
18. *Ibid.*
19. *Hearings on Governmental Intervention*, Pt. 3, p. 1,294.
20. Fred C. Allvine and James M. Patterson, *Highway Robbery: An Analysis of the Gasoline Crisis*, Indiana University Press, Bloomington, 1974, pp. 166–167 (emphasis added).
21. *1973 FTC Staff Report*, p. 11. To simplify exposition quantities represented by imports, transfers to districts outside Districts 1 and 3, and exports, have been omitted.
22. *Hearings on Governmental Intervention*, Pt. 3, pp. 1,271–1,272.
23. Fred C. Allvine, "Petroleum Product Shortages Prior to the Arab Oil Embargo," Paper given before the Annual Convention of the Southern Economic Association, Atlanta, Georgia, Fall 1974, mimeographed.
24. *Ibid.*
25. Allvine and Patterson, *op. cit.*, p. 83.
26. *Ibid.*, pp. 88–89.
27. OEP Memorandum of meeting with Humble on July 17, 1972 (cited by Allvine, *loc. cit.*).
28. Exxon letter dated June 27, 1974 (cited by Allvine, *loc. cit.*). See also 93rd Cong., 1st Sess., Senate Permanent Subcommittee on Investigations, *Staff Study of the Oversight and Efficiency of Executive Agencies with Respect to the Petroleum Industry, Especially as It Relates to Recent Fuel Shortages*, November 8, 1973, p. 108.
29. Allvine, *loc. cit.*
30. Exxon submission dated June 27, 1974 (cited by Allvine, *loc. cit.*).
31. Allvine and Patterson, *op. cit.*, pp. 171–185.
32. *U-Filler-Up, Inc.*, vs. *Crown Central Petroleum Corp. and Exxon Corp.*, U.S. District Court for the Middle District of North Carolina, Greensboro Division, Civil Docket No. C-174-C-73, pp. 11, 12.
33. Allvine and Patterson, *op. cit.*, p. 179.
34. *Ibid.*, p. 172.
35. *Ibid.*, p. 172.
36. *Ibid.*, p. 174.
37. Allvine, "Petroleum Product Shortages Prior to the Arab Embargo," *loc. cit.*
38. Senate Permanent Investigating Subcommittee, *Staff Study, op. cit.*, p. 46.
39. *Ibid.*, p. 46. The increase, approved by President Nixon on May 23, 1972, was 230,000 b/d.
40. Letter of June 27, 1974, Allvine, *loc. cit.* (emphasis added).
41. These included such companies as Ashland, Coastal States, and Standard of Ohio.
42. Senate Permanent Investigating Subcommittee, *Staff Study, op. cit.*, p. 46.
43. Allvine and Patterson, *op. cit.*, pp. 192–194.
44. The pattern of distribution was subject to an unusual degree of distortion in Florida, one of the South's two largest gasoline-consuming states, by the common practice of basing allocations on use in prior years, thereby ignoring the state's subsequent growth rate—the most rapid in the country.

45. In 1974, these states accounted for 89% of total U.S. gasoline consumption.

Chapter **11.** THE PRICE EXPLOSION

1. *Hearings on Governmental Intervention*, Pt. 1, pp. 432–433.
2. *Report on Multinational Corporations and U.S. Foreign Policy*, p. 149.
3. The changes in posted prices between Oct. 1, 1973, and Feb. 1, 1975, are shown below for various important grades of Mideast and African crudes:

Posted Price of Leading Crudes (per bbl.)

		1/1/73	10/1/73	1/1/74	12/1/74	2/1/75
Arabian light	34	$3.01	$5.12	$11.65	$11.25	$11.25
Iranian, medium	31	2.93	4.99	11.63	11.23	11.23
Iraq, Basrah	35	2.98	5.06	11.67	11.27	11.27
Kuwait	31	2.98	4.90	11.54	11.14	11.14
Abu Dhabi	39	3.08	6.04	12.64	12.24	12.24
Qatar	40	3.14	5.34	12.41	12.01	12.01
Libya	40	4.60	8.92	15.77	15.77	15.77

Source: The Petroleum Economist, various issues.

4. *The Petroleum Economist*, February 1974, p. 46.
5. 93rd Cong., 1st Sess., Hearings before the Permanent Subcommittee on Investigations of the Committee on Government Operations, *Current Energy Shortages Oversight Series*, December 14, 1973, Pt. 1, p. 7.
6. *Ibid.*, p. 7.
7. *Ibid.*, Pt. 5, p. 606.
8. *Ibid.*, p. 605.
9. *Ibid.*, Pt. 2, p. 268.
10. *The Petroleum Economist*, March 1974, p. 98.
11. *Ibid.*, p. 97.
12. *The Petroleum Economist*, June 1974, p. 218.
13. *The Petroleum Economist*, February 1974, p. 52.
14. *The Petroleum Economist*, April 1974, p. 125.
15. For the five-month period November 1973–March 1974, actual domestic production totaled 1,382,351 barrels; at the October 1973 rate, it would have amounted to 1,412,152 barrels. The corresponding figures for imports (crude and refined products) were 837,384 and 960,964 barrels. The shortfall of imports below the October rate totaled 123,580 barrels, compared to a total supply of 2,219,735 barrels. (Compiled from American Petroleum Institute, *Weekly Statistical Bulletins*, Vols. 54 and 55.)
16. Output also continued to rise in Iraq which, following the nationalization of the Iraq Petroleum Co., had suffered an extreme reduction in output earlier in the year.
17. *Hearings on Governmental Intervention*, Pt. 1, p. 173.
18. The price and most of the cost entries are virtually identical with those shown in the hearings for "Iranian light," with the exception that a special OPEC discount of some $.10 a barrel, scheduled to expire in 1974, has been omitted.
19. *The Petroleum Economist*, July 1973 to February 1974.
20. *Hearings on Governmental Intervention*, Pt. 1, pp. 174–175.

21. *The Petroleum Economist*, October 1974, p. 362.
22. *Hearings on Multinational Corporations*, Pt. 7, pp. 426–427 (emphasis added). The wording used above is from the actual telegram of October 25, reproduced as Exhibit 16, pp. 530–531, which differs in immaterial respects from the passage quoted in this exchange.
23. *The Petroleum Economist*, January 1974, p. 9.
24. World Bank, Report No. 477, July 1974.
25. Morgan Guarantee Co., "World Financial Markets," January 21, 1975.
26. Irving Trust Co., "The Economic View from One Wall Street," March 20, 1975.
27. First National City Bank, "Monthly Economic Letter," June 1975.
28. World Bank, "Prospects for Developing Countries," Report No. 802, July 1975.
29. Hobart Rowen, *Washington Post*, November 30, 1975.
30. Walter J. Levy Consultants Corp., "Future OPEC Accumulations of Oil Money: A New Look at a Critical Problem," 30 Rockefeller Plaza, New York, 1975. For an earlier appraisal by Levy, see "World Oil: Cooperation or International Chaos?" *Foreign Affairs*, July 1974.
31. Cited by Hobart Rowen, *Washington Post*, August 17, 1975.
32. International Monetary Fund, *Annual Report*, 1974.
33. Hobart Rowen, *Washington Post*, August 1, 1975 (the World Bank document referred to is Report No. 802).
34. Hobart Rowen, *Washington Post*, July 23, 1975.
35. For a critique of policies followed by the World Bank with regard to OPEC, see columns by Hobart Rowen, *Washington Post*, 7/22/75, 7/23/75, 8/1/75, 8/24/75, and 9/28/75.

Chapter 12. THE CURTAILMENT OF OUTPUT

1. For an analysis suggesting that the recent domestic offshore production has been unduly restricted, see Statement by Walter S. Measday before the Senate Subcommittee on Antitrust and Monopoly, *Hearings on Multinational Corporations*.
2. Anthony Sampson, *The Seven Sisters*, Viking Press, New York, 1975, p. 300.
3. *The Petroleum Economist*, March 1975, pp. 84–85.
4. *The New York Times Magazine*, September 14, 1975, p. 32 (Interview with Oriana Fallaci).
5. *The Petroleum Economist*, September 1974, p. 33.
6. Columbia Broadcasting Company, *Face the Nation*, April 20, 1975.
7. *The New York Times Magazine*, loc. cit., p. 19.
8. *Ibid.*
9. *The Petroleum Economist*, April 1974, pp. 129–130.
10. *The Petroleum Economist*, October 1974, p. 388.
11. *Ibid.*
12. P. R. Odell in *The Large International Firms in Developing Countries*, by Edith Penrose, George Allen & Unwin, Ltd., London, 1968, pp. 296–297.
13. *Ibid.* A logical corollary of the cause of restrictionism is a preference for dealing with large enterprises, which Venezuela has made no effort to disguise.

Venezuela has been particularly hard in recent years towards the production plans of the smaller companies which secured concessions in 1956–57. Their export prices have been closely vetted and challenged immediately if the discounts were considered too high: in contrast the major companies' prices have in general only been vetted retroactively. Additionally, regulations designed to prevent the flaring of associated gas and other conservation measures have been vigorously implemented for the smaller companies, thus restricting their production. The international companies have not suffered the same degree of supervision. A former oil minister, Perez Alfonzo, indicated clearly that he would prefer Venezuela to deal only with the international major companies. Some of the independents have reacted to this by selling out their interests to the larger companies. (*ibid.*)

14. *The Petroleum Economist*, February 1975, p. 51, and June 1975, p. 240.
15. United Nations, *Statistical Yearbooks*, Tables 18 and 77.
16. *The New York Times*, September 21, 1975.
17. *The Petroleum Economist*, August 1975, p. 299.
18. *Ibid.*
19. *Ibid.*, p. 291.
20. *The Petroleum Economist*, January 1975, p. 3 (emphasis added).
21. Marwin Inlander, "Have the Arabs Lost the Oil War?" *Atlas*, September 1975, p. 14 (originally published in the Beirut, Lebanon, weekly, *Monday Morning*).
22. *The Petroleum Economist*, August 1975, p. 299 (emphasis added).
23. Zuhayr Mikdashi, "The OPEC Process," *Daedalus*, Journal of the American Academy of Arts and Sciences, Fall 1975, pp. 207, 208. (Symposium on the "Oil Crisis in Perspective," edited by Raymond Vernon.)
24. *Ibid.*, p. 207.
25. Columbia Broadcasting System, *Face the Nation*, November 16, 1975 (emphasis added).
26. *Ibid.* (emphasis added).
27. *The Petroleum Economist*, January 1975, p. 14.
28. *Petroleum Intelligence Weekly*, November 10, 1975 (Reproduced in Hearings of the Senate Subcommittee on Antitrust and Monopoly on S.2387 [Nov. 12, 1975].)

Chapter 13. PROFIT CENTERS AND TARGET RETURNS

1. *The Petroleum Economist*, November 1973, p. 403.
2. *The Petroleum Economist*, March 1974, p. 117.
3. *Ibid.*, September 1974, p. 322.
4. Jean-Marie Chevalier, *The New Oil Stakes*, English edn., Allen Lane, Penguin Books, Ltd., Middlesex, 1975, p. 130.
5. *Ibid.*, p. 49.
6. See Chart 13-1: "Middle Distillate."
7. *The Petroleum Economist*, February 1974, p. 42.
8. Edith Penrose, "The Development of Crisis," *Daedalus*, Journal of the American Academy of Arts and Sciences, Fall 1975, p. 51.
9. *Hearings on Multinational Corporations*, Pt. 7, p. 454.
10. *Journal of Commerce*, May 1, 1975.
11. For the original formulation of the target return concept, see Donaldson Brown, "Pricing Policy in Relation to Financial Control," *Management and Administration*, February–April 1974, pp. 195–198, 283–286, 417–422. For the leading postwar study, see Robert F. Lanzillotti, "Pricing Objectives in Large Companies," *American Economic Review*, December 1958, pp. 921–940.
12. Richard B. Heflebower, "Full Costs, Cost Changes and Prices," in *Business Concentration and Price Policy*, National Bureau of Economic Research, 1955, p. 363 (emphasis in original).
13. Donaldson Brown, *op. cit.*
14. Blair, *Economic Concentration*, pp. 640–642.
15. *Ibid.*, pp. 489–490. (See also Chapter 7 above.)
16. Senate Permanent Subcommittee on Investigations, *Hearings on the Current Energy Situation*, January 1974, Pt. 2, p. 257.

17. *Ibid.*, p. 258.
18. *Ibid.*, p. 259.
19. *Ibid.*, pp. 258–259 (emphasis added).
20. *Ibid.*, p. 259.
21. *Ibid.*, p. 260.
22. *Ibid.*, p. 261.
23. *Ibid.*, p. 262 (emphasis added).
24. *Ibid.*
25. *Ibid.*, p. 262.
26. *Ibid.*, p. 258.
27. *Ibid.*, pp. 264–265.
28. See Table 6-1.
29. Chase Manhattan Bank, *The Petroleum Situation*, August 29, 1975, p. 4.
30. *The Petroleum Economist*, November, 1975, p. 410.
31. John M. Blair, "Market Power and Inflation: A Short-Run Target Return Model," *Journal of Economic Issues*, June 1974, and *Economic Concentration*, Ch. XVIII.
32. Bureau of Labor Statistics. Reflecting the seasonal decline in demand, the price of residual fuel declined by 21.7%.
33. In order to provide a company of approximately the same size to compare with Standard (Ind.), SoCal was included in the "international" group although its average percentage of foreign taxes to net income fell below 50%; in 1974, its percentage was 40.4%.
34.

Rate of Returns on Net Worth (after taxes)

	Five Int. Majors	Six Dom. Majors	Differences
1972	12.0%	9.1%	2.9% pts.
1971	12.2	8.8	3.4
1970	11.5	8.5	3.0
1969	11.5	9.9	1.8
1968	12.1	10.9	1.2
1967	11.8	11.5	0.3
1966	11.8	11.3	0.5
1965	11.5	10.5	1.0

Source: Compiled from Federal Trade Commission, *Rates of Return of Selected Manufacturing Companies.*

35. *Hearings on Governmental Intervention*, Pt. 2, p. 835.
36. *Ibid.*, p. 810.
37. Federal Trade Commission, *Rates of Return of Selected Manufacturing Industries*, annually. The unique values of this source are that (a) profits are grouped in the relatively narrow (for profit comparisons) three-digit industry groups of the Standard Industrial Classification; (b) more than half of the companies' income comes from the industry in which they are classified; and (c) profit figures are shown for individual companies.
38. The Chase Manhattan Bank, *Capital Investments of the World Petroleum Industry*, 1973, pp. 8–9.
39. *Ibid.*
40. Frankel, *Mattei*, p. 105 (emphasis in original).

41. *Ibid.*, p. 106.

42. *Ibid.*, pp. 106–107 (emphasis in original).

43. *Wall Street Journal*, March 15, 1976.

Part FOUR   PUBLIC POLICY

1. 90th Cong., 1st Sess., Senate Subcommittee on Antitrust and Monopoly, *Hearings on Competitive Aspects of Oil Shale Development*, Pt. 1, 1967, p. 152 (emphasis added).

2. H. S. Houthakker and Lester D. Taylor, *Consumer Demand in the United States 1929–1970, Analysis and Projections*, Harvard University Press, Cambridge, Mass., 1966.

3. Data Resources, Inc. "A Study of the Quarterly Demand for Gasoline and Impacts of Alternative Gasoline Taxes," 1973.

4. Louis Phlips, "A Dynamic Version of the Linear Expenditure Model," *Review of Economics and Statistics*, November 1972, pp. 450–458.

5. Charlotte Chamberlain, "Policy Options: Gas Tax vs. Gas Rationing and/or Auto Excise Tax," U.S. Department of Transportation, Transportation Systems Center, Cambridge, Mass., July 1974.

Chapter 14. THE TECHNOLOGICAL POTENTIAL

1. Cf., e.g., Federal Trade Commission, *Concentration Levels and Trends in the Energy Sector of the U.S. Economy*, 1974 (Mimeo); Hearings before the Senate Subcommittee on Antitrust and Monopoly on S. 487 (Testimony of Thomas Gale Moore), June 19, 1975.

2. *The Petroleum Economist*, July 1975, p. 270. (The source cited is a study of energy consumption for the various forms of transport made by the Dutch Institute for Road Vehicles.)

3. *Congressional Record*, October 7, 1975, p. S17,671.

4. In 1913 Fredrick Bergens developed a hydrogenation process for converting brown coal to crude oil by squeezing heated coal and hydrogen together at extremely high pressures. In 1925 Frank Fischer and Hans Tropsch invented a catalytic process for transforming coal gas directly into gasoline. Used in the early years of World War II to provide the fuel for Hitler's war machine, important technical details of these processes appear to have been lost.

5. Cf. e.g., "Design of a Coal-Oil-Gas Refinery," by M. E. Frank and B. K. Schmid, and "Converting Coal into Non-Polluting Fuel Oil" by P. M. Yovarsky, S. Arktar, and S. Friedman, *Chemical and Engineering Progress* (Vol. 69, No. 3), March 1973.

6. For a recent account of the status of research on coal conversion, see 93rd Cong., 2nd Sess., Subcommittee on Science, Research and Development and Subcommittee on Energy of the House Committee on Science and Technology, *Hearings on Synthetic Liquid Fuel Research and Development Act of 1974*, December 1974.

7. Christopher Welles, *The Elusive Bonanza*, E. P. Dutton and Co., New York, 1970, p. 25. This is an excellent account of the history of oil shale by the former business editor of *Life* Magazine.

8. *Ibid.*, pp. 22–23.

9. 90th Cong., 1st Sess., Senate Interior and Insular Affairs Committee, *Hearings on the Federal Oil Shale Program*, 1967, p. 202, n.

10. 90th Cong., 1st Sess., Senate Subcommittee on Antitrust and Monopoly, *Hearings on Competitive Aspects of Oil Shale Development*, Pt. 1, 1967, p. 147.

11. Welles, *op. cit.*, p. 85 (emphasis added). The correspondence quoted was introduced in proceedings conducted by the Bureau of Land Management,

Colorado Contests, Nos. 359 and 360. See also Testimony of Captain Albert G. Miller, former director of Naval Petroleum and Oil Shale Reserves.

12. *Hearings on the Federal Oil Shale Program*, p. 99.

13. William O. Metz, "Oil Shale: A Huge Resource of Low-Grade Fuel," *Science*, June 21, 1974.

14. According to former Secretary of Interior Udall, "Research to date demonstrates that the production of crude shale oil itself—the processes of mining, crushing and retorting—requires relatively little water. Refining of shale oil is comparable to petroleum refining in requiring large amounts of water for cooling and steam generation" (*Hearings on the Federal Oil Shale Program*, p. 12). In the pilot plant constructed by Union Oil Co., "A key feature . . . was that the shale oil vapors flowed through the rising shale. They were thus condensed and cooled to near atmospheric temperatures while the shale was being preheated. *No cooling water was required*" (Welles, *op. cit.*, p. 83, emphasis added).

15. Metz, *op. cit.*

16. *Science*, August 18, 1967. (Letter from John W. Hand, Cameron and Jones, Inc., Denver, Colorado.)

17. Welles, *op. cit.*, pp. 131–132, 175.

18. *Hearings on the Federal Oil Shale Program*, p. 174.

19. *Ibid.*, p. 11.

20. Cf. Welles, *op. cit.*, pp. 83–85.

21. *Hearings on the Federal Oil Shale Program*, p. 255.

22. *International Petroleum Cartel*, p. 212 (see Ch. 6).

23. See Chapter 1.

24. Welles, *op. cit.*, p. 90.

25. Quoted in *ibid.*, pp. 92–93 (emphasis added).

26. The use of nuclear explosion has been suggested for this purpose. See *Hearings on the Federal Oil Shale Program*, pp. 60–73.

27. *Chemical and Engineering News*, March 19, 1973.

28. *Business Week,* April 28, 1975, p. 87.

29. Department of Interior, Bureau of Mines, Division of Mineral Studies, "Estimated Costs of Producing Capacity of a Government Assisted Shale Oil Industry, 1970–1980," by L. W. Schram.

30. 94th Cong., 1st Sess., Senate Small Business Committee, *Hearings on Energy Research and Development and Small Business* (Statement of Dr. John M. Teen, Assistant Administrator of the Energy Research and Development Administration), May 14, 1975. (Hereafter referred to as *Hearings on Energy Research.*)

31. Types of collectors now under study include flat plates with honey-comb cores, evacuated glass tubes containing tubular absorbers, concentrating and tracking collectors, and absorbing liquid, air and water bed designs. Energy Research and Development Administration, *National Plan for Solar Heating and Cooling*, Interim Report, March 1975, p. 65.

32. *Ibid.*, p. 6.

33. *Hearings on Energy Research* (Statement of Dr. John M. Teen).

34. Energy Research and Development Administration, *op. cit.*, p. 100.

35. *Hearings on Energy Research* (Statement of Dr. Jerry D. Plunkett).

36. *The New York Times*, September 21, 1975.

37. Central Policy Review Staff, *Energy Conservation*, Her Majesty's Stationery Office, London, July 1974, pp. 20–21.

38. *Ibid.*, p. 22.

39. *St. Petersburg (Fla.) Independent,* May 30, 1975.

40. *Hearings on Economic Concentration*, Pt. 6, pp. 2,841–2,842.

41. *Ibid.*, pp. 2,842–2,843.

42. *Ibid.*, p. 2,854. In 1966, a year of relatively high automobile output, production of less than the 70,000 minimum "crossover point" was not uncommon; e.g., General Motors: Toronado (33,000), Riviera (46,000) and Fleetwood (24,000); Ford: Thunderbird (67,000), Lincoln (49,000); Chrysler: Barracuda (28,000), Charger (35,000), and Imperial (15,000); and American Motors: Rambler (67,000), Ambassador (54,000), and Marlin (6,000) (*ibid.*, p. 3,275).

43. *Ibid.*, p. 2,855.

44. Owens-Corning Fiberglas Corp., *The Economics of Fiberglas Reinforced Plastic in Automotive Bodies*, June 1962.

45. According to Artinian and Terry, a 1.0 lb. change in the weight of an automobile part can change the overall weight of the automobile by 1.3–1.5 lbs. (L. Artinian and S. L. Terry, "The Total Cost of Weight," Paper 325D, *Society of Automotive Engineers*, March 1961.)

46. In Pontiac's side-window louver, the original zinc die cast component weighed 20 lbs.; the fiberglass replacement only 4.7 lbs.; a saving of 75%. The front end of the Chrysler Newport was reduced from 22 lbs. to 12 lbs., a saving of 45%. A combination fender extension-lamp bezel on the Oldsmobile Toronado weighed 7.1 lbs. in metal but only 2.5 lbs. in fiberglass, a saving of 65%. With the heavy emphasis placed on mileage claims in the 1975 advertising campaigns, this trend may be expected to continue. "Weight Savings Approaches through the Use of Fiber Glass-Reinforced Plastic," Society of Automotive Engineers, February 24–28, 1975, by Eldon D. Trueman, Transportation Materials Div., Owens-Corning Fiberglas Corp.

47. *Ibid.*

48. *Hearings on Ecoomic Concentration*, Pt. 6, p. 2,616.

49. See, e.g., U.S. Department of Commerce, *The Automobile and Air Pollution*, 1967, Pt. I, p. 2. For a criticism, see the Statement by Lloyd D. Orr, Senate Commerce Committee and Senate Public Works Committee, *Hearings on the External Combustion Engine*, May 27–28, 1968.

50. See, e.g., Federal Power Commission, *Development of Electrically Powered Vehicles*, February 1967, p. 8.

51. Senate Antitrust Subcommittee, *Hearings on Economic Concentration*, Pt. 6, p. 2,608.

52. *Ibid.*, p. 2,786.

53. That electric vehicles do in fact enjoy an advantage in terms of operating costs is shown by an unusual body of evidence provided by the United Parcel Service. This company has been operating electric trucks in New York City since the 1920's, and in 1963 had sixty-seven electric trucks in service, all purchased between 1925 and 1952. Based on data for its entire fleet, the company reported a daily operating cost for its electric trucks of $7.96, or 11.1% below the $8.85 cost for internal combustion engine trucks and 19.2% below the $9.73 figure for the diesel trucks. (*Electric Vehicle News*, October 1969, p. 1.)

54. Alvin J. Salkind, "Battery Power," March 1972, p. 3.

55. *Hearings on Economic Concentration*, Pt. 6, p. 2,601.

56. Shrade F. Radtke, "Charging Up for a Changing World," Paper presented at Battery Council International Convention, May 7, 1970.

57. *Hearings on Economic Concentration*, Pt. 6, p. 2,564.

58. *Ibid.*, p. 2,568.

59. *Ibid.*, p. 1,572.

60. *Ibid.*, pp. 2,863–2,876.

61. U.S. Patent 3,280,015 (October 18, 1966).

62. In addition to the power savings, other advantages for the new process included good thermal control, higher yield from the reactor, flexibility,

low materials costs, and a small addition to the capital investment of the existing process.

63. *Hearings on Economic Concentration,* Pt. 6, pp. 2,874–2,875.

Chapter **15.** THE REMEDIES AT LAW:
The Regulatory Approach

1. Library of Congress, "Energy Policy and Conservation Act—Summary Analysis of the 5.622 Conference Report," *Congressional Record,* December 16, 1975, p. S22,421.
2. *Business Week,* December 1, 1975, p. 20.
3. *Congressional Record,* December 16, 1976, p. H12,961.
4. The figure of $5.25 was itself an average based on prices for different grades as of May 15, 1973, which, depending on quality, ranged from $3.50 to $7.00.
5. The Commission formally adopted an "allowable cost" rule and a limitation on profits as a percentage of sales, which, however, did not govern the term-limit agreements.
6. Robert F. Lanzillotti, Murry T. Hamilton, R. Blaine Roberts, *Phase II in Review,* The Brookings Institution, Washington, D.C., 1975, pp. 34–35.
7. *Congressional Record,* December 16, 1975, p. H12,689.
8. *Congressional Record,* December 17, 1975, p. S22,499.
9. *Congressional Record,* December 16, 1975, p. H12,694.
10. *Ibid.,* p. H12,686.
11. *Congressional Record,* December 17, 1975, p. S22,474.
12. Quoted in *ibid.,* p. S22,474.
13. Federal Trade Commission, Staff Report, "The Effects of Decontrol on Competition in the Petroleum Industry," September 5, 1975 (mimeo).
14. *Ibid.,* pp. 7, 38.
15. *Congressional Record,* December 16, 1975, p. S22,410.
16. *Congressional Record,* December 15, 1975, p. H12,588.
17. *Congressional Record,* December 16, 1975, p. S22,413.
18. *Congressional Record,* December 17, 1975, p. S22,524.
19. *Congressional Record,* December 16, 1975, p. H12,691.
20. *Congressional Record,* December 15, 1975, p. H12,589.
21. *Congressional Record,* December 16, 1975, pp. H12,691–12,692.
22. *Congressional Record,* December 15, 1975, p. H12,589.
23. *Congressional Record,* December 17, 1975, p. S22,518.
24. *Congressional Record,* December 16, 1975, p. H12,699.
25. *Congressional Record,* December 17, 1975, p. S22,517.
26. Letter from Frank O. Zarb to Senator Henry Jackson, December 6, 1975, reproduced in *Congressional Record,* December 17, 1975, p. S22,402.
27. Note the complaint by Saudi Arabia that Aramco had neglected its low and middle grades (Chapter 1).
28. *Congressional Record,* December 17, 1975, p. S22,524.
29. *Hearings on Governmental Intervention,* Pt. 1, p. 221.
30. Bureau of Mines, "Depth and Producing Rate Classification of Oil Reservoirs in the 14 Principal Oil Producing States," Information Circular 8362, 1968.
31. *Hearings on Governmental Intervention,* Pt. 1, p. 212. Among the shallowest wells (those with a depth of under 2,000 feet) costs per barrel fell from $.58 for wells with the lowest to $.13 for wells with the highest daily output. The same inverse relationship was apparent in all depth categories. Among the deepest wells (those with depths of over 8,000 feet) the decline was from $1.82 per barrel for wells with the lowest daily output to $.40 for wells with the highest output (*ibid.,* p. 442).

32. "In Texas, for example, the calculation shows that only 54 percent of the productive capacity of the nonstripper wells was utilized; hence, to produce at capacity, actual production rates would have to be increased by forty-six fifty-fourths, or by 84 percent" (*ibid.*, p. 218).

33. *Hearings on Governmental Intervention*, Pt. 1, p. 223.

Chapter 16. THE REMEDIES AT LAW:
The Competitive Approach

1. C.C.A. 9th 1902 (118 Fed. 120). In 1921 the Supreme Court, in *American Column & Lumber Co.* vs. *U.S.*, held illegal a scheme to control and discourage "over-production" in the hardwood lumber industry, which had been carried out through an elaborate program of trade statistics and through suggestions and exhortations by the statistical manager of the trade association to limit the production of its members (257 U.S. 377 (1921)).

2. U.S. vs. Southern Pine Assn., Cr. 19903, Civil 275; CCH Trade Reg. Rpts., 8th ed., Vol. 3, Par. 25,394; U.S. vs. Western Pine Assn., CCH Trade Reg. Rpts. Supp. 1741–43, Par. 52,548; U.S. vs. West Coast Lumbermen's Assn., CCH Trade Reg. Rpts. Supp. 1941–43, Par. 52,588; U.S. vs. National Lumber Manufacturers' Assn., CCH Trade Reg. Rpts., Supp. 1941–43, Par. 52,593.

3. U.S. vs. Aluminum Co. of America, et al., CCH Trade Reg. Rpts., 8th ed., Vol. 3, Par. 15,125 (1941).

4. U.S. vs. American Can Co., et al., CCH Ct. Decs. 1944–47, Par. 54,121.

5. FTC Order No. 3868, May 31, 1940.

6. FTC Order No. 3556, May 15, 1945.

7. FTC Order No. 4657, May 29, 1945.

8. Interstate Circuit, Inc. vs. United States, 306 U.S. 208 (1939); American Tobacco Co. vs. United States, 328 U.S. 781 (1945); Federal Trade Commission vs. Triangle Conduit, 168 Fed. 2 at 175.

9. See e.g., *Hearings on Multinational Corporations*, Pt. 8, p. 956.

10. *Hearings on Multinational Corporations*, Pt. 8, p. 956.

11. *Ibid.*, pp. 956, 957.

12. Interstate Circuit, Inc., vs. United States, 306 U.S. 208 (1939), at 222.

13. 328 U.S. 781 (1945), at 809.

14. Walter Adams, "Comment," *Journal of Economic Issues*, June 1975, p. 342 (emphasis in original).

15. *Congressional Record*, October 7, 1975, p. S17,684.

16. *Congressional Record*, October 8, 1975, p. S17,866.

17. *Ibid.*, p. S17,825.

18. *Congressional Record*, October 7, 1975, p. S17,674–17,675.

19. *Ibid.*, p. S17,677.

20. *Congressional Record*, October 8, 1975, p. S17,869.

21. *Ibid.*, p. S17,836.

22. *Ibid.*, p. S17,861.

23. *Congressional Record*, October 22, 1975, p. S18,587.

24. *Congressional Record*, October 7, 1975, p. S17,680.

25. *Congressional Record*, October 8, 1975, p. S17,871.

26. *Ibid.*, p. S17,835.

27. *Congressional Record*, October 7, 1975, p. S17,690.

28. Quoted in *Congressional Record*, October 8, 1975, p. S17,835.

29. *Congressional Record*, October 8, 1975, p. S17,826.

30. *Ibid.*, p. S17,859.

31. *Congressional Record*, October 22, 1975, p. S18,586.

32. *Congressional Record*, October 7, 1975, p. S17,686.

33. *Congressional Record*, October 8, 1975, p. S17,860.
34. *Congressional Record*, October 7, 1975, p. S17,681.
35. *Congressional Record*, October 8, 1975, p. S17,860.
36. *Ibid.*, p. S17,835.
37. Joe S. Bain, *Barriers to New Competition*, Harvard University Press, Cambridge, Mass., 1965, pp. 72, 158, 233.
38. Senate Subcommittee on Antitrust and Monopoly, Statement of January 30, 1975. Based on Frederick M. Scherer, *Economies of Scale at the Plant and Multi-plant Levels*, privately published, 1975, pp. 15–19.
39. A. C. Eastman and Stefan Stykolt, *The Tariff and Competition in Canada*, Macmillan Company, New York, 1967; N. G. Brathen and R. M. Dean, *The Economies of Large-Scale Production in British Industry*, Cambridge University Press, 1965.
40. Scherer, *op. cit.*
41. *Ibid.*
42. For a further discussion of these potential economies and diseconomies, see John M. Blair, *Economic Concentration*, Harcourt Brace Jovanovich, New York, 1972, Ch. VII.
43. *Ibid.*
44. Access to markets and distribution channels; procurement of materials; outboard transport pooling; and product specialization and lot-size economies.
45. Peak spreading, risk spreading, and other massed reserves; research, development, and technical services; advertising and image differentiation; and optimal investment staging.
46. John L. Enos, "Invention and Innovation in the Petroleum Refining Industry," in the *Rate and Direction of Inventive Activity*, National Bureau of Economic Research, 1962, pp. 299ff. Reprinted in *Hearings on Economic Concentration*, Pt. 3, pp. 1,481–1,503.
47. *Ibid.*
48. *Ibid.*
49. *Ibid.* (emphasis added).
50. Edwin Mansfield, *Firm Size and Technological Change in the Petroleum and Bituminous Coal Industries*, prepared for the Energy Policy Project, Ford Foundation, 1973.
51. *Ibid.*
52. *Ibid.*
53. *Ibid.*
54. *Ibid.*
55. Mansfield, *op. cit.*
56. John Wilson, "Market Structure and Interfirm Integration in the Petroleum Industry," *Journal of Economic Issues*, June 1975.
57. *Ibid.*

AN ACTION PROGRAM

1. John M. Blair, *Economic Concentration*, New York, Harcourt Brace Jovanovich, 1972, Chs. 9 and 10.
2. Harold Barnett in *The Energy Question: An International Failure of Policy*, edited by Edward W. Erickson and Leonard Waverman, University of Toronto Press, 1974, p. 295.
3. See, e.g., *Report of the Special Review Committee of the Board of Directors of Gulf Oil Corporation*, John J. McCloy, Chairman, U.S. District Court for the District of Columbia, in the matter of Securities and Exchange Commission v. Gulf Oil Corporation and Claude E. Wild, Jr., December 30, 1975.

Index

428

Market concentration, downward trend in, 257

Market Demand Act (1932), 161

Market demand prorationing, in domestic control, 159–62

Marketing control, 54–76. *See also* Control

Market share, growth rate and, 289

Marland, Ernest W., 163

Massachusetts Institute of Technology, 341

Mathers, Charles McC., 361

Mattei, Enrico, 91, 96, 226

McCloy, James D., 224–5

McGhee, George, 74, 78, 196, 200, 202

McGovern, George, 384

McKellar-Black Airmail Act (1934), 386

McKelvey, V. E., 11

McLaren, Richard W., 224 n.

McIntyre, Thomas J., 384

McQuinn, W. Jones, 271–2

Mead, Walter J., 138

Measday, Walter J., 141, 169 n., 180

Memorandum for European Markets (1930), 56, 58–9, 65, 98

Memorandum of Conversation, in Iraq concession case, 87

Menefee, J. M., 153

Mergers and acquisitions, 378–81

Mesopotamia. *See* Iraq

Metcalfe, Lee, 384

Metz, William O., 333–4

Mexican imports, "Brownsville turn-around" for, 176

Mid-Continent Oil and Gas Association, 191

Middle East
American exclusion in, 34–5
bilateral symbiotic oligopoly in, 293
Caltex role in, 38–41
concessions in, 35, 74
control of oil in, 29–53
discovery of oil in, 29–30
foreign tax credit and, 196–7
Japan and, 29
oil reserves of, 15–23, 27
"open door" policy of, 32–4
restrictionism in, 81–4
"seven sisters" in, 31

Middle East crude. *See also* Major oil companies
base price for, 114–15
costs and profits for, 47–53
curtailment of, 279
"developing" vs. "operating" cost of, 48
"equity" vs. "participative" types in, 270–1
freight costs in, 116
Italy and, 90–4
price explosion in. *See* Price explosion
prices and profits in, 49, 51, 294–5

return on investment for, 49–50
Western resources and, 74

Middle East Economic Consultants, 290

Middle East Energy Committee, 3

Midwest Refining Company, 127

Mikdashi, Zuhayr, 50, 78–9, 290

Miller, Otto N., 184 n., 296

Mintz, Morton, 291

Mobil Oil Corp., 19, 31, 63, 127, 388–9. *See also* Socony-Vacuum
in Far East, 36
interlocking directorates of, 146
Iranian oil and, 43–7
Montgomery Ward and, 318
Persian Gulf oil and, 81
profit performance of, 307–8
restrictionism of in Iraq, 81–3
Rockefeller holdings in, 149–50
target return for, 306
transportation costs for, 170

Mock, H. Byron, 334

Monopoly power, legal remedies for, 354–70

Monroe, Archie, 93–4

Moody, J. D., 19, 21

Morrison, Robert S., 344

Mossadeq, Muhammed, 34, 78, 80

Mother Hubbard case, 394

Motor fuel, supply-demand relationship for, 326–7. *See also* Gasoline

Motor vehicle companies, taxes paid by, 187

Motor vehicles, *See* Automobiles

Multiplant operations, efficiency of, 389

Murchison, Clint, 173–4

Murray, Allen E., 306

Murray, William J., Jr., 168

Muskie, Edmund S., 46–7, 84, 105

National Academy of Sciences, 12, 22, 330–1

National Association of Swedish Farmers, 68

National cartels, 63–70
classifying customers of, 67
price fixing and, 67

National Iranian Oil Company, 294

National Petroleum Council, 305 n., 337

National Petroleum News, 251

National Plan for Energy Research, Development, and Demonstration, 326

National Security Council, 73–4, 198
International Petroleum Cartel and, 73–5

Nationalization of oil operations, 44, 78, 80, 90, 103, 375

Net income, increase in (1965–74), 313

New England Gas and Electric System, 230

New England Petroleum Company, 231–4

About the Author

A graduate of Tulane University, Dr. John M. Blair received his Ph.D. from the American University in Washington, D.C. Entering the Civil Service in 1938, he spent thirty-two years in the federal government, first as author of monographs for the pre-war investigation of the concentration of economic power (the TNEC), followed by nearly a decade as Assistant Chief Economist of the Federal Trade Commission and finally by fourteen years as Chief Economist of the Senate Subcommittee on Antitrust and Monopoly.

At the Federal Trade Commission Dr. Blair wrote and directed the preparation of reports on mergers, economic concentration, and cartels. After transferring to Congress, he directed under Senator Estes Kefauver the Antitrust Subcommittee's inquiry into administered prices in the steel, automobile, drug, and bread industries. Later, he directed under Senator Philip Hart the Subcommittee's inquiry into economic concentration which produced hearings on industry structure, mergers, divisional reporting, size and efficiency, new technologies, and invention and innovation. The empirical material gathered in these Congressional investigations formed much of the basis for his encyclopedic book *Economic Concentration*, published in 1972.

Dr. Blair first gained his special competence in the petroleum industry as director and co-author of the classic study *The Staff Report on the International Petroleum Cartel*, prepared at the Federal Trade Commission and published in 1952 by the Senate Small Business Committee. Later he directed the Antitrust Subcommittee's investigation of the mandatory oil import quota, culminating in four volumes of hearings published in 1969–70 on *Governmental Intervention in the Market Mechanism*.

Throughout, Dr. Blair remained active in the academic world, writing some twenty articles and papers for academic journals and symposia, teaching at the American University and the Free University of Berlin, and lecturing at many universities at home and abroad. He retired from the federal service in 1970, resides in St. Petersburg, and is Professor of Economics at the University of South Florida.